Frances Larson
By Sister
Rhodia Guest.

GOSPEL TRUTH
Vol. I

Gospel Truth

DISCOURSES AND WRITINGS
OF

President George Q. Cannon

FIRST COUNSELOR TO PRESIDENTS
JOHN TAYLOR, WILFORD WOODRUFF AND LORENZO SNOW
(1880-1901)

Volume 1

Selected, Arranged, and Edited
by
JERRELD L. NEWQUIST

PUBLISHED BY DESERET BOOK COMPANY
1974

Library of Congress No. 57-35445

ISBN No. 0-87747-519-9

Lithographed by

DESERET PRESS

in the United States of America

GOSPEL TRUTH

VOLUME I

Too great a value cannot be placed upon the possession of the truth. It is indeed beyond estimate. . . . Everything untrue, no matter how widely believed and advocated, must sooner or later perish. . . . The great strength of the latter-day work in which we are engaged is found in its truth. This constitutes its great power and makes it all powerful. . . . Truth cannot be changed. It cannot be altered. It is eternal. All other things may perish; the heavens and the earth may pass away; but the truth cannot be destroyed.

—George Q. Cannon
Juvenile Instructor
30:273-74 (May 1, 1895)

I know that God lives. I know that Jesus lives, for I have seen Him. I know that this is the Church of God and that it is founded on Jesus Christ, our Redeemer. I testify to you of these things as one that knows—as one of the Apostles of the Lord Jesus Christ that can bear witness to you today in the presence of the Lord Jesus Christ that He lives and that He will live and will come to reign on the earth, to sway an undisputed sceptre.

—GEORGE Q. CANNON
Deseret Weekly 53:610
(October 6, 1896)

We must remember that God's work is not confined to this life, that God's plan of salvation extends throughout eternity, that according to our belief it began to operate in eternity, if it ever began at all. It always operated from eternity and will operate to eternity for all the children of men, for every human soul.

—GEORGE Q. CANNON
Journal of Discourses 26:79
(November 9, 1884)

CONTENTS

SECTION 3: AUTHORITY AND COMMUNICATION
FROM GOD

VOLUME 2 CONTAINS THE FOLLOWING: Truth—The Only Anchor; The Gospel—A Practical Religion; Temptations, Trials, and Persecutions; Mormonism—The Leaven of the Earth; The Church of God—The Kingdom of God; True and False Religion; Preaching the Gospel to the World; God's Covenant Peoples; Salvation for the Dead; Courtship and Marriage—Home and Family; The Sabbath—The Lord's Day; The Sacrament of the Lord's Supper; Fasting and Fast Days; Prayer—The Bulwark of the Saints; The Word of Wisdom—God's Law of Health; Administering to the Sick; Virtue, Chastity, and Love; Habits—Good and Bad; True Education—Literature for the Saints; The Standard Works—Our Scriptures; Apostasy from the Truth—Some Causes; Evil Spirits and Secret Combinations; The Law of Tithing—A Law of God; Temporal Affairs and Economic Prosperity; America—A God-Inspired Nation; Constitutional Government and Politics.

PREFACE TO THE FIRST EDITION

Few men in our Church have had such remarkable understanding of the gospel of Jesus Christ as President George Q. Cannon. An apostle for more than forty years and the first counselor in the First Presidency for approximately twenty years, he was also editor of such publications as the *Juvenile Instructor*, *The Millennial Star* and the *Deseret News*, and wrote several books. President Heber J. Grant once wrote: "When the records of the achievement and life's labors of the prophets of this dispensation shall be made up, the record made by President George Q. Cannon shall stand out as one of the brightest."

Several years ago I had the privilege of reading early copies of the *Juvenile Instructor* and was greatly impressed by President Cannon's editorials. Later, I read many of his discourses and felt even more strongly that the membership of the Church today should have access to this inspirational material.

Hesitantly I undertook the pleasant task of reading published discourses and editorial writings and selecting what I considered the most appropriate material. It was a project of greater magnitude than I anticipated. But I feel sure the reader will agree with President Joseph F. Smith, who said that George Q. Cannon was a "man in whom the Spirit of God dwelt, a man of great intelligence, one of the wisest men I ever knew. . . . He was a mighty man—A chieftain in the hosts of Israel."

As compiler, I wish to express sincere thanks and appreciation for the help and encouragement given: first, to Samuel Weller of Zion's Book Store for his suggestion that I undertake the work and for obtaining research material; to the Church Historical Department, especially to Earl E. Olson for his assistance and to Joseph Peterson for making available autostatic copies of some discourses; to Harold Lundstrom for his helpful suggestions; to Edwin Q. Cannon for writing the foreword; to George J. Cannon, Theodore L. Cannon, Rosannah C. Irvine, Marba Josephson, and others of the Cannon family for their interest and encouragement; to Evelyn Playfair for manuscript typing, and to Mary Lou Gillison and Sharon Whitaker for assisting her; and to Erma Provost and many other friends for their encouragement.

Portland, Oregon　　　　　　　　　—JERRELD L. NEWQUIST
February 1957

PREFACE TO THE SECOND EDITION

Since the appearance of the first edition of this volume, President George Q. Cannon has become one of the most widely quoted of the early leaders of the Church. *Gospel Truth* has long been out of print, and the reissuing of this popular volume will be welcomed by those who are already familiar with this great leader's inspirational messages as well as many new converts and younger members who will find clear, explicit expositions of important gospel truths.

President Cannon was a gifted speaker and writer. For many years he ranked among the foremost public speakers of the nation. Few have ever had such a remarkable understanding of the gospel of Jesus Christ as has President Cannon. He developed to a high degree the ability to adapt his words to convey important thoughts to the minds of children as well as the most cultivated audiences of mature persons.

This volume, as well as Volume 2, compiled from his numerous discourses and extensive writings, will bring to the reader some of the finest material on the gospel yet to appear in print. Those who read and study these books will find them to be a most important source of gospel doctrine and truth.

As was written at the time of his death, "In faith, few were his equals. As a servant of the Most High, he was among the favored few who saw the face of the Lord while yet in the flesh and heard the Divine voice, and yet remained in mortality."

JERRELD L. NEWQUIST

Seattle, Washington
March 1974

HIGHLIGHTS IN THE LIFE OF GEORGE Q. CANNON

1827—January 11	Was born in Liverpool, England.
1840—June 18	Was baptized into the Church of Jesus Christ.
1842—September 17	Left Liverpool for America on ship *Sidney*.
1843—April 12	Saw Joseph Smith for the first time.
1845—February 9	Was ordained on elder by his uncle, John Taylor, and also ordained a seventy.
1847—October 3	Arrived in Great Salt Lake Valley with the Saints.
1850—December 12	Landed on Sandwich Islands on his first mission.
1852—January 27	Commenced the translation of the Book of Mormon in the Hawaiian language at Wailuku, Maui, finishing it two years later.
1854—July 29	Sailed from Honolulu on his return to America.
November 28	Was set apart as president of the 30th Quorum of Seventies.
December 11	Married Elizabeth Hoagland.
1856—January 28	Completed publication of the Book of Mormon in the Hawaiian language.
February 23	Issued first number of the *Western Standard*, a weekly paper in San Francisco.
1858—September	Was called on a mission to the Eastern States.
1860—August 26	Was ordained a member of Council of Twelve Apostles by President Brigham Young.
September 26	Left Salt Lake City for England to preside over European Mission.
1862—January 23	Was elected a delegate to Congress.
1864—Fall	Was appointed private secretary of Brigham Young.
Early winter	Organized and taught a Sunday School in Salt Lake City.
1866—January 1	Published first number of the *Juvenile Instructor*.
November 4	Appointed as the first General Superintendent of the Sunday Schools.
1867—	Became editor and publisher of the *Deseret News*.
November 21	Issued first number of daily *Deseret Evening News*.
1872—August 5	Was elected a delegate to Congress.
1873—April 6	Was chosen as one of five additional counselors to President Brigham Young.
1877—August	Again became editor of the *Deseret News*.
1880—October 8	Was selected by John Taylor to be the first counselor in the First Presidency.
1886—February 13	Was arrested at Humboldt, Nevada.

1888—September 17	Was sentenced to 175 days in penitentiary.
1889—April 7	Was sustained as first counselor to President Wilford Woodruff.
1898—October 9	Was sustained as first counselor to President Lorenzo Snow.
1900—November 29	Left Salt Lake City to attend jubilee of Sandwich Islands Mission.
1901—April 12	Died in Monterey, California.

Key To Abbreviations

CR—Conference Reports, annual and semiannual (1897-.)

DEN—Deseret Evening News (1867-.)

DNW—Weekly Deseret News (1850-88).

DW—Deseret Weekly (1888-1898).

Era—Improvement Era (1897-1970).

JD—Journal of Discourses (26 volumes, 1851-86).

JH—Journal History (Mss.) of The Church of Jesus Christ of Latter-day Saints.

JI—Juvenile Instructor (later known as *Instructor*) (1866-1970). A magazine published and edited by George Q. Cannon during his lifetime.

MS—Millennial Star (1840-1970).

WS—Writings from the Western Standard (Liverpool, 1864). A compilation of editorials written for the newspaper *Western Standard,* which George Q. Cannon published in San Francisco, 1856-57.

Titles of any other sources are written out in full.

The abbreviated references are preceded by a date, which is the date the discourse was given or the date the article was published. All references are verbatim quotations, except where ellipsis points (. . .) indicate that some material has been left out.

GEORGE Q. CANNON
A BIOGRAPHICAL SKETCH

"I know that God lives. I know that Jesus lives, for I have seen him." (*Deseret Weekly* 53:610.)

How the people assembled in general conference in the Salt Lake Tabernacle must have thrilled when they heard that powerful testimony. President George Q. Cannon was nearly seventy years old when he spoke those words. Having such a knowledge and being able to bear such a testimony must have contributed greatly to the success he attained in life.

In 1895 B. F. Cummings, Jr., told of a few of the accomplishments of this man so loved and respected by the Saints. He wrote:

> George Q. Cannon stands forth a central figure of commanding influence among the "Shining Lights" of Latter-day Israel. In him are seen qualities and an organization that makes of him a distinct type among our leading men, and in his career we witness experiences and achievements the like of which we could not credit to any other man, without feeling that we were violating a natural law of association and propriety. . . .
>
> How natural it is to remember George Q. Cannon as the father of the Sandwich Islands Mission, and the typical journalist among the people of these mountains, and the champion of the Church in Congress in the days when the lowering clouds of the nation's anger hovered threateningly over the Saints! What eternal fitness there has always seemed to be in his taking the lead whenever appeals were to be made to, or negotiations conducted with, men in power, in behalf of his persecuted people.
>
> The precision with which the personal history of George Q. Cannon fits into the historical superstructure of the Church, constituting, as it does, an indispensable portion of it, proves that his place and part in its affairs were predetermined by the Designer, who foreordained the destiny of both. . . . He is, above all else, the diplomatist of his people, the greatest master of practical statecraft that has ever appeared among them. (*Contributor* 16:118-32.)

George Quayle Cannon was born in the humbler ranks of life but not among the lower classes; his parents had a wealth of honesty, integrity, and Christian devotion, which made them respected and esteemed. He was the eldest child; the other children were Mary Alice Cannon, who later married a Charles Lambert; Anne Cannon, who married Orin N. Woodbury; Angus M. Cannon; David H. Cannon; Leonora Cannon, who married Robert Gardner; and Elizabeth Cannon (the daughter of his father by a second marriage), who married William Piggott. (*Historical Record* 6:174.)

George Q. Cannon was born January 11, 1827, at Liverpool, England. His parents, George and Ann Quayle Cannon, were natives of Peel, Isle of Man, the family line being traceable on the island for centuries back.

Young George Q. was a careful reader of the Bible. The knowledge thus acquired of the dealings of God with his children founded his deep and abiding faith. As he later said:

> When I have read this Bible as a child, I have wept because I did not live on the earth when Jesus wandered among men. And I have asked myself, why is it that men cannot receive those blessings as they who were the associates of Jesus received them? I asked my teachers, and I asked my parents, "Are there men now who receive these blessings?" and they answered me that there were none, and I wondered why it was so. (*Millennial Star* 24:563.)

His aunt, Leonora Cannon, had moved to Canada, where she became the wife of John Taylor, a Methodist preacher. Elder Parley P. Pratt arrived in Toronto in 1836 and baptized John Taylor and his wife.

Two years later John Taylor was called to the apostleship, and on the day that George Q. Cannon was thirteen, January 11, 1840, John Taylor and Wilford Woodruff, two of the most ardent followers of the Prophet Joseph Smith, and members of the Council of the Twelve Apostles, landed at Liverpool to fill their missions in the British Isles.

Elder Taylor called at the house of his brother-in-law, George Cannon, where he met the mother and her son George. Finding that the head of the household was at work, he departed, promising to return. As he walked away from the door, the mother said to her boy, "George, there goes a man of God. He has come to bring salvation to your father's house." (*Instructor* 79:67.)

As soon as Elder Taylor preached the gospel to her family, Mrs. Cannon was ready to be baptized, knowing for herself, as she said, that the principles he taught were the true gospel of the Son of God. Her husband read the Book of Mormon carefully twice before his baptism. After finishing it the second time, he remarked, "No wicked man could write such a book as this; and no good man would write it, unless it were true and he were commanded of God to do so." (Andrew Jenson, *Historical Record* 6:174.)

George Q. Cannon always believed he was born with a testimony of the gospel and so stated years later:

Did you ask how I got my testimony of the truth of Mormonism? Why, I never got one. . . . The reason why I received none was because I did not have to get one. It was born with me. Since I first heard the Gospel, or Mormonism as it is called, I have always known it to be true. It seemed to be a part of my very nature. I can remember, though, in my early boyhood that I felt very badly because I had no especial gift, and I used to think I was not a favored child of God, else I would have received the gift of tongues or some other such gift. (*Young Woman's Journal* 4:123.)

After being baptized, the family was filled with the "spirit of gathering to Zion." To fulfill this irresistible desire, they saved and planned for two years. Prior to his marriage, the father of the family had had a dream concerning the death of his wife, and when migration was talked about, they both seemed aware that she would not live to reach Zion. But she was determined to undertake the journey for the sake of her children.

The family started for Zion, sailing from Liverpool on the ship *Sidney* on September 17, 1842, but the mother died and was buried at sea. The others continued their journey to Nauvoo.

At the time of their arrival, a general conference of the Church was in session, and a great crowd was on the landing stage to greet them. Although George had never seen a picture of Joseph Smith, he instantly knew and pointed him out to the others. All his life he treasured that inspired recognition. He later wrote:

It was the Author's privilege to thus meet the Prophet for the first time. . . . Nearly every prominent man in the community was there. Familiar with the names of all and the persons of many of the prominent Elders, the Author sought, with a boy's curiosity and eagerness, to discover those whom he knew, and especially to get sight of the Prophet and his brother Hyrum, neither of whom he had ever met. When his eyes fell upon the Prophet, without a word from any one to point him out or any reason to separate him from others who stood around, he knew him instantly. He would have known him among ten thousand. There was that about him, which to the Author's eyes, distinguished him from all the men he had ever seen. (*The Life of Joseph Smith, the Prophet*, p. xxvi.)

Young George was seventeen when the Prophet Joseph and his brother Hyrum were martyred. He shared the grief of the people at the tragedy and had an additional sorrow because his beloved uncle, John Taylor, had been wounded by the mob. He saw his father construct the coffins in which the martyrs were to rest. He may even have been with his father when that skillful man made the death masks. (*Instructor* 79:162.)

There was confusion in the minds of some of the Saints following the loss of the Prophet and his brother, but the Cannons had no doubts. George was present at the meeting in the grove at Nauvoo when the mantle of Joseph fell upon Brigham Young in a miraculous manner, and he spoke of it many times throughout his life.

> A more wonderful and miraculous event than was wrought that day in the presence of that congregation we never heard of. The Lord gave His people a testimony that left no room for doubt as to who was the man He had chosen to lead them. . . . On that occasion President Brigham Young seemed to be transformed. . . . The tones of his voice, his appearance, everything he said and the spirit which accompanied his words, convinced the people that the leader whom God had selected to guide them stood before them. (*Juvenile Instructor* 5:175, 182.)

On August 19, 1844, George Cannon died at St. Louis while on a short visit. After the death of his father, young George went to live with his uncle, John Taylor, until October 1849. At that time John Taylor was the editor and publisher of the *Times and Seasons* and the *Nauvoo Neighbor*. George learned the printing business while living and working with his uncle. He wrote:

> When a youth, it was my good fortune to live in the family of President John Taylor. It was my chief delight in those days to listen to him and other Elders relate their experiences as missionaries. Such conversations were very fascinating to me. They made a deep impression upon me. The days of which they spoke were the days of poverty, when Elders traveled without purse and scrip, among strange people who were ignorant of our principles, and too many of whom were ready to mob and persecute. They traveled by faith and were pioneers for the Lord in strange lands, and He was their only reliance. Their missions were rich in instances of His power exhibited in their behalf. What I heard strengthened my faith and increased the desire in my heart to be a missionary. No calling was so noble in my eyes as that of a standard-bearer of the Gospel. (George Q. Cannon, *My First Mission*, Preface.)

While still in Nauvoo, George Q. Cannon was given the higher priesthood. He was ordained an elder by John Taylor on February 9, 1845, and on the same day was ordained a seventy. The quorum of which he became a member was organized the day he was ordained, and he was chosen to be its clerk.

When the Saints were exiled from their beautiful city, Nauvoo, Illinois, in 1846, Elder Cannon accompanied the main body to Winter Quarters. There he remained until the next year, when he made his way with other exiled Saints across the plains to Salt Lake Valley. He arrived October 3, 1847, and thus became one of Utah's earliest pioneers.

In the fall of 1849, with a number of other brethren, he was called to California, under the direction of Elder Charles C. Rich of the Council of the Twelve. After a hazardous journey, the company reached lower California. George Q. worked in the gold mines until the fall of 1850, a work in which he had little interest.

> There was no place that I would not rather have gone to at that time than California. I heartily despised the work of digging gold. (*JI* 4:13.)

It was great news to him when he was called with nine others to go on a mission to the Sandwich (Hawaiian) Islands. This mission to the islands emphasized a prominent trait in his character. The missionaries had expected to preach to the white population, but the opportunity to do so was very limited. Consequently, most of the elders were in favor of returning home. Elder Cannon was impressed by a sense of his duty to preach the gospel; he could not feel that he had performed his part by stopping at the very threshold of his work. The white people would not listen, but the native population was in need of gospel teaching; Elder Cannon determined to do his part in supplying that need.

> I felt resolved to stay there, master the language and warn the people of those islands, if I had to do it alone; for I felt that I could not do otherwise and be free from condemnation. (*My First Mission*, p. 22.)

His unflinching devotion to duty and unwavering faith that the Lord would bless his labors were the means of a great triumph in disseminating the gospel message among the Hawaiian people. Four elders remained with him, and in three-and-a-half years there were more than four thousand members of the Church on the islands.

On one of his first speaking assignments, Elder Cannon had a wonderful experience.

When he commenced to speak the Spirit of the Lord rested upon him as it never had done before. The people had faith, and their hearts were prepared to receive the truth. For upwards of an hour he spoke, and he was so carried away in the Spirit, that he was like a man in a trance. Joy filled his heart and the hearts of the people. They wept like children, and that day was the beginning of a good work in that place. (Ibid., p. 11.)

The elders had to learn the language—an accomplishment that came with remarkable ease to Elder Cannon.

My desire to learn to speak was very strong; it was present with me night and day, and I never permitted an opportunity of talking with the natives to pass without improving it. I also tried to exercise faith before the Lord to obtain the gift of talking and understand the language. One evening, while sitting on the mats conversing with some neighbors who had dropped in, I felt an uncommonly great desire to understand what they said. All at once I felt a peculiar sensation in my ears; I jumped to my feet, with my hands at the sides of my head, and exclaimed to Elders Bigler and Keeler who sat at the table, that I believed I had received the gift of interpretation. And it was so. (Ibid., p. 23.)

From that time on he had little difficulty in understanding what the people said. He refrained from speaking or reading English as much as possible and even trained himself to think in the native tongue.

He prayed often to the Lord, and many comforting things were revealed to him by the power of the Holy Ghost.

I had never been so happy in my life before as I was then. When I prayed I could go unto God in faith; He listened to my prayers; He gave me great comfort and joy; He revealed Himself to me as He never had done before, and told me that if I would persevere, I should be blessed, be the means of bringing many to the knowledge of the truth, and be spared to return home after having done a good work.

Many things were revealed to me, during those days, when He was the only Friend we had to lean upon, which were afterwards fulfilled. A friendship was there established between our Father and myself, which, I trust, will never be broken nor diminished, and which I hope has continued to grow stronger from those days to these. (Ibid., p. 26.)

No sooner had Elder Cannon begun to travel among the natives in an earnest endeavor to search out those who would receive the truth, than the direct interpositions of Providence began to be manifested. He was led, at times in a singular manner, to individuals whose hearts were in a condition to receive the gospel, and within a short time numerous baptisms occurred. This was in fulfillment of a blessing upon the head of Elder Cannon by John Taylor, who had predicted that he "should stand in the waters as a Saviour, and call upon the multitudes to come forward and be baptized." (*MS* 14:493.)

The history of the Sandwich Islands Mission reads like a romance, with the young missionary as its central figure. His eloquence charmed the natives and overwhelmed his opponents. His personal traits won the hearts of hundreds. From village to village and from island to island he passed, kindling in the hearts of thousands of the simple, honest, and affectionate islanders faith in the gospel, a remarkable and contagious religious zeal, and an unbounded and undying affection for himself. "Dreams, visions and revelations were given to me," he wrote, "and the communion of the Spirit was most sweet and delicious." (*My First Mission*, p. 43.)

Elder Cannon had hardly commenced his labors among the Hawaiians when he was seized with an overpowering desire to translate the Book of Mormon into their language. He believed they were of the house of Israel, a branch of the race descended from Lehi, and he longed to place before them, in their own tongue, the record of their forefathers. His fellow-laborers, the elders, encouraged him, and from the First Presidency at home— Presidents Young, Kimball, and Richards—came words of cheer, counseling him to persevere.

This translation demanded much care. He could get no aid from the white men in this labor, but he had the assistance of several of the natives. He read his translation to them as it progressed and discussed with them the principles to see if they obtained the same idea from the translation that the English edition gave to its readers. He afterwards examined the translation carefully with the aid of William Farrer and a native named Kauwahi, a man of acute intellect and talent, who was known as the most eloquent and best reasoner in the Hawaiian nation. (Ibid., p. 71.) During this revision, they went through the Book of Mormon twice to see that no words or sentences were omitted and to correct any inaccuracies in the translation or the idiom.

The work was finished January 31, 1854, a labor of nearly two years. The original idea had been to purchase a press and materials to publish the Book of Mormon in Hawaii, and money for that purpose was raised by selling advance copies of the book and by loan.

In the meantime, on July 29, 1854, George Q. Cannon and the four faithful elders sailed home, carrying with them the love, almost adoration, of literally thousands of the people who had believed their words and been baptized into the true church of Christ. Speaking of this fifty years later, President Cannon said:

> Of all the experiences in the intervening years there are none more dear to my memory than the blessed experiences of those years upon the Islands, where I saw the miracles of the Gospel repeated in the healing of the sick, by faith and the laying on of hands; where I grew strong in my own duties and certain of the divine help of God; where the sowing of the seed brought so bountiful a harvest. It was then that I was filled with prophecy for the future of Hawaii, and my prophecy has been fulfilled. (*Church News*, July 17, 1949, p. 6.)

Arriving in San Francisco sometime in August, Elder Cannon remained there some forty days and assisted Parley P. Pratt in copying his *Autobiography*. He then went on to Salt Lake City. Upon his arrival he was named to be one of the presidents of the 30th Quorum of the Seventy.

Waiting for him was a lovely young schoolteacher, Elizabeth Hoagland, whom he had known as a girl when they crossed the plains together. They were married on December 11, 1854, less than two weeks after his return. In later years he wrote of his marriage:

> When I went on my first mission, I was engaged to a young lady. After a lengthy absence, I came back as poor as missionaries generally do. But I got married twelve days after my return. I tried to get employment, but up to the day of my marriage had not obtained it. The next day after marriage I secured employment. I had only been home five months when I went on another mission; and though it was in the winter time, I made means so fast that when I started on this mission, having been called to take my wife with me, I left Salt Lake City with a very excellent outfit— mules and wagon, provisions, etc. (*JI* 33:65.)

Soon after his return to Utah Elder Cannon received an intimation from President Brigham Young that he would be called to return on a mission to Hawaii. However, before this Parley P. Pratt wrote to the First Presidency from San Francisco asking that Elder Cannon be sent to aid in the publication of a newspaper, and also to publish the translation he had made in Hawaiian of the Book of Mormon. Consequently, Elder Cannon was called, at the Church's annual general conference in April 1855, to go on a mission to California to labor in connection with and under the direction of Elder Pratt.

Upon Elder Cannon's arrival at San Francisco, he found that Elder Pratt had already started on his return home. Elder Cannon followed him and soon caught up with him. Elder Pratt set him apart to preside over the Pacific Mission, subject to the direction of any of the Twelve Apostles who might visit or be called to labor in that area.

The first order of business for the young elders (Elders Joseph Bull and Matthew F. Wilkie had accompanied him) was to secure a suitable office, set up the press, and go to work. Elder Cannon later wrote:

> An office was secured on the principle street in town, and we immediately commenced the publication of the translation of the Book of Mormon in the Hawaiian language. Two thousand copies of this work were issued and sent down to the Islands. While publishing this work, and attending to the other labors which devolved upon me, I maintained a constant correspondence with President Brigham Young. He still favored the publication of a newspaper, and appointed me to be its editor, and, by his kind, fatherly and hopeful counsels, gave myself and the Elders laboring with me continual encouragement in our labors. . . .
>
> Prospects in San Francisco for the establishment of a printing-office and newspaper, I found to be of the most discouraging character. . . . The Lord opened our way in a most signal manner. . . . It really seemed to me that money grew in our hands, and . . . would go further and accomplish more, than four times the amount would under ordinary circumstances. . . . Friends were raised up on every hand, and though our pathway was not free from obstacles, yet the work moved off so successfully that we felt greatly favored and blessed of the Lord. (George Q. Cannon, *Writings from the Western Standard*, pp. vii-ix.)

The last form was run off the press January 28, 1856, just over six months after the arrival of Elder Cannon and his associates in California. Thus was the Book of Mormon first translated and published in the Hawaiian language.

The publication of a paper, the *Western Standard*, and the fulfillment of duties involved in the mission called for all of Elder Cannon's mental and physical energies for a period of nineteen months. The *Western Standard* became a powerful agency for good and permanently established its editor's reputation as a writer. Later his editorials were compiled and published under the title *Writings from the Western Standard.*

When the news of the approach of Johnston's Army toward Utah was received, Elder Cannon closed the mission affairs and returned home, reaching Salt Lake City on January 19, 1858. He left this parting word with the people of San Francisco:

> The editor of the Herald deceives himself and those who believe what he writes, when he says that "the days of Mormonism at Salt Lake are numbered." The cannon are not cast, the muskets or rifles not made, the powder and ball not manufactured nor the men to use them either born or conceived, that will destroy "Mormonism." Mark our words, gentlemen, it will live, though all earth and hell array themselves against it. (*Western Standard,* September 18, 1857.)

Upon his arrival home, he was appointed adjutant general of the army being organized for defense against invasion. Soon afterwards he was directed by President Young to take a printing press and material to Fillmore to issue the *Deseret News* in a reduced size, which he did from April to September, 1858.

On his return north, an incident occurred that illustrates his great faith.

> At Payson at noon on Monday, as I was unhitching my team at Brother William B. Preston's, . . . Brother John Bollwinkle drove up with a carriage and mules and handed me a note. It was from President Young, and was dated the day previous, Sunday. He informed me that I had been appointed to go East on a mission. The company I was to go with expected to start the next day (the day I received the note), and he wished me to come to the city as quickly as I could. In reply to my inquiry the messenger said he would be ready to start back as soon as he had eaten his dinner and fed his mules.
>
> While he was gone, I gathered up what clothing and bedding and weapons I needed for the journey, and in about three-quarters of an hour we were on our way to Salt Lake City, where we arrived the next morning as day was breaking. As I had only been home from a mission a few weeks before I went to Fillmore, and had been absent several years before on another mission, I had no home in Salt Lake City. In leaving my family at the roadside, therefore, I left them with no bright prospect for comfort and ease during my absence. But they uttered no complaints. They put their trust in the Lord and during the two years of my absence, He was their benefactor and friend. (*JI* 28:220.)

On seeing him, President Young turned to others in the office and said, "Didn't I tell you it would be so? I knew I had but to call; here he is." (Bryant S. Hinckley, *The Faith of Our*

Pioneer Fathers. p. 169.) Probably this was as short notice as any elder in the Church ever received for a mission of such duration.

The eastern mission was of a delicate nature; so much prejudice against and misinformation concerning the Church prevailed that correcting false impressions had to be done judiciously to be effective. Elder Cannon began with characteristic zeal and energy; and, by means of letters of introduction from General Thomas L. Kane and others, he was able to meet many editors, members of Congress, and other public men and to present to them the true state of affairs in Utah.

In addition to this special assignment, he had charge of the branches of the Church in the East, and in 1859 and 1860 he acted as Church emigration agent, in which position his careful attention to detail made his services highly valuable.

While on this mission Elder Cannon was selected to fill the vacancy in the Council of the Twelve occasioned by the assassination of Parley P. Pratt. On his return home, August 26, 1860, he was ordained an apostle by President Brigham Young. He was then thirty-three years of age. This calling fulfilled the prophecy made by Elder Pratt a few years previously that George Q. Cannon would succeed him as a member of the Council of Twelve.

Elder Cannon's calling as an apostle also fulfilled a revelation he himself had received many years earlier.

> The Lord revealed to me when I was quite young that I at some time would be an Apostle. I never told it to any human being; but on more than one occasion I have gone out and besought the Lord to choose some one else and to relieve me of that responsibility. I have besought Him earnestly, time and again, that if I could only get my salvation and exaltation without being called to that high and holy responsibility, I would much rather He would choose some other person. (*DW* 40:377.)

Soon after this he was appointed, together with Elders Charles C. Rich and Amasa M. Lyman, to preside over the European Mission. His duties were to take charge of the *Millennial Star* and the publishing business connected therewith and also emigration.

These three apostles presided over the European Mission until May 14, 1862, when Elders Lyman and Rich returned home, and Elder Cannon went to Washington, D. C., where he had been called. He and W. H. Hooper had been elected United States

Senators, and he was to join Senator Hooper in endeavoring to get the Utah Territory admitted to the Union. They labored faithfully in this assignment until the adjournment of Congress, when Elder Cannon returned to England.

Until his return home in 1864, he presided over the European Mission, visiting twice the branches of the Church in Scandinavia, Germany, Holland, Switzerland, and France. During the four years of this mission more than thirteen thousand Saints sailed from Liverpool for Zion. And it was a cause of joy to all engaged in the work at that time to know that more persons had joined the Church in the same period than had emigrated.

During the next three years Elder Cannon was private secretary to President Brigham Young and enjoyed the great leader's personal friendship. He also became well informed regarding Church affairs at headquarters. He was a careful, thoughtful observer, a constant reader, a student of men and measures, with the power of assimilating and turning what he saw and heard to practical account. A natural diplomat, with polite address and easy conversation, he impressed favorably and had great personal magnetism.

But Elder Cannon was not to lay aside his missionary work. Thousands of youths needed to receive the same testimony as their parents of the divinity of the gospel restored to earth, that they might in turn be valiant in its behalf and enjoy its blessings. At the Sunday School Jubilee in 1899 he spoke of how he had felt:

When I returned from Europe, after filling continuous missions for a long time, I felt there was an immense field in Zion for the labors of the Elders. I had seen how few souls could be gathered abroad, and when I reflected upon the numbers of our children at home, I felt a burning desire to spend all the time I could in trying to teach them the principles of the Gospel.

Upon my return, in 1864, I organized a Sunday School in the Fourteenth Ward, and other schools were organized directly afterwards. (Conference Report, October 1899, p. 88.)

The great object for which Sunday Schools are established is to make of our children earnest, sincere and intelligent Latter-day Saints—nothing short of this. To fill their hearts with love for God and his work. To inspire them with faith in the Gospel. To make the Gospel a part of their life, of their whole being. (Instructor 84:389.)

In January 1866, he commenced the publication of the Juvenile Instructor. His experience as a writer and his love for children aptly qualified him to issue such a paper, and he served as editor and publisher until his death more than thirty-five years later. He never failed in devoting time and attention to this publication for the development of faith and purity in the hearts of the young people.

In an editorial entitled "Salutatory" in the first issue, Elder Cannon wrote:

> No other community, with which we are acquainted, indulge in such high hopes respecting their young as do the inhabitants of this Territory. . . . To have these hopes and expectations gratified, steps should be taken to train our children and to do all in our power to prepare them for the duties that will devolve upon them. It is to aid in this work and to supply a want which has been long felt to exist that the publication of this paper has been undertaken. (*JI* 1:3.)

George Q. Cannon's name has long been identified with the Sunday School movement. He became general superintendent in 1867 when the Deseret Sunday School Union was organized and served in that capacity the balance of his life. He publicly stated that he knew of no work that had given him greater satisfaction. It has recently been written that the Sunday Schools "owe their permanence and vitality as an institution to George Q. Cannon." (*Instructor* 84:261.)

In educational matters he was connected with the public school system, being at one time chancellor of the Deseret University, and he was a strong supporter of the Church schools. From the day of its organization, April 5, 1888, he was a member of the Church's general board of education and never relaxed his interest and energies in that capacity.

Elder Cannon's field of usefulness as a writer was greatly enlarged in the autumn of 1867 by his appointment by President Young to edit the *Deseret News*. It was then issued weekly and semiweekly, but he instituted the *Deseret Evening News,* a daily, the first issue being dated November 21, 1867.

Upon him fell the labor of conducting, in behalf of the Church and through its official organ, one of the mightiest controversies that ever agitated the minds of men. Not only was it necessary for the peculiar features of the faith and practice of the Latter-day Saints to be explained and defended before the world, but it was also necessary to teach the members of the Church at home; the *Deseret News* was a great power in this

work of defense and education. Its teachings aided in giving form
to the faith of the Saints, and its utterances and arguments were
cues and texts that were used by thousands of speakers at home
and abroad.

Under the editorial direction of George Q. Cannon, the
Deseret News became an eloquent exponent of the principles of
the American Constitution and the Declaration of Independence.
Powerful expositions of these principles were his work, and they
left an impress upon the people of Utah that still endures.

During the fall of 1871 a great many articles appeared in
various papers on the subject of admitting Utah to the Union,
on the condition that the Latter-day Saints relinquish their practice of plural marriage. So much was said in favor of, and so
little in opposition to, this method of dealing with the question
that Presidents Brigham Young and George A. Smith, who were
then at St. George, felt there was danger of the Latter-day Saints
being put in a false position. They telegraphed Elder Cannon
to proceed at once to Washington, D.C., to define the true position of the Saints on this important point. He remained in
Washington until Congress adjourned for the holidays.

In August 1872, he was elected to Congress as a delegate
from Utah. In that position he served for ten years. Although
not entitled to vote as a representative, he exercised a marked
influence among leaders in that notable body. Because of the
intense prejudice against Utah and her people, his experience
in Congress was frequently difficult. In spite of this he made
many warm friends in the national capitol.

It is interesting to read from George Q. Cannon's journal
his comments on the day he was to be sworn in as a new member
of Congress.

> I am here without a man who is in sympathy with me; but I have
> a Friend more powerful than they all. In this I rejoice. I feel there are
> angels with me, and as one of old said, they that are for us are more than
> they who are against us. When I pray, I feel comforted and filled with
> joy. Of myself I feel very weak; but in my Lord I feel strong. (*Instructor*
> 80:157.)

In 1873, when Congress adjourned for the Christmas holidays, Elder Cannon made a hurried trip to St. George to see
President Young. He recorded the following advice he received:

He said that I ought to be careful about my movements in Washington—that I would be watched and everything I did scrutinized and I ought to keep a journal of my movements that I could prove where I was at any time. If anything should occur to General Grant, he (the President) would be accused of having prompted its commission, and I would probably be charged with having had it done. He said that next to himself I was the most hated of any of the authorities. . . . They would seek my life with the greatest of anxiety after seeking his, and I ought to be careful of myself. In all the publications of our enemies my name was generally held up to the public next to his own. (Ibid., p. 158.)

Finally, in March 1882, the outcry against the Latter-day Saints culminated in the passage of law that rendered Elder Cannon ineligible to the office of delegate. This was the Edmunds Act, disfranchising those who practiced polygamy as a religious rite. Before retiring from Congress, however, he had the opportunity of speaking in vindication of the people of Utah; and under the trying circumstances he discharged his duty with boldness and emphasis, yet with diplomatic delicacy.

It has been stated that the House of Representatives, which expelled George Q. Cannon for believing and practicing a principle of his religion, allowed two other members to retain their seats, one of whom had killed a man in cold blood, while the other had been convicted of bribery. (MS 44:367.)

One amusing item concerning him appeared in the *Washington Telegram*:

Bishop Cannon will be astonished to see the *Chronicle* classifying him as a Democrat. If there is one square-built, iron-clad Independent in the House, who knows his own mind and paddles his own canoe, it is the journalist Bishop from Utah. (MS 38:111.)

Many members of Congress parted from their friend, "the Mormon Delegate," with unfeigned regret. He had won his way to their hearts, not more by his uniform courtesy and his affable and engaging manner than by his great knowledge of Congressional affairs. He had made it a point to acquaint himself with all departments and functions of the government and with the names, personal history, and constituencies of every member in both houses of the national legislature, and his retentive memory and quick recollection enabled him to give information at a moment's notice.

One historian paid him the following tribute:

His forte, in secular affairs, was statecraft, and in the field of
diplomacy, Utah, among all her gifted sons, has not seen his equal. Much
of the prestige he possessed was undoubtedly due to his ecclesiastical prominence; . . . but it was not office that gave him intellect, eloquence, magnetism, and all those rare qualities which enabled him to mould and sway
the minds and hearts of men. He would have been a man of mark in any
community. Had he remained in his native England, he would probably
have been heard of in Parliament, and it is within the bounds of conserva-
tive calculation to imagine such a one the peer of Gladstone, Disraeli and
other premiers of the realm. (Orson F. Whitney, *The History of Utah*
4:663.)

President Brigham Young died August 29, 1877. Under his
direction, George Q. Cannon had prepared his will and was made
the principal executor with Brigham Young, Jr., and Albert Car-
rington as co-executors. Elder Cannon, then editor of the *Deseret
News*, stood close to his leader when death came. He had been at
the President's bedside constantly for thirty-six hours. At the
request of the family, he conducted the services.

Among the noble traits of character possessed by George Q.
Cannon, none was more conspicuous than his profound respect
for the Lord's anointed. This is evidenced by his journal at the
death of Brigham Young:

To describe my feelings upon the death of this man of God, whom I
loved so much and who had always treated me with such kindness and
affection is impossible. . . . On my part, he was in my eyes as perfect a
man as I ever knew. I never desired to see his faults; I closed my eyes to
them. To me he was a Prophet of God, the head of the dispensation on
the earth, holding the keys under the Prophet Joseph, and in my mind
there clustered about him, holding this position, everything holy and sacred
and to be revered. . . . I never criticized or found fault with his conduct,
his counsel or his teachings at any time in my heart, much less in my words
or actions. (*Instructor* 80:258.)

In October 1880, the Council of the Twelve reorganized
the Quorum of the First Presidency, the Church having been
without that quorum since the death of President Brigham Young.
Under the date of October 8 Elder Cannon records the following
in his journal:

Elder Woodruff's motion [that John Taylor be the first President of
the Church] was then called for and carried unanimously. President Taylor
said he was prepared to name his counselors and being requested to do so,
named me as his first and Joseph F. Smith as his second. The mention
of my name was a great surprise to me. As I had been nominated again

for Congress and would be absent this winter and probably half at least of the next two years, I had felt free in expressing my feelings upon the subject of the First Presidency and in favor of it, not thinking for a moment that my name would be mentioned for this position and feeling satisfied that no one could suspect me under the circumstances of having any personal ambition in connection with this matter.

I could scarcely express my feelings. Before the names of the counselors were called, I had a presentiment that my name would be mentioned, and I trembled all over. My nerves twitched all over my body, and I could scarcely control myself. When my name was mentioned, I rose to my feet and begged of the brethren to excuse me from filling that position. I told them that I would much rather remain in the Quorum of the Twelve. I could think of at least twelve or thirteen men who could fill that position, in my opinion, better than I could. My agitation was extreme, and I was completely overcome. President Taylor said it was not a matter of personal choice. Several of the brethren also spoke very kindly, approving of the nomination, and it was carried unanimously on motion of Brother Woodruff. (Ibid., p. 411.)

In 1884 an extremely persecutive assault on the Latter-day Saints began, particularly aimed at the plural marriage doctrine. Owing to the intense bitterness of this crusade, it was felt adviseable for the leading brethren of the Church to avoid coming directly within the power of the persecutors. This anti-polygamy crusade, which raged from 1884 to 1890, singled out President Cannon as one of the main objects of its malevolence. His influence being so great, it was thought that if he could be compelled to surrender, the entire Church would soon follow his example. However, he preferred exile and imprisonment to such a course, and in common with most of the Church leaders he went into retirement, remaining "underground" for several years, though helping to direct the general policy of the Church. The most strenuous efforts were made for his arrest, with not only the Church offices but also his homes being raided repeatedly and members of his family being taken before magistrates and grand juries to testify.

One of his most trying experiences occurred in 1886. A reward of five hundred dollars had been posted for his arrest. He was at that time "underground," and, in view of this reward, it was decided he should leave the area. With two or three others, he boarded a train for California. However, at Humboldt Station, Nevada, he was arrested. He was brought into Salt Lake City under military escort and placed under bonds set at $20,000 and $25,000, totaling the enormous sum of $45,000.

The feeling against the Church leaders was so bitter that President Taylor counseled him not to appear when his case was called, so his excessive bail was declared forfeited. Subsequently the amount was restored by an act of Congress. President Cannon's sole reason for not appearing in court was President Taylor's advice. During the night it had been revealed to President Taylor that if President Cannon went to trial, he would be killed. (*The Faith of Our Pioneer Fathers*, page 174.)

Finally, the fury of the persecution began to diminish. President Cannon and other leaders met the issue as early as it was reasonably safe for them to do so and were subjected to fine and imprisonment. President Cannon served four months in the Utah Penitentiary. Altogether about 800 men and a few women were imprisoned. All of this tended to advance the interests of the cause and proved the Saints to be superior to their persecutors in morals, sobriety, patience, and faith. Their prison life, rather than a stain, was a credit, indicating their fidelity to conviction of right.

The period of President Cannon's greatest power and influence followed his incarceration as a prisoner. President Taylor having died in exile, Wilford Woodruff became head of the Church, the First Presidency being reorganized in April 1889. Again George Q. Cannon was chosen first counselor. He bore a heavy part of the burden of that administration, the most notable events of which were the issuance of the famous Manifesto, discontinuing plural marriages, and the completion and dedication of the Salt Lake Temple. In the establishment of the Pioneer Power Plant and the Utah sugar industry, the promotion of mining, the building of Saltair, and many other enterprises, the weight of responsibility told upon him, notwithstanding his great vitality, conserved and perpetuated by a life of temperate and abstemious self-denial.

In addition to his duties in the First Presidency, he was engaged in many enterprises of importance. He was at various times a director of the Union Pacific Railroad Company and of the Salt Lake and Los Angeles Company; vice-president and director of ZCMI; founder of the publishing firm of George Q. Cannon and Sons Co., of which he was president; president of the Utah Sugar Co.; vice-president and director of Zion's Savings

Bank & Trust Co.; director of the Cooperative Wagon and Machine Co.; president of Brigham Young Trust Co.; president of the Utah Light and Power Co.; and director of the Bullion-Beck and Champion Mining Co. and the Grand Central Mining Co. He also organized the George Q. Cannon Association, of which he was the president and in which he placed all his property. He was president of the Trans-Mississippi Commercial Congress for one term and attended all its sessions. He was also president and afterwards vice-president of the Irrigation Congress and addressed its meetings on several occasions as an authority on irrigation.

In addition, President Cannon wrote many interesting and important works: *My First Mission,* the initial volume of the *Faith-Promoting Series; The Life of Nephi,* the ninth volume of that same series; *The Life of Joseph Smith,* and *The Latter-day Prophet;* he also assisted in writing *The Life of Brigham Young* and other publications. During his lifetime more than three hundred of his discourses were printed in various publications. His editorials for the *Juvenile Instructor* numbered well over a thousand, and the editorials written for the *Millennial Star* and the *Deseret News* were uncounted hundreds. He wrote *A Review of the Decision of the Supreme Court of the United States in the Case of George Reynolds vs. the United States.* He had begun a compilation of the *History of the Church* when death called him. President Heber J. Grant wrote, "The record made by him in writing is a great one, equaled by but few who have devoted their entire life to literary pursuits." (*Young Woman's Journal* 12:243.)

After the death of President Woodruff, Lorenzo Snow succeeded to the Presidency on September 13, 1898. The Lord revealed to him who his counselors should be, and he named George Q. Cannon and Joseph F. Smith, both of whom had been counselors to Presidents Taylor and Woodruff. He remained in this important position until his death.

In 1900 President Cannon attended the jubilee of the Sandwich Islands Mission. He landed at Honolulu on December 10 and the next day received a magnificent greeting. He was crowned with the yellow lei, the emblem of royalty, and several prominent people in the present and former governments waited upon him. Ex-Queen Liliuokalani attended a meeting at which he spoke half an hour in Hawaiian, which he was able to recall in a surprising manner. He wrote in his journal on December 17:

> The ex-queen Liluokalani sent me word that she would like to see me at one o'clock today as she expects to sail for Hilo. . . . She welcomed me very cordially and expressed the pleasure it gave her at meeting me. She also dwelt on the good my visit had done and would do, how the people's feelings had been aroused and their love awakened and strengthened by my visit. Many more remarks of this character were made by her, and when I arose to bid her goodbye, she said she would like me to give her a blessing; then she led the way to another room. Before I was aware of what she was doing, she was on her knees at my feet to receive the blessing. I felt very free in blessing her, and the Spirit rested upon us both. (*Era* 53:624.)

It was during this visit that President Cannon prophesied that one day a temple would be built in Hawaii. This was fulfilled in 1919. (*Era* 53:669.)

He returned home late in January 1901. His health, which for two years had been impaired, withstood poorly the Utah winter as compared with the Pacific Islands climate, and in March he deemed it advisable to seek relief on the Pacific coast. However, his illness almost immediately assumed a fatal form. In the early morning of April 12, at the peaceful old Spanish town of Monterey, the end came. His body was brought home for burial, and after a public funeral in the presence of mourning thousands, it was consigned to the family vault in the city cemetery.

Many wonderful tributes were paid to George Q. Cannon. Elder Orson F. Whitney closed his sketch with these words:

> President Cannon was a man of varied gifts and wide experience. A natural counselor, his eminence and influence as such were well warranted. As an orator he shone among the brightest, and almost equal to his powers as a speaker were his abilities as a writer. . . . No man in Utah, after the passing of President Brigham Young, wielded with all classes so great an influence as President George Q. Cannon, and this influence was felt up to the very close of his life. (*History of Utah* 4:663.)

President Heber J. Grant made the following observation:

> There has been no other man in Utah who has shown such marked ability in so many different ways as has he. . . . The broad educational views held by President Cannon entitle him to be ranked as one of the foremost men from an educational standpoint that Utah has ever produced. . . . Speaking of the estimate in which President Cannon was held in the world, . . . I was informed upon one occasion, when a number of leading statesmen were discussing different men and were endeavoring to decide as to who were the eight brightest minds in America, President Cannon was named as one of the eight. . . .

One thing which aided President Cannon very greatly was his marvelous memory. Never have I come in contact with a man possessed of such a remarkable capacity to remember faces and incidents and family relationships. . . .

It seems when one stops to think of all that he has accomplished . . . that figuratively speaking, during his life-time, he removed mountains. . . . (*Young Woman's Journal* 12:243-45.)

The *Juvenile Instructor* carried an editorial entitled "Our Late Superintendent," an excerpt of which read:

President Cannon in intellectual gifts was richly endowed beyond the great majority of his fellows. In faith, few were his equals. As a servant of the Most High, he was among that favored few who saw the face of the Lord while in the flesh and heard the Divine voice, and yet remained in mortality. (*JI* 36:274.)

The *Improvement Era* spoke editorially as follows:

No man has set a better example to the young men of Zion than President Cannon. In Congress, in the business world, in politics, and in all the common affairs of men, it was never forgotten that George Q. Cannon was a "Mormon." That fact distinguished him, and he upheld his reputation as a genuine representative of the Latter-day Saints and their system of ethics, by an integrity as unimpeachable as truth itself. . . . With President Cannon, his personality was foremost in any company, and on no occasion was it ever forgotten that he belonged to the peculiar people called Latter-day Saints. . . .

George Q. Cannon was a powerful man whose intellectual personality enlarged him in men's eyes, so that, while his physical being was small, he yet appeared large in body to most people who saw him or heard him speak. His strength consisted largely in his humility; and his power as a wise counselor lay in his deference for the opinions of others, and in his willingness to listen to and respect their views. As a diplomat, he had few equals; as a forceful public speaker, he bound his hearers, as in a spell, to the views he advocated. (*Era* 4:546-57.)

At his funeral his fellow counselor in the First Presidency, President Joseph F. Smith, said:

He was a mighty man . . . a man remarkable in many ways, whose actions inspired confidence in those with whom he was associated. Something about him won the love and confidence of all who met him. (*Millennial Star* 63:312-13.)

Elder Bryant S. Hinckley, in his book *The Faith of Our Pioneer Fathers* (page 175), includes this interesting information:

George Q. Cannon . . . attained a fame that spread far beyond the confines of the community in which he was one of the most illustrious leaders; being reckoned among America's greatest statesmen and holding even an international prominence in reputation.

At the close of 1901, the year of his death, the show windows of the celebrated commercial emporium of the most noted avenue in Berlin, Germany, the magnificent Unter den Linden, displayed his portrait along with six others, as the principal world personalities whom death had taken during the previous twelve months. His seat was indisputably among the mighty.

THE GOSPEL PLAN

Now, if a man can only know whence he came, why he is here, and that which awaits him after this life, it seems to me that he has abundant causes of happiness within his grasp.

If we are the children of our God, then God our Eternal Father has had an object, a great object to accomplish in placing us here on the earth. . . . This earth has been created for a purpose. Man is here for a purpose. Death is in the world for a purpose, just as much as life, and all these are a part of the Divine plan connected with man's existence in the past, at the present and for the future.

—GEORGE Q. CANNON
Journal of Discourses
26:184, 187
(September 28, 1884)

CHAPTER 1

PREEXISTENCE AND THE MORTAL PROBATION

THE TRUE ORIGIN OF MAN. It cannot be a question with any person of faith in our Church as to the origin of man. We did not have monkeys for ancestors, nor any inferior order of beings. We have not grown up to our present position as human beings through various stages of development from a very low order of creation. We descended from God. Man was created in His image. He is our Father. We have not ascended to reach our present position; but many of the human family have fallen from their high estate into dreadful degradation. (Dec. 1, 1892, *JI* 27:720)

GODS IN EMBRYO. There was a period when we, with Jesus and others, basked in the light of the presence of God and enjoyed His smiles. We are the children of God, and as His children there is no attribute we ascribe to Him that we do not possess, though they may be dormant or in embryo. The mission of the Gospel is to develop these powers and make us like our Heavenly Parent. I know this is true, and such knowledge makes me feel happy. (Oct. 4, 1863, *MS* 25:722)

LITERAL OFFSPRING OF GOD. God in His infinite mercy has revealed to us a great truth. It is a truth that, when understood by us, gives a new light to our existence and inspires us with the most exalted hopes. That truth is that God is our Father, and we are His children. What a tender relationship! What a feeling of nearness it creates within us! What? God my Father? Am I indeed His son? Am I indeed His daughter? Do I belong to the family of God? Is this literally true? The answer is, "Yes." God has revealed it, that we are literally His children, His offspring, that we are just as much His children as our offspring are our children, that He begot us, and that we existed with Him in the family relationship as His children.

What an immensity of vision is given to us in this truth! What a field for reflection! And how our hearts should be inspired with great hopes and anticipations to think that the Being under whose direction this earth was organized, who governs the planets and controls the universe, who causes the rotation of the seasons and makes this earth so beautiful and such a delightful place of habitation, is our Father and that we are His children, descended from Him! What illimitable hopes the knowledge of this inspires us with!

ANGELS GIVEN CHARGE CONCERNING US. Now, this is the truth. We humble people, we who feel ourselves sometimes so worthless, so good-for-nothing, we are not so worthless as we think. There is not one of us but what God's love has been expended upon. There is not one of us that He has not cared for and caressed. There is not one of us that He has not desired to save and that He has not devised means to save. There is not one of us that He has not given His angels charge concerning. We may be insignificant and contemptible in our own eyes and in the eyes of others, but the truth remains that we are the children of God and that He has actually given His angels— invisible beings of power and might—charge concerning us, and they watch over us and have us in their keeping. . . .

Those who otherwise might be thought to be contemptible and unworthy of notice, Jesus says, be careful about offending them, for "their angels do always behold the face of my Father."[1] We are in their charge. They watch over us, and are, to a certain extent, doubtless, responsible for the watchcare that they exercise over us, just as we are responsible for any duty that is assigned us.

PREEXISTENCE A REASONABLE DOCTRINE. This is one great truth that has been revealed to us. And with this truth is this kindred truth: We dwelt in the presence of our Father; we are the brothers and sisters of that great and exalted Being who helped create the heavens and the earth, namely, Jesus Christ, our Savior and our Redeemer; and as He dwelt in the presence of the Father and afterwards descended and took upon Himself the form of man, being born as a babe, so we have done. It is no more wonderful for us to be born in this manner— as babes—than it was for Him to be born a babe—the babe of Bethlehem. It is just as reasonable to suppose that the whole family of man had a pre-existence as it is to suppose that Jesus, and He alone, had a pre-existence. (1890, *Contributor* 11:476-7)

[1]Matthew 18:10.

PREEXISTENCE OF JESUS. Was He, the Son of God, born of a woman? Yes. Well, then, if one God was born of a woman, why not other Gods be born of women? Is He the exception to the entire race? Is He the only Being born of woman that can attain to the Godhead? That is not logical. It is not reasonable to suppose this. . . .

Jesus, who was the Son of God, who was God Himself, was born of a woman. When Jesus said, "I am that I am,"[2] when He appeared unto the brother of Jared, when He appeared unto Moses, He was doubtless then at the full stature of a man. Yet He was born of a woman. I do not wonder at Paul saying, "Great is the mystery of godliness."[3] God manifested in the flesh! It is a mystery to human beings, for they do not comprehend these things.

If Jesus, who was at one time at the full stature of a man, was compressed that He could enter the world as an infant, is it unreasonable to say that the rest of mankind could be born in that way? I think not. It appears to me that if Jesus could be born that way we could be, that our spirits could be compressed, although we might be six feet six inches in height or weigh 300 pounds, so as to be born as a little infant. It is a strange thing to state; but because we do not understand all things, shall we reject truths? Or shall we wait until a full revelation comes to us? . . .

KNOWLEDGE OF PREEXISTENCE FORGOTTEN. There is no doubt in my mind that we were familiar with the principles of the Gospel, and though they had faded from our memories, yet when we heard them again the recollection was revived. I believe that when we see our Father in heaven we shall know Him; and the recollection that we were once with Him and that He was our Father will come back to us, and we will fall upon His neck, and He will fall upon us, and we will kiss each other. We will know our Mother, also. We will know those who have begotten us in the spirit world just as much as we will know each other after we pass from this state of existence into another sphere. . . .

---

[2]Exodus 3:14.   [3]I Timothy 3:16.

SPIRIT MEMORIES. I was a boy when my people gathered with the Saints of God. I was very curious to know the Prophet Joseph, having heard a great deal about him. I happened to be in a large crowd of people where the Prophet was, and I selected him out of that large body of people. There were no means of recognition that I know of which would suggest him to me as the Prophet; but I recognized him as though I had always known him. I am satisfied that I had known him and been familiar with him. There are instances which all of us doubtless have known which have proved to us that there has been a spiritual acquaintance existing between us. We frequently say, "How familiar that person's face is to me." In this way kindred spirits are brought together. We are drawn together by this knowledge and this acquaintanceship which, I have no doubt, was formed anterior to our birth in this state of existence. (April 7, 1889, *DW* 38:676-7)

A SON OF THE MORNING. We are told that there was once a rebellion in heaven. The Prophet Joseph and Sidney Rigdon beheld in vision, and they recorded that which they saw in this language:

> And this we saw also, and bear record, that an angel of God who was in authority in the presence of God, who rebelled against the Only Begotten Son whom the Father loved and who was in the bosom of the Father, was thrust down from the presence of God and the Son,
> And was called Perdition, for the heavens wept over him—he was Lucifer, a son of the morning.[4]

Some have called him "the" son of the morning, but here it is "a" son of the morning—one among many, doubtless. This angel was a mighty personage, without doubt. The record that is given to us concerning him clearly shows that he occupied a very high position, that he was thought a great deal of and that he was mighty in his sphere, so much so that when the matter was debated concerning the earth and the plan of salvation, he was of sufficient importance to have a plan, which he proposed as the plan by which this earth should be peopled and the inhabitants thereof redeemed. His plan, however, was not accepted; but it was so plausible and so attractive that out

---

[4]D. & C. 76:25-6.

of the whole hosts of heaven one-third accepted his plan and were willing to cast their lot with him.

THE DIFFERENCE BETWEEN LUCIFER AND JESUS. Now, the difference between Jesus and Lucifer was this: Jesus was willing to submit to the Father. He had His plan which was accepted. Everything that has come down to us, coupled with our own experience in relation to the effect of the Spirit of God upon the heart, leads us to the conclusion that if Jesus had proposed a plan that would not have been accepted by the Father, He would not have rebelled against the Father nor against the Son of God, who might have proposed the plan which was accepted.

How different it was with Lucifer! Because he could not have his way, he was determined to wreck everything. He would pull down the throne of the Eternal Father and destroy everything. He was not one with the Father. If he had been, that rebellion would not have occurred.

SPIRIT OF LUCIFER MANIFESTED ON EARTH. Now, it is a remarkable fact, which completely verifies and establishes the truth of the record concerning this rebellion in heaven, that from the time Adam appeared on the earth and children began to multiply and increase the spirit that Lucifer exhibited in heaven has been manifested on the earth. When he has had power to influence men and women, he has filled them with precisely the same spirit that he manifested in heaven before man came upon the earth. That spirit made its appearance in Cain, and the Bible shows us that it was continued from generation to generation. The Book of Mormon is filled with the same testimony.

But we need not depend upon the records that have come to us for illustrations of this and testimony concerning it. We ourselves, in our own persons, in our own organization as a Church, have seen the same spirit and the same results that attended its manifestation in ancient times and even as far back as the time of which I speak—before the earth was peopled. We have seen the spirit of rebellion exemplified in our Church as it was when we were in our spiritual existence. . . .

SPIRIT OF LUCIFER VS. SPIRIT OF GOD. History has repeated itself all the time in the Church of God. The Book of Mormon is full of it. That record shows how the sons of Lehi divided, some listening to Lucifer and entertaining the spirit of rebellion, and others entertaining the Spirit of God and seeking for its love and union. Those who yielded to the spirit of Lucifer sought the destruction of the others, and not being willing to submit to that which was right, they rebelled against their father. They determined to have their own way, regardless of the rights of others.

That history, from the beginning of it to the end, shows clearly the operation of these two influences, the Spirit of God bringing the people into union and love, and the spirit of Lucifer —which God in His own wisdom and for His own purposes has permitted to come upon the earth to test us—working out destruction wherever it could get possession of the people to manifest itself through, until it wrought the entire destruction of two races of people on this continent—the Jaredite race and the Nephite race. (April 7, 1895, DW 50:641-2)

THIS ESTATE A PROVING GROUND. We have been sent here with our agency, for the express purpose of being tested and proved. We have had this second estate granted unto us that it may be ascertained whether we shall keep it or not. . . . We are left to exercise our agency, just as we did in our first estate at the time of our trial, to see whether we will be faithful to God in this second estate.

We are shut out, as I have said, but God points out to us the way in which we should walk. He tells us what to do and entreats us to be obedient to Him. He asks us to cultivate His Spirit, to seek to Him for light and guidance; and He promises us that if we will do this and be faithful to Him in this earthly existence, He will crown us with glory and will give unto us eternal happiness.

We are the children of God. God is our Father. He wants us to be like Him. He wants us to enter upon a career that will lead us to as great heights as He has attained to. Therefore, it is well that we should be tested—tested even unto death, if necessary—because He intends to make us His heirs and to bestow upon us the glory that He possesses, leading us along in the path of progress till we will be in our sphere as He is in His sphere. But Satan has determined to destroy this plan. He has determined to lead away as many of the children of men as he possibly can. (Feb. 27, 1898, *MS* 60:213-4)

CHURCH MEMBERS WERE FAITHFUL SPIRITS. We have got to be watchful, for I tell you God has sent us here to test us and to prove us. We were true in keeping our first estate. The people that are here today stood loyally by God and by Jesus, and they did not flinch. If you had flinched then, you would not be here with the Priesthood upon you. The evidence that you were loyal, that you were true and that you did not waver is to be found in the fact that you have received the Gospel and the everlasting Priesthood.

THIS LIFE A HIGHER TEST. Now you are in your second estate, and you are going to be tested again. Will you be true and loyal to God with the curtain drawn between you and Him, shut out from His presence, and in the midst of darkness and temptation, with Satan and his invisible hosts all around you, bringing all manner of evil influences to bear upon you? The men and the women that will be loyal under these circumstances God will exalt, because it will be the highest test to which they can be subjected.

A VEIL BETWEEN GOD AND MAN. It is not as it was before. We were then in the presence of God. Now there is a veil between us and our Father, and we are left to ourselves, to a certain extent. We are left to be governed by the influences that we invite, and there are any number of evil influences around us, whispering into our ears and hearts all manner of things. If we will open our hearts to receive them or allow them to enter our hearts, we will think evil of our brethren and of our sisters; we will have malice towards them; we will envy them; and we will say bad things about them. God will test us in all this. (Oct. 9, 1892, *DW* 45:621)

It is a part of the plan of salvation, I say, connected with man's existence upon the earth that God should thus withdraw Himself, as it were, from man and that a veil should be drawn between Himself and man and that if knowledge of Him be obtained, it should be obtained by the exercise of great faith and continued labor on the part of His children. . . . (Sept. 28, 1884, *JD* 26:187)

Never since Adam and Eve partook of the forbidden fruit has man beheld the face of God except under some very peculiar circumstances. After they fell they were banished from His presence, then they heard the voice of God, but they did not behold Him. He withdrew Himself from them, and there was a veil drawn between God and man. A few men such as Moses and the brother of Jared and Joseph Smith and a few others of the children of men were able through faith to penetrate, as it were, the veil and to behold God under certain conditions. But to the whole world of the children of men God has been willing to communicate through His Spirit, through the manifestations of His power, through angelic visitations, through dreams and visions and through methods of communication that He has adopted or that come within the power of man to receive—He has communicated His mind and His will and revealed Himself with sufficient plainness to enable His children to do that which He requires at their hands, to press forward and to keep His commandments and to rejoice in the knowledge He has bestowed. He has done sufficient to enlighten men and women to cause them to rejoice. (Jan. 18, 1885, *DNW* 34:50)

GLORIES FROM BEYOND VEIL WISELY WITHHELD. If we could understand the glory we once had with our Father in heaven, we would be discontented in dwelling in this condition of existence. We would pine for the home we left behind us. Its glory and its beauty, its heavenly graces and delights were of such a character that we would pine for it with that homesickness that men have some partial knowledge of here on the earth. . . .

Wisely, in the providence of God, this knowledge is withdrawn from us. We can have a glimpse occasionally, through the revelations of the Spirit to us, of the glory there is awaiting us, and sometimes when men and women are approaching death —when they are ready to step out of this existence into the other —the veil becomes so thin that they behold the glories of the eternal world, and when they come back again—as some have . . . —they come back to this mortal existence with a feeling of regret. They have had a foretaste of the glory that awaited them; they have had a glimpse of that glory that is behind the veil; and the love of life is so completely lost, the love of earthly home and friends is so completely taken from them, that they desire with all their hearts to take their exit from this life into that glorious life which they knew was on the other side of the veil. (Sept. 28, 1884, JD 26:192-3)

ADAM A PERFECT IMMORTAL MAN. We are told in the Bible that "God created man in his own image, in the image of God created he him."[5] Adam was no gorilla, no squalid savage of doubtful humanity, but a perfect man in the image of God. When placed on the earth he was immortal. Eve was no degraded, loathsome creature, but a lovely, admirable being, a suitable partner for an immortal man.

> The loveliest pair
> That ever yet in love's embraces met:
> Adam, the goodliest man of men since born.
> His sons; the fairest of her daughters, Eve.

Man when placed on the earth was not far from God. But through the practice of sin he has fallen. The most perfect men and women on earth to-day are physically far beneath their great progenitors, Adam and Eve. We are not the offspring of monkeys but are the children of God, and Jesus is our brother.

The Book of Mormon shows us how the Lamanites became the degraded beings they are. Revelation informs us also concerning the negroes. They are not more perfect than their ancestors; they have not been progressing towards a better type but have fallen, by the transgression of some of their parents, far below what they were originally. (Jan. 31, 1874, JI 9:30)

TRUE EVOLUTION. We hear considerable about evolution. Who is there that believes more in true evolution than the Latter-day Saints?—the evolution of man until he shall become a god, until he shall sit at the right hand of the Father, until he shall be a joint heir with Jesus! That is the Gospel of Jesus Christ, believed in by the Latter-day Saints. That is the kind of evolution we believe in, but not the evolution of man from some low type of animal life.

---

[5]Genesis 1:27.

There is a tendency today in the scientific world to entertain and advocate such ideas concerning the origin of man. The attempt is made to prove that man has come up from the lowest depths through the stone age, the bronze age, the iron age, until he has reached his present condition. This is incorrect.

Man is the son of God and came here perfect from the eternal worlds. Adam was made in the image of God, and he stood upright before Him. His children, however, fell into darkness and sin, and corrupted themselves; and probably there were times when they used flints, just as geologists now attempt to prove, and afterwards, bronze and iron. But that was not man's original condition. He came from God perfect, and he was so intelligent as to give names to all the animal creation, and he became their lord and master. He knew God and walked with Him.

ADAM WAS VERY INTELLIGENT. God was not a simpleton then. He knew just as much as scientific men do now, I think. It has not been necessary for Him to go to school since the days of Adam in order to learn knowledge. He always knew what He comprehends today, and He could teach Adam everything that was necessary to be taught. Not only that, but men who lived as long as they did must have learned an immense amount. Think of it, Adam living nearly a thousand years! What progress he would make in the knowledge of earthly things, even supposing he started out ignorant! So with the others, until the earth was filled with knowledge. But men corrupted themselves and fell into darkness and sin, and became so wicked that God, in order that wickedness might not destroy His purposes, had to send a flood to wipe them out, excepting a few.

Enoch walked with God three hundred and sixty-five years, and the Bible says he was not for God took him. If he walked with God that length of time, he must have known something about Him, and about the heavens, and about the organization of the earth, and something about what is called science now, geological as well as astronomical. Our revelations tell us that not only he but his city was translated. They were all taken, with the exception of Methuselah, who was left on the earth, because the promise had been made to him that through him one should arise who should be the progenitor of a new world. This proved to be Noah, his grandson. After that the earth waxed worse and worse until the flood was sent and destroyed the world. (Sept. 24, 1893, *DW* 47:506)

PURPOSE OF MORTALITY NOT FULLY UNDERSTOOD. God has placed us here upon the earth to accomplish important purposes. These purposes have been in part revealed unto us. Probably it is not possible for men and women in this mortal state of existence to comprehend all the designs of God connected with man's existence upon the earth; but much has been revealed upon this subject to us as a people. . . .

Now, if a man can only know whence he came, why he is here, and that which awaits him after this life, it seems to me that he has abundant causes of happiness within his grasp. . . .

AN IMPORTANT QUESTION. The Bible tells us we came from God. The Bible tells us He is the Father of our spirits. How is He the Father of our spirits? This is an important question and one that each of us should endeavor to understand. I think it is of the utmost importance that the Latter-day Saints should understand and be able to comprehend this question thoroughly, because upon the proper understanding of this must, to a great extent, depend their actions in this life. . . .

SAVIOR AND APOSTLES FOREORDAINED. The Lord Jesus was undoubtedly selected for the great mission of redeeming the world because of His great qualities and His peculiar fitness as one of the Godhead. It is written of Him, "Thou lovest righteousness, and hatest wickedness; therefore God, thy God, hath anointed thee with the oil of gladness above thy fellows."[6]

Who were his fellows? Were not all the distinguished of heaven's sons there—they who afterwards made their appearance on the earth as Prophets, Apostles and righteous men? If He was chosen above all His fellows and anointed with the oil of gladness, is it not consistent and reasonable to suppose that His faithful Apostles were also chosen and anointed to perform their part in the great drama of human existence for the enact-

---

[6]Psalms 45:7.

ment of which the earth was to be prepared? If He had companions in the heavens, or to use the language of the Scriptures— "fellows," is it reasonable to suppose that He left them there while He came down here and took upon Himself mortality? Does it violate in the least any idea that we derive from the sacred records to think that His "fellows" also came here and, as He did, also obtained mortal tabernacles? . . .

His disciples had the right to think, from all that He taught, that if He had been with the Father before coming into this mortal life, they also had been there. If they were to be so closely associated with Him in the great future, what was there to suggest to them that they had not been intimately connected with Him in the past? If He had been chosen from before the foundation of the earth to do the work which He was then doing, what inconsistency would there be in their being chosen also, as His ministers and associates, at the same time? . . .

A DIVINE PLAN. If we are the children of our God, then God our Eternal Father has had an object, a great object to accomplish in placing us here on the earth. . . . This earth has been created for a purpose. Man is here for a purpose. Death is in the world for a purpose, just as much as life, and all these are a part of the Divine plan connected with man's existence in the past, at the present and for the future. . . . (Sept. 28, 1884, JD 26:184-7)

WHY ARE WE HERE? It is necessary, in His wisdom and according to the laws of exaltation, that we should descend from our heavenly abode and come here and take upon us mortal tabernacles and forget all that we knew. The reason of this is that we should be tempted, that we should be tried, that we should be purified, that the dross of our nature should be cleansed by obedience to the laws of God and that by obedience to His laws these tabernacles which we have received and which belong to this fallen world may be redeemed and be fitted and prepared to dwell in a higher and purer abode—in an element that is far beyond anything that we know anything of at the present time. These tabernacles of ours, which are so full of humanity and its weaknesses, God has given unto us, and He has told us how we can redeem them—by obeying the laws He has taught. . . .

WHY IS THE DEVIL PERMITTED TO TEMPT MAN-KIND? It is necessary that we should be tempted, that we should be tried, that we should be purified, by going through these trials and passing through this furnace of affliction which this life furnishes. . . .

Human nature desires an easy path to tread. It wants to go with the stream, to float with the current. We therefore avoid the hardships of life if we can. But after we have passed through these trying scenes and endured these afflictions, we look back at them and are thankful and say they have been more fruitful in profitable experience to us than any other scenes that we have passed through. This is not only the case in relation to parts of our lives, it is the case in relation to the whole of our lives.

When we have passed through this probation, if we have been faithful, we shall look back at all that we have experienced and thank God with all our hearts that He permitted us to come on the earth and have the opportunities that we had of showing our fidelity to God, our willingness to keep His commandments and our determination that we would not be seduced from the path of obedience and rectitude by the blandishments and the temptations of Satan.

It is necessary, I say, to exaltation that we should pass through these scenes. (1890, *Contributor* 11:477-8)

THIS LIFE A MISSION TO BE FAITHFUL. We are sent here as missionaries, so to speak. God has given to each of us a mission. He has sent us forth and has said unto us: "Go, now, and be faithful. I have blessed you with everything that is necessary to fill a good mission on the earth. You are going in to new scenes, and you will be exposed to temptations such as you have never known. You are going to take upon you a tabernacle of flesh, and Satan is going to be there with you. He has tempted you here; you have been exposed to his allurements and his sophisms, but you resisted his propositions, and you clung to me and to Jesus, my well beloved Son.

"Now, go down on the earth and receive tabernacles of flesh and bones and be proved there and see whether you will be faithful there in the midst of the darkness that will prevail; for there will be a veil drawn between your present life and that life, and you will have to live by faith. If you will exercise faith in

Me, I will always be with you; My spirit will be with you; and if you will keep My commandments, you will come back into My presence, and you will dwell with Me eternally, and you will enter upon a career of never ending glory. Now, go and be faithful."

I have just described to you in my crude way something of that which I know occurred when we came from the abode of our Father in heaven. He wants us to be faithful. He does not want us to listen to Satan. (April 21, 1895, *DW* 51:291)

A FAITH TESTING STATE OF PROBATION. There is a characteristic about the faith of the Latter-day Saints in which they perhaps differ from most of the professed followers of Jesus Christ—they do not believe that God expects or desires them to put off acquiring these perfections, powers, gifts and graces which belong to the heavenly world until they reach that world; but they believe that God has placed them here in a state of probation and that He has hid himself only to a certain extent from them. He has drawn a veil of darkness between Himself and His children on the earth for the purpose of trying their faith, developing their knowledge and testing their integrity, so that those who will feel after Him in faith, persevering in the midst of ignorance, darkness, doubt, confusion and the temptations of Satan, and all the evils with which we come in contact in this state of being may receive His blessings and the gifts, graces and favors which He bestows upon His most favored children. Hence, the Latter-day Saints believe in doing everything here that will help to prepare them for life eternal in His presence. They look upon this world as a place where they should attend to these things. (Oct. 8, 1874, *JD* 17:230)

THIS LIFE A PREPARATION. His reason for placing us here was to develop our divine natures. If we were not surrounded by darkness, we could not develop. We must taste the bitter in order to relish the sweet, that our spirits might be purified and that we might exercise our free agency. Good and evil must be presented before us. We are as free agents in our sphere as the angels are in theirs. We are free to do right or to do wrong and to choose the path we shall tread in. . . .

God will force no man to heaven, because we would be of

no value if there. When we get to heaven it will be because we have developed within ourselves the qualities that make heaven. We must develop heaven within ourselves, so that there will be perfect harmony between us and our surroundings. . . .

MUST CONQUER EARTHLY DESIRES. I thank God for giving us our agency, because I think this earth will be a furnace to cleanse me and prepare me for a better condition of affairs and a better life, and I believe this of all of us. . . . It is just as necessary that our bodies should be subject to law as it is that our spirits should be. These bodies of ours are naturally rebellious—full of strange appetites. We are here to conquer these desires. All of us will be sanctified and redeemed if we are faithful. But we must bring this earthly substance in subjection to the will of God.

When men die, their bodies do not leave this planet. Our spirits leave here, not being created out of the elements of this planet, but if these spirits of ours are subject to the Spirit of God and are controlled by its influence and our tabernacles have been subject to the law of God, they will be redeemed, exalted and glorified. Every law of God that we obey tends to our exaltation. The spirit that we have here will be the spirit that will animate us in the resurrection. If it is a spirit of evil, it will have power over us; if it is one of truth and righteousness, it will direct us. All the progress we make here will be to our advantage in the next life. The intelligence acquired here will not be lost. We will keep adding to it, and the more we seek understanding the greater will be our endowment of knowledge. Fidelity, industry and all the other good qualities exhibited on earth will be manifested in heaven. . . .

I do not believe we will go immediately to celestial glory. There must be a preparation—some means by which we shall become nearer and nearer to the glory which is promised. . . . We are not going to receive blessings unless we comply with the conditions on which they are predicated. God will not force these things upon us. (Feb. 1, 1891, MS 53:195-7)

WE ARE HERE TO EXPERIENCE POWER OF EVIL. It seems as though evil is as eternal as good, error as eternal as truth, and therefore He wants us to know this power. I do not know what the Father has in store for us to the full extent; but I suppose that evil will always exist, and though we shall be emancipated from the power and dominion of evil, it will be by keeping the commandments of God. We shall understand in eternity that which we have learned in the flesh, and we shall know the dreadful effect of doing evil. This is the object that God has had in placing us here and leaving us to the exercise of our agency.

The days of our probation are not many. We shall have but one probation. This is the opportunity for us to gain this experience, and we should make use of it carefully. We should not allow the day to pass without profiting by it. We should look upon this existence as an exceedingly precious one, in view of the object of our Father in placing us here. (Nov. 2, 1895, *DW* 51:802-3)

OBTAINING A KNOWLEDGE OF GOOD AND EVIL.

The devil in tempting Eve told a truth when he said unto her that when she should eat of the tree of knowledge of good and evil they should become as Gods. He told the truth in telling that, but he accompanied it with a lie as he always does. He never tells the complete truth. He said that they should not die. The Father had said that they should die. The devil had to tell a lie in order to accomplish his purposes; but there was some truth in his statement. Their eyes were opened. They had a knowledge of good and evil just as the Gods have. They became as Gods; for that is one of the features, one of the peculiar attributes of those who attain unto that glory—they understand the difference between good and evil.

In our pre-existent state, in our spiritual existence, I do not know how extensive our knowledge of good and evil was. That is not fully revealed. But this I do know that when we come to earth and become clothed with mortality, we do arrive at a knowledge of good and evil, and that knowledge prepares us for that future existence which we will have in the eternal worlds; it will enable us to enter upon a career that is never ending, that will continue onward and upward throughout all the ages of eternity.

It is for this purpose that we are here. God has given unto us this probation for the express purpose of obtaining a knowledge of good and evil—of understanding evil and being able to overcome the evil—and by overcoming it receive the exaltation and glory that He has in store for us. . . . (Sept. 28, 1884, JD 26:190-1)

A PRECIOUS PROBATION. The admonition conveyed to the living by the death of our friends is one that should be taken to heart. Every one should so live each day that no duty will be unperformed or neglected. The days of our probation are given unto us in which to perform certain work. We cannot live twice; there is but one life given unto us, and during that life we must lay the foundation for future existence.

It must be a terrible feeling to become conscious on the other side of the veil that while we had opportunities afforded us of doing the work assigned to us in this mortal existence we failed to do it. What a reflection it must be, for instance, for a man who is a member of the Church and has abundance of means to find himself tormented by the consciousness that he has failed to contribute of his means as the Lord requires towards the work of salvation by the payment of tithing and other things. He has left his money behind him, and somebody else possesses it, and he is poor indeed. It must be torment for one who calls himself a Latter-day Saint to wake up in eternity and find himself in such a condition. And so with every other duty that devolves upon us. The command of the Savior is to lay up treasures in heaven, and every young person should remember how important this is.

The days of your probation, children, are more precious to you than gold. Be careful of them. Avoid all manner of sin, and so live that the spirit and power and blessing of God will attend you, whether you live long upon the earth or only for a short period. (Sept. 15, 1881, JI 16:210)

THE ANTAGONISM OF SATAN. We have a foe opposed to us that is the most wily, that is the most cunning, that is the most determined, that is the most unscrupulous, that can be imagined, and that foe is one who was once a great angel holding authority in the presence of God. He was our brother, sitting side by side with our Redeemer, having equal opportunities with Him. But he rebelled. . . .

Over this earth he has wielded for generations great sway; his dominion has been almost unquestioned, and he has imagined that he would gain supremacy in the earth and be successful in preventing the Father from fulfilling his designs concerning the earth. Therefore, he has sought by every means within his power to destroy the work of the Father. He has shed the most precious blood which has coursed in the veins of mortal man to accomplish his purposes. He has filled the earth with lies. He has circulated every abominable thing. He has stirred up the children of God one against the other and has inspired them with the most deadly and hostile sentiments against everything that is holy and pure and god-like. . . .

SATAN RESTRAINED BY GOD. If he had the power, he would sweep this entire people from the face of the earth. If he could, he would destroy us all. . . . It is because he has not the power that he does not do it; it is because our Father and God checkmates him and restrains him and overrules his acts that he does not do this. The disposition is there; the willingness is there; the murderous spirit is there, everything is there that is necessary to accomplish this except the power to do it, which God in His providence withholds or controls, so as to prevent its exercise. We know this. . . . We have this kind of a foe to contend against. (Aug. 23, 1884, JD 25:301-2)

SATAN SERVES A PURPOSE. This earth is not always going to be the pandemonium it is today, in some respects. It is not always going to be the hell it is today for millions of human begins who are suffering and toiling and going down to the grave in misery, as they are in almost every land. He is not going to allow this to continue; for this fair earth was created for man's abode and happiness.

Satan, however, has obtained power over man, and it seems as though he had got possession of this earth and that it would always remain as it is now. But not so. Men have said, "Why don't the Lord kill the devil?" Well, the devil answers His purpose, in his place. (March 11, 1894, DW 48:479)

MUST OVERCOME ALL INFLUENCES. One of the great objects, as I imagine, which God has in view in sending us here upon the earth is to give us experience in the influences of the earth that we may contend with them successfully and overcome them, that when we pass beyond the veil, we may be in a position to comprehend them to a greater extent than we could had we not come here and felt the influences to which human nature is subject. (Nov. 13, 1864, *JD* 11:29)

EFFECT OF EVIL INFLUENCES. Every properly constituted person can feel the influence of the various spirits that are in the world and that seek to bring us in subjection to them. To some it is given to see these influences, but all can feel them. . . . You will see a man all at once seized with a spirit of anger; another time you will see a person seized with a spirit of jealousy or some other evil influence infuriated sometimes, so much so that he or she is transformed. You have seen people's faces completely changed by the spirit that takes possession of them. They cannot see that power; but it is undoubtedly a spiritual entity. We may not be conscious of it, but it takes possession of us if we yield to it.

EVERYONE HAS POWER TO RESIST EVIL. The Lord our God has sent us here to get experience in these things so that we may know the good from the evil and be able to close our hearts against the evil. . . . It is true that some have greater power of resistance than others, but everyone has the power to close his heart against doubt, against darkness, against unbelief, against depression, against anger, against hatred, against jealousy, against malice, against envy. God has given this power unto all of us, and we can gain still greater power by calling upon Him for that which we lack. If it were not so, how could we be condemned for giving way to wrong influences?

There could be no condemnation for our doing what we could not help; but we can help doing these things. We can help yielding to wrong influences and being quarrelsome and selfish. We can help giving way to the spirit of theft, and we can resist the spirit of lust. God has given us power to resist these things, that our hearts may be kept free from them and also from doubt; and when Satan comes and assails us, it is our privilege to say, "Get thee behind me, Satan, for I have no lot nor portion in you, and you have no part in me. I am in the service of God, and I am going to serve Him, and you can do what you please. It is no use you presenting yourself with your blandishments to me. You come and try to insinuate into my heart evil thoughts about the servants of God or about the work of God, and I will not listen to you; I will close my heart against you. . . ."

Whenever darkness fills our minds, we may know that we are not possessed of the Spirit of God, and we must get rid of it. When we are filled with the Spirit of God, we are filled with joy, with peace and with happiness no matter what our circumstances may be; for it is a spirit of cheerfulness and of happiness. . . .

THIS LIFE OUR SECOND ESTATE. This is our second estate. We kept our first estate. In the time of trial in the eternal worlds, when the spirits had to choose between Satan and Jesus, we and all the children of men who are on the face of the earth adhered to our Father. There was one-third of the hosts of heaven who joined Satan in his rebellion. The plan which he proposed for the salvation of the children of men was so specious and attractive that one-third of the children of God thought Satan was right and the Father wrong. These did not keep their first estate, and therefore they were denied the privilege of coming on earth and receiving a tabernacle. They are consigned to darkness—to hell—and are in torment. They are angels to the devil. . . .

Now, the Lord our God has given unto us this probation, which we call our second estate. . . . We consented to come here. For when the foundations of the earth were laid, the sons of God sang together, and rejoiced because an earth was prepared to which they could come and receive tabernacles and enjoy the blessings connected therewith. It was a step in our progress towards the glory that our Father has attained unto.

The Lord has given unto all the children of men His Spirit; not the Holy Ghost with its gifts, for that is only received by obedience to the commandments of God; but every man receives the light of the Spirit, and every man that has listened to and cherished it has joined this Church. Those who have not listened to the voice of the Spirit have not received the Gospel. (Aug. 26, 1894, DW 49:449-50)

CHOICE SPIRITS BORN NOW. We have been told repeatedly that God has reserved in the heavens choice spirits to come forth in this last dispensation, because of the greatness and the magnitude of the work to be accomplished. Of course, among the spirits of men, as we have proved in our mortal existence, there are differences of degree. It has required apparently the most valiant men and women to come forth in the last days for reasons which ought to be plain to those who reflect.

This is not a short lived dispensation; it is to go on increasing in power and volume until it shall fill the whole earth, and the earth be redeemed and sanctified. And, of course, it requires great valor, great obedience and great gifts in order to accomplish the end that is to be attained under the promises of God. The Lord has permitted spirits to be born among the various races of mankind that are fitted and qualified to accomplish this great work. He has called His servants as fishers and as hunters to go forth to the various nations of the earth, and hunt and gather out therefrom those spirits who shall be drawn to the Gospel. (Oct. 7, 1894, *DW* 49:738)

I know that the Lord, for a wise purpose, has called the noblest spirits that he had around him to come forth in this dispensation. He called them to come in humble circumstances that they might receive the experience necessary to try and prove them in all things, that they might descend below all things and gradually begin to ascend above all things; there was a wise design in this. (Mar. 19, 1865, *JD* 11:100)

God has reserved spirits for this dispensation who have the courage and determination to face the world and all the powers of the evil one, visible and invisible, to proclaim the Gospel and maintain the truth and establish and build up the Zion of our God fearless of all consequences. He has sent these spirits in this generation to lay the foundation of Zion never more to be overthrown and to raise up a seed that will be righteous and that will honor God and honor Him supremely and be obedient to Him under all circumstances. (May 6, 1866, *JD* 11:230)

CONSTANT STREAM OF NOBLE SPIRITS BEING BORN. I feel sure that this work will lose nothing by the departure of those who are called to go; for . . . there is a constant stream of emigration from the spirit world of noble spirits to take the places of those who are going hence. As they pass away, having filled their probation, others are pressing forward to the gates of life, anxious to emerge into this sphere of existence, pressing forward, a vast column of them, noble and holy beings, ready to take their part in the probation which God has assigned unto all his children. (July 6, 1884, *DNW* 33:498)

God has chosen us out of the world and has given us a great mission. I do not entertain a doubt myself but that we were selected and fore-ordained for the mission before the world was, that we had our parts allotted to us in this mortal state of existence as our Savior had His assigned to Him. (May 1, 1887, *JI* 22:140)

A LIFE OF PROGRESS. It should be the aim of every Latter-day Saint to be godly, to understand godliness, and to carry out godliness in his or her life, so that we all shall be like our Father in heaven as near as we possibly can be. Jesus has given us to understand that it is possible for His disciples to be perfect; for He says: "Be ye therefore perfect, even as your Father which is in heaven is perfect."[7] He did not mean by that that we should attain to the fulness of godhood in this life, but that we should carry out in our lives and exemplify in our conduct those laws and principles which God has revealed and which are the principles of perfection and godliness.

If we do this every day, we shall eventually be permitted to enter into the presence of our Father and God and dwell with Him. But unless we take this course we cannot approach perfection. Therefore, the life of a Latter-day Saint is a life of progress—a life of continued improvement. The Latter-day Saint who is living as he should do is better today than he was yesterday; he will be better tomorrow than he is today. If there be any imperfections in his life, he is eager to discover and correct them, that he may become more perfect and more like our Father. (May 19, 1889, *DW* 39:17)

ALL MUST PROGRESS OR RETROGRADE. We cannot value our calling too highly. And I say to you that you have entered upon a pathway that leads back to God. You may dally by the wayside; you may fool away your time; you may be idle, indifferent and careless; but you only lose thereby the progress that you ought to make. Unless you commit the unpardonable

[7]Matthew 5:48.

sin, you will have to progress. It is written in the eternity of our God that every soul must progress that does not retrograde.

Therefore, make good use of the time you have. Now is the time of your probation; now is the time of harvest; now is the summer of your days. Let it not be said, "the harvest is past, the summer is ended, and my soul is not saved." But let us bear in mind that now is the probation that God has given us. Let us make use of it by doing the works of righteousness, by keeping the commandments of God, by having our eye on the mark of our high calling in Christ Jesus. (Nov. 9, 1884, *JD* 26:86-7)

PERFECTION IN OUR SPHERE. The main thing for us is to cherish in our hearts the spirit that God gives, cherish those good and holy influences that He pours out upon His children, live up to the light that He has revealed. If we do this, we are as perfect in our sphere as God our Eternal Father is in His. . . . Every being, no matter what his condition or circumstances, no matter what his race or his nationality, no matter what his creed may be—every being who lives up to the light that God has given, whether it be much or little, is perfect in his sphere just as God the Eternal Father is, and will receive a reward according to the light that he has received. (July 6, 1884, *DNW* 33:498)

CHAPTER 2

THE FALL AND THE ATONEMENT

ADAM FELL THAT MEN MIGHT BE. I rejoice myself in the fall of man. I rejoice that Adam partook of the forbidden fruit, for he did so knowingly and understandingly, comprehending fully the results that would attend his partaking of that fruit. It was not so with Eve. Eve was deceived; Eve was beguiled. The adversary, Lucifer, through the serpent, beguiled Eve and deceived her and induced her to eat of the forbidden fruit.

It was not so with Adam. He was aware of all the consequences that would follow that which he did; but he knew that unless he did partake there would be an eternal separation between him and the partner that God had given to him, so he transgressed the law. Death would inevitably come upon her because of the transgression, and she would be thrust out from the presence of God. He knew this, comprehended it, and knowing it he nevertheless partook of the fruit, and he fell. As Lehi says: "Adam fell that men might be; and men are that they might have joy."[1] Because had he not partaken of the fruit, they would have been eternally separated. (Jan. 18, 1885, *DNW* 34:50)

THE FALL FORESEEN BY GOD. It was a part of the plan that was understood in the heavens before Adam was placed in the garden. God by His foreknowledge understood perfectly that Adam, in the exercise of his agency, would fall. Therefore, He prepared a Redeemer in the person of His Son Jesus Christ, who we are told was "the lamb slain from the foundation of the world."[2] God having seen that Adam would fall, that death would come upon him and that a Redeemer would be necessary in order to redeem man from the effects of the fall—for unless there had been a Redeemer provided, Adam and all his posterity would have slept an eternal sleep, they would have been consigned to the tomb and there would have been no redemption therefrom because of the penalty that had been pronounced by the Father upon him if he committed this act—God, knowing all this, provided a Redeemer. That Redeemer was the Son of

---

[1] 2 Nephi 2:25.   [2] Revelation 13:8.

God, Jesus our Savior, in whose name we all approach the Father, in whose name salvation is given unto the children of men. It was arranged beforehand that He should come and perform His mission in the meridian of time—lay down His life, as it was known that He would do, through the wickedness of bad men. . . .

A WAY FOR SALVATION PREPARED. It would be in violation of those eternal laws which our God Himself recognizes, for Him to have interfered and deprived man and woman of their agency. But, knowing the consequences of their actions, He prepared a way for their salvation and their redemption, and thus it is that we are born on the earth. It was part of the design that we should be subjected to all these afflictions and trials and ordeals that belong to this mortal state of existence. This was part of the plan. (Sept. 28, 1884, *JD* 26:189)

RACE OF GODS REDEEMED. It was necessary that a probation should be given to man. The courts of heaven were thronged with spirits that desired tabernacles. They wanted to come and obtain fleshly tabernacles as their Father had done. Their progenitors, the race of Gods with whom they associated and from whom they have descended, had had the privilege of coming on earthly probations and receiving tabernacles, which by obedience they had been able to redeem. Hence, I say, the courts of heaven were thronged with spirits anxious to take upon themselves tabernacles of flesh, agreeing to come forth and be tested and tried in order that they might receive exaltation. . . .

DEATH A CONSEQUENCE OF THE FALL. One of the consequences of the fall was that in the day that man ate of that fruit he should surely die—die so far as the temporal body was concerned; that body should be consigned to the tomb, from which it could not be resurrected until the redemption was effected. To effect this resurrection, before man was placed upon this earth, before Eve was exposed to the temptation of the adversary, God prepared a Redeemer in the person of our Lord and Savior Jesus Christ. . . . Thus has a means been prepared by which the spirits—our spirits and the spirits of all men—should come forth and receive tabernacles, and a work of probation commence here upon the earth. (Jan. 18, 1885, *DW* 34:50)

Now the penalty of the sin that our father Adam committed was death—"In the days that thou eatest thereof thou shalt surely die"[3] was the proclamation of the Creator; and when Adam sinned, he paid the penalty and died and entailed death upon every generation of his posterity, and that sleep of death would have been eternal had it not been for the death of the Son of God. (July 14, 1872, JD 15:114)

EARTH CURSED BY THE FALL. The earth has been cursed because of man's transgressions. When the earth was first organized and man was placed upon it, everything was lovely and beautiful. The earth was fair and yielded its fruits in great abundance. Every living thing dwelt on the earth in peace. But man soon began to listen to Satan, and broke God's laws. The evils which now exist then commenced to appear.

When men began to steal, blaspheme, quarrel, hate one another and murder, then love and peace were withdrawn, and enmity also extended to the animals and birds. Earthquakes tore up the face of the ground, and mountains and valleys were seen. Floods came, and the sea spread and covered parts of the earth and divided it up. Fruitful spots were turned into deserts and many changes took place all over the earth, through God's judgments being poured out upon wicked men. Man's sin changed earth in many places from a heaven into a hell. (Dec. 15, 1866, JI 1:95)

ATONEMENT SHOULD BE UNDERSTOOD. The atonement of the Son of God is a principle that should be clearly understood by us, because unless there is an intelligent comprehension of it, we fail to appreciate the value of the salvation that has been extended to us through the atonement of our Redeemer. It is a great mystery to many people that Christ should die and that through His death redemption should come; and because it is a mystery and they cannot comprehend it by their human wisdom, they are inclined to reject Him as their Savior. Now, there are many things connected with life that we cannot understand, and, of course, there are many more things connected with eternal salvation that in our present finite condition we cannot grasp.

---

[3]Genesis 2:17.

NECESSARY TO WALK BY FAITH. It is necessary that human beings should walk by faith, that they should have faith in God and in the plan of salvation that He has revealed. It being an infinite plan, a divine plan, a plan prepared by the Creator for our salvation, it would be presumptuous in us to imagine that we can comprehend it all at once, or that failing to comprehend it, or failing to have it fully explained to us, we are therefore at liberty to reject it.

Man in his present condition is not equal with God. He cannot grasp the fulness of the plan of salvation. It reaches into eternity; and . . . it had its origin before the earth was framed. It was necessary that there should be, in the wisdom of God, an infinite atonement, that a Being pure and holy, such as the Son of God was, should come here and die, in order to make amends for the broken law. (May 10, 1891, *MS* 53:561-2)

JESUS SUBJECT TO TEMPTATION. Jesus, our Great High Priest and Elder Brother, when He was upon the earth, had to contend against evil. He was not free from temptation. He was tempted in all things like unto us, but He differed from us in being able to overcome temptation, in being sinless through the power that He had through His sonship. But He set us the example. He knows, through that which He had to contend against, the weakness of human nature. He stands as mediator at the right hand of the Father pleading for his brethren and sisters who, like Himself, are subject to the trials, temptations and afflictions that exist in this mortal life.

But because of this shall we say that God does not speak? Because we do not see His face, shall we say He does not exist? Because we do not hear His voice, shall we say He has no voice? Because we do not see His hand or His arm, . . . shall we say that He has neither hand nor arm? Certainly not. (April 24, 1881, *JD* 22:239)

CHAPTER 3

DEATH AND THE RESURRECTION

REINCARNATION A FALSE DOCTRINE. That a belief in reincarnation should prevail among the Latter-day Saints seems strange for there is nothing in the Gospel, as taught in the Bible, in the Book of Mormon, in the Book of Doctrine and Covenants or in the teachings of inspired men, that furnishes the least foundation for such a conception. It is true that pre-existence is taught; but the pre-existence in which we believe is confined to our first estate. We are taught that our present life is our second estate, and this is a probation given unto us in which to gain experience and to be tried and purified to prepare us for our next estate. The teachings of men who have had a deep understanding concerning the purpose of our Great Creator in placing us here in this condition of existence show that this is the grand opportunity which is given to man—an opportunity which he must not fail to avail himself of as it is the only opportunity that he will have on the earth; his earthly existence is confined to one appearance in the flesh.

When a child comes forth, it possesses a tabernacle. That tabernacle is the house of its spirit, intimately associated with the spirit, separated, it is true, for a time by death, but designed to be re-united in the great hereafter. The Savior says that His disciples looked upon the long absence of their spirits from their bodies to be a bondage. . . . We are taught that all holy beings looked forward with joyful anticipation to the time when their bodies and spirits will be re-united in the resurrection. They do not look forward to reincarnation or to another birth as a baby but to the union of their spirits and their bodies—the bodies that they possessed and in which they had passed through all the trials and temptations and vicissitudes incident to a mortal career.

This is the doctrine taught in the Gospel; and the doctrine of reincarnation is utterly foreign to every principle which God has revealed in the last days to His Church.

Since the revelation of the Gospel to the world through the Prophet Joseph Smith, there has been a great disposition manifested by many people to investigate the oriental religions and to appropriate from them strange ideas entirely foreign to those that have been believed in by the people of Christendom. An itching for something new seems to have been the incentive in many instances to adopt strange views and to announce beliefs that are antagonistic to Christianity. Prompted by this feeling numbers have adopted Buddhism and other forms of oriental belief.

In this way Satan seeks to divert the children of men from the truth; for although his power is not visible to mortal eyes, yet he exercises it to a wonderful extent, and the children of men are led hither and thither by his influence and the agencies through which he operates. When Latter-day Saints do not escape these false doctrines, how much less likely to resist error are those who do not know the truth as revealed in these days from heaven?

The Latter-day Saints should be warned on these points and not be carried about by "every wind of doctrine, by the sleight of men, and cunning craftiness, whereby they lie in wait to deceive,"[1] but cling to the simple and plain truth, as God has revealed it and as He teaches it unto those who will receive it, not seeking to dive into mysteries and to adopt strange and startling ideas but confining themselves to that which God has written, cultivating within themselves continually His Holy Spirit that through it they may be led into all truth. (Nov. 1, 1893, JI 28:675-6)

THE VALUE OF LIFE. It is a dreadful sin for one to destroy his own body. Everything should be done among us to show the abhorrence of the people to the practice and how great a crime it is in the sight of heaven. No man has the right to rush unbidden out of this life into the life beyond. God has given us a probation, and He has had a wise purpose in doing this. A man who, when sent on a mission, leaves his post and returns home contrary to the counsel of those who preside over him is held by the Latter-day Saints as a deserter and as unworthy of the Priesthood. Dishonor attaches to such conduct, and men who do this among us are viewed as weak and unreliable. But this is a trivial act compared with the taking of one's own life and

---

[1]Ephesians 4:14.

leaving the place which God has assigned to us in this world by an act of self-destruction. Human life is too sacred to be extinguished in this manner without incurring the severe displeasure of heaven.

We should by every means in our power impress upon the rising generation the value of life and how dreadful a sin it is to take life. The lives of animals even should be held far more sacred than they are. Young people should be taught to be very merciful to the brute creation and not to take life wantonly or for sport. The practice of hunting and killing game merely for sport should be frowned upon and not encouraged among us. God has created the fowls and the beasts for man's convenience and comfort and for his consumption at proper times and under proper circumstances; but he does not justify men in wantonly killing those creatures which He has made and with which He has supplied the earth.

Much less can anyone be justified for wantonly taking human life, as it can scarcely be compared with the life of animals. Man is the lord of creation. He has descended from God, and having received a tabernacle of flesh he should value it as beyond price and do all in his power to preserve it. God has given us laws and instructions concerning the best manner of preserving our bodies, and at no time has He given the least encouragement to anyone to destroy the temple of the spirit which He has provided for them. (April 15, 1896, JI 31:218-9)

SUICIDE IS MURDER. Man did not create himself. He did not furnish his spirit with a human dwelling place. It is God who created man, both body and spirit. Man has no right, therefore, to destroy that which he had no agency in creating. They who do so are guilty of murder, self-murder it is true; but they are no more justified in killing themselves than they are in killing others. What difference of punishment there is for the two crimes, I do not know; but it is clear that no one can destroy so precious a gift as that of life without incurring a severe penalty. (Sept. 15, 1886, JI 21:275)

FUNERALS OF SUICIDES. Anyone committing this crime should not expect a public and honorable funeral. There is a wide distinction between the condition of one who dies a natural death and one who dies by his own hand. No one should be led to believe that if he commits this sinful act he will still receive the same respect and honor at his burial from the Priesthood and people of God that others do who die as faithful members of the Church.

No encouragement of this kind should be given to anyone who has an inclination to commit suicide. For this reason a person who commits suicide should be buried privately and without ostentation, and certainly the funeral services should be conducted without the authorities of the Church lending their presence to the funeral. All should be taught that it is a sin of great magnitude to take the life which the Creator has given to them. (June 1, 1893, JI 28:352)

WHO RESURRECTED JESUS? In dealing with this subject, care should be taken not to advance mere opinions. It is a very important subject and one that should be treated with the utmost seriousness, and no one should indulge in theories outside of the written word concerning it. There is plenty written upon this subject to give food for reflection and to furnish comfort for mankind, and there is not the least necessity to go beyond that which the Lord has made plain upon it.

It is recorded that Jesus said,

Destroy this temple, and in three days I will raise it up. . . . But He spake of the temple of His body.[2] . . .

Verily, verily, I say unto you, The hour is coming, and now is, when the dead shall hear the voice of the Son of God: and they that hear shall live. For as the Father hath life in himself; so hath he given to the Son to have life in himself; and hath given him authority to execute judgment also, because he is the Son of man. Marvel not at this: for the hour is coming, in the which all that are in the grave shall hear his voice.[3] . . .

Therefore doth my Father love me, because I lay down my life, that I might take it again. No man taketh it from me, but I lay it down of myself. I have power to lay it down, and I have power to take it again. This commandment have I received of my Father.[4]

From these passages it is evident that the Savior had the power of the resurrection within Himself and held the keys. This power He has received from His Father; for as He says:

As the Father hath life in himself, so hath he given to the Son to have life in himself.[3] . . .

[2]John 2:19, 21.
[3]Ibid., 5:25-8.

[4]Ibid., 10:17-8.

Jesus was, as He says, "the resurrection and the life."[5] (April 1, 1891, *JI* 26:219-20)

THE RESURRECTION—TO BE UNIVERSAL. Concerning the resurrection of the dead the word of the Lord is very clear and definite. It leaves no room to doubt that through the redemption of the Son of God all the children of men will be resurrected. . . .

The word of the Lord being so plain and free from doubt upon this subject, can anyone, after this, question the completeness of the redemption of our Savior or place a limit upon the number of the children of men to be resurrected? The deeds of men, whether good or evil, cannot prevent the resurrection of their bodies. Their resurrection will be accomplished without any agency of theirs and independent of them. But their deeds can hasten or delay that event; and to that extent only is their resurrection affected by that which they themselves do. The spirits of the righteous will be resurrected with their bodies much speedier than the spirits of the wicked will be; in other words, death does not have power to retain the bodies of the righteous for any great length of time in its grasp. But not so with the wicked for the Lord says:

These are the rest of the dead; and they live not again until the thousand years are ended, neither again, until the end of the earth.[6]

Yet then they all will be brought forth by the power of the Lamb of God. (June 15, 1891, *JI* 26:378-380)

THE RESURRECTION AS AFFECTING THE SONS OF PERDITION. In many minds there has been a great misapprehension on the question of the resurrection. Some have had the idea and have taught it that the sons of perdition will not be resurrected at all. They base this idea and draw this conclusion from the 38th and 39th verses of Section 76 of the book of Doctrine and Covenants, where the Lord says:

Yea, verily, the only ones who shall not be redeemed in the due time of the Lord, after the sufferings of his wrath.

For all the rest shall be brought forth by the resurrection of the dead, through the triumph and the glory of the Lamb, who was slain, who was in the bosom of the Father before the worlds were made.

---

[5]*Ibid.*, 11:25.   [6]D. & C. 88:101.

A careful reading of these verses, however, and especially of the preceding verses will show that the Lord does not, in this language, exclude even the sons of perdition from the resurrection. It is plain that the intention is to refer to them explicitly as the only ones on whom the second death shall have any power. . . .

This is by no means to say that they are to have no resurrection. Jesus our Lord and Savior died for all, and all will be resurrected—good and bad, white and black, people of every race, whether sinners or not; and no matter how great their sins may be, the resurrection of their bodies is sure. Jesus has died for them, and they all will be redeemed from the grave through the atonement which He has made. . . .

It is abundantly evident that all mankind will be redeemed from death and the grave, and all will stand before the judgment seat of God to be judged for the deeds done in the body. It is therefore an entirely false conception of the great and divine plan of existence which is entertained by those who believe that there will be no resurrection of the body in the case of the sons of perdition. (Feb. 15, 1900, *JI* 35:123-4)

THE DESTINY OF SONS OF PERDITION. As to the future punishment of the sons of perdition, the Lord says that they shall go away into everlasting punishment, to reign with the devil and his angels. But, He adds:

> The end thereof, neither the place thereof, nor their torment, no man knows; neither was it revealed, neither is, neither will be revealed unto man, except to them who are made partakers thereof. Nevertheless, I, the Lord, show it by vision unto many, but straightway shut it up again; wherefore, the end, the width, the height, the depth, and the misery thereof, they understand not, neither any man except they who are ordained unto this condemnation.[7]

Some have entertained the idea that after being resurrected the sons of perdition would be deprived of their bodies and forever be companions to the devil and his angels, being like them without a body. . . . But some others equally as intelligent believe that the sons of perdition would never be raised, or if they were, the spirit would then be destroyed and go back into its native element, and this would be the second death and of course the end of their torment.

---

[7] *Ibid.,* 76:45-8.

In view of what the Lord says upon this subject, these ideas are, to some extent at least, speculative. Where the Lord has shown something concerning this by vision to those whom He had favored in this respect, they would not be justified in making it known. But the Elders are entirely safe in confining their views and teachings to the written word. That the sons of perdition will be resurrected there can be no doubt if we rely upon what has been said by many of the Prophets and Apostles, as well as the Savior Himself. Argument beyond this concerning their future can scarcely be profitable. (May 1, 1892, *JI* 27:287-8)

NOT HEIRS OF SALVATION. They will be redeemed and brought forth, but they will not be brought forth in the manner that we will be resurrected; they will not receive that redemption which the rest of the children of men will receive. God, in this glorious revelation through His servant Joseph, taught this to us, that there will be a time when every human being, except the sons of perdition, will partake of the salvation of our God. And even it is said concerning them of the telestial glory that they are heirs of salvation. But the sons of perdition are not heirs of salvation; they will not receive redemption, they having committed the unpardonable sin, from which they never can be redeemed, so far, at least, as God has taught us in His revelations. . . .

No matter what a man's sins may be, whatever crimes he may have committed, the resurrection of the mortal body is assured to him by the redemption of the Lord Jesus Christ. But after that comes the second death; and they who are sons of perdition will partake of that. . . .

All men will come forth from the dead regardless of their condition, regardless of their sins, the just and the unjust; all will stand before the judgment seat of Christ, and they will have His judgment passed upon them. Some will receive and have pronounced upon them the blessings of eternal lives, as promised to the faithful, and be exalted; another class will not receive exaltation, but they will nevertheless be redeemed, and there will be degrees in the condition of the children of men there, just as there are degrees in our condition here. There will be this difference, however; the righteous and the wicked will not mingle together as they now do, but a great separation will take place. (Oct. 6, 1889, *DW* 39:594)

DEATH HOLDS NO TERROR FOR RIGHTEOUS. Many people in the world are afraid of death. They think of it with terror. But it should not be a cause of dread to Latter-day Saints. And it is not. No true Saint is afraid to die. The Saints know that God is their friend. When they pass from this life, they go home to Him. He has promised that they "shall not taste of death, for it shall be sweet unto them."[8] He smooths their pathway to the spirit world and makes it a pleasant one for them to walk in; they can tread it without fear. But He says, respecting them who die not in Him, "wo unto them, for their death is bitter." . . .[9]

How is it with the wicked and the apostate? They have no real joy or satisfaction in this life. In their secret hearts they despise themselves, and they are despised and distrusted by others. Their lives are miserable; and, then, with what horror and dread do they look forward to the time of their death! In their sight death is a grim and terrible monster. They have no cheering promises of God to lean upon. The road before them, which leads to the spirit land, is dark and dismal; they have a foretaste of that which awaits them, and they shrink back with affright. (July 1, 1868, *JI* 3:100)

A TANGIBLE FAITH IN RESURRECTION. We know when a man dies, inasmuch as he dies faithful to the truth, having kept the commandments of God and obeyed the ordinances of the house of God as far as they have been revealed and as he has had an opportunity, that he is secure, that his future is assured. He goes, as we are taught, to the Paradise of God, there to await the morning of the first resurrection. We know that his body will be called forth from the dust and from the tomb and that his spirit will re-animate it, and he enter upon that glorious condition of existence concerning which so many promises have been made. In this respect the faith of the Latter-day Saints is not a chimera; it is something tangible. . . .

A PROMISE TO THE FAITHFUL. It is not a strong assurance or hope that the Latter-day Saints have that they will

---

[8]*Ibid.,* 42:46.   [9]*Ibid.,* 42:47.

receive these blessings in the eternal worlds; but when the promise is sealed upon their heads that they shall come forth in the morning of the first resurrection and be crowned with glory, immortality and eternal lives, there is a testimony from God, our Eternal Father in the heavens above, which rests down upon them and confirms the truth of these words upon the soul of a faithful man or woman. They know, when words are pronounced upon them by a man who has the authority, sealing upon them blessings, keys, thrones, principalities, powers and exaltations in the eternal Kingdoms of God our Father, . . . that these words are not the words of men but that they are the words of the Spirit of God inspiring that man and that God takes a record of that ordinance in the heavens and that it is sealed upon them and upon their children and that they will actually come forth in the morning of the first resurrection according to the promise. Hence, there is no fear of death in the minds of the Latter-day Saints.

If the stake was standing before us prepared for our execution—if we had that faith that we should have and which animated the Saints of God in ancient days—we would walk as calmly to that stake and be bound to it as we would walk to eat a meal of victuals, knowing that God, our Heavenly Father, will bestow all the blessings that have been sealed upon us.

This was the faith which animated the ancients and sustained them in the midst of persecutions, and this is the faith that we should cherish and cultivate as a people and as individuals. Woe to the man who has lost that faith! Dreadful is his condition if he has not that faith living within him. Woe to that man, for his condition is far worse than his first condition, that is, before he had these blessings sealed upon him. (July 19, 1874, *JD* 17:136-8)

THE DOCTRINE OF TRANSLATION. "Does translation imply an entire change in the body?"

There is nothing written upon this subject concerning Elijah, who was translated. But we have the words of the Lord in the Book of Mormon concerning the three Nephites unto whom the promise was made, in the words of Jesus, "For ye shall never taste of death."[10] They were told that they should "never endure the pains of death,"[10] but when Jesus should come in His glory they were to "be changed in the twinkling of an eye from mortality to immortality."[10] They were not to have pain while they should "dwell in the flesh, neither sorrow save it be for the sins of the world."[10] They were caught up into heaven, and it is recorded that they could not tell whether they were in the body or out of the body; "for it did seem unto them like a transfiguration of them, that they were changed from this body of flesh into an immortal state."[11] In speaking of them, the Prophet Mormon says, "Whether they were mortal or immortal from the day of their transfiguration"[11] he knew not.

The Prophet Mormon afterwards added that he had enquired of the Lord concerning these three Apostles, and He made it manifest unto him "that there must be a change wrought upon their bodies, or it needs be that they must taste death; therefore, that they might not taste of death there was a change wrought upon their bodies, that they might not suffer pain nor sorrow save it were for the sins of the world."[12] But, he adds, "this change was not equal to that which should take place at the last day."[12] By this change "Satan could have no power over them, that he could not tempt them; and they were sanctified in the flesh."[12] At the judgment day of Christ, however, "they were to receive a greater change."[12]

This gives us a clear idea of the change that was wrought in these three Apostles. In the translation of Elijah and others who may have been translated there doubtless were similar changes made such as the Prophet Mormon describes as having taken place in the case of the three Nephites. (Jan. 15, 1898, JI 33:75)

TRANSFIGURATION. The evangelists Matthew and Mark give an account of the Transfiguration of our Lord Jesus Christ. . . . Both the narratives are very brief but very significant. It is stated that "his face did shine as the sun, and his raiment was white as the light."[13] This was a transfiguration in the appearance of His person and raiment and not of the form of either. This change was of a heavenly character but not one of continued duration.

---

[10]3 Nephi 28:7-9.
[11]Ibid., 28:15, 17.

[12]Ibid., 28:37-40.
[13]Matthew 17:2.

This circumstance is one of the most wonderful and instructive incidents in the life of our Savior. The scene was at the top of a "high mountain" but the name of the mountain is not given. It has been supposed by some biblical scholars to have been Mount Tabor, but as this height is fifty miles from Caesarea Philippi, where Jesus last taught, it is now believed that it was a mount less distant, possible Mount Hermon. It may have been neither, and nothing forbids us to imagine that it was that "exceeding high mountain"[14] from whence the devil showed the Redeemer the kingdoms of the world and the glory of them. However that may be, it was without doubt on a mount that was not the resort of the multitude but a place removed from the familiar haunts of men.

There is nothing said by either of the evangelists of any preparatory arrangements for this important visit of Jesus and His three specially chosen disciples, Peter, James and John. That arrangements had been made there can be but little doubt. The top of the mountain was reached. A supernatural light enveloped the scene; a divine radiance pervaded the countenance of Jesus and His garments were matchless in their whiteness. Near Him were disclosed two personages from the world of spirits in the person of Moses and Elias. The Elias being, as the Prophet Joseph Smith informs us, John the Baptist.[15] These heavenly messengers came without doubt in answer to prayer. What they said and what they did is not revealed. But the glory of God overshadowed and overpowered the three Apostles insomuch that they were sore afraid; and Peter who apparently thought it was his duty to say something, but not knowing exactly what, proposed that they erect three tabernacles. Then they heard a voice in this excellent glory saying, "This is my beloved Son, in whom I am well pleased; hear ye him."[16] This voice was no other than the voice of God the Father bearing record of His only begotten Son. What transpired between Jesus and His heavenly visitors the Apostles were forbidden to tell until He had risen from the dead.

---

[14]*Ibid.*, 4:8.

[15]The Prophet Joseph said, in relation to that which is written by Mark, (9:4) that it should read: "And there appeared unto them Elias with Moses, or in other words, John the Baptist and Moses, and they were talking with Jesus." (*Inspired Version,* Mark 9:3)

[16]Matthew 17:5.

The difference between resurrection and transfiguration appears to be this: The former implies an entire change in the body, while the latter leaves the body unchanged and implies only an enveloping of the body by divine glory for the time being. The only instance besides the transfiguration of Christ of which we have any record in the old Scriptures is of Moses who, when coming from the presence of Jehovah, was obliged to cover his face for it shone so brightly with the divine glory that the people could not look upon him. (Jan. 15, 1898, *JI* 33:74-5)

CHAPTER 4

ZION AND ITS REDEMPTION

AN IMPORTANT PERIOD OF EARTH'S HISTORY.
We are living in one of the most important periods of the earth's
history. Events are of such a character connected with us as to
excite the greatest interest, and no one connected with this people
who feels as he or she should can help being interested in the
way in which this work is progressing and attracting attention
throughout the earth. . . .

God is dealing with us in a most remarkable manner and
is fulfilling, through His people, the predictions of the holy Prophets, and we behold on every hand, when we open our eyes to
see and our hearts to understand, the great events which God
said should transpire in some day and age in the future. (Oct. 11,
1874, *JD* 17:260)

THIS CONTINENT IS ZION. The whole of this continent
is the land of Zion. But it is impracticable to organize Wards
and Stakes in the old states. There has been a peculiar providence
manifested in the gathering of the Saints to new or unoccupied
lands where they could live together and have the organizations
which the Lord has instructed His people to enter into. A popu-
lous state—such as are all the old settled states from which the
Saints have been gathered—is not a fit place in which to organize Wards or Stakes. There could be no separation between
the members of the Church and those who are not of the Church.
This would defeat the purpose of the Lord; for the object of the
gathering is to have the Latter-day Saints gather together in
places where they can have such organizations as they now enjoy.

In the due time of the Lord the whole land of Zion will
be occupied by the Church of Christ. When that happy day
arrives, the organizations of the Church will be carried out in
perfection. But a great many things must take place and a
great many changes must be effected before that day arrives.
(Aug. 1, 1898, *JI* 33:539)

BOTH JERUSALEMS TO BE RESTORED. At the present time the sites of both the Old and the New Jerusalem are occupied by strangers. Israel has not yet been gathered home, and the Latter-day Saints are still awaiting permission to go back to Missouri. But the day is at hand when the Lord will restore these places to their rightful owners, and then there will be manifestations of divine power equal to those shown ancient Israel, combined with the integrity, the virtue and the unfaltering faith of those who sought to establish Zion in this dispensation. (Oct. 1, 1898, *JI* 33:668)

REDEMPTION OF ZION NOT UNDERSTOOD. The Lord acts with us as we act with our children, to some extent. He does not tell us everything. I suppose that if the early Elders of this Church could have seen all that we had to pass through and the length of time that would elapse before the redemption of Zion was achieved, they would have fainted by the wayside and have felt that human nature could not endure such trials.

I know, in my early recollections of the teachings of the Elders, they imagined, judging from their remarks, that it would be only a few years before Zion would be redeemed. When we were coming to these valleys, I happened to be present when some of the Twelve Apostles were talking concerning the future, and the recollection of that conversation is in my mind now; and I know that, though they were inspired men and filled with revelation, they did not conceive, as we now can conceive, of the events that would take place before Zion would be redeemed. It was necessary, seemingly, according to the mind of the Lord, that they should be encouraged with the hope that their efforts would result in complete triumph. . . .

MANY REVELATIONS NOT OBEYED. Well, many were tried because those revelations concerning the order of Enoch were not carried out, and they thought that Joseph was not a true prophet. They argued in this way: "God knows His children, and if He gives a revelation to His children, He knows whether they can carry it out or not. Now, if Joseph were a Prophet and inspired of God, he would know whether the people were prepared for this, and the Lord would not have inspired him to give a revelation if they were not prepared;" and the failure of the people to do this was laid to Joseph's charge, as though he had received false revelations and had attempted to do something that ought not to have been done.

The facts are that God reveals His truth continually to His children, and He lays before them principles to obey as they are able to obey them. So it has been from that day until the present. There have been a great many revelations given to us that we have not had faith to carry out as they should be. (Nov. 1, 1891, MS 54:2, 16)

REDEMPTION OF ZION DEFERRED. I do fear that we will defer the redemption of Zion indefinitely through our unwillingness to do the things that God requires at our hands. I have not an earthly doubt that this revelation given in 1834 would have been fulfilled to the very letter had our people obeyed the Lord as He desired; neither do I believe now that the redemption of Zion will be long deferred if the people will obey the Lord and keep His commandments. But the difficulty is, our hearts are hard and almost impenetrable in many instances. . . .

SOME TO LIVE TO HELP BUILD CENTER STAKE. Let us labor continually for the redemption of Zion and for the time when the promises which God has made to Zion will be fulfilled that we may build the center Stake of Zion and rear the house of the Lord there. There are men standing in this generation that will see it accomplished; but we do not want it put off to the very last. Let us all strive to fit and qualify ourselves and our families by obeying the commandments of God to the fullest extent so that we and our families may be remembered among those who shall be counted worthy to take part in the glorious work of redeeming Zion and enjoying the blessings thereof. (Oct. 8, 1899, CR 50, 53)

PREPARATION FOR CHRIST'S COMING. God in His revelations has informed us that it was on this choice land of Joseph where Adam was placed and the Garden of Eden was laid out. The spot has been designated, and we look forward with peculiar feelings to repossessing that land. We expect when that day shall come that we will be a very different people to what we are today. We will be prepared to commune with heavenly beings; at any rate the preparation will be going on very rapidly for Jesus to be revealed.

We expect that a society will be organized there that will be a pattern of heavenly society, that when Jesus and the heavenly beings who come with him are revealed in the clouds of heaven, their feelings will not be shocked by the change, for a society will be organized on the earth whose members will be prepared through the revelations of God to meet and associate with them, if not on terms of perfect equality, at least with some degree of equality. (March 3, 1867, *JD* 11:337)

WHEN WILL ZION BE REDEEMED? When will the Saints possess the Kingdom? Of this we may rest assured, they will not possess the Kingdom, if by that is meant the power to rule and exercise dominion over the earth, until they themselves have made such progress in the knowledge of God and the principles of truth as to be willing to yield an implicit obedience to Him and to be governed in all things by His laws. No matter how long a period may elapse before the Saints attain unto this condition, they must attain unto it (whether it be they who are now recognized as Saints or their children or another people who may be raised up) before the important and immense interests which God has promised shall yet be in their hands can be entrusted to them. If it were otherwise than this, the triumph of the Kingdom of God would be anything but a blessing to His people, for the power they would thus obtain they would not know how to use, except for their own destruction.

Before the Kingdom of God can have the power which every Saint anticipates and desires to see enjoyed, there must be a growth and development of the whole people suited to the new power and position which will be laid upon them. It is not only necessary that the authorities of the Church should comprehend the truth and be willing to be governed by its laws, but the whole people must become educated in the truth and be equally obedient to its requirements. The Kingdom cannot have power only as the people are willing to be governed by its laws.

However desirous the Almighty might be to bestow power and dominion upon the people, He could only do so, to be consistent with His designs, in proportion to their willingness to be thus governed; and they cannot be thus governed until among the people of God themselves there shall be found a majority of the Saints understanding the truth and having faith in the work and willing to render unmurmuring obedience to every requirement that may be made of them. When the time shall come—if it has not already come—when the majority of the people are in this condition and the remainder are approximating towards it, then may we indulge in the hope that the redemption of Zion and the triumph of the Kingdom are nigh at hand. . . .

It is folly for the Saints to neglect their duties and still think, while doing so, that without some given period Zion will be redeemed. Zion will be redeemed, and it may be within the period estimated by them; but they will not be in a position to be benefited by it if they are neglectful and dilatory in seeking for and acquiring that knowledge of the truth which their position and relationship to God and His work admits of their obtaining. (Aug. 31, 1861, *MS* 23:563-5)

A DUTY TO BUILD UP ZION. Joseph said in the beginning that it was the duty of the Elders of this Church to labor constantly to build up Zion and not to build up that which is opposed to Zion. . . . God has not required it of me that I should build up anything that is opposed to Zion but on the contrary that I should always keep in my thoughts and be influenced by it in my actions that which will advance the cause of Zion and that which will not retard it or operate against it in any manner. (Aug. 26, 1883, *JD* 26:320)

I do not know any better thing that we can engage in than to build up the Zion of God. It is as good and as great a labor as we can be engaged in; in fact, it is the labor which God has assigned unto us as a people and as individuals, and if any of us are engaged in anything else, we are not in the line of our duty, and we should turn aside from that and pursue the path which God has marked out. (Oct. 11, 1874, *JD* 17:263)

CHAPTER 5

THE LAST DAYS — A TESTIMONY OF JUDGMENTS

PROPHECIES FULFILLED BY NATURAL MEANS. Even Latter-day Saints have, doubtless, in many instances entertained erroneous views respecting the fulfillment of revelation and prophecies of the Bible. . . .

The Lord works in the midst of this people by natural means, and the greatest events that have been spoken of by the holy Prophets will come along so naturally as the consequence of certain causes that unless our eyes are enlightened by the Spirit of God and the spirit of revelation rests us, we will fail to see that these are the events predicted by the holy Prophets. . . .

They will come along in so natural a manner, the Lord will bring them to pass in such a way that they will not be accepted by the people, except by those who can comprehend the truth, as the fulfillment of the predictions of the Prophets. It requires the Spirit of God to enable men and women to understand the things of God; it requires the Spirit of God to enable the people to comprehend the work of God and to perceive His movements and providences among the children of men. The man who is destitute of the Spirit of God cannot comprehend the work of God. (Nov. 2, 1879, JD 21:266-7)

FULFILLMENT OF PROPHECY. A reader of the prophecies of ancient and modern times would naturally imagine that when the stupendous events which they mention should take place the world would be convinced of the work of God and would repent of their sins. But it is a remarkable fact that prophecy may be fulfilled in the plainest and most unmistakable manner and yet the great bulk of mankind refuse to believe that that which they see is the fulfillment. . . .

The Prophets have plainly predicted that before the coming of the Lord there should be a variety of signs given to the people by which the righteous might know that the day of the Lord was near at hand. The Savior Himself predicted that before His coming wars and rumors of wars should be heard, the whole earth should be in commotion, and men's hearts should fail them. Through the Prophet Joseph the Lord has told the people that after the testimony of the servants of God in these days wrath and indignation should come upon the people; there should be the testimony of earthquakes, that should cause groanings in the midst of the earth; there should be the testimony of the thunderings, of lightnings, of tempests, the waves of the sea heaving themselves beyond their bounds, and all things should be in commotion. Through Joseph also the Lord says that He would say to the nations of the earth:

> How oft have I called upon you by the mouth of my servants, and by the ministering of angels, and by mine own voice, and by the voice of thunderings, and by the voice of lightnings, and by the voice of tempests, and by the voice of famines and pestilence of every kind, and by the great sound of a trump, and by the voice of judgment, and by the voice of mercy all the day long, and by the voice of glory and honor and the riches of eternal life, and would have saved you with an everlasting salvation, but ye would not.[1]

A VOICE OF WARNING. From these things it appears that not only are the inhabitants of the earth called by the mouth of God's servants, by the ministering of angels, and by His own voice, but also by the voice of thunderings, and lightnings, and tempests, and earthquakes, and great hailstorms, etc., all these judgments proclaiming the will of God to the people and bearing testimony to them as a voice of warning.

Yet, notwithstanding these things have been fulfilled no attention is paid to them. The inhabitants of the earth are deaf and blind to all these evidences of God's displeasure and warning.

One of the most notable features in the news of the day is the frequency with which catastrophies of various kinds are published. The inhabitants of the earth are suffering from judgments of the most terrible character; but they appear to make no impression upon them. The remark is frequently heard, when allusion is made to these events, "Oh, these disasters always have occurred. We hear more of them now because of the telegraph, which collects details from all parts of the earth."

In this way mankind console themselves with the idea that there is nothing in these occurrences to be startled at, and their hearts are hardened against the testimony of the servants of God and the testimony of God's judgments. . . .

---

[1]D. & C. 43:25.

So it will be to the end. The Lord calls in vain upon the impenitent and the wicked. They will not listen to His voice nor to the voice of His servants nor to the voice of His judgments but are determined to harden their hearts and go on their way in the downward course. If we did not have evidence of this blindness on the part of the people, it would be almost impossible to convince anyone that it could exist and that men could be so stupid and obstinate as to resist testimonies of so wonderful a character, especially when they have been foretold with such great plainness. (Aug. 15, 1890, JI 25:527-8)

AN AGE OF DISASTERS. An age of disasters is the present. All the signs foretold by the Savior and the Prophets which were to precede the second coming of the Lord are being witnessed at the present time. The news that comes to us every day over the wires brings word of calamities of every description. We hear of cyclones, of shipwrecks, of floods, of the sea heaving itself beyond its bounds, of earthquakes, of collisions upon railroads, of murders and suicides, of wars and rumors of wars, until the ear is vexed with the tidings. We read of more calamities in one day than formerly were known in a month. Yet, these things have come along so gradually that men attach no importance to them. Though they are intended as signs of the coming of the Lord and the near approach of the end, mankind fail to perceive in these events any of the signs which the Prophets have described. (Oct. 1, 1889, JI 24:452)

THE TESTIMONY OF JUDGMENTS. The scriptures inform us that there will be earthquakes and other terrible calamities given unto man for the accomplishment of the purposes of the Almighty; but they do not lead us to expect that repentance and an acknowledgment of the hand and the power of the Lord, on the part of mankind, will follow these visitations. They intimate, on the contrary, that feelings directly the opposite of these will be indulged in and that men will feel more like cursing God and dying than repenting.

Jesus predicted to his disciples that there should be "famines, and pestilences, and earthquakes in divers places;"[2] but these were to be only "the beginning of sorrows."[2] They were to be testimonies to men given in the language of Almighty power.

---

[2]Matthew 24:7-8.

When the voice of heaven-inspired man failed to have the
desired effect upon his fellow-man, and the latter resisted his
testimony and warning because he was a man like himself, then
there was to be heard and felt testimonies and warnings in voices
of a more potent and terrible character. The earth itself, at the
impulse of its Almighty Creator, should be moved to add its
testimony in language peculiar to itself—language of terrible
significancy and portentous character—to its inhabitants. Universal creation should join to testify unto blind and self-righteous
and conceited and rebellious man, in manifestations and voices
of awful and sublime power, to the truth of the words declared
in meekness unto them by their fellow-mortals, who had been
inspired and sent forth by the Almighty with the message and
warning.

The Lord has said unto his servants that "After your testimony cometh wrath and indignation upon the people, for after
your testimony cometh the testimony of earthquakes, that shall
cause groanings in the midst of her, and men shall fall upon
the ground and shall not be able to stand. And also cometh
the testimony of the voice of thunderings, and the voice of
lightnings, and the voice of tempests, and the voice of the waves
of the sea heaving themselves beyond their bounds."[3] (Oct. 24,
1863, MS 25:682)

AS IT WAS IN THE DAYS OF NOAH. The inhabitants
of the earth did this in the days of Noah. They did not believe
there would be any flood. They went on enjoying themselves
in their way, notwithstanding the message that Noah delivered
to them. But still the flood came, and the hardened nations were
drowned, and the earth was cleansed from their presence.

In these last days the Lord has made many predictions concerning the judgments with which mankind shall be visited if
they would not repent. Destruction should come upon them as
a whirlwind. In the very beginning and before this Church was
organized the Lord foretold what would happen if the people
hardened their hearts against the testimony of His servants. He
said:

For a desolating scourge shall go forth among the inhabitants of the
earth, and shall continue to be poured out from time to time, if they

[3]D. & C. 88:88-90.

repent not, until the earth is empty, and the inhabitants thereof are consumed away and utterly destroyed by the brightness of my coming. Behold, I tell you these things, even as I also told the people of the destruction of Jerusalem; and my word shall be verified at this time as it hath heretofore been verified.[4]

These are the words of Him who rules and who does not speak in vain. Whether the world heed or believe them or not, they will be fulfilled as surely as were the words of the Lord in the days of Noah. (Dec. 15, 1900, *JI* 35:825)

PLAGUES AND SCOURGES. The Lord has spoken very plainly on the subject of pestilences, and many predictions have been made concerning the dreadful judgments that will fall upon mankind. In one revelation the Lord says:

There shall be men standing in that generation, that shall not pass until they shall see an overflowing scourge; for a desolating sickness shall cover the land.[5]

The generation referred to here is the generation in which the Gospel was to be revealed—in these last days. In another revelation the Lord says:

For I, the Almighty, have laid my hands upon the nations, to scourge them for their wickedness. And plagues shall go forth, and they shall not be taken from the earth until I have completed my work, which shall be cut short in righteousness.[6]

Among the other judgments which were to come, the Lord said in the revelation concerning our Civil War, was plague. The inhabitants of the earth, through plague and other judgments, were to be made to feel the wrath of an Almighty God.

In another revelation the Lord says that His "scourge shall pass over by night and by day, and the report thereof shall vex all people."[7]

THE RIGHTEOUS TO ESCAPE. From all these predictions it is very evident that among the many judgments which were to fall upon the wicked in these last days plagues or, in other words, pestilences are to perform an important part. The Lord's disciples were promised that they "Shall stand in holy places,"[8] in the midst of these judgments, "and shall not be

---

4*Ibid.*, 5:19-20.
5*Ibid.*, 45:31.
6*Ibid.*, 84:96-7.
7*Ibid.*, 97:23.

moved; but among the wicked, men shall lift up their voices and curse God and die."[8]

Of course, if the disciples shall stand in "holy places," they must obey the commandments of God. They cannot hope to escape without such obedience, for the Lord, in connection with these predictions, has said concerning judgments:

"Nevertheless, Zion shall escape if she observe to do all things whatsoever I have commanded her. But," the Lord continues, "if she observe not to do whatsoever I have commanded her, I will visit her according to all her works."[9] She was to be visited with pestilence and plague in case she should prove disobedient. . . .

If we escape these dreadful judgments which the Lord has said He will pour out upon the wicked, we must keep His commandments and obey Him in all things. This is our only safety. The Lord has given unto us "A Word of Wisdom,"[10] and He has said concerning this that "All saints who remember to keep and do these sayings, walking in obedience to the commandments, shall receive health in their navel and marrow to their bones; and shall find wisdom and great treasures of knowledge, even hidden treasures; and shall run and not be weary, and shall walk and not faint; and I, the Lord, give unto them a promise, that the destroying angel shall pass by them, as the children of Israel, and not slay them."[11]

To fully understand the meaning of this promise about the destroying angel passing by them, our juveniles should read the 12th chapter of Exodus. There they will get a full understanding of what the Lord means by this promise; for there they will see that through doing what the Lord commanded the destroying angel did pass by all the houses of the children of Israel. (Oct. 15, 1899, *JI* 34:624-5)

PREDICTED JUDGMENTS WILL COME. Because the Almighty does not proceed to execute His decrees in the manner that men anticipate, many fall into the error of supposing that He governs the universe by great and inflexible laws without regard to the events that are taking place among men. The Elders of this Church, inspired by the Almighty, have made many pre-

---

[8]*Ibid.*, 45:32.   [10]*Ibid.*, 89:1.
[9]*Ibid.*, 97:25-6.   [11]*Ibid.*, 89:18-21.

dictions in this nation concerning the judgments which the Lord was about to pour out upon the people if they did not repent. This has been more especially the case since the martyrdom of the Prophet and Patriarch and other faithful Saints and the expulsion of the Church of Christ from the lands which they occupied. A civil war has rent this nation, and the blood of thousands has been freely shed. The nation has recovered so rapidly from the effects of this war that men cease to look upon it in the light of a judgment but rather as a natural consequence which attends the growth of all nations.

So with all the calamities that are taking place. They are attributed to every cause but the true one. For instance, these dreadful cyclones of which we read in every issue of the daily papers which are so destructive in their effects upon life and property are undoubtedly a part of those judgments which God inspired His servants to foretell. But who, outside of the members of this Church, looks upon them as a fulfillment of the word of God? Who thinks that the predictions of the Elders of this Church are being fulfilled in these destructive storms? Who imagines that the shedding of the blood of a mighty Prophet and of faithful followers of Jesus Christ, or the mobbing and persecuting and driving out of the people of God, has anything to do with the occurrence of these dreadful disasters? Yet, they are a part of those calamities which the Lord has said He will pour out upon the people if they do not repent. (July 1, 1883, *JI* 18:200)

A SPIRITUAL DESTRUCTION. It is true, He is not coming out in every case in His anger to destroy us; but the work of destruction is operating silently among us. I do not mean physical destruction altogether but spiritual destruction. It is operating among us, and because of the process being silent, the people do not perceive it. Men and women are dropping off like worm-eaten apples from our trees. They are losing their faith and their standing; and family after family, member after member is disappearing and being forgotten. I call this a work of spiritual destruction, for when men and women lose their faith, they are spiritually destroyed. Their names are blotted out of the records of the just, and their condition is a most awful one. (Nov. 2, 1895, *DW* 51:803)

FAMINE AND PESTILENCE. Famine is one of the dreadful scourges which the Lord has told us by the mouths of His servants will fall upon the inhabitants of the earth in the last days. It is often accompanied or followed by pestilence; and no widespread famine can occur in any country without the danger of pestilence following in its train and carrying off thousands upon thousands of unhappy victims. . . .

It may be that our land in its turn will also receive some of the scourges which are to come upon the earth in the last days. It seems scarcely possible, in so fruitful a land as America, that there should be famine; yet we have good reason to believe that sooner or later even this country, now so bountifully supplied with every product of nature, may be visited by famine; and we should not waste the bounties of the earth because of their abundance and their cheapness. We should garner our grains and the fruits of the earth and preserve them so that we may have on hand sufficient to meet our wants should crops fail for one or more seasons. This is true prudence on our part and should be acted upon by every wise man and woman in this country, especially those who have faith in the prediction of God's servants. (Nov. 1, 1891, *JI* 26:666)

TWO YEARS' SUPPLY OF FOOD. The Lord has only to let loose the grasshoppers throughout this country, and we should soon have a famine for food. Many may think this will never come, that it is folly to talk about a famine in this land. . . . If grasshoppers were let loose, they could soon spoil the prospects for crops in those regions where food has hitherto been so plentiful. But whether this shall come or not, I think it a wise precaution for the Latter-day Saints to keep a year or two's bread-stuff on hand. (Aug. 6, 1893, *DW* 47:347)

Do not forget the teachings you have heard and which have been repeated in our hearing for so many years; I refer to the saving and storing of grain. The day will come when you will see the wisdom of doing so, and many of you will doubtless wish you had profited by it. For I tell you that wars and desolation will cover the land just as Prophets have declared they would; and these are coming, coming, coming as plainly and as surely as the light comes in the morning before the sun rises above the summit of yonder mountains and before we see his rays. (July 21, 1878, *JD* 25:258-9)

A CLASS-WAR FORESEEN. Secret organizations are also multiplying in number and increasing in power—a menace and a sign concerning which the Latter-day Saints have had full notice from the beginning. Year by year these organizations increase in magnitude and in boldness, and the difficulty of dealing with them is made more apparent. The relations of employers and employed become more and more strained, even in prosperous and peaceful times, and there is an ever-present threat of outbreak and violence. A general conflict between these classes, such as might occur at any time, would be so dreadful and far-reaching in its effects that no parallel in history could be found for it. Even the rising of slaves against their masters, of which the records of the past furnish us some examples and which is a conflict notoriously cruel and ferocious, gives only a feeble idea as to what this class-war might become because of the strength and organization of the respective parties and the bitterness of feeling which has been engendered.

A SOCIAL VOLCANO. A thought as to what the future may bring forth in this respect adds another to the many fears which already oppress men's minds. If to the dread and misgiving which mankind feel as to the fury of the elements be added the feeling that the people of many civilized governments today are walking upon the thin crust of a slumbering social volcano, it will be easy to see how men's hearts shall fail them and they be found running here and there in the search for safety, which they know not how to find. (Sept. 15, 1900, *JI* 35:616)

WAR A SCOURGE FOR SHEDDING INNOCENT BLOOD. There is no sin that a nation can commit which the Lord avenges so speedily and fearfully as He does the shedding of innocent blood or, in other words, the killing of His anointed and authorized servants. No nation which has been guilty of this dreadful crime has ever escaped His vengeance. The thunderbolts of His wrath have been always launched forth for the destruction of the perpetrators of such wickedness. It is a rank offense against the majesty of Heaven and the authority of the

Creator which He never suffers to pass unrebuked, for such men act in His stead and are His representatives on the earth. . . .

Men acting in this ambassadorial capacity for the Lord, having been selected by Him to officiate in His name, were sent to the people of the United States. After diligent labor and the endurance of indignities and wrongs of a very gross character, the principal ones were at last cruelly murdered, others were persecuted to their graves and all were threatened with the most dreadful and outrageous violence if they persevered in their mission of mercy in the name of heaven's King. By these acts the authority of the Almighty was defied and treated with the greatest possible contempt, and they could not, consistently, be overlooked by Him; for He had declared to them beforehand what the results of such a course of conduct would be to them if they adopted it. . . .

Innocent blood, the blood of Apostles and Prophets, has been shed, and it must be avenged. That vengeance cometh speedily upon the nation who suffers such crimes to be perpetrated in its borders without taking steps to punish the guilty; for we live in a day when God's work will be cut short in righteousness. The land of America, also, is a land upon which such wickedness cannot long flourish unpunished. It is written respecting that land, in the record of it which has been preserved, that the Lord had sworn in His wrath that whoso should possess that land from that time henceforth and forever should serve Him, the true and only God, or they should be swept off when the fulness of His wrath should come upon them; also, that "cursed shall be the land, yea this land (America), unto every nation, kindred, tongue, and people, unto destruction, which do wickedly, when they are fully ripe; . . . for this is the cursing and blessing of God upon the land. . . ."[12]

America will yet emerge from the dreadful difficulties in which she is now involved [Civil War] and will yet obtain that position which has been designed by God for her to hold. She will yet occupy the chief place among the nations and enjoy a form of government that will be copied, as a model, by surrounding peoples. But England stands, at the present time, in a slippery and dangerous path; she is encircled by evils and

[12]Alma 45:16.

dangers that seriously threaten her peace and security and from which she will yet find that it will require more than the wisdom of her statesmen to deliver her. Instead, therefore, of deluding herself with the idea that she enjoys an immunity from the evils which afflict other nations, rather let her examine well the causes which have involved them in trouble, and seek to profit by their experience. (June 4, 1863, *MS* 26:361-4)

ENGLAND TO SUFFER AND MOURN. There is a time coming and not far distant, as sure as God has spoken it, when all the nations of the earth shall fall in pieces before the Kingdom of the great I AM, and all that compose the image which Daniel saw shall crumble in fragment before the advancing march of the Kingdom of God. Let no man, therefore, glory in man nor make the arm of flesh his strength for the sword of God's justice shall fall upon all the nations of Babylon.

Hear it all ye people, as an Apostle of Jesus Christ I prophesy in the name of my Master that England will suffer and mourn even as America is now doing and as all other nations shall do unless they repent and receive the message that has been sent unto them. They shall weep tears of blood and bewail in bitter anguish the miseries which they shall be forced to endure. The blood of the Prophet Joseph and the Patriarch Hyrum and of the martyred Apostles and Saints who have been slain for the truth's sake cry aloud for vengeance to heaven, and the Lord will demand a just retribution. You may think and say that the American nation is alone guilty and that the Lord will demand retribution from them alone, but all nations who viewed the persecutions we have endured and looked on with admiring gaze participated in the guilt by consenting to the act in their feelings. . . .

The hour is rapidly approaching when all nations shall feel the sword of God's justice. If the storm has burst in the United States, the clouds which presage its near approach are rapidly gathering over the nations of Europe. . . . In a few years you will see the entire prediction fulfilled as you have already seen it fulfilled in part. The sign which God said should warn mankind of the approach of these things was the rebellion of South Carolina. God said these scenes of war and misery should commence there, and all nations should know of it. . . .

It shall be but a short time till the sword of justice shall fall upon her as well as upon every other nation that will pursue a similar course. As England rejects the Gospel, she must bear the same load of misery which other nations shall be compelled to endure. (Jan. 5, 1862, MS 24:725-7)

We can perceive the judgments of God coming upon the nations as clear as the sun that shines in the heavens, yet the people shut their eyes and will not see them. Because you have enjoyed peace in this land [England] so long, the people do not think it will ever be any different. They imagine it will be so all the time, as the inhabitants of the United States believed it would be with them. But it will not always be peace and prosperity for this land. There is a day of trouble and gloom awaiting England such as she never saw since she was a nation, a day of wrath and misery fearful to contemplate. (Aug. 10, 1862, MS 24:551)

THERE WILL BE NO PEACE. It is worse than useless for men to cry "peace, peace," when there is no peace or to flatter themselves that the terrible issue of war can be avoided. The decree has gone forth respecting the nations of Christendom. War in their midst is inevitable unless they take the course pointed out by the Lord which, however, they seem determined not to take. They are to be wasted away by war. . . .

Babylon must fall; no power can avert her destruction. Machines of warfare, machines of offense and defense of every description will be needed in great abundance to complete her destruction; and it must be confessed that the nations of which she is composed are doing all in their power to furnish them for the occasion. . . . Until Babylon meets with her long-promised fate, the manufacture of machines and weapons of war will be continued and peace may be looked for in vain among the nations of the earth. (Sept. 21, 1861, MS 23:612)

PEACE CONGRESSES TO FAIL. Elaborate and beautiful theories may be constructed, but they will crumble to atoms before the stern logic of facts and leave those who adopt them in a worse predicament than they were in before they attempted to put them into practice. While man remains as he is and as he has been since God's revelations and direct manifestations and guidance have been withheld from him, all such schemes as these for Peace or International Congresses must be barren of all good and permanent results. . . .

The demon of war, when once aroused, cannot be easily exercised, as Europe will yet find to her cost. The political elements are thoroughly disturbed, and it is not too much to assert, in the presence of the events that are crowding prominently forward and the knowledge which the Lord has revealed upon the subject, that complications are likely to arise at any moment which may destroy the peace of Europe and enkindle a conflagration in which several nations may be involved who now deem themselves secure from peril.

ONLY WAY TO AVERT WAR. Conferences and Congresses are but a delusion and a snare in the present condition of affairs in Europe; they serve to lure their authors and participants and all who place confidence in them into greater and more inextricable difficulty and are more than likely, in the most of instances, to bring about that which they are designed to avert. God's fiat has gone forth concerning Babylon, and no man or nation or combination of nations can prevent its fulfilment.

War is one of the scourges which man, by his sinfulness, has brought upon himself. There is one way—and but one way—to avert it and that is for the people to obey God's commands, through whose power alone can this and other threatened evils be stayed. This is too simple for the great men of the earth to believe. Like their class in every preceding generation they view such a proposition as ridiculous and treat it with contempt, practically asserting by their actions that they consider their wisdom and plans as being infinitely superior to the Lord's. The day will come when they will see their folly and be constrained to acknowledge it; but in the most of instances it will be when they will not have the power to avail themselves of the knowledge.

There was a king in ancient times who learned the lesson and profited by it during his lifetime. His sentiment was "Believe in the Lord your God, so shall ye be established; believe His Prophets, so shall ye prosper."[13] (May 28, 1863, MS 26:346)

---

[13]II Chronicles 20:20.

COUNSELS OF CHURCH LEADERS TO BE SOUGHT
AFTER. Just as sure as we live and as the Lord has spoken this
people will at some time—and the distance of that time depends
upon our faithfulness—be sought after; their counsels will be
sought for, and men will say, "Those Latter-day Saints are capable of governing themselves and of maintaining good government; they love their fellow men and respect their rights, and we
want to live among them, or we want to have their influence
among us."

The time will come in this land—I tell you now, ye faint-
hearted ones—the time will come when the counsels of the servants of God will be sought for in our own land and in all the
states where our people live because our conduct and our management will stand out in such bold relief in comparison with the
management and conduct of others that they will want to get
our counsel and our help in their extremity. This will be the
case not only right here but elsewhere. (April 5, 1897, *DW* 54:
676)

You will see the day, and it is not far distant, when these
mountains will be the stronghold of a free people, and when men
will come here because the principles of the Constitution will be
maintained here; and they will be protected in their political and
religious rights. (July 21, 1878, *JD* 25:260)

THOUSANDS TO FLEE TO ZION. If all those who had
embraced the Gospel from the beginning of the Church until the
present time had remained true and faithful to their covenants,
what a mighty host they would be! If every man who has been
warned had warned his neighbor, as the Lord has required, how
few of the children of men there would be left who would be
ignorant concerning this great latter-day work! As it is, millions
have been warned and are left without excuse for their rejection
of the work of God. The Elders have traveled and preached and
borne testimony, and their fame has gone to the ends of the
earth. There are but few people who have had opportunities of
reading who have not heard something of what the Lord is doing.

Our enemies have greatly helped to advertise us, and while
they tell the most abominable lies and misrepresentations, still
they make us known, and many people suspect that their statements concerning us are mainly false. When the judgments of

the Almighty shall be poured out in such a manner as to cause men to look around for a place of peace and safety to which they can flee, then will the testimony of the Elders come vividly to their minds. They will cast their eyes towards Zion, and thousands will yet flee there to enjoy the blessings God will vouchsafe to His people but which will be denied to those who live among the ungodly.

While people are rich and prosperous, they seldom care about the eternal riches to be found in the Gospel. It is when they are poor and in straitened circumstances that the Gospel is listened to as a message of glad tidings. Let calamity fall upon this nation, as it most assuredly will, then the warnings of the Elders will be remembered and people will inquire for them that they may receive the ordinances at their hands. Proud cities will be humbled; judgments will fall upon them, and though the people may say it is long delayed, it will nevertheless come, just as the Lord has said. (March 15, 1884, *JI* 19:85)

SAFETY IN ZION. I look for the time to come and expect to see it when a great deal of wealth will roll into this community because of the probity and honesty of the Latter-day Saints—because they can be trusted to do that which is right and not take advantage of their neighbor. I say, the people of the nations will turn their eyes to Zion and admire the good qualities developed in the Latter-day Saints and enter into dealing with them; therefore, the Latter-day Saints should do nothing to injure their credit, their name, nor the Kingdom of God. The time will come, as predicted, when all those who will not take up their sword against their neighbor must flee to Zion for protection. They will bring their wealth with them. This prediction was made a great many years ago, but it will have its fulfilment. . . .

Those desiring peace . . . will come to Zion for personal safety and for personal liberty. Zion will be the only place where peace can be found on the earth, and people desiring peace will come here and bring their wealth with them in order that it may be put in a place of safety. (July 5, 1891, *MS* 53:500)

WICKED MUST BE DESTROYED. We have in the neighborhood of two thousand Elders out in the world preaching the Gospel. All the Christian world have thousands of ministers

laboring among the nations. What do they accomplish? Are the
inhabitants of the earth, take them as a whole, any better? We
have to confess they are not. Then, what are we doing with our
Elders? Why, the Lord has sent them forth with a message and
to gather in the honest. What for? To separate them from the
wicked.

We have been gathered for this purpose, that we may stand
in holy places and, if faithful, escape the judgments that are
about to be poured out upon the nations. There is no other way
of cleansing the earth. Preaching does not do it. Ministers of
religion have been engaged in preaching now for hundreds of
years, and they must confess, if they are honest, that their efforts
have failed to bring about a better and purer state of society. Consequently, if purity ever reigns on this earth, if righteousness ever
prevails, there will have to be a destruction of wickedness and of
those who practice it. . . .

I do not level these remarks at any particular class of society. Every man can be a righteous man, if he wishes to. The
Latter-day Saints have not got the exclusive patent to this for
themselves. It is for everybody—Jew and Gentile. All can embrace righteousness; all can forsake iniquity; all can turn to the
Lord. And those who will not but will continue to practice iniquity, I tell you, as a servant of God, they will be destroyed,
whether they be "Mormons" or non-"Mormons". Those who
wish to have themselves and their posterity perpetuated in the
earth must practice righteousness, for righteousness alone will
save the people from the calamities that are coming upon the
earth. (*DEN*, Jan. 27, 1900)

WICKED TO BE DESTROYED BY FIRE. I expect that
before Satan is fully bound the wicked will be destroyed. You
are familiar with the history which the Book of Mormon gives of
that period. There was a great destruction among the people.
The Lord visited them in a most terrible manner. Dreadful calamities fell upon them, and the wicked were literally wiped out,
just as much as the antedeluvian world was wiped out by the
flood. That wicked generation was completely extirpated, and
those only were left who were righteous.

I look forward to the same kind of destruction preceding the
glorious events that will take place in the near future. The earth

will be visited by fire. President Smith yesterday told us that "he that is tithed shall not be burned at His coming."[14] I believe that there will be literal fire come upon the earth and calamities and destructions of so universal a character that the earth will be burned, so to speak, so that there will be but few men left. . . .

In coming to these mountains we hoped to find a place where we could live secluded from the abominations of Babylon. But here in this secluded place wickedness intrudes itself and is practiced in this land which we have dedicated to the Lord as a land of Zion! How can this be stopped? Not while those who have knowledge of these filthy crimes exist. The only way, according to all that I can understand as the word of God, is for the Lord to wipe them out, that there will be none left to perpetuate the knowledge of these dreadful practices among the children of men. And God will do it as sure as He has spoken by the mouths of His prophets. He will destroy the wicked, and those who will be left will be like the Nephites after the wicked were all killed off; they were righteous men and women who lived for over two hundred years according to the law of heaven. . . .

DETAILS OF WICKED PRACTICES TO BE KEPT SECRET. When will these things end? When God visits the wicked with His judgments, as He will do. Then these practices and the wicked and the knowledge of their wickedness will be destroyed. Then, I hope, the filthy details and the exact forms and methods of these abominations will be kept secret, as the Prophet Alma counseled his son Helaman concerning the secret oaths and covenants of the Jaredites that had come down from the days of Master Mahan, of whom we read in the new translation and who was the head of that secret organization that banded themselves together to commit murders and works of darkness. Alma said to Helaman:

> Therefore, ye shall keep these secret plans of their oaths, and their covenants from this people, and only their wickedness and their murders and their abominations shall ye make known unto them; and ye shall teach them to abhor such wickedness and abominations and murders; and ye shall also teach them that these people were destroyed on account of their wickedness and abominations and murders.[15]

---

[14]D. & C. 64:23. [15]Alma 37:29.

So, I trust, it will be with us. The knowledge of the wicked and their destruction will be preserved in our midst; but the abomination and the wickedness itself will be concealed from human knowledge so that wickedness may be abolished in the earth and the reign of righteousness be ushered in. . . .

CHURCH BEING CLEANSED. Now, if we want our generations to live in the earth and to have them go down through the thousand years, if we want to have representatives among the children of men during that happy period, we have to lay the foundation for that now. . . . The day of the Lord cometh; it is near at hand; and if we and our children live, it will be because we try to be pure. No generation from this time forth can live for any length of time unless they are pure; God has said it, and His word does not return unfulfilled.

Even now you can see how this Church is being cleansed as we go along. Look at the families that we have known in the Church, and see how they are being thinned out, just as though we were passing through a sifting machine. And when we see how few of those whom we have known have clung to the iron rod and maintained their faith, we are led to ask, "who then can be saved?" Then, how many families there are who, after the death of the father and mother, are not numbered among the Saints of God! This is a cleansing process which is going on, and it will continue to go on more and more, because we are advancing. The Lord will hold us to a stricter accountability than He ever has done because we have more light and because of the near approach of the end. (Oct. 6, 1897, CR 52-54)

CHAPTER 6

THE LORD'S SECOND COMING

THE SECOND COMING OF THE SAVIOR. If we take the revelations which the Lord has given unto us, it appears that nothing plainer can be set forth than the great truth that the coming of the Lord will precede the Millennium or the thousand years of rest. Those interested in this question can find what the Lord has said upon this subject in many sections of the Book of Doctrine and Covenants[1]. x x x x

It would appear very plain that before the coming of the Lord there will be signs in the heavens and in the earth of blood and fire and vapors of smoke; the earth will tremble and reel to and fro as a drunken man; the sun will be darkened, the moon turned into blood and the stars fall from heaven. The Saints also who are alive upon the earth will be caught up to meet the Lord in the clouds, as well as those who have slept in their graves; their graves will be opened, and they will be brought forth at the sounding of the trump of the angel. Satan will be bound and will not be loosed for one thousand years, and a reign of righteousness and of peace will prevail for Satan will have no place in the hearts of the children of men. (Feb. 1, 1892, JI 27:92-3)

TIME OF COMING NOT REVEALED. We have had no authority given unto us, no message to designate the hour nor the day, nor even the year when the Lord would make His appearance. That has been kept by the Father. The angels did not know the hour nor the day when our Savior spoke the words that I have read in your hearing;[2] and if the angels have since been informed of it, we have not been advised to that effect. (Dec. 7, 1884, JD 26:40)

I will tell you what men can know. They can know that such and such a time is not the time. Men can prophesy that 1891 is not the year. Although they cannot tell you the day nor the hour, they can tell you that He will not come this year or

---

[1]D. & C. 29:9-11, 33:7-9, 43:17-29, 45:36-50, 88:87-110, also others.
[2]Matthew 24.

next year according to the words of God already given. There are several revelations which speak plainly upon this point. . . .

There are a great many events to take place that have not yet occurred, and the Savior will not come until they do take place. Be assured of this and be not concerned in your minds and agitated on these matters; it is easy to understand that there are many things yet to be fulfilled before that grand and glorious event will come. Yet, as he has told us, He will come as a thief in the night. He will come when the inhabitants of the earth are unprepared for him. . . .

GOD WORKS IN NATURAL WAYS. You need not look for the coming of the Son of Man either this year or next. Though we cannot prophesy the day or the hour, we can prophesy some things concerning His coming—that is, that will take place before His coming. God has not left us in doubt upon these points. . . .

Therefore, Latter-day Saints, go ahead and perform your duties carefully, consistently and with a determination to do that which God requires at your hands. Do not look for some great cataclysm to occur which will show all the world that this is the Kingdom of God. Perhaps such a thing will occur; but I will tell you what I have observed during my life, that God works in natural ways. His purposes come around seemingly perfectly natural—so natural that the world cannot see the hand of God in them. It requires faith and the Spirit of God to show these things. . . .

My conclusion is that God works in this way among the children of men, and they will continue to harden their hearts against all the evidences of the divinity of this work, notwithstanding the continued fulfilment of the prophecies of the Elders of this Church. The inhabitants of the earth are not converted by the fulfilment of the prophecies because they come along so naturally. (Oct. 5, 1890, DW 41:652)

A MEANS OF MEASURING OUR READINESS. That the Lord will appear when his people are prepared for His presence is a gladdening truth; that that day is rapidly hastening on is fully evidenced by the progress of the Saints and the development of Jehovah's purposes among the nations. . . . There is a means by which we can measure our progress to meet that auspicious event. If the breach is daily widening between ourselves and the world, as it is between the community of the Saints and the world, then we may be assured that our progress is certain, however slow. On the opposite hand, if our feelings and affections, our appetites and desires, are in unison with the world around us and freely fraternize with them, if our faith and our actions are cold and barren of good fruit, we should do well to examine ourselves. Individuals in such a condition might possess a nominal position in the Church but would be lacking the life of the work, and, like the foolish virgins who slumbered while the bridegroom tarried, they would be unprepared for His coming when it bursts upon them unexpectedly. (Oct. 5, 1861, *MS* 23:645-6)

THE COMING OF THE LORD IS NEAR. I have had resting upon my mind now for some time a feeling to call upon the Latter-day Saints and tell them that the coming of the Lord is near, even at our doors. I have been greatly impressed with this feeling. . . .

Many who are now within the sound of my voice have been promised that they shall live, if they have faith, to behold the second coming of the Lord. The Lord has also promised that certain events shall take place while men that are standing in the generation in which these promises were made will yet be alive. . . .

THIS LAND HAS BEEN WARNED. This land has been warned. I feel that we can stand before the judgment seat of our great Creator free from the blood of this generation in these United States. It is true we have not told every man, woman and child about these things. God requires us to preach His Gospel and to warn the inhabitants of all lands, and then if they do not take warning and warn their neighbors, their sins rest upon their own heads, and our garments are clean.

How long has this great work which God has established been a theme for newspaper writers? Ever since we came to these valleys they have known about us; they have had thousands of testimonies borne to them concerning this work; they have seen it grow and spread; they have seen and heard of our Elders traveling through their cities and visiting foreign lands. . . .

The Lord's judgments are following the warning voice that has been raised by the Elders of this Church. If another Elder did not lift his voice and if another tract were not distributed in this land of ours, the Elders have done their duty, and this nation cannot in the day of judgment rise up against the Elders of this Church and say that they did not bear testimony to them concerning this work. I am now telling you my own views. . . .

BLOOD OF MARTYRS A TESTIMONY AGAINST WICKED. In this land of ours what warnings there have been. The blood of the martyrs shed upon this soil is crying to God. The expulsion of the Saints from Ohio, the expulsion from Jackson County, from Clay County, from Caldwell County, in Missouri and from Illinois—are they not testimonies? I take it that they are, and God will hold them as testimonies against the guilty men and women who have done these things, as well as against those who have never lifted their hands or their voices to redress any wrong that has been practiced upon the Latter-day Saints. Then, since we came to these mountains, this whole nation has been almost convulsed by this Mormon question. It has agitated the people everywhere. All the newspapers in the land have discussed it in all its phases. Is not this a warning? What more can we do than we have done in this direction? Or shall we all go out and allow ourselves to be martyred. . . .

MANY NATIONS YET TO BE WARNED. There are many nations yet to be warned, and we have this work to do. I will not say that we ought to do it before the Lord comes, for I do not know when He will come. But this duty is incumbent upon us; by people out of every nation under heaven Zion is to be built up. Every land and every nationality will have to contribute of its strength and numbers, in greater or lesser degree, to fulfill the words of God concerning the building up of Zion. Oriental lands now untouched by the Elders of the Church have to be penetrated and sought out. In this work God will precede His Elders. He will send His angels before them, as He has done, to prepare the people to receive them and to listen to their message.

SEND GOSPEL TO LANDS WHERE TYRANNY REIGNS. My feeling is that we should withdraw our efforts to a great extent from the countries where we have been spending so much time and means with so little fruits. Let the Gospel be sent to lands afar off where tyranny reigns; and when the Gospel goes there, God will soften the hearts of the rulers and greater freedom will follow. It has been so in Germany; it will be so in Russia, in the Latin countries and in the countries of Europe. God is working with the nations, and He will work with us if we will do our duty. Then, we can stand before our Father with our skirts clean from the blood of this generation, having done our whole duty.

WE MUST BE WILLING TO SACRIFICE LIVES. If it should cost us our liberty, as it may do at times, if it should cost us our lives, as it may do to carry this Gospel to every land, it would be no more than others have suffered in the same cause. God has said:

And whoso layeth down his life in my cause, for my name's sake, shall find it again, even life eternal. Therefore, be not afraid of your enemies, for I have decreed in my heart, saith the Lord, that I will prove you in all things, whether you will abide in my covenant, even unto death, that you may be found worthy.[3]

And again he says:

And all they who suffer persecution for my name, and endure in faith, though they are called to lay down their lives for my sake yet shall they partake of all this glory. Wherefore, fear not even unto death; for in this world your joy is not full, but in me your joy is full.[4]

In another revelation the Lord tells us:

Let no man be afraid to lay down his life for my sake; for whoso layeth down his life for my sake shall find it again. and whoso is not willing to lay down his life for my sake is not my disciple.[5]

It is a test by which His disciples may be known. But while we should not shrink from complying with every requirement, we ought to avoid persecution and death by every means in our power that would be honorable and consistent with our duties and obligations. But in preaching this Gospel to the nations of the earth we ought not to be afraid of our liberty or our lives. (Oct. 7, 1900, *MS* 63:17-20, 33-5, 50)

---

[3]D. & C. 98:13-4.   [5]*Ibid.*, 103:27-8.
[4]*Ibid.*, 101:35-6.

CHAPTER 7

ANGELS, SPIRITS, AND SPIRIT WORLD

THE ANGELS WHO VISIT US. In the broadest sense, any being who acts as a messenger for our Heavenly Father is an angel, be he a God, a resurrected man or the spirit of a just man; the term is so used in all these senses in the ancient scriptures. In the stricter and more limited sense an angel is, as the Prophet Joseph states, a resurrected personage, having a body of flesh and bones. But it must be remembered that none of the angels who appeared to men before the death of the Savior could be of that class for none of them were resurrected. He was the first-fruits of them that slept. He Himself appeared often to His servants before He took His mortal body—for instance, to the brother of Jared, to Abraham, to Moses, to the seventy Elders of Israel and to many others. The Holy Ghost, who, we are directly informed, has never yet taken a body, was seen and conversed with by Nephi, who bears record, "that he was in the form of a man."[1]

We have no doubt of the correctness of the statement of the Prophet Joseph Smith that "there are no angels who minister to this earth but those who do belong or have belonged to it;"[2] but that does not necessarily imply that they did not belong to the earth before they took a mortal body. In our opinion they belonged to this earth from the time of its creation, when they covenanted to come and take bodies thereon, at the time that the morning stars sang together and all the sons of God shouted for joy. In just this same way was Jesus "the Lamb slain from the foundation of the world."[3]

We are taught to believe that Adam was the first man who took a body on this earth. There was no death before he fell. Who, then, was the angel who taught him the law of sacrifice, or of faith and baptism, or who was the cherubim with the flaming sword who guarded the tree of life? We cannot admit that the scriptures are false and that these beings were not angels; neither can we admit that Adam was not the first man

---

[1] 1 Nephi 11:11.
[2] D. & C. 130:5.
[3] Revelation 13:8.

and that the Savior was not the first-fruits of the resurrection. Therefore, we are forced to the conclusion that the word "angel" is used in the scriptures for any heavenly being bearing God's message or fulfilling His commands; and, further, all beings who were created with the design that they should inhabit this earth belong to it and to no other planet. Taking this view all difficulty in understanding this matter vanishes. On the other hand, if this is not the case, how can the sayings of Joseph and the scriptures—the Bible, Book of Mormon and modern revelation—be harmonized as these all declare that angels were frequent visitors to this earth from the time of the creation to the days of the coming of the Redeemer? (Jan. 15, 1891, JI 26:53-4)

DO ANGELS HAVE WINGS? It is an erroneous idea to believe that angels have wings.

It is true that in Isaiah's vision the "seraphim" is described as having "six wings; with twain he covered his face, with twain he covered his feet, and with twain he did fly."[4]

It is not, however, upon this statement of Isaiah's that the popular idea of angels having wings is based, because if modern artists described them with wings at all, it is only with two wings.

The early artists, long centuries ago, are credited with the idea of painting angels with wings. They represented angels as human beings in form but with the addition of wings springing from the shoulders and halos round their heads—symbols of their higher nature.

From that time to the present this has been accepted as the proper form in which to present angels. It has become a firmly fixed tradition in the Christian world that angels must have wings. Yet, there is nothing in the scriptures to justify the idea. All the descriptions that we have of the visits of angels to the servants of God make them to appear in the image of man.

The people of Sodom saw nothing unusual in the appearance of the two "men"[5] who visited Lot at that place, yet in our translation of the Bible they are called "angels."[5] It is very

---

[4]Isaiah 6:2.   [5]Genesis 19:5, 1.

probable that if they had appeared in any but a human form, the men of Sodom would have refrained from conducting themselves as they did. Jacob is said to have wrestled with "a man;"[6] but we are led to believe that he was an angelic being. The angel who appeared to Joshua outside of Jericho, described as "a man . . . with a sword drawn in his hand,"[7] was not known by Joshua to be an angel until he had announced himself; then Joshua recognized him.

Daniel says of the visit of Gabriel to him, "there stood before me as the appearance of a man."[8] The angel at the sepulchre of the Savior is described by Matthew in this language: "His countenance was like lightning, and his raiment white as snow."[9] Mark, in describing the same, says, "They saw a young man sitting on the right side, clothed in a long white garment."[10] Luke says, "two men stood by them in shining garments."[11] John's description is, "two angels in white."[12] When Peter was released from prison by an angel, there is nothing said to convey the idea that he was in any other form than that of a man; but when he appeared, it is said "a light shined in the prison."[13]

In the various accounts given of angels visiting men, there is nothing to impress the reader with the idea that they appeared in any but human form.

The Prophet Joseph gives us his description of angelic ministrations. Other Elders also have described the appearance of angels; for many have been ministered unto by angels in our generation. The Prophet has told us, "When the Savior shall appear, we shall see him as He is. We shall see that He is a man like ourselves."[14] In answer to a question which was asked of him he said, "There are no angels who minister to this world but those who do belong or have belonged to it;"[15] that is, they had been mortal men but after each death were immortal. No wings had grown upon them subsequent to their departure from this life; but they appeared in the form which they possessed while on earth. Of course, they were glorified and changed in that respect. An angel that has been resurrected has a body of

[6]*Ibid.*, 32:24.
[7]Joshua 5:13.
[8]Daniel 8:15.
[9]Matthew 28:3.
[10]Mark 16:5.

[11]Luke 24:4.
[12]John 20:12.
[13]Acts 12:7.
[14]D. & C. 130:1.
[15]*Ibid.*, 130:5.

flesh and bones. In this respect they are like the Savior, who, when He appeared to His disciples, said:

"Handle me, and see; for a spirit hath not flesh and bones, as ye see me have."[16]

A just man made perfect, who has not received the resurrection, if he appears, will be seen in his glory; for that is the only way he can appear. (June 15, 1897, JI 32:387-8)

MINISTRATION OF ANGELS NOT EXPECTED. We often talk about and desire to see angels. Every person who has joined this Church has had a desire to have revelations from God our Heavenly Father and have knowledge poured out upon him as it was poured out in abundance upon the Prophets of old. I merely suppose that this is so with everybody else because I have these feelings myself and judge others in this respect by myself. But, until we can learn to control and resist those evil influences that are now invisible, I think it would be unprofitable to have the administration of angels personally or visibly unto us. Until we can do this, I do not expect that we can have those other blessings profitably bestowed upon us. I do not expect that in the providence of God we will be favored with those other blessings until we can listen unto and obey the counsels of those appointed to preside over us.

I know it is natural for people to be anxious to have some ministered spirit wait on them and reveal itself unto them. For my own part my reflections have caused me to view this in a different light than I viewed it in the beginning. I then thought it would be a great blessing to have that favor bestowed upon me. But when I have reflected upon the character and calling of the men whom God has called and sent in this generation, when I have thought of Brother Joseph Smith and his greatness, his magnanimity and his faith, I have thought and still think it is one of the greatest blessings of God upon me to have been permitted to behold his face and to listen to his teachings. I feel the same now towards the present leaders of Israel.

MUST APPRECIATE LIVING PROPHETS. I am satisfied that this generation has been honored by as great Prophets as ever stood before God upon the earth, excepting the Lord

[16]Luke 24:39.

Jesus Christ; and, how could I expect, if I disobeyed Brother Joseph Smith's counsel, that I could be favored with the presence and instruction of any being further advanced than he was when he was in the flesh? And, so I feel in relation to Brother Brigham, whom we now have with us; he is one of the noblest sons of God, a man whom God has endowed with the wisdom of eternity, with the power in part that is exercised in its fulness by the Gods of eternity. If we disobey his counsel, disregard his warning voice and are careless respecting his teachings and the teachings of those associated with him, we are indeed unworthy of the presence of personages who have been glorified and who now dwell in the presence of God.

I do not expect the day to come when this people will be favored with the administration of angels—with the presence of those holy and immortal beings—until we can learn to appreciate the teachings and instructions of the men of God in our midst. When that day does come that this people will implicitly obey the voice of those whom God had placed over them and give heed to every instruction imparted to them by the spirit of revelation through the servants of God, then I shall expect visits from holy angels and the glory and power of God to rest upon us to that extent it has never done hitherto; but I cannot well expect it before that time arrives; if these blessings were to be bestowed upon us before we are prepared to receive them, I should fear they would turn to our condemnation as they have done to many in the early history of this Church. (Nov. 13, 1864, JD 11:30-1)

THE WORLD OF SPIRITS. Alma . . . states:

The spirits of all men, as soon as they are departed from this mortal body, yea, the spirits of all men, whether they be good or evil, are taken home to that God who gave them life. And then shall it come to pass, that the spirits of those who are righteous are received into a state of happiness, which is called paradise, a state of rest, a state of peace, where they shall rest from all their troubles and from all care and sorrow.[17]

We are asked how this can be reconciled with the statement of the Savior . . . when He told the penitent thief on the cross, "Today shalt thou be with me in paradise;"[18] and His other statement . . . where He says to Mary, after His resurrection,

---

[17]Alma 40:11-12.   [18]Luke 23:43.

"Touch me not; for I am not yet ascended to my Father: but go to my brethren, and say unto them, I ascend unto my Father, and your Father; and to my God, and your God.'"[19] In this connection also reference is made to the statement of Peter, where he says that "Christ also . . . went and preached unto the spirits in prison; which sometime were disobedient, when once the long-suffering of God waited in the days of Noah, while the ark was a preparing, wherein few, that is, eight souls were saved by water."[20]

Though there may seem to be some conflict between these passages, it is only seemingly so for there is no real conflict between these various statements. Alma, when he says that "the spirits of all men, as soon as they are departed from this mortal body, . . . are taken home to that God who gave them life," has the idea, doubtless, in his mind that our God is omnipresent—not in His own personality but through His minister, the Holy Spirit.

He does not intend to convey the idea that they are immediately ushered into the personal presence of God. He evidently uses that phrase in a qualified sense. Solomon . . . makes a similar statement: "Then shall the dust return to the earth as it was: and the spirit shall return unto God who gave it."[21] The same idea is frequently expressed by the Latter-day Saints. In referring to a departed one it is often said that he has gone back to God, or he has gone "home to that God who gave him life." Yet it would not be contended that the person who said this meant that the departed one had gone where God, the Father Himself is, in the sense in which the Savior meant when He spake to Mary. . . . Neither is it to be supposed that Alma made this declaration in such a sense. In fact, this is demonstrated by what he says afterwards. . . . Alma says plainly that the spirits of the righteous go into a state of happiness, etc. He says the spirits of the wicked are cast into outer darkness, etc. Now, then, how can those spirits who are cast into outer darkness be in the personal presence of God? God does not dwell where they are, and they certainly do not go where He is.

And yet He is there by His Spirit and by His power, for as

---

[19]John 20:17.
[20]I Peter 3:18-20.

[21]Ecclesiastes 12:7.

the Psalmist David beautifully expresses in . . . his 139th Psalm:

Whither shall I go from thy spirit? or whither shall I flee from thy presence? If I ascend up into heaven, thou art there: if I make my bed in hell, behold, thou art there. If I take the wings of the morning, and dwell in the uttermost parts of the sea; even there shall thy hand lead me; and thy right hand shall hold me. If I say, Surely the darkness shall cover me; even the night shall be light about me. Yea, the darkness hideth not from thee; but the night shineth as the day: the darkness and the light are both alike to thee.[22]

Now, respecting the words of the Savior to Mary recorded by John, to the effect that He had not yet ascended to His Father, even though He had been resurrected, it is plain that He meant, in this expression, that He had not met His Father personally.

Alma understood this matter and makes it very plain. Alma harmonizes with Christ. Christ harmonizes with Alma. Alma says the righteous go to paradise. Christ said the thief would go to paradise. Whether the thief, because of his penitence, may be classed with the righteous or not is not altogether clear. Probably the Savior considered him worthy to go to paradise. At any rate, it is evident that He accepted the thief's humble petition, "Lord, remember me when thou comest into thy kingdom,"[23] and He gave him the assurance that he should be with Him in paradise. It may be possible that the word "paradise," in this instance, is a mistranslation, and that the spirit world is meant.[24] An evidence in favor of this is the statement by Peter that Jesus, while His body lay in the tomb, went and preached unto the spirits in prison. Be this as it may, however, there is no doubt that Alma perfectly understood that there were places prepared both for the righteous and the wicked and that the latter class, at least, would not go where God is as soon as they departed this life. (June 1, 1891, JI 26:353-4)

[22]Psalm 139:7-12.
[23]Luke 23:43.
[24]The Prophet Joseph, in commenting on this passage, said this: "What is paradise? It is a modern word: it does not answer at all to the original word that Jesus made use of. . . . There is nothing in the original word in Greek from which this was taken that signifies paradise; but it was—This day thou shalt be with me in the world of spirits: then I will teach you all about it and answer your inquiries. . . . What is hell? It is another modern term, and is taken from hades. . . . Hades, the Greek, or Sheol, the Hebrew, these two significations mean a world of spirits. Hades, Sheol, paradise, spirits in prison, are all one: it is a world of spirits. The righteous and the wicked all go to the same world of spirits until the resurrection." (Teachings of the Prophet Joseph Smith, page 309-10)

OUR TIES WITH SPIRIT WORLD. We are in reality, while in this mortality, aliens and strangers. We are far distant from our Father's house, living in a cold world far removed from those affections which we doubtless have experienced in the spirit world and which we will again enjoy if we are faithful to the trust reposed in us on the earth.

In one of the revelations given to Enoch it is said: "And the Lord said unto Enoch, then shall thou and all thy city meet them there, and we will receive them into our bosom, and they shall see us; and we will fall upon their necks, and they shall fall upon our necks, and we will kiss each other; and there shall be mine abode, and it shall be Zion, which shall come forth out of all the creations which I have made, and for the space of a thousand years the earth shall rest."[25] This quotation describes how happy will be the meeting of the faithful with their Father in heaven. Our old affections, of which we know but little at this time, will be revived, and we shall enjoy ourselves with a joy that to us is inexpressible now.

It is right that the ties should be strengthened between us and the spirit world. Every one who departs from this mortal state of existence only adds another link to the chain of connection—another tie to draw us nearer to our Father and God and to those intelligences which dwell in His presence. . . .

DEATH STIMULATES INTEREST IN SPIRIT WORLD. Those of us who have lost children, brothers, sisters and parents feel an increased interest in the spirit world; the ties between such and the spirit world have become binding, and we can contemplate, if not with delight, at least with no great sorrow, our removal from this state of existence to the next. In the providence of God it is right that these earthly ties should be weakened to convince us that we are not in the condition the Lord wishes us to remain. We are here in a state of temptation, sin and sorrow, and He desires us to look forward to a better world—to a state of happiness far beyond that which we at present enjoy. As our friends continue to pass from this state to that better world, we who remain feel an increased interest therein and feel stimulated to look forward with increased joy to the time when we shall be united. . . .

[25]Moses 7:63-4.

The Latter-day Saints have hopes and anticipations which none besides them can indulge in because we have a knowledge of the Gospel which buoys us up under these earthly afflictions and assures us that we shall be united with our friends again. It is not a matter of doubt or speculation with us; it is with us a matter of knowledge. God has given us the testimony of His Spirit, which bears witness to our spirits that we shall again be united with our departed friends after death. Our mortal tabernacles may sleep, but our spirits are eternal, and, if faithful here, we shall enjoy an immortality in the presence of God that will amply reward us for all that we may suffer on the earth. (Nov. 29, 1864, *DNW* 14:82)

OUR CONDITION IN SPIRIT WORLD. We shall enter into the other sphere of existence with the same spirit that we have here. If we were animated by the spirit of the Telestial Kingdom we shall have that, if by the spirit of the Terrestrial Kingdom we shall have that, if by the spirit of the Celestial Kingdom we shall have that. We shall go from this condition of existence into the other sphere with the same feelings, to some extent at least, as we have here. If we have had knowledge, we shall have it there.

There will be just as much distinction between spirits there as you find between spirits here. Those who have made good use of their opportunities here will have the benefit of their diligence and faithfulness there. Those who have been careless and indifferent and have not acquired knowledge and power through the exercise of faith will find themselves lacking there.

We will have to work there to grow and to make progress just as we have here, though the facilities will be better there than they are here. If we can only pass into the paradise of God without Satan having any power over us, our condition will be a very happy one. But we shall find that knowledge and power will not come to us there as the rain that falls upon us, without any effort of ours to acquire them. We shall have to exercise ourselves and exert our powers there just as we have to here. We shall be rewarded according to our diligence and faithfulness in the exercise of our agency. (Nov. 2, 1895, *DW* 51:803)

OUR MEMORIES TO BE QUICKENED. Memory will be quickened to a wonderful extent. Every deed that we have done will be brought to our recollection. Every acquaintance made will be remembered. There will be no scenes or incidents in our lives that will be forgotten by us in the world to come. You have heard of men who have been drowning or have fallen from a great height describe that in about a second or two every event of their lives passed before them like a panorama with the rapidity of lightning. This shows what power there is latent in the human mind, which, when quickened by the power of God, will make men and women recall not only that which pertains to this life, but our memories will stretch back to the life we had before we came here, with the associations we had with our Father and God and with those bright spirits that stand around His throne and with the righteous and holy ones. (April 7, 1889, *DW* 38:677)

DEATH HAS NO TERRORS FOR RIGHTEOUS. How delightful it is to contemplate the departure of those who have been faithful, as far as their knowledge permitted, to the truth which God has revealed! There is no sting nor gloom nor inconsolable sorrow about the departure of such persons. Holy angels are around their bedside to administer unto them. The Spirit of God rests down upon them, and His messengers are near them to introduce them to those who are on the other side of the veil. . . .

Satan has power here over us to a certain extent. He can afflict us; he can tempt us; he can annoy us in many ways. These are the consequences of the fall and for a wise purpose belong to our probation here in the flesh. But, if we listen to the Lord, if we strive to keep His commandments, if we seek to be governed by His Spirit, when death comes, Satan's power ceases. He can no more afflict or torment or tempt or annoy those who are thus faithful. His power over them ceases forever.

But not so with those who disobey God, who keep not His commandments, who yield to the power and spirit of Satan. They are his servants; they are under his influence. He takes possession of them when they pass from this mortal existence, and they experience the torments of hell. (Sept. 1, 1885, *JI* 20:264)

SATAN HAS NO POWER OVER FAITHFUL DEAD.

Satan is bound as soon as the faithful spirit leaves this tabernacle
of clay and goes to the other side of the veil. That spirit is
emancipated from the power and thraldom and attacks of Satan.
Satan can only afflict such in this life. He can only afflict those
in that life which is to come who have listened to his persuasions,
who have listed to obey him. These are the only ones over
whom he has power after this life.

The Latter-day Saints who have been faithful, the men and
the women who have kept the commandments of God, those
who have lived according to the light that they have had,
whether it be much or little, when they leave this state of existence, they are placed in such a position that Satan has no power
over them; he cannot tempt them; he cannot afflict them; he
can do nothing to interfere with their happiness; but the wicked,
those who list to obey him, those who give heed to his spirit,
will only be still more completely in his power in the life that
is to come. . . .

Already we have a foretaste of it. You watch the men who
yield to the temptations and allurements of Satan; you watch the
men and women who give heed to his spirit, and you will find
written legibly upon their faces that misery that awaits them
in the world to come. (July 6, 1884, *DNW* 33:498)

If you are faithful to the truth, . . . you will then be
ushered into the presence of the holy and the just. You will dwell
in the paradise of God, waiting with delightful anticipations the
time when your spirits and your bodies will be re-united, and
when you shall dwell together with the holy, the just and
exalted ones in the presence of God and the Lamb, nevermore,
as the Prophets have said, to depart or to go out thence. . . .

Those who are unfaithful, those who will listen to Satan,
who will lend a willing ear to his blandishments and to his
allurements, when they go from this state of existence, they go
into a condition where they are subject to his power. They
will dwell in darkness, and according to their sins their punishment will be. Some will be consigned to "outer darkness,"
where there is weeping and wailing and gnashing of teeth; and
they will remain in that condition until they will be visited
by some servant of God to unlock the prison doors to them and

to preach to them again the Gospel of salvation, through repentance and faith in the Lord Jesus Christ.

The condition of these spirits will be similar to that described by Alma. You remember when he was stricken down to the earth, in company with the sons of Mosiah. He was visited by an angel of God. His astonishment was so great that he became dumb, and they carried him home. His father and his brethren prayed over him and for him. After they had fasted and prayed two days and two nights, Alma was restored. He then described the agony of mind and the torment that he had endured. He was in hell during that period. His "soul was racked with eternal torment."[26] While he was in this condition, he remembered that his father had taught about one Jesus, who should come as a Savior; and when that thought came across his mind, he clung to it, and he besought Jesus to come to his deliverance and deliverance came.

So it will be with those who are damned in the way that I have described and who are consigned to torment. They will remain in that condition, according to the enormity of their offenses, until punishment will be meted out to them sufficiently to bring them to a condition that they will receive the Gospel of salvation. That Gospel which is taught to us will be taught to them, and they will have an opportunity of obeying it in their damned condition and through repentance will receive salvation.

CONFESS SINS DAILY. Now, how much better it is for us, while this day of probation lasts and while God gives us life and power and opportunities, to live according to the laws of God, so that every day our sins will be remitted. Let us confess our sins to our Father every day, and if we have sinned against our brethren and sisters, obtain forgiveness of them. Then, when the hour of death approaches, no matter where it may find us, we shall be found prepared to enter into the presence of our God. How much better it is to be in this condition than to lead a life of sin and then go into torment and remain there till we embrace the opportunities that we now reject. (1890, *Contributor* 11:478-9)

A PRISON HOUSE FOR THE UNRIGHTEOUS. The

[26]Mosiah 27:29.

first resurrection, we are told, will be in the beginning of the Millennial era. One thousand years will elapse before the wicked will have the opportunity of coming forth; they will sleep in their graves for that thousand years, and they will await with dread the time when they shall receive punishment for their sins. In the meantime they will be in a state of utter darkness, where there is weeping and wailing and gnashing of teeth.

The Latter-day Saints do not believe, however—God having taught us better things—that there is a place of torment to which the souls of the children of men will be consigned throughout the never ending ages of eternity—that is, those who have not committed the unpardonable sin. He has revealed to us a sufficient amount to show us how dreadful is the condition, even under the best of circumstances, of those who sin against light and knowledge and break the commandments of God.

We are told that those who lived in the days of Noah who refused the Gospel, the message of life and salvation that He offered to them, were consigned to a prison house, that they remained in that prison house until the time when Jesus descended into hell and unlocked the door and preached to them the Gospel of repentance. Twenty-five hundred years—according to our chronology—had elapsed since those spirits had been consigned to this place of torment, this prison house, from which they could not emerge, into which no heavenly messenger had access. There they were locked up in the prison house of God for this long period of 2500 years.

With what expectations they must have awaited the arrival of some messenger who had the power to unlock the door and enter into this house and bring them some comfort and some help. How much better for them to have obeyed the message of God through His Prophet Noah! How much better it would have been to have repented and borne all the afflictions, all the pain and all the persecution that Noah and his household bore or that any servant of God had borne than that they should be in such a condition as this! (July 6, 1884, *DNW* 33:498)

GOSPEL PREACHED TO SPIRITS OF DAMNED. The spirits of the damned—those who have committed abominable crimes—will have this doctrine preached to them, and they will be kept in torment until they repent of their sins. The labors of

the men who have received the Priesthood in this life will be
continued in the life to come in this glorious work of carrying
the glad tidings of salvation to those who sit in darkness because
of their sins, who may be in the condition of the antediluvians,
whom the Lord consigned to prison after destroying them with a
flood because they rejected the testimony of Noah and those
associated with him.

The Lord had promised His servants, however, that these
people should be visited after they had atoned to some extent
for their violation of His laws; and this was the glorious mission
of our Lord and Savior Jesus while His body lay in the sepulchre.
He went into the spirit world and visited these spirits in prison,
unlocked the doors of their prisons and started again the work
of preaching salvation to them to see whether, after having endured the wrath of God from the time when they were overwhelmed with the flood until then, they would receive the Gospel
of salvation and repent of their sins. That is the labor that we
have upon us as a people, both here and hereafter. (Jan. 22,
1898, MS 61:115-6)

INVISIBLE SPIRITS AROUND US. I believe there are
places and circumstances in which people can be placed where
there are influences brought to bear upon them that are more
difficult to resist than there would be under other circumstances
and in other places. I have often heard it remarked by the
brethren, and I have remarked it myself, that in some places
there is a greater disposition entertained by the people to commit
adultery and indulge in kindred sins of this description than
there is in this country. There seem to be influences in the
atmosphere in those lands of such a character that unless a person
is on his guard and constantly watching and resisting them he
will be led down to destruction by them. A spirit and disposition
will creep over the people unless they are careful to lead them
astray. . . . This is undoubtedly the case. There are spirits
in the atmosphere that are filled with that disposition and who
seek to influence those with whom they are brought in contact,
impressing those who are in the tabernacle of flesh to indulge
in the same sin.

There are influences in the atmosphere that are invisible
to us that, while we are here upon the earth, we ought to resist

with all our might, mind and strength—influences which, if we would be led by them, would lead us to destruction—influences that are opposed to the Spirit of God—influences that would bring upon us destruction here and hereafter if we would yield to them. These influences we have to resist.

We have to resist the spirit of adultery, the spirit of whoredom, the spirit of drunkenness, the spirit of theft, and every other evil influence and spirit that we may continually overcome, and, when we have finished our work on the earth, be prepared to govern and control those influences and exercise power over them, in the presence of our Father and God. I have no doubt that many of my brethren and sisters have sensibly felt in various places and at various times evil influences around them.

PROPHET JOSEPH'S EXPLANATION. Brother Joseph Smith gave an explanation of this. There are places in the Mississippi Valley where the influence or the presence of invisible spirits are very perceptibly felt. He said that numbers had been slain there in war and that there were evil influences or spirits which affect the spirits of those who have tabernacles on the earth. I myself have felt those influences in other places besides the continent of America; I have felt them on the old battle grounds on the Sandwich Islands.

I have come to the conclusion that if our eyes were open to see the spirit world around us, we should feel differently on this subject than we do; we would not be so unguarded and careless and so indifferent whether we had the spirit and power of God with us or not; but we would be continually watchful and prayerful to our Heavenly Father for His Holy Spirit and His holy angels to be around about us to strengthen us to overcome every evil influence.

NUMEROUS AGENCIES AT WORK. When I see young men indulging in drunkenness and in stealing, I come to the conclusion that they are led captive by the evil spirits around them. We call it the spirit of the evil one; but he has numerous agencies at work even as the Lord has numerous agencies to assist Him in bringing to pass the consummation of His great designs. The adversary has numerous agencies at his command,

and he seeks to control and lead to destruction the inhabitants of the earth who will be subject to them.

If we could see with our spiritual senses as we now see with our natural senses, we should be greatly shocked at the sight of the influences that prompt us to disobey the counsels of God or the Spirit of the Lord in our hearts. But we cannot see them for they are spiritually discerned; and he who discerns the most is the most fully impressed by the Spirit of God; he who does not discern has not profited by the instructions given to him and yields to those evil influences in an unguarded moment and is taken captive in his blindness.

He who is imbued with the Spirit of God is sensibly aware when the evil power approaches, but he does not welcome it to his bosom; he resists it with all the might and strength God has given unto him; he obtains power over it, and it no more troubles him; if it does, its influence is more weakened than previously. (Nov. 13, 1864, *JD* 11:29-30)

GOD'S CARE FOR ALL HIS CREATIONS. The agencies which our Father in heaven has at His control are utterly beyond our conception. Every department of His heavenly and illimitable Kingdom is under the immediate supervision of His agents. . . .

Lord Jesus plainly informs us concerning certain agencies which the Father uses to watch over his little ones—guardian angels, who always behold His face in heaven. They watch over those who are put in their charge, and no one can offend or despise them with impunity.

What a consolation is this knowledge to the people of God. In distress, in trouble, in the midst of affliction or of persecution, they can go with confidence to the Lord. They can cry unto Him with faith, knowing that He will hear their supplications. They know, too, that His angels have charge concerning them and that they can have access to their Father in heaven in their behalf. Despised though they may be by the wicked, insignificant even in their own estimation, they may rest assured they are not overlooked or forgotten. The Lord watches over them; nothing can befall them without His knowledge. This is a glorious position to be in. (Jan. 15, 1889, *JI* 24:37)

POWERS OF HEAVEN AT WORK. There are agencies

laboring for the predictions of the holy Prophets of which we have but little conception at the present time. . . .

There are powers engaged in preparing the earth for the events that await it and fulfilling all the great predictions concerning it which we know nothing of, and we need not think that it depends upon us Latter-day Saints alone and that we are the only agents in the hands of God in bringing these things to pass. The powers of heaven are engaged with us in this work. (June 29, 1873, JD 16:120-1)

God is doing a great work among us, much greater than many of us imagine. We do not see Him, but He is nevertheless in our midst. We do not see Jesus, but He is nevertheless in our midst. We do not see angels, but they are nevertheless in our midst. God is working to get this people to the perfection that He desires them to attain. . . . God demands of us a holiness of life that we cannot conceive of at the present time. . . .

A CONTEST BETWEEN GOD AND SATAN. There are unseen influences on both sides. There are unseen and invisible agencies that God our Heavenly Father has brought to bear upon this work to aid us, and there are on the other side those unseen agencies of evil. We can tell them by their fruits and by the results of their actions upon the children of men.

Let us remember that it is not that which is before us alone that we have to contend with but that there are powers behind those that we see in the flesh, and those powers are determined to destroy this work. It is a contest between Satan and God, and there can be no doubt as to the result. (Sept. 2, 1883, JD 25:1-3)

INVISIBLE INFLUENCES. Those evil spirits, . . . invisible to our eyes, yet palpable to our senses, are constantly seeking to instill into our minds evil thoughts and wrong desires, to prompt us to commit sin and thereby grieve the Spirit of God and to lead us, as Cain was led, to perpetrate crime which resulted in his becoming Perdition. But there are also angels around us. Though invisible to us they are continually inviting us and pleading with us to do that which is right. The Spirit of God, too, rests upon us, and it prompts us to keep the commandments of God. By means of these influences, therefore, we are receiving experience and we are growing in knowledge. (May 19, 1889, *DW* 39:17)

A man that has had the light, the truth, the Spirit of God and has grieved that Spirit, when the other spirit takes possession of him, there is a complete transformation. Those who know see it in his face and feel it in his spirit. They cannot associate with him without discerning that there is a spirit of darkness and evil taken possession of him, and so it is with all who take this course. They already begin to have a foretaste of that dreadful misery that awaiteth those who break the commandments of God and listen to the spirit of the evil one. (July 6, 1884, *DW* 33:498)

HELL A REAL PLACE—MANY TO GO THERE. I have thought sometimes that some of our people are inclined to think there is no hell and that nobody is going to hell. I tell you there will be a large number of people go to hell; they will suffer torment and will go where there is weeping and wailing and gnashing of teeth; they will be in outer darkness and suffer far beyond anything we can conceive of. Latter-day Saints especially who commit sin, if they die in their sin, will go to hell, and they will suffer torment there until the day of redemption. But think of the length of time during which they will be in this torment! You remember what the Lord said to Martin Harris when He told him that unless he repented his sufferings would be sore—"how sore you know not, how exquisite you know not, yea, how hard to bear you know not! . . . of which in the smallest, yea, even in the least degree you have tasted at the time I withdrew my Spirit."[27] If any of you have the Spirit of God withdrawn from you, you can have a little foretaste of what the punishment of sinners will be. (Feb. 16, 1896, *DW* 52:388)

---

[27]D. & C. 19:15, 20.

CHAPTER 8

THE MILLENNIUM—A THOUSAND YEARS OF PEACE

HOW SATAN WILL BE BOUND. We talk about Satan being bound. Satan will be bound by the power of God; but he will be bound also by the determination of the people of God not to listen to him, not to be governed by him. The Lord will not bind him and take his power from the earth while there are men and women willing to be governed by him. That is contrary to the plan of salvation. To deprive men of their agency is contrary to the purposes of our God.

There was a time on this continent, of which we have an account, when the people were so righteous that Satan did not have power among them. Nearly four generations passed away in righteousness. They lived in purity and died without sin. That was through their refusal to yield to Satan. It is not recorded that Satan had no power in other parts of the earth during that period. According to all history that we have in our possession Satan had the same power over men who were willing to listen to him. But in this land he did not have power, and he was literally bound. I believe that this will be the case in the Millennium. (Oct. 6, 1897, *CR* 52)

MAN'S AGENCY TO BIND SATAN. Satan only gains power over man through man's exercise of his own agency; and when Satan shall be bound, as the Lord says he will be for a thousand years, one of the great powers that will help bring this to pass will be man's agency. The Lord has never forced men against their will to obey Him. He never will do so. If Satan, therefore, has power with man, it is because man yields to his influence.

Children can resist Satan. They can obey the Lord. They can be righteous. They can take a course which will give them power over Satan. And every child which takes this course helps bring to pass the fulfillment of the words of the Lord concerning the binding of Satan.

SATAN LOOSED AT END OF MILLENNIUM. When Satan will be bound, he will have no power to tempt the children of men. This happy period will cover one thousand years. Then Satan will be loosed again. Why will he be loosed again? Because a generation will arise, some of which in the exercise of their agency will listen and yield to him. Thus he will have power over them. They will become his willing servants. In this way wickedness and all the evils under which the earth now groans will be introduced among men; for whenever men will listen to Satan and exercise their agency in that direction, wickedness flourishes and righteousness lessens.

DESTRUCTION OF WICKED TO END SATAN'S POWER. The time is not far distant when great judgments will be poured out upon the wicked inhabitants of the earth. Every Prophet who has looked forward to our day has seen and predicted that the wicked would be destroyed. Their destruction means the destruction of Satan's power. The righteous will be left, and because of their righteousness the Lord will have mercy upon them; they, exercising their agency in the right direction, will bring down His blessings upon them to such an extent that Satan will be bound. (Nov. 15, 1891, *JI* 26:693)

SATAN BOUND BY LIVING GOSPEL. My view of the Gospel is that when it is obeyed by mankind the power of the devil will cease. That is my view respecting a part of the power that will be brought to bear to bind Satan. Satan will be bound because he will not have power over the hearts of the children of men. Why? One reason will be because they will have obeyed the more perfect law which will have relieved them from his power. . . .

In the Gospel of the Lord Jesus Christ as God has revealed it unto us there are laws so perfect that when this people called Latter-day Saints shall obey them they will be so far lifted up above the power of Satan that he will have but little power to tempt them. We never shall be emancipated from the power of Satan until we do obey these laws of God. An obedience thereto will bring emancipation to us and to every human being on the face of the earth, and it is upon no other principle that emancipation can be brought.

It will not be as many suppose by our being withdrawn without volition on our part from the influences of Satan; but it will be by our obedience to the laws of God, by our conforming to the requirements which He makes of us, by our putting into practice all those higher laws which God has revealed and which He designs we shall practice. Any soul that is waiting for some outward deliverance, waiting for some time to come when by some extraneous means and independent of our action and the exercise of our agency deliverance will be brought, will wait in vain, I am afraid.

Not that I would convey the idea that God is not going to help us, that God is not going to do it by His power; I would not convey any such idea because I know and you know that without God's help all our efforts are powerless, and it is vain to seek to do anything in and of ourselves; we cannot do it. Human nature is too fallible to do anything of this kind; but we must exercise the powers God has given to us by obeying His law, by conforming to His requirements.

In this way we will be emancipated through the blessing and aid of God upon us, and in this way the earth will be redeemed from the power of Satan. The more people obey the laws of God as God has revealed them and as they are embodied in the Gospel of Jesus Christ, the nearer they approach unto God, the more they become like Him, the more power they get over themselves and over the adversary. (May 6, 1883, JD 24:145-6)

BINDING SATAN IN HOMES. By the Saints refusing to be led by the influences of Satan and not yielding to his seductive temptations, he is virtually bound so far as they are concerned; and, when the head of the family can attain unto this power and persuade his wife and family to do likewise, the power of Satan will be bound in that habitation, and the Millennium will have commenced in that household; and, if all should take this course, man and the earth would soon be prepared for the coming of Jesus and the ushering in of the full millennial glory and the complete binding of Satan, all of which glory they would already have a foretaste. (July 17, 1863, MS 26:514)

DESTRUCTIONS TO CLEANSE THE EARTH. If the destruction of the wicked among the Nephites was necessary in order to bring about a reign of peace and righteousness for three or four generations, do you not think that there will have to be great and overwhelming destructions to cleanse the earth of the wicked and to lay the foundation of a thousand years of peace and righteousness? Will wickedness be allowed to flourish? I tell you, no.

The wicked will be destroyed, according to the words of all the Prophets, and the righteous only will survive. There will be a cleansing of the earth from the wicked as great in its place as the cleansing of the earth by the flood that came in the days of Noah, though this time it will be by fire. Malachi says the day will come when the wicked shall be ashes under the soles of the feet of the righteous.

Already, as I have said, you can see the operation of this cleansing process among us. The wicked are gradually being purged from among us. It is not very perceptible; we have got to think about it and call it to mind to become aware of it; but we can become aware of it if we will reflect. And this will be more and more the case as the power of God increases and the responsibility of the Latter-day Saints becomes greater.

Therefore, I am looking for destructions and for judgments; I am looking for the cleansing power of God among us as well as among the nations of the earth, in order that the foundation of that great and glorious time shall be laid when Jesus shall reign upon the earth. (DEN, Sept. 21, 1895)

MILLENNIAL CONDITIONS. Now, how will it be on this earth when Christ reigns? . . . When the Millennium dawns, Satan bound and the elements of the earth at our disposal and under our control, there will be no hunger, no thirst, no nakedness, no vagrants, no houseless people; all will have that which is necessary to supply their physical wants. But there will be no waste. One man will not be allowed to lord it over another and take possession of more than he needs; but all will have a fulness, Satan will be bound. He will not have power to inflict the misery he has done and is doing.

But how has Satan obtained such power? By men obeying him instead of God. That is the root of all the misery that comes upon mankind. When Satan is bound, this will be stopped. He will not be able, for a thousand years at least, to inflict upon mankind the misery and the sorrow that they have suffered through their obedience to him.

After the thousand years he will regain some of his present power. It will be as it was among the Nephites. . . . Men will arise who will object to working for the benefit of others; class distinctions will once more make themselves apparent; Satan will regain his power and will maintain it until the great battle shall take place which is spoken of in the scriptures.

We have a good prospect before us. We are at the beginning, not the end, of the thousand years of peace. If we are faithful, we are to be the happy pioneers of this new order of things that is to be established upon the earth. Our children, if they are faithful, will live generation after generation in this glorious condition. (April 16, 1899, MS 61:631)

We shall build temples, and we shall go forth in peace and in righteousness, doing the works of redemption that have to be done for those that have died in ignorance of the Gospel and without receiving these saving ordinances. We shall find plenty of employment during the thousand years in doing these works, and the earth will be cleansed from sin. . . . There will be no war, for swords will be beaten into plowshares, and spears into pruning hooks, and there shall be peace from one end of the earth to the other. (Oct. 9, 1892, DW 45:620)

THE EARTH TO BE RENEWED. The tenth Article of Faith of the Latter-day Saints states among other things their belief "that the earth will be renewed and receive its paradisiacal glory." The question is sometimes asked if this change is to take place before the millennial reign of peace, during that period or afterwards.

That the earth is to be renewed and glorified is evident from the words of the New Testament writers. The Savior told His disciples that "heaven and earth shall pass away;"[1] John the Revelator says that in his vision of future events he "saw a new heaven and a new earth: for the first heaven and the first earth were passed away."[2] He continues by describing the glories of the holy city, the New Jerusalem which should come down upon this new earth "from God out of heaven."[2] The Revelation of St. John depicts both past and future events. These events are evidently set forth by the Apostle in the order in which

---

[1]Matthew 24:35.   [2]Revelation 21:1-2.

they should occur. According to the order of description the renewing of the earth is to take place after the millennial reign, for the occurrences of the thousand years of peace, as well as those that should follow that glorious era, are mentioned before the event of the earth passing away and being restored as the glorified abode of immortal beings.

The revelations given to the Prophet Joseph Smith make it clear that the earth is to be renewed and receive its paradisiacal glory after the peaceful reign of a thousand years is past. In a revelation given him in September, 1830, are recorded these words: "When the thousand years are ended, and men again begin to deny their God, then will I spare the earth for a little season; and the end shall come, and the heaven and the earth shall be consumed and pass away, and there shall be a new heaven and a new earth, for all old things shall pass away, and all things shall become new, even the heaven and the earth, and all the fullness thereof, both men and beasts, the fowls of the air, and the fishes of the sea."[3]   March 1, 1899, *JI* 34:139-40)

---

[3]D. & C. 29:22-4.

Chapter 9

The Glory of the Future

PERFECT JUSTICE. The Lord says that He is coming "to recompense unto every man according to his work, and measure to every man according to the measure he has measured to his fellow man." This is in keeping with the words of Jesus:

> Judge not, and ye shall not be judged: condemn not, and ye shall not be condemned: forgive, and ye shall be forgiven:
> Give, and it shall be given unto you; good measure, pressed down, and shaken together, and running over, shall men give into your bosom. For with the same measure ye mete withal it shall be measured to you again.[1]

This is perfect justice. No one can complain with any good cause if he is recompensed according to his works or if he receives the same measure that he measures to his fellow man. But do we always think of this in all our transactions? If we all do, then we are in a happy condition and will not be afraid to meet the consequences of all our acts when the Lord judges us.

But that there is such a judgment coming too many forget; at least it would appear so from their conduct. Would any man do a wrong to his fellow man or take advantage of his fellow man in any direction if he had in mind the great fact that the Lord is coming and that He will repay him according to his works and measure back to him as he has measured to his fellow man? If it is not forgotten by many, then they do not act as though they believed that the Lord would do any such thing. (Oct. 1, 1891, JI 26:604)

JUDGMENT ACCORDING TO LAW. The Gospel of Jesus Christ teaches that all will be judged according to the law that has been taught unto them. . . . "This is the condemnation, that light is come into the world, and men loved darkness rather than light."[2] "Where no law is," the Apostle says, "there is no transgression."[3] Men cannot be held accountable for that which they never knew. God will never consign his creatures to a

---
[1]Luke 6:37-8.   [3]Romans 4:15.
[2]John 3:19.

never-ending misery for not obeying the Gospel of His Son when they never had it taught unto them, and it is as great a fallacy and as great a libel on our God as ever was propagated about any being to make such an assertion. . . .

God's salvation is not confined to this brief space which we call time, but as He is eternal, so are His mercy, love and compassion eternal towards His creatures. . . .

SAINTS HELD TO STRICTER ACCOUNTABILITY. Who are they who are under condemnation and who need fear at the prospect of the same? Men and women who, living in the day when the Gospel is preached in its fullness and purity, hear it and reject it. Against such the anger of God is enkindled, and they are in a far worse condition than those who die and never hear it. Says Jesus, "It were better for him that a millstone were hanged about his neck, and that he were drowned in the depths of the sea,"[4] than to do such and such things; and in another place He says, "It had been good for that man if he had not been born."[5] Why? Because light having been presented to him and truth proclaimed in his hearing, he rejects the same.

The Latter-day Saints, I hold, will be held to stricter accountability than any other people on the face of the earth. . . . We must be a pure people or we will be scourged; we must be a holy people or God's anger will be kindled against us. . . . In proportion to the light which men have will they be judged, and God will reward them according to the deeds done in the body. (July 14, 1872, JD 15:118-9)

DESIRE FOR SALVATION SHOULD DOMINATE LIVES. We have started out to obtain salvation. Everything on the earth ought to be brought into subordination to this. It should be the dominant feeling of our hearts. The love of this Gospel, the love of our standing in the Church of God, our love for the fellowship of the Saints ought to be uppermost within us. . . .

Is there anything that you love more than you do this work? Is there anything that you love more than your standing in this Church? If there is, then I am sorry for you for I think there is nothing that ought to be more desirable than salvation

---

[4]Matthew 18:6.　　　　　　[5]Ibid., 26:24.

and exaltation in the Celestial Kingdom. (Apr. 21, 1895, *DW* 51:291)

SALVATION IS INDIVIDUAL. Each individual should seek to do that which he himself knows to be right regardless of what others do. We should have clear convictions as to the truth and then carry out those convictions in the proper spirit. . . .

It is our duty to do that which we ourselves know to be right. What matters it to me if man chooses to do a thing which is not right? Is it for me to do as he does? No! It is for me to conceive correctly that which is right, then carry it out in my life and teach others to do the same. Until we do this we shall never attain unto that glory that He has promised.

God has made great promises to us connected with the Celestial Kingdom. Some have imagined that as soon as they leave this state of existence they enter upon celestial glory, especially after they get their resurrected bodies. I do not believe that we will ever reach there unless we develop within us those qualities which will fit us for that exaltation. The promise is given to us, but we must live so as to realize it. No being can be exalted only by self development and self exertion. God will bestow His blessing, but we must be developed under His power and blessing upon us. . . .

MUST DO AS SAVIOR DID. If we are to associate with our Father in Heaven and with the Savior, it must be because we become like them. If there is a quality which Jesus possesses, we must possess it. If there is faithfulness which He has exhibited, we must exhibit it. If there is obedience which He has manifested while in the flesh, similar obedience must be shown in our lives. We must do all this or we will not be like Him.

I would like to impress this truth upon the minds of the Latter-day Saints that they need not fold their arms and imagine because they are members of the Church that that is all that is necessary. We can see for ourselves the powers that God had endowed us with. We are conscious that God has endowed us in a very wonderful manner. When our minds are lit up with the Spirit of God, we are filled with exalted ideas. It is right that we should exercise these powers.

I would not, however, by any expression of mine convey the

idea to you that it is a difficult matter to do what I have been talking about and to serve God. Jesus said His yoke was easy and His burden was light. It is so. The weakest of us carry it. God stands ready on our right and on our left to give unto us all the aid that we need; but He wants us to exercise faith and the powers that He has given unto us and not follow someone else blindly and do things that are wrong because others do them. . . .

OUR REWARD CARRIED WITH US. Each will have to stand for himself or for herself, and each will receive reward or punishment. We carry our punishment with us; we cannot escape it. We carry blessing with us. We carry heaven or we carry hell with us. Heaven is not altogether a question of locality, neither is hell. Hell is with the individual that deserves it. He may go where he pleases; hell will be with him. If he deserves heaven, wherever he goes heaven will be with him.

Of course, it is a desirable thing to be in good society, and people who keep the laws of God will be in the society of heavenly beings and live in heavenly places eternally, and it will intensify their pleasure and happiness. We know this by experience in this life. But you put a man who is a sinner and who is carrying the penalty of his sins into the society of heavenly beings, and he could not endure it; he would be in hell. (Oct. 14, 1894, MS 56:754-6)

INDIVIDUAL SALVATION MOST IMPORTANT. I would like to have the power to impress upon your minds the importance of this great truth. There is nothing so important to me as an individual as my own salvation. This is the most important thing to me that can be—that I myself shall be saved, that I myself shall so live as to be counted worthy by the Almighty to receive an exaltation in His Kingdom. This is of the utmost importance to me individually. . . .

After all, the great labor, the most honorable labor that any person can perform is . . . to improve ourselves, to be Latter-day Saints in deed and in truth, to live our holy religion. (Oct. 5, 1879, JD 21:79-80)

REWARD ACCORDING TO WORKS. I tell you that God's providence is over all His children, and He will reward every man and every woman according to his or her works, and

He will reward those who have lived exemplary lives, those who have been moral, whether they be heathen or Christian, whether they have known the name of Jesus or not, whether they have the Bible or the Koran or some other book or no book at all; whatever may have been their condition and circumstances, if they have lived according to the light that God has given them and to laws that they understood, God will reward them and will eventually bestow every blessing upon them which they are capable of receiving. (Nov. 9, 1884, JD 26:82)

THE IMPORTANCE OF SMALL THINGS. We are often indifferent to the importance of small things. . . . All that we will know at the end of our lives will be the sum total of the ideas we have daily accumulated. In like manner our moral characters are made up little by little from the impressions we receive from our surroundings.

For these reasons every act of our lives is of some importance, for it helps to shape our destiny or that of those around us. The accumulated good works of our lives must be the measure of our salvation in the world to come. . . .

SURROUNDED BY WITNESSES. We are evidently surrounded by a cloud of witnesses. Every act of our lives, no matter how secret we have thought it, has had its witnesses. Every act of our lives is a testimony to those numerous witnesses of the spirit and motive that actuate us. If all our acts are in the spirit and power of the Gospel, then we are constantly bearing the testimony of Jesus to all the intelligences, good or bad, that surround us. Thus we show by our lives that we have received the testimony of Jesus, which is another essential condition for gaining a part in the resurrection of the just. It is by these testimonies that we will be judged, not altogether by what mortal man may see us do. . . . (June 1, 1880, JI 15:126)

A GLORY SUITED TO OUR CONDITION. We shall have the spirit of that glory which we shall attain unto; and just as there are grades in this life among men, so it will be in the resurrection. There will be grades of happiness, of glory and of exaltation. You put a man that has not lived so as to receive the spirit of a certain glory with those who have received that glory, and he would be entirely out of his element and unhappy.

God will give to every man a glory that will be suited to his condition. So, if a man obeys every law that God gives and maintains his integrity, he will receive the highest glory that God has to bestow, even the celestial glory.

There are some who cannot do this. As the revelation that Joseph received teaches us, there are honorable men who do a great many good things but who have not faith enough to receive the Gospel in its fulness. All of us have met such individuals. We have also seen men and women who gladly obeyed the Gospel when they heard it. They were baptized; they had hands laid upon them, and they received the Holy Ghost; but they did not have faith enough to go beyond this. . . . Such persons will receive a reward in proportion to their obedience.

You will find others who have faith enough to obey the first principles of the Gospel and perhaps receive the Priesthood and gather with the Saints; but when they are taught the doctrine of tithing, they have not faith enough to obey that; or if they do pay tithing, they pay but very little. Persons who have no more faith than this will not get a reward like those who are obedient to tithing.

So with all these works that God requires at our hands. There are some men that have not faith enough to go upon missions when they are called, and they offer excuses. They will get their reward according to their diligence and faithfulness; but they will not get the reward of the man who is always willing to do that which he is required to do and whose life is crowded with good works, who is liberal to the poor, honest in his dealings, just and merciful in his actions and who is willing to suffer wrong rather than do wrong. . . .

JUDGED ACCORDING TO WILLINGNESS TO OBEY. There are some laws that we are prevented from obeying that have been declared to be necessary to exaltation in the Celestial Kingdom of our God. What will be the condition of those who do not obey these laws? God, knowing all our desires, if He should see a spirit of willingness and obedience in our hearts, will judge us accordingly. That which we cannot do we are not expected to do. God does not ask impossible things from His children. But He asks us to be obedient to Him and to carry out His laws in our lives; and if for any reason we cannot do this but are willing to do it, He will accept the offering and the good desires that we entertain in our hearts. . . .

The widow's mite is as much as the thousand dollars of the rich man, if it is only given in the right spirit. The Lord looks at the hearts of His children. The woman who is poor but who gives to the extent of her ability, God accepts that, and she is blessed accordingly and will be rewarded just as much in her place as the rich man that has done to the extent of his ability. Our God is a just God, and He deals with His children in justice and mercy. (Oct. 9, 1892, *DW* 45:618)

SALVATION BY USE OF AGENCY. It is a remarkable fact that there is no blessing that God has promised unto us that any human being, that any angel or any devil can take from us. There is no power of that kind that can take it from us. But a man himself, by sinning, can rob himself of his blessing; he can prevent its fulfilment; but no human being can do it beside himself.

Remember this, Latter-day Saints; remember it and treasure it up in your hearts that you have salvation within your own keeping. If you are damned, you damn yourselves; you will be the instrument of your own damnation. It will not be because God will damn you; it will not be because Satan has such power that he can take away every blessing from you; it will not be because of anything of that kind.

How will it come about? It will come to every soul by wrong-doing on the part of that soul. He or she alone can bring condemnation on himself or herself. There is no other power can do it. Hence, if we are damned we shall have no one to blame but ourselves; we shall have no one to condemn but ourselves; it will be the result of our own agency, the exercise of that power which God gave to Adam and Eve in the Garden of Eden. . . . Every one of us will bring upon ourselves either salvation or condemnation as the case may be, according to the manner in which we exercise our agency before God. It is by this Priesthood and the exercise of it that the blessings of God will flow up to us. . . .

PROMISED BLESSINGS FOR RIGHTEOUS. A man who practices wrong may have all these blessings pronounced upon him; he may have been baptized and have had hands laid upon

him; he may go through the temple and have wives sealed to
him and have every blessing promised unto him that is promised
to the most faithful of the children of God, and yet, if he does not
live so as to be worthy of these blessings, he will not receive them;
he will, sooner or later, be bereft of them and left destitute.

This is the glorious feature of this great tie that God has
restored to the earth. It only binds the righteous. It does not
bind the wicked to the righteous. It does not bind the wicked
to the wicked. Its power and saving force can only be exercised
or enjoyed where righteousness prevails. Hence, when the people
of God come forth in the resurrection, they will come forth pure.
There will then be a separation of the wicked from the righteous.
The righteous will enjoy their own society. (Oct. 18, 1884,
JD 26:249-50)

HEAVEN IS WHAT WE MAKE IT. There are a great
many people who are thinking all the time about the celestial
glory and want to get there. It is a very good wish. It certainly
is a most desirable blessing. But do you know that if we were
in the celestial glory and were not fitted for it, we would not
enjoy it?

Whence comes your enjoyment? Whence come the glorious
feelings that you have when you feel the best? Do they come
from the outside? Do external circumstances produce real happiness of the kind that I describe? Doubtless, they contribute
to happiness; but the purest joy, the greatest happiness, that
which is most heavenly proceeds from within. A man must carry
the principles of happiness and the love of God in his own breast,
or he will not be happy.

It is not true enjoyment when it comes from any other
source. Not from without, therefore, must we expect happiness
and exaltation but from within. Deity is within us, and its development brings happiness and joy inexpressible. (Jan. 14, 1894,
DW 48:350)

MORE THAN A GOOD MORAL LIFE NECESSARY.
The idea is quite popular in the Christian world that belief in
Jesus and sincerity of heart are the only necessary requisites to
insure an entrance into the Kingdom of heaven. The expression
is heard from hundreds of mouths, "Oh, if I live a moral life, if

I do unto others as I would be done by, I think it will all be right with me. God is a Being of mercy, and He will not cast off any one who leads a moral life." Hundreds delude themselves with this idea and pass through life without making an exertion to obey a single given law of the Lord other than to be what they consider honest and neighborly. They seem to entirely overlook the fact that God is a Being of justice as well as mercy, that He is a God of truth and cannot lie, and that were He to do as they expect He will towards them, He would divest Himself of the attributes which constitute Him a Being worthy to be adored and would, therefore, cease to be God.

ALL LAWS MUST BE OBEYED. The Lord has revealed certain laws which He says in plain and unmistakable language must be obeyed, or the being who dares to disobey must suffer the consequences. . . . Jesus told Nicodemus that "except a man be born of water and of the Spirit, he cannot enter into the king- dom of God."[6] An entrance into the Kingdom of God, then, cannot be obtained by a man who has not been born of water and of the Spirit. Neither sincerity nor morality will avail, except these essential ordinances have been attended to. Though the Lord is full of mercy and love for His creatures, yet His justice and truth would not permit so flagrant a violation of His laws, as the neglect of these ordinances would be, to pass unpunished; much less would He break His own word . . . by admitting them therein. . . .

There are some who call themselves Latter-day Saints who seem to think that if it is not quite convenient for them to attend to all the requirements which the Lord has made of them that it will all be right; they need not be at any particular trouble to attend to these things as the Lord will overlook any negligence they manifest in this respect, and they will get the reward they are looking for. "Ah," say such individuals, "I know that such and such things are right and ought to be attended to; but my circumstances are such that I cannot do it; when it comes con- venient, I will attend to it." Their circumstances not coming convenient, the performance of these things is put off, the time of probation is frittered away, and they come short of obtaining

[6]John 3:5.

the blessings and the reward they might have received had they been faithful and diligent.

LEARN TO CONTROL CIRCUMSTANCES. There may be circumstances of such a nature that the person who is subject to them cannot do as he would wish; but in the great majority of instances it is for us, if we expect to gain a celestial glory, to exercise such faith that we can control circumstances and make them subservient to our purpose. It would be folly for men to expect, in the great day of reward, that the excuse of their circumstances not being convenient for them to obey the law which the Lord says must be obeyed by all those unto whom it is revealed would cause Him to bestow the same reward and exaltation upon them that he would upon those who obeyed it.

The Lord says in explicit terms that we must abide that law and that covenant, or we cannot enter in or attain to His glory. Can we expect, then, to enter therein and not obey it? The Lord cannot falsify His word but will be compelled to exclude from celestial glory all those who do not comply with the laws which He has sent forth.

The requirements of every law of God are inexorable and cannot be set aside. He never gave a commandment unto the children of men without opening a way by which they could fulfill it; if they do not fulfill it, therefore, through lack of diligence or faith on their part, they must be the losers. He has done all that He can, consonant with justice, in revealing the law, with the rewards and penalties attached to obedience and disobedience, and in promising the necessary assistance to enable them to fulfill it if they will but seek for it. All who have ever sought for this assistance have obtained it and have proved for themselves that the Lord requires nothing of mankind but what, if they seek it, he gives them power to perform; and there are no circumstances—however seemingly difficult—which conspire to prevent them from obeying His commandments but what the Spirit of the Lord will enable them, in His own due time, to surmount and control. . . .

PROCRASTINATION TO BE REPENTED OF. Those who are guilty of procrastination in regard to these principles and commandments, thinking that there will be a time in the future when they can better attend to them, will come short of the glory of God unless they heartily repent. Celestial glory, which is the burden of all our prayers, will be obtained by none such; for those who obtain this glory permit no circumstances to deter them, no fears to assail them but rise superior to every obstacle, putting their trust in their God and, Abraham-like, obey every commandment and ordinance so soon as it is revealed to them. Experience will yet teach mankind that strict obedience to every law of God is the only means by which they can obtain a seat and an exaltation in His Kingdom and that disobedience or neglect of these laws—however sincere or moral the person who does so may be—will effectually exclude them from a participation in the fulness of His glory. (May 1, 1857, *WS* 402-5)

HOW TO OBTAIN CELESTIAL GLORY. There is, as Paul says, one glory of the sun or the celestial glory. Who shall attain unto that? Those who keep the law that pertains to that glory; those who do everything that is commanded them of God; those who are willing to endure everything for His sake and to do that which He requires at their hands. There have been, no doubt, millions of people on the earth who have had this willingness. They will attain, we are told, unto the celestial glory. (April 27, 1890, *DW* 40:835)

We have but entered upon the path that leads to the exaltation we anticipate and desire; and the individuals who believe, when they have been baptized into the Church, that they have done all that is requisite to secure their salvation have made but a poor commencement and understand but very little of the nature of the work in which we are engaged.

What, then, is there for us yet to do? We have to become acquainted more and more with the principles which govern the heavenly beings, to put them into practice, each day bringing us fresh duties and new responsibilities, as principle after principle is revealed to us, the righteous fulfilment of which will bring us ever increasing happiness. (Nov. 10, 1861, *MS* 23:796)

MUST BE WILLING TO SACRIFICE ALL. We must obey the Holy Priesthood, which He has placed in our midst, at the cost of everything, if it be required, and not allow any sordid or self-aggrandizing feeling to enter into our hearts or to have place therein. I cannot conceive of any man being able to attain unto celestial glory who is not willing to sacrifice everything that he has for the cause of God. If I have a piece of land, house, money, cattle, horses, carriages or powers of mind and body and am not willing to devote any or all of these to the rolling forth of the work of God, as they may be required by Him, I cannot conceive that it will be possible for me to enter into the Celestial Kingdom of God our Heavenly Father.

Do you understand, do you comprehend that everything we have is required by God our Father, to be laid upon the altar? (June 29, 1873, *JD* 16:116-7)

MUST ENDURE TO THE END. They are the ones who shall be saved—those who endure to the end, faithfully keeping the commandments of God, not those who run well for a season and then cease to run or endure and yield to temptation and sin. They cannot be saved; better for them if they had never heard the Gospel; better for them if they had never, I was going to say, be born. Indeed, I think I might say it correctly. (May 26, 1889, *DW* 38:709)

TO BE TESTED TO UTMOST. God will have a tried and peculiar people. We have been tried to some extent but not to the extent which we probably will be; there are many things in which we will be greatly tried before we get through. Every Latter-day Saint who gains a celestial glory will be tried to the very uttermost. If there is a point in our character that is weak and tender, you may depend upon it that the Lord will reach after that, and we will be tried at that spot for the Lord will test us to the utmost before we can get through and receive that glory and exaltation which He has in store for us as a people. When we think about the character of the exaltation promised unto us, we can understand why this should be the case. . . .

When we talk about celestial glory, we talk of the condition of endless increase; if we obtain celestial glory in the fullest sense of the word, then we have wives and children in eternity; we have the power of endless lives granted unto us, the power of propagation that will endure through all eternity, all being fathers and mothers in eternity, fathers of fathers and mothers of mothers, kings and queens, priests and priestesses, and shall I say more? Yes, all becoming gods. For this is the power of God; it is the power by which God presides over the universe and fills the universe with power and which we pray unto Him to bestow upon us.

This being the case, do you think that we are going to attain unto these things without we show ourselves perfect before the Lord? Do you expect that God will save you and me and exalt us and give unto us this inestimable, this indescribable glory if we are full of sin, if we yield to temptation and are not tested and are not tried in all these things? . . .

MUST BE PERFECT IN OUR SPHERE. The words of Jesus which he spoke unto his disciples are intended for us: "Be ye therefore perfect, even as your Father which is in heaven is perfect.'"[7] We, as a people and as individuals, should seek to attain to that perfection, to be as perfect in our sphere as God our Eternal Father is in His; and we cannot attain to that exaltation and glory which He has promised unto us unless we are thus perfect. . . .

I, therefore, do not expect that any man will ever enter into the Celestial Kingdom of our God until he is tested and proved in all things. Some men think they can slip around—I have heard such men talk—they think they are going to get into the Celestial Kingdom without obeying the law of celestial marriage. I do not have any such ideas about exaltation; and yet I am perfectly satisfied there are men who will be counted worthy of that glory who never had a wife; there are men probably in this world now who will receive exaltation who never had a wife at all, or probably had but one. But what is necessary for such a case? It must be perfection before God and a proof of willingness on their part if they had the opportunity. . . .

COMPLETE SUBJECTION TO WILL OF GOD. If we live in the flesh, you may depend upon it we shall be tried in all things. If I have an appetite, if I have a passion, if I have an inclination which is in conflict with the law of God, if I do not subdue it and bring it into complete subjection to His law, I do not see how I can enter into celestial glory. . . . I must bring every appetite, I must bring every passion, I must bring every

---

[7]Matthew 5:48.

desire of my being into complete subjection to the will and mind and law of God, or I cannot receive the exaltation He has promised unto His faithful children. . . . If there is anything about us, if there is selfishness in us, if there is a disposition in our hearts not to yield upon a certain point or to have our own way and own will and carry that will into effect in opposition to the will of God, we cannot in that condition receive exaltation at His right hand. And if we die in that condition, we will have in some other state of existence to get rid of it, or we cannot get exaltation. . . .

If there is anything that stands between me and the will of God which would prevent me from doing that will perfectly as He requires of me, if there is anything which I love more than God, I am not in a condition to receive that glory. If I think more of my own life, if I think more of my own will, if I think more of a wife or child or of all my wives and children or of my property or of my time or of anything over which I have control or which belongs to me and is part of me than I do of God, then I am not in the condition to receive the exaltation; I am not worthy to receive it; I am not willing to bring everything I have or which belongs to me into complete subjection to Him and to what He requires of me. When He says, "Go," to go; when He says, "Come," to come; to do that which he requires or to refrain from doing so as He may require and to do this not only when He, Himself, tells me I must do it but to do it also through the voice of those whom He has chosen to hold control. (Oct. 31, 1880, JD 22:123-5)

MANY SAINTS WON'T ATTAIN CELESTIAL GLORY. Experience has proved that it is not all of those who are called Latter-day Saints who cry "Lord, Lord, shall enter into the kingdom of heaven,"[8] for there are many who have a nominal membership in the Church of Christ who will never succeed in entering that "strait gate"[9] and "narrow . . . way"[10] which would lead them to an exaltation in the Celestial Kingdom of our God.

When we realize what is required on the part of the Saints to constitute them worthy to receive and enjoy all these glorious blessings and then contrast it with the works which their actual lives afford, wonder need not be indulged in even if some of them

---

[8]Ibid., 7:21.
[9]Ibid., 7:13.
[10]Ibid., 7:14.

come short of celestial glory. When we see a so-called Saint indulging in a spirit of fault-finding, murmuring against his brethren who bear the Priesthood and talking about the follies of every one with whom he is connected, the conclusion that we are forced to adopt is that he must repent and thoroughly reform or he can never enter into the celestial glory of God.

When we hear a so-called Saint parading his little acts in favor of the Work of God, talking about the efforts which he has made in paying money to sustain it or in giving the Elders a meal or two occasionally, as though he had done something that was very meritorious indeed and for which he should receive great praise, then we are compelled to think that unless he gets rid of feelings such as these and cultivates a different spirit, he can never enter into the strait gate and pursue the narrow path which leadeth to the exaltation and glory of God. . . .

A LIFE OF DEVOTED SERVICE REQUIRED. Brethren and sisters, be not deceived upon these points. Flatter not yourselves with the idea that ye can enter into the Celestial Kingdom of our God and hug to your bosom those weaknesses and impurities which characterize fallen human nature. Purity and perfection can alone enter there. Our lives and all that we have must be devoted to the service of our Maker. We must be filled with a steadfast integrity which nothing can move. And we must not only labor cheerfully and gladly in doing those things which God has commanded, but we must be anxiously engaged in the good cause and do many things and bring to pass much righteousness of our own free will for the power is in us. "He that doeth not anything until he is commanded, and receiveth a commandment with doubtful heart, and keepeth it with slothfulness, the same is damned."[11]

The man who seeks for the possession of celestial glory is not content with treading the well-beaten road travelled in by the world, but his mind soars aloft with an intense desire to comprehend and put into practice every law pertaining to exaltation, though it may be far off in the (to him) dim future. His continual struggle will be to obey those higher laws which can only be perceived and understood by those who attain unto very powerful faith. (Feb. 7, 1863, MS 25:88-90)

[11]D. & C. 58:29.

FEW TO ATTAIN CELESTIAL GLORY. There will be but comparatively few of the human family that will attain to celestial glory because they will not listen to the voice of God. Many there will be that will fall by the wayside and will yield to an influence that is not of God, and the result will be that they will lose that exaltation which God is desirous to bestow upon His children. (Aug. 26, 1894, *DW* 49:450)

The price of such a glory is great for the reward is great, and much is required from our hands before we can obtain it. We must lay everything upon the altar, subdue every evil desire and the propensities common to our nature before we can dwell in the exalted presence of God. (Dec. 31, 1863, *MS* 26:83)

The exaltation which God has attained to has been through obedience to these self-same laws that are now taught to us. (Jan. 6, 1884, *JD* 25:26)

THE GLORY OF THE FUTURE BEYOND COMPRE- HENSION. Why, human imagination fails. "Eye hath not seen, nor ear heard, neither have entered into the heart of man, the things which God hath prepared for them that love him."[12] In our present condition we cannot conceive of these things because they are beyond our comprehension. But we have a foretaste of that glory given unto us in the outpouring of the Holy Spirit when it rests upon us. You have felt, no doubt, many times in your lives as though you were filled to overflowing and had no room for another drop of happiness. The peace and love of God have filled your hearts. Of course, we are but mortal beings at the present time, and we are not prepared for that glory and immortality that God has in store for us. But we will grow up to it, and we will be prepared for it when it comes. . . .

TO BE MADE GODS. God has removed doubt from our hearts and our minds concerning these things. We know them. The testimony of God is with us. He bears testimony to us that we are His children. And he wants to draw us to Him, in His arms of love. He wants to save us and exalt us and make us like Himself, clothe us with glory and make us indeed gods in the eternal world, wielding dominion and power. For this purpose

---

[12] I Corinthians 2:9.

He has sent us here. For this purpose He has given us His laws, which we understand to some extent. (1890, *Contr.* 11:480)

THE JOYS OF THE FUTURE ESTATE. There is something tangible about the views of the Latter-day Saints concerning the future. We do not expect to sit upon a cloud, playing a harp throughout the endless ages of eternity. There will be work for us to do—work of the most glorious and exalted character. Oh! what joy will fill the hearts of those who are faithful when they meet the Lord, and He welcomes them back to His presence, having been true and unswerving in their integrity while they were in the flesh.

You welcome your sons home from missions; gladness inexpressible fills your hearts if they have been faithful to the cause of God and have magnified their Priesthood. By this you can have a faint idea of the joy that our Father in heaven will have over us if we are true to Him and go from here pure. And think of our joy! Though we have been separated from our Father, though there has been a veil between Him and us in order that we might be tested and proved, now the mission is ended, the probation has been performed and we go back emancipated from the power of Satan. (Feb. 27, 1898, *MS* 60:215)

INDESCRIBABLE GLORY. God our Eternal Father intends to endow those of His children who are faithful to Him in their second estate with indescribable glory. Even if the human mind could conceive, the human tongue could not describe that glory. We cannot, though our minds be fully illumined by the Spirit of God, conceive in our mortal estate the greatness of the glory that God has in store for His faithful ones. When we even approach the understanding of it, it must be by vision. Yet, to those who are true to Him in the midst of the numerous temptations that abound in the world that glory will be given. (Aug. 26, 1894, *DW* 49:449)

FUTURE IS GLORIOUS TO FAITHFUL. We may have our trials and afflictions here. But let our eyes look forward with faith to that glorious future that God has prepared for us and the great reward that He will bestow upon us. For we shall have crowns; we shall have thrones; we shall have dominion; we shall have power. God will give all this to us just as fast as we are prepared for it; and if we enter into these holy temples and receive there the ordinances that He has commanded His servants to give, these promises will be fulfilled to the very letter, if we are faithful. Not one will fail.

How was it when you were baptized by one having authority? Did you not have the testimony that your sins were remitted? God accepted the offering. He accepted the administration of the ordinance. He accepted the laying on of hands, and He gave the Holy Ghost to those upon whom hands were laid. And when you come to the altar, and the servant of God says, "I seal upon you the blessings of the holy resurrection with power to come forth in the morning of the first resurrection clothed with glory, immortality and eternal lives, and I seal upon you the blessings of kingdoms, thrones, principalities, powers, dominions and exaltations, the blessings of Abraham and of Isaac and of Jacob," when the servant of God pronounces these words upon those who come to the altar and he seals the wife to the husband, just as sure as God lives, just as sure as the heavens are above our heads and the earth beneath our feet, so sure will those words be fulfilled upon the heads of those upon whom they are pronounced, if they are faithful to the covenants which they make; and they will come forth in the morning of the first resurrection clothed with glory, immortality and eternal lives.

DEATH HAS LOST ITS STING. When we lay down our dead after having received these holy ordinances—our husbands, our wives, our children, our fathers, our mothers—we lay them down without a shadow of doubt in our hearts as to the future. "O death, where is thy sting? O grave, where is thy victory?"[13] Under such circumstances as these death has lost its sting; the grave has lost its victory; it is robbed of its terrors by the glorious promises that God has made unto His servants and His children. Others may fear death. Others may dread the future. Others may think that it is a leap in the dark. But not so the Latter-day Saints!

The future is illumined by the glory of God and the promises that He has made to us; and when the time comes for us to lay down these mortal lives, we will do so just as we do when we go on missions and the time comes for us to return home;

---

[13]*Ibid.*, 15:55.

we will go home, with regrets of course for those we leave behind but with gladness and joy to think that our missions are ended and that we have been faithful, and we will be welcomed by our brothers and sisters and our families. We will look forward with joyful anticipation to the delightful reunion that we will have with those whom we have left, who have been our fellow laborers and companions in the afflictions of this life, and it will be a heavenly time. Therefore, I say that death has lost its terrors, and the grave no longer triumphs over people who have received such blessings as these. (Oct. 9, 1892, *DW* 45:621)

SONS AND DAUGHTERS OF A KING. It is a glorious thing . . . to know that our religion is true and given us from God and that in obedience to it we may attain to the exalted position occupied by Him and our Lord and Savior Jesus Christ. . . . We are of the race of God, the sons and daughters of a King. What monarch's children do not hope and look forward to sovereignty. May we, who are the offspring of the Almighty King, not hope for crowns and kingdoms in eternity?

OUR ETERNAL DESTINY. Some believe our eternal destiny is to sit upon clouds, thrum harps and sing forever. What an occupation! What a monotony! No matter how sweet this music might be it would become very wearisome if extended so long. But such is not our destiny. Our mission hereafter is to perpetuate and continue the work of our Father and our God, to perpetuate our species and to create worlds from the elements by which we are surrounded.

Go out at night and behold the starry firmament. The millions of shining orbs we see are the work of God—worlds created and peopled by the Almighty. Such works are for us to do. Eternity is before us, and every man and every woman will find ample room for the exercise of every faculty he or she may possess. How glorious to think that we have the spark of divinity within us. (*DEN*, March 28, 1881)

ALL THE FATHER HATH. Speaking of those who receive the testimony of Jesus and who overcome by faith, the Lord says:

They are they who are the church of the Firstborn. They are they into whose hands the Father has given all things.

Now, these are not idle words given merely to round out a sentence; but they are full of meaning.

They are they who are priests and kings, who have received of his fulness, and of his glory; and are priests of the Most High, after the order of Melchizedek, which was after the order of Enoch, which was after the order of the Only Begotten Son. Wherefore, as it is written, they are gods, even the sons of God wherefore, all things are theirs, whether life or death, or things present, or things to come, all are theirs, and they are Christ's, and Christ is God's.[14]

I wish to emphasize the following:

And also all they who receive this priesthood receive me, saith the Lord; For he that receiveth my servants receiveth me; and he that receiveth me receiveth my Father; and he that receiveth my Father, receiveth my Father's kingdom; therefore all that my Father hath shall be given unto him.[15]

Notice the last clause, "All that my Father hath"—not a part, but "all that my Father hath shall be given unto him." That language admits of no mistake. It corresponds with the other language that I have read in your hearing. It also corresponds with what the Lord says in Section 93:

I give unto you these sayings that ye may understand and know how to worship, and know what you worship, that you may come unto the Father in my name, and in due time receive of his fulness. For if you keep my commandments you shall receive of his fulness, and be glorified in me as I am in the Father; therefore, I say unto you, you shall receive grace for grace.[16]

This same revelation goes on to say:

The Spirit of truth is of God. I am the Spirit of truth, and John bore record of me, saying: He received a fulness of truth, yea, even of all truth; and no man receiveth a fulness unless he keepeth his commandments. He that keepeth his commandments receiveth truth and light, until he is glorified in truth and knoweth all things.[17]

These are sufficiently plain to reveal to us that which God has in contemplation for His faithful children. The Latter-day Saints are promised, if they are faithful, that they shall receive the fulness as Jesus received it; and Jesus received it as the Father received it. In the words of Paul they become "heirs of God, and

---

[14]D. & C. 76:54-9.
[15]Ibid., 84:35-8.

[16]Ibid., 93:19-20.
[17]Ibid., 93:26-8.

joint heirs with Christ."[18] There is nothing that the Savior has attained unto that God's faithful children are not promised. They are promised the same blessings, the same power, the same authority, the same gifts, the same graces.

AN EQUAL INTEREST IN POWER AND AUTHORITY OF GOD. I know that we are apt to think that heaven is a sort of spiritual place. It is spiritual; but God our Eternal Father is a being of power. He controls the earth and the inhabitants thereof; He controls the elements of the earth; and we are promised that we shall be sharers with Him. He will give us an equal interest in all this power and authority. What is more desirable to man, generally speaking, than to wield power? Mankind aim for it. To what lengths will ambitious men go to wield power, to sit upon thrones and to wield a sceptre of authority. History tells us that men have been willing to wade through seas of blood to gratify this ambition.

Now, this ambition can be gratified righteously by keeping the commandments of God; and a righteous man will exercise righteous authority. That is the object God had in view in sending us here. Through faithfully keeping His commandments we may attain unto power—not illegitimate power, but lawful power —and wield it for our own exaltation and for the exaltation of other human beings.

PRIESTS AND KINGS UPON THRONES. It is God's design to make us priests and kings, not to have an empty title, not to sit upon thrones without power but to be actually and really priests and kings. The promise is that all things that He hath shall be given unto us. We will be His heirs; we will be (if I may use the term without irreverence) co-partners with Him in all this power and authority. . . .

CONSECRATE ALL TO GOD. Those who have faith and who rise to the comprehension of the dignity and exaltation that God intends to bestow upon us will not hesitate to give everything they have to the Lord, but it requires faith. The Lord might require us to lay down our lives. That would require faith, would it not? Yes. But what is the promise? That we shall have eternal

---

[18]Romans 8:17.

life and be exalted in His presence. Therefore, those who wish to attain to this exaltation must cherish sublimity of feeling, sublimity of self-sacrifice. They must not only be willing to pay their tithing but be willing to give everything they have got on the earth—wives and children and everything else. If I cannot give up my wife and all my children, if required, if I cannot lay down my life, if necessary, God help me. I do not know what I might do, but God help me to do it if the test ever comes. But if I am not willing to do this, I cannot hope to attain to that exaltation and receive that fullness which the Lord has promised unto us, if we are faithful. . . .

I say to you this day, in the presence of God and the holy angels and of this assembly, if we expect to attain the fulfillment of the promises God has made to us, we must be self-sacrificing. There is no sacrifice that God can ask of us or His servants whom He has chosen to lead us that we should hesitate about making. In one sense of the word it is no sacrifice. We may call it so because it comes in contact with our selfishness and our unbelief; but it ought not to come in contact with our faith. . . .

TRIALS ARE FOR OUR OWN BENEFIT. Why did the Lord ask such things of Abraham? Because, knowing what his future would be and that he would be the father of an innumerable posterity, he was determined to test him. God did not do this for His own sake for He knew by His foreknowledge what Abraham would do; but the purpose was to impress upon Abraham a lesson and to enable him to attain unto knowledge that he could not obtain in any other way. That is why God tries all of us. It is not for His own knowledge for He knows all things beforehand. He knows all your lives and everything you will do. But He tries us for our own good that we may know ourselves; for it is most important that a man should know himself.

He required Abraham to submit to this trial because He intended to give him glory, exaltation and honor; He intended to make him a king and a priest, to share with Himself the glory, power and dominion which He exercised. And was this trial any more than God Himself had passed through? God the Eternal Father gave His Only Begotten Son to die for us; and He wanted to see whether Abraham was as willing to sacrifice his son of promise as He Himself was to sacrifice His well beloved, His first born, Jesus Christ.

And what of Isaac? Josephus tells us that Isaac was old enough to carry the wood for the sacrifice; and after his father had told him what the Lord wanted, Isaac, in the spirit of submission that such a son had for such a father, said to him, "If the Lord had not commanded you to do this, father, I would have been willing to have done whatever you required of me." In this Isaac exhibited a spirit akin to that manifested by the Lord Jesus; and Abraham showed a willingness akin to that exhibited by the Father in offering up His Only Begotten Son for the rest of His brethren and sisters. (April 9, 1899, CR 64-7)

HEIRS OF GOD. Remember the word! If we are heirs of God, why then we shall inherit the power and the blessings and the glory of God our Eternal Father. This is what the Latter-day Saints ought to have constantly in view, "How can I live so as to become an heir of God and a joint heir with Jesus Christ? What course can I take to secure to myself celestial glory—a never-fading crown?" Not an empty bauble, not a barren sceptre but a sceptre of power, a sceptre of dominion, a crown that means something real, a throne that means the kingly and queenly authority. This is what the Latter-day Saints have in view when they have their hearts fixed as they should be and their eyes open to the glory that God has in store for the faithful. (April 27, 1890, DW 40:836)

TO HAVE EXTENSIVE DOMINIONS. If we are heirs of God and joint heirs with Jesus Christ, we expect to have control over many things, and there is reason to believe that our dominion will be very extensive. But before we attain to that dominion we must learn to be wise rulers over the few things that God has placed in our charge and to use them for His glory and the advancement of His purposes on the earth.

When He sees that our eyes are single to His glory and that our hearts are pure and free from avarice and every sordid and selfish feeling, He will multiply His blessings upon us because He will then know by testing us that we are fit to be trusted; and it will be said to us according to the words of the Scriptures, "When he shall prove himself faithful in all things that shall be entrusted unto his care, yea, even a few things, he shall become ruler over many."[19] (April 21, 1867, *JD* 12:43)

We talk about kings and nobles, and we have admired their glory; but the day is not far distant when there will be thousands of men in Zion holding more power and having more glory, honor and wealth than the greatest and the richest of the nobles of the earth. The earth and its fulness are promised unto us by the Lord our God as soon as we have the wisdom and experience necessary to wield this power and wealth. (Oct. 8, 1865, *JD* 11:175)

KINGS WITH KINGDOMS. We build temples and we administer and submit to ordinances and perform those things within them which will prepare us to dwell eternally with our God, with Jesus and the Apostles in the heavens. There each man will have his family and kingdom. It is said that God is Lord of lords and King of kings; but how can He be King of kings unless there be kings under Him to give Him homage and pay respect unto Him and acknowledge Him as their Lord and their King?

When God led forth Abraham and told him that as the stars of the firmament were innumerable so should his seed be, He proclaimed to him the greatness of his kingdom in eternity. He told Abraham that he should be a king over this innumerable host; for, if Abraham were not to be king over them, of what use or glory would his posterity be to him? When God pointed Abraham to the sand on the sea shore and told him that as it was countless so should his seed be, He told him in accents that could not be mistaken of the future glory of his eternal kingdom. And if all mankind attained to the same promises as Abraham, they also would have an innumerable posterity to reign over. (April 8, 1871, *JD* 14:128)

REIGN ON THE EARTH. Many men wonder how it is that we can believe in celestial marriage. We believe in it because it lies at the foundation of all future greatness. If a man rules in heaven, he will rule over his own posterity. The Apostle John said that they sang a new song in heaven—"And hast made us unto our God kings and priests: and we shall reign on the

---

[19]D. & C. 124:113.

earth."[20] Reign on the earth! This was the song. Over whom were they to reign? Over whom more properly than their families? (Aug. 10, 1873, JD 16:143)

THE GLORY OF AN ENDLESS INCREASE. As the Prophet says concerning our Lord and Savior Jesus Christ, "of the increase of his government . . . there shall be no end."[21] It shall go on increasing with every cycle of eternity as long as time endures. There shall be no end to the increase of His Kingdom. His glory consisted of this; and the glory of God consists in the number of His posterity; and as generation succeeds generation, until the earth is filled and glorified, other worlds will be rolled into existence upon which the posterity of God, our Heavenly Father, shall increase throughout the endless ages of eternity. . . .

The godlike power has been given us here on the earth to bear and perpetuate our own species. Shall this power, which brings so much joy, peace and happiness, be confined and limited to this short life? It is folly to talk about such a thing; common sense teaches us better. It teaches that we have been organized not for time alone, that we have been endowed as we are in the image of God not for thirty, forty, fifty, seventy or a hundred years but as eternal beings, exercising our endowments and functions for all eternity, if we live faithful or take a course that God approves. Therefore, there is great sense, beauty and godliness in the idea that God taught Abraham with respect to his posterity becoming as numerous as the stars of the firmament. . . .

We look forward to the time when this earth will be redeemed from corruption and cleansed by fire, when there shall be a new heaven and a new earth and when the Saints shall possess their native inheritance purified from sin, redeemed from corruption, with the power of Satan curtailed and when we shall be able to increase and multiply and fill this earth, go to other earths and carry on the work of emigration through the endless ages of eternity. (April 8, 1871, JD 14:128-9)

He has revealed to us that these relationships that are so tender and that make life so delightful will exist beyond the grave. Wife will be united to husband. Children will be united to parents. The family relationship will exist in eternity, and the glory

---

[20]Revelation 5:10.   [21]Isaiah 9:7.

of a man and a woman will be in dwelling in the midst of their posterity and seeing that posterity increase. For after God seemingly had exhausted every blessing that He could give to Abraham or that human heart could desire, He took him out and showed him the stars of heaven and said to him: "In blessing I will bless thee, and in multiplying I will multiply thy seed as the stars of the heaven, and as the sand which is upon the sea shore."[22] That seemed to be the crowning blessing—the blessing of all blessings—that He pronounced upon His faithful servant Abraham, after he had expressed a willingness to sacrifice his son Isaac.

And this is the blessing that God has promised to every faithful man and woman—that to the increase of their seed there shall be no end. This will constitute the great glory of eternity— the man presiding over his family and being lord over them. Thus it is that Jesus is called Lord of lords. He is Lord of lords because His brethren will exercise this power and authority over their posterity. And then what? Why, the creative power will be given to men. . . .

OTHER WORLDS TO BE CREATED. What will be their occupation? The exercise of that creative power that our Father and God has exercised in preparing this earth as the abode for man. He called together the elements and formed the earth as a habitation for man; and man, if he is faithful, will progress until he will do that very same thing for his posterity.

Abraham, standing at the head of an innumerable posterity, will find it necessary to have room. He will want to emigrate after awhile from this earth and find a new habitation for there will not be room enough on the glorified earth for him and his posterity in the coming eternity. Thus it is that the heavens are bespangled with the glorious orbs that we see at night—the creations of God, peopled by the children of God.

And all this God promises to us, if we are faithful. He says, "You shall be kings; you shall be queens; you shall sit upon thrones; you shall sway scepters, and you shall have power and dominion, if you prove yourselves faithful and true to Me; and you shall be My heirs, and joint heirs with My beloved Son, Jesus Christ, your Redeemer." (Oct. 9, 1892, DW 45:619-20)

[22]Genesis 22:17.

NO STANDING STILL. There is progress for our Father and for our Lord Jesus. There is no such thing as standing still in the eternal work of our God. It is endless progress, progressing from one degree of knowledge to another degree. Thus the children of men will be continually exalted and drawn up toward God. (Jan. 22, 1898, *MS* 61:117)

HEAVEN A PLACE OF ACTIVITY AND PROGRESS. Heaven is something to be desired; . . . heaven is a place of activity, a place of progress; that which furnishes man his highest enjoyment on the earth, that which develops and calls out his highest and noblest qualities, we are to have in heaven. And this is no new revelation; but it is beclouded and misunderstood by the world.

"He hath been faithful over a few things, . . . and he shall be made ruler over many,"[23] the Scriptures say. What does that mean? That the man who has done his duty in his sphere here on the earth faithfully will have an enlarged sphere hereafter, will have greater power, more opportunities for development, shall have every God-like power, every power and attribute that we have derived from our ancestry—that is, from God our Eternal Father. We shall have room for infinite gratification, unlimited gratification, going on from one degree of power to another and exercising it as our Father exercises it in the midst of the eternities. Is there not something delightful in this thought and in the contemplation of such a future?

POWER OF PROCREATION PROMISED. If I have children, if I have a wife, I shall have them in eternity. I shall preside over that family no matter how small it may be or how large it may extend. They will be my kingdom; for this is the promise of God. What is there that is more delightful in the contemplation of the future than this thought, that those with whom we are associated here, with whom our lives and happiness is entwined, who give unto us the greatest pleasure because of the love we have for them and they have for us, that that union shall be perpetuated throughout eternity and that there shall be an increase of that love and of that union and an increase also of that power, because the power of procreation is promised

[23]D. & C. 132:53.

—the greatest power that man possesses on the earth. That is promised unto those who are faithful.

I know the world say this is materialistic, that we take wrong views of this, that we are not spiritual enough. Well, I am willing to have that charge levelled against me. I want to be materialistic in this sense. I want to enjoy that which we enjoy here, purified, exalted and increased beyond my comprehension or your comprehension at the present time; and we are to have this glory and this power; the Lord promises it unto us.

Therefore, it can be said of us as it was said of our Lord and Savior, "of the increase of His government there shall be no end."[24] Why? Because of this principle that I spoke of—the principle of procreation. By it and through that principle the worlds are peopled. The planetary orbs which stud our heavens so gloriously are peopled by that principle—the principle of procreation. God possesses it, and we as His children inherit the power. If we do what is right, He promises to bestow it upon us.

A SPIRITUAL HEAVEN. Our heaven, then, is materialistic in this sense; it is not altogether spiritual. But it is spiritual also. We shall have spiritual joy; we shall have spiritual pleasures such as have been described to us this day, for it is the highest pleasure or joy the human soul is capable of to worship God, to do His will, keep His commandments and to serve Him. This is the highest pleasure that human beings can attain unto, and we shall have it in eternity, and it shall be the chief source of our enjoyment and of our happiness in the world to come. (April 6, 1899, CR 19-20)

ENDOWMENTS NECESSARY FOR CELESTIAL GLORY. Can a man attain unto celestial glory without receiving his endowments? Under some circumstances he can. If he should die, as some of our faithful brethren have, before endowments were given, no doubt he would be judged by the Lord according to his opportunities and his willingness. But speaking generally, men and women cannot receive celestial glory without having the ordinances that pertain to the endowments. Men and women cannot be united for eternity unless they are united by the Priesthood of God in the place appointed for the administration of

---

[24]Isaiah 9:7.

that ordinance. The union of husband and wife, of parents and children depends upon obedience to law, and they cannot get into the Celestial Kingdom without they obey these laws. Other commandments of the Lord might be mentioned in this connection. We are commanded to live by every word that proceedeth from the mouth of God. We must do this. The Lord reveals His word to His Church; that word must be obeyed, if we expect to reach the celestial glory. (April, 1900, CR 54-5)

SUSTAINING THE IMMORTAL BODY. We can have but little conception at the present time of the life that lies beyond. The sustaining of the immortal body, we have reason to believe, will not involve the toil and the other burdensome conditions which the sustenance of the mortal body does. It is by obedience to law that immortality is brought to pass, for the Lord has said, "that which is governed by law is also preserved by law, and perfected and sanctified by the same." Laws are given, but unto every law there are certain "bounds and conditions." Those who abide those conditions are justified and preserved.

It will be by a comprehension of and obedience to certain laws that immortality will be preserved. The immortal body will, doubtless, derive its sustenance from the elements as the mortal does; and those elements will be applied to immortal man's use and benefit by the knowledge which he will possess in the same manner as the mortal body derives its benefits from the knowledge which mortal man possesses of those earthly elements to which he has access and over which he exercises control. (March 15, 1895, JI 30:186)

WHO CAN BECOME A DEVIL? God has not predestined any of us to be damned. On the contrary He has desired and does desire the salvation of all the children of men; and He will save all with certain degrees of salvation if they do not go so far as to commit the unpardonable sin. Some people think they have done this when they have not. A man must have attained to considerable knowledge about God and eternal things before he is in a condition where he can commit the unpardonable sin. ... There are comparatively few who get so far as this.

A man must have sufficient knowledge to make him a God

in order to be a devil. Lucifer had to be a great and a powerful being. He stood high in the presence of God, and his fall was greater than it would have been if he had occupied an inferior station. Therefore, the more we know concerning God, the more power and the more gifts we get from God, if they are abused, the greater will be our condemnation and the greater will be the depth to which we shall fall when we do fall.

On the one hand there is glory and exaltation in proportion to faithfulness, to knowledge and to gifts and opportunities enjoyed. On the other hand there is damnation and a withdrawal of these blessings, and the depth to which that soul will fall will be in proportion to the knowledge, to the understanding, to the gifts, to the opportunities and to the blessings that he possessed and that he enjoyed. . . .

God has devised a plan of salvation that will bring us all to a certain amount of glory, and each one of us will receive a glory far beyond anything that we can possibly conceive of, even if we have been sinners. But it is far better to repent of our sins and have them blotted out, so that we may receive the greater glory and the greater exaltation. (May 10, 1891, MS 53:577-80)

NO FORGIVENESS FOR MURDERERS. The Apostle John says: "Ye know that no murderer hath eternal life abiding in him."[25]

The Prophet Joseph, speaking upon this subject, says as follows:

> Remission of sins by baptism was not to be preached to murderers. All the priests of Christendom might pray for a murderer on the scaffold forever, but could not avail so much as a gnat towards their forgiveness. There is no forgiveness for murderers; they will have to wait until the times of redemption shall come, and that in hell. Peter had the keys of eternal judgment, and he saw David in hell, and knew for what reason, and that David would have to remain there until the resurrection at the coming of Christ.

No Elder in the Church of Jesus Christ of Latter-day Saints who understands his duty would baptize a man who had been guilty of wilful murder. For such a crime, according to the law of God, his blood should be shed; it is a crime which tears and repentance alone cannot entirely wash away. What a horrible

---

[25]I John 3:15.

doctrine it is to teach that men who have been steeped in vice all their days and been guilty of the most horrible crimes are going, when they die, into the society of the holy and the pure and of those whose entire lives have been devoted to works of righteousness! Jesus and many of the Prophets and Apostles were killed for their righteousness; how could men strangled for their murders and other abominable crimes abide their presence? (Dec. 15, 1883, *JI* 18:376)

SECTION 2

FUNDAMENTALS OF MORMONISM

The Lord is the same yesterday, today and forever. This is the corner-stone, it may be said, of our faith. It is upon this foundation we have built; that He is an unchangeable God; that He does not manifest His mind and His will in plainness and simplicity to one people, and hide the same from a succeeding people who are equally faithful. . . . God is no respecter of persons; He is today as He was yesterday and as He ever was, and He will continue to be the same Being as long as time endures or eternity continues.

—GEORGE Q. CANNON
Journal of Discourses
21:72-73
(October 5, 1879)

CHAPTER 10

DEITY—THE MORMON CONCEPTION

THE BASIS OF TRUE INTELLIGENCE. God is the fount of all true knowledge. Belief and faith in Him is the basis of all true intelligence. To know Him is the greatest of all knowledge, to lose Him is to incur a penalty from which no worldly learning can save. By proper conduct every soul may learn to know Him with as much certainty as anything that can be seen with the eyes or felt with the hands. (March 15, 1892, JI 27:184)

One of the great duties devolving upon us is to teach the world that there is a God and that he has power to save today, as much as in ancient days, those who are willing to trust him. It is this peculiar feature that makes everything connected with this work so incomprehensible to men. (July 12, 1874, JD 17:123)

KIND OF GOD THE SAINTS BELIEVE IN. We who belong to the Church of Jesus Christ of Latter-day Saints believe in God, not a God who lived a few thousand years ago but a God who lives today, a God who has a voice with which to speak to-day and who has arms and a head and bodily as well as spiritual powers, who can communicate His mind and His will unto His children with the same facility in the days in which we live as He did in the days of the Savior and His disciples or in the days of the Prophets. . . .

JESUS CHRIST A MAN LIKE US. Our Lord and Savior Jesus Christ whom we worship as God, was a man like unto us, so much so that His divinity was not recognized through any external signs by the Jews. There was nothing about His person that they could discover that would make Him a God, the creator of the heavens and the earth. . . . He was in all respects a man, so far as the outward appearance was concerned; His exterior was that of a man; but, nevertheless, He was a God. He was the first begotten Son of the Eternal Father, who sits enthroned in glory and majesty, surrounded by burning fire. He was the Son of that Being and was the express image of His person, like Him, having a head, having the senses that men have, having all the bodily features that we have, and His Father was precisely like

Him, or He, in other words, was precisely like His Father.) (May 4, 1884, JD 25:149-155)

A TRUE CONCEPTION OF GOD NECESSARY. Now, it was meant that this knowledge should be restored first of all. It seems so, at least, from the fact that God Himself came; it seems that this knowledge had to be restored as the basis for all true faith to be built upon. There can be no faith that is not built upon a true conception of God our Father. Therefore, before even angels came, He came Himself accompanied by His Son and revealed Himself once more to man upon the earth.

PROPHET JOSEPH LAID THE FOUNDATION. The set time had come, the instrument had been born—the instrument that had been selected doubtless as much as the Son of God had been selected to accomplish His mission—that is, He had also been selected from before the foundation of the world to come and to be the instrument in the hands of God to again lay the foundation of His Church upon the earth—that instrument had been born and the set time had come for the establishment of the work of the Lord.

Joseph Smith had the necessary gifts and qualifications by which he was enabled to seek unto God with such irresistible faith that God heard his prayer and granted unto him the desire of his heart by revealing Himself unto him and giving unto him the instructions which He did. This was followed by other ministrations— the ministrations of angels. . . .

ANGELS NOT FEATHERED BEINGS. When Joseph received the ministrations of an angel—or angels, for he was visited by more than one—he saw that they were men and that they had not feathered after death, that they did not have wings, but that they were glorified men, or men who had received glory from God; they were personages like they were on the earth. Thus, a true conception began to dawn upon the minds of at least a few individuals who believed Joseph's testimony concerning these beings. (Sept. 2, 1883, JD 24:372-3)

AN UNCHANGEABLE GOD. The Lord is the same yesterday, to-day and forever. This is the corner-stone, it may be said, of our faith. It is upon this foundation we have built, that

He is an unchangeable God, that He does not manifest His mind and His will in plainness and simplicity to one people and hide the same from a succeeding people who are equally faithful. The great truth has been impressed upon us, the great truth that runs through all the writings of every man of God concerning whom we have any account from the beginning down to the last revelation that has been given, that God is no respecter of persons, that He is to-day as He was yesterday and as He ever was and that He will continue to be the same being as long as time endures or eternity continues.... . .

We worship Him; we adore Him; we lift up our eyes to Him; we rely upon Him as the Supreme Being, the Creator of the heavens and the earth, the Founder of the universe, the Builder of the planet which we inhabit and which we tread, the Being over whom centuries have passed without making any change to His injury; eternity has rolled and continues to roll and will continue to roll without in the least affecting His power or His capacity for good; His eye does not grow dim by the lapse of ages; His ear does not become heavy by the passage of time; neither does His arm become short or feeble.

He is the God whom we worship. When we call upon Him, though he may be remote from us, dwelling in His holy habitation in the midst of the eternities, the very thoughts of our hearts, the very conceptions of our minds, the feeble whisperings of our voices, they ascend to Him, are carried to Him; His ear comprehends them; His bowels of compassion are moved towards us His children; His all-piercing eye penetrates eternity, and the glance of His vision reaches us.

There is not a single thought of our hearts which He does not comprehend; there is nothing connected with us He does not know. We may hide ourselves in the bowels of the earth, but we cannot conceal ourselves from His all-piercing sight. We may climb the highest mountains or descend into the deepest valleys, or we may go to the uttermost parts of the earth; but wherever we may go, He is there; His power is there; His vision is there to hear and to comprehend the desires and the wishes of our hearts. (Oct. 5, 1879, JD 21:72-3)

GOD HAS A FATHER. Jesus, our Lord and Savior, was once a child upon the earth as you are now. He was the Son of God on earth, and He is now God in heaven. It was He who spoke to Moses in the wilderness, and it was He who revealed Himself to the brother of Jared and came to him before He was in the flesh. He gave revelations to His servants in ancient days; and He afterwards came upon the earth just as you have done. He came here, was born, had a father and mother like you have. Well, who was His father? Why God was His father; and who was God's father? Why God had a father like you and I have.

Now, what I want to say in connection with this is, it is your privilege to become just what Jesus and God our Heavenly Father have become, if you, while on earth, take a course to serve God and keep His commandments; for He is actually the Father of your spirits, just as your earthly parents are of your bodies. (June 4, 1871, JI 6:155)

HEAVENLY FATHER ONCE A MORTAL MAN. Every child knows that its earthly father had a father, and its grandfather had a father, and so on back as far as they can be traced; it can believe also that if it lives to become a man or a woman, it will also have children.

The Prophet Joseph teaches us that our Heavenly Father was once a man and dwelt on an earth like we do upon this[1] and that He has gone on from step to step, from one degree of glory and exaltation to another, until He now rules and governs.

Now, with this information children can begin to understand something about their Heavenly Father. They can see that if Jesus is His Son, and we are His sons and daughters, that He must be the Son of some other personage,[2] for He could not beget Himself, but must have a father even as He is our Father. (Sept. 11, 1869, JI 4:148)

GOD HAS TROD THIS SAME PATH. Our Heavenly Father is a loving and a kind and beneficent Parent. He, Himself, has trod the path we are now treading. He is familiar with every step of the road, with all the meanderings of this life, for He has

---

[1]"God himself was once as we are now, and is an exalted man, and sits enthroned in yonder heaven. . . . I say, if you were to see him today, you would see him like a man in form. . . . He was once a man like us; yea, God himself, the Father of us all, dwelt on an earth, the same as Jesus Christ himself did." (*Teachings of the Prophet Joseph Smith*, pages 345-6)

[2]"Where was there ever a son without a father? And where was there ever a father without first being a son?" (Ibid., page 373)

had the experience in it. He knows how to guide us and how to time His blessings to our wants; and when you feel impatient and dissatisfied because He does not give you more than you now have, and when you are afflicted and bowed down in sorrow and pain, let the reflection enter into your hearts to comfort you that our Father and God, our Lord and Savior Jesus Christ, trod the path we are now treading, that there is no affliction and sorrow that we are acquainted with, or can be, that the Lord has not already had an experience in; and He knows our condition; He knows what is good for us. If we need a gift and a blessing, He knows when to bestow it upon us. (Oct. 8, 1865, *JD* 11:174)

THE FAMILY OF GOD. The Mormons believe that all men were born in the spirit world of the union of the sexes, having a literal father and a literal mother before coming to this world, that the spirits are just the same in appearance as the body, that God is a married Being, has a wife at least, as Jeremiah said the angels were offering incense to the queen of heaven. The Latter-day Saints believe that God is an exalted Man, and that we are the offspring of Him and His wife. (April 15, 1884, *Salt Lake Herald*)

The "Mormons" believe that God is the Father of our spirits —that we are His offspring; and we think it just as consistent and reasonable to believe that He has a partner or partners as to think that He sits, isolated and solitary in lonely grandeur, in a state of bachelorship, and yet a Parent of so innumerable a progeny. (March 29, 1856, *WS* 47)

OFFSPRING OF DEITY. There are many people who imagine that we are the children of God because He is our Creator. But we differ from all other people in this respect. We believe that we are the literal descendants of our Eternal Father, that we are the offspring of Deity, that those aspirations which man has and which cause Him to perform the mighty works that we see on every hand as we travel throughout the earth are inherited from our Eternal Father. They come to us by descent; or, to use another phrase, they are hereditary. The doctrine of heredity is manifested in the works of man. We descend from this great Father who formed the earth and who governs this universe. Therefore, it is natural that man, being

His offspring, should have these glorious aspirations which prompt him to attempt these wonderful works and to succeed in carrying them out.

This is the belief of the Latter-day Saints; and, having this belief, we should have with it a corresponding desire that, when we shall see our Father, we shall be like Him. If we have this hope within us, we will seek to purify ourselves, even as He is pure, that we may be counted worthy to come into His presence. . . .

A GOD OF REVELATION. We believe in a God of revelation. We believe in a God who communicates His mind and will to His children. And if we seek for it, we believe that He will reveal Himself more and more unto us and in greater and greater fulness, until we shall comprehend Him as well as it is possible for mortal man to comprehend God. We do not worship a Being that we have created in our own imaginations; we worship a Being who has revealed Himself to us—a Being who has communicated to us His character and His attributes and revealed unto us the greatness of His Godlike character.

It was necessary in the very outset of this work that there should be a revelation of this character. Up to that time men for generations had been ignorant of the character of God. It was believed, as many now believe, that He was a Being diffused through space—a spiritual Being, without an entity or without a tabernacle. But the first revelation that was given in our day, in answer to the prayer of the boy, Joseph Smith, Jun., and seemingly the most necessary one that could be given to lay the foundation of faith in the human mind, was the appearance of God the Father and His Son Jesus Christ. . . .

There were two Personages appeared unto Joseph Smith, Jun.,—God the Father and His Son Jesus Christ. Whatever errors had existed, whatever doubts had prevailed up to that time concerning the being of God were swept away, never to return, from the minds of those who believed in that revelation at that time. God was then understood to be the Being who walked in the Garden of Eden and spoke with a voice—Whose finger was seen by the brother of Jared and Whom the Prophets declared to be the Being that He is. This testimony came with power on this occasion. . . .

In the very outset of this work the Father and the Son were revealed in ineffable glory, and they were seen by mortal man; his testimony stands on record today, corroborated and sustained by the testimony of others who have since seen the Lord Jesus Christ and who are living witnesses that He lives and that He is indeed the Son of God and one of the two Personages that form the Godhead. . . .

AS MAN IS GOD ONCE WAS. Among the Latter-day Saints there is a knowledge concerning the Personage of God. We have some conception of Him. We know that He is a Being of tabernacle. A remark suggests itself to my mind which I heard a few days ago from one of our Apostles—Brother Lorenzo Snow. It was something to this effect: That as God now is, we will be; as man is, God was. It is very comprehensive. And we descend from this Father. We are His offspring. We possess His attributes. It is true they are not developed, but we possess them; and He desires to lead us forward until we shall be like Him. This is the object of the Gospel.

Men talk about evolution. This is the true evolution—being such as we are and developing and advancing and progressing in that upward and onward career until we shall become like Him, in truth, until we shall possess the powers that He possesses and exercise the dominion that He now exercises. This is the promise that is held out to us. It is an incentive to faithfulness on our part. (April 7, 1889, *DW* 38:675-6)

PROGRESSION FROM AN INFANT TO A GOD. What is there more helpless, weak, puny, insignificant, it may be said, in many respects, than a human being when it is born into the world. Yet that being, if nurtured properly, if trained as it should be, has before it a career of never-ending glory. That little puling infant may become, in the eternity of our God, a god, to sway power and dominion in the eternal worlds, to be the father of unnumbered millions. Yet at its birth who would anticipate such a future for it. (Oct. 5, 1884, *JD* 25:319)

JESUS THE GOD OF ANCIENT ISRAEL. There is in modern Christendom a strong tendency to ascribe to the Father visits and communications with mankind that were really made by the Lord Jesus. There is even a respectable percentage of the members of His Church, established in these days, who have the idea that it was the Father and not the Son who appeared to the Patriarchs and Prophets of old, who delivered Israel from Egypt, who gave the law on Sinai, and who was the guide and inspirer of the ancient Seers. This was not the understanding of the true servants of God either before or after His coming.

Those who preceded that advent of the Messiah understood that He whom they worshiped as Jehovah should in due time tabernacle in the flesh, and the writings of Justin Martyr and other of the early fathers show that this was the belief of the early Christian Church on the eastern continent. The writings of the Hebrew Prophets, as we have them in the Bible, are perhaps not as plain on this point as are those of the Nephite Seers that are revealed to us in the Book of Mormon. But we have in this latter record some quotations from the earlier Hebrew Prophets that make this point very clear. Nephi writes:

> And the God of our fathers, who were led out of Egypt, out of bondage, and also were preserved in the wilderness by him, yea, the God of Abraham, and of Isaac, and the God of Jacob, yieldeth himself, according to the words of the angel, as a man, into the hands of wicked men, to be lifted up according to the words of Zenock, and to be crucified, according to the words of Neum, and to be buried in a sepulchre, according to the words of Zenos. . . .[3]

About four hundred years later another Nephite seer, King Benjamin, testifies that an angel came to him and made this glorious promise:

> For behold, the time cometh, and is not far distant, that with power, the Lord Omnipotent who reigneth, who was, and is from all eternity to all eternity, shall come down from heaven among the children of men, and shall dwell in a tabernacle of clay, and shall go forth amongst men, working mighty miracles, such as healing the sick, raising the dead, causing the lame to walk, the blind to receive their sight, and the deaf to hear, and curing all manner of diseases.[4]

A little further on he says:

> And he shall be called Jesus Christ, the Son of God, the Father of heaven and earth, the Creator of all things from the beginning; and his mother shall be called Mary.
> And lo, he cometh unto his own, that salvation might come unto the children of men, even through faith on his name; and even after all this,

---

[3] 1 Nephi 19:10.   [4] Mosiah 3:5.

they shall consider him a man, and say that he hath a devil, and shall scourge him, and shall crucify him.[5]

But we have the word of the Savior Himself on this point that puts controversy to an end. When, after His resurrection and ascension into heaven, He first appeared to His Nephite disciples on this land, He declared:

Behold, I am Jesus Christ, whom the prophets testified shall come into the world. . . . I am the God of Israel, and the God of the whole earth, and have been slain for the sins of the world.[6]

Later during His ministry among the Nephites he affirms:

Behold I say unto you that the law is fulfilled that was given unto Moses. Behold, I am he that gave the law, and I am he who covenanted with my people Israel; therefore, the law in me is fulfilled.[7]

Should any still have a lingering doubt that the Jehovah who revealed Himself to Abraham, to Moses and to others was any other than He who we know in the flesh as Jesus Christ, that doubt is set at rest by the revelations given in these days. In the vision seen by the Prophet Joseph Smith and by Oliver Cowdery in the Kirtland Temple, 3rd of April, 1836, the following appears:

We saw the Lord standing upon the breastwork of the pulpit, before us; and under his feet was a paved work of pure gold, in color like amber.

His eyes were as a flame of fire; the hair of his head was white like the pure snow; his countenance shone above the brightness of the sun; and his voice was as the sound of the rushing of great waters, even the voice of Jehovah, saying:

I am the first and the last; I am he who liveth, I am he who was slain; I am your advocate with the Father.[8]

Somewhat curiously an ancient Syriac manuscript has within the last few months been unearthed that is known as the Gospel of the Twelve Apostles. Whether the Twelve Apostles had anything to do with writing it has nothing to do with the point under consideration. The writing was originally in Hebrew, and what we wish to draw attention to is that, whenever this manuscript was first written, the writers of the original believed that Jesus was He who spake with the ancient Israelites. It commences:

[5]*Ibid.*, 3:8-9.
[6]3 Nephi 11:10, 14.

[7]*Ibid.*, 15:4-5.
[8]D. & C. 110:1-4.

The beginning of the Gospel of Jesus Christ, the Son of the living God, according as it was said by the Holy Spirit, I send an angel before his face, who shall prepare his way.

It came to pass in the 309th year of Alexander, the son of Philip the Macedonian, in the reign of Tiberius Caesar, in the government of Herod, the ruler of the Jews, that the angel Gabriel, the chief of the angels, by command of God went down to Nazareth to a virgin called Mariam, of the tribe of Judah the son of Israel (her who was betrothed to Joseph the Just), and he appeared to her and said, Lo! there ariseth from thee the one who spake with our fathers, and he shall be a Savior to Israel; and they who do not confess him shall perish, for his authority is in the lofty heights, and his kingdom does not pass away. (Feb. 1, 1900, *JI* 35:90-1)

THE SAVIOR SEEN—A PERSONAL TESTIMONY.

I know that God lives. I know that Jesus lives; for I have seen Him. I know that this is the Church of God, and that it is founded on Jesus Christ, our Redeemer. I testify to you of these things as one that knows—as one of the Apostles of the Lord Jesus Christ that can bear witness to you today in the presence of the Lord that He lives and that He will live, and will come to reign on the earth, to sway an undisputed sceptre. (Oct. 6, 1896, *DW* 53:610)

THE WORSHIP OF FEMALE DEITIES.

In the days of Jeremiah the Prophet the worship of "the queen of heaven,"[9] a feminine deity, was very common. The people of Judah attributed great power to this female deity, so much so that Jeremiah declared the word of the Lord unto them concerning their idolatrous practices and their departure from the true God. . . .

It appears from the record of Jeremiah that it was chiefly the women who worshiped this deity. . . . It was in vain that the Prophet of the true God pled with them and endeavored to show them that they were deceived and that by continuing this course they were sure to bring down the anger and the hot displeasure of the true God. . . .

It has not been uncommon for different nations to worship female deities. Pele, a female deity, was worshiped by the Sandwich Islanders. In ancient days Isis was the principal goddess worshiped by the Egyptians. . . . Perhaps this was the deity whom the Israelite exiles worshiped in Egypt, they living at Pathros, in Egypt, at the time when the interview took place between Jeremi-

---

[9]Jeremiah 44:17.

ah and them, though Aphrodite is said to have been worshiped by the Israelites in the days of their idolatry. . . .

The Greeks and Romans also indulged in the worship of female deities. Juno, a celebrated deity, was worshiped by both Greeks and Romans. Ceres was the goddess of Corn, Clio of History, Diana of the Chase, Erato of Lovers, Hygeia of Health. Minerva was also a noted name in their mythology. She was supposed to represent Wisdom, War, and the Liberal Arts, as Pallas also did Wisdom, and as Vesta did the domestic hearth. . . .

The tendency to attribute God-like powers to members of the female sex is exhibited nowadays in the adoration which is paid to the mother of the Savior, the Virgin Mary. . . .

That great care must be exercised among the Latter-day Saints upon this point there can scarcely be a question. . . . There is too much of this inclination to deify "our mother in heaven". . . . As Latter-day Saints we cannot be too careful concerning the use of language that may lead to wrong impressions, especially regarding the Being whom we worship.

One of the great commandments which the Lord gave to Israel after He led them out of Egypt and from the midst of the idolatrous people of Pharaoh, who had many false gods, was: "Thou shalt have no other gods before me."[10] The Lord also told the children of Israel, "I, the Lord, am a jealous God."[11]

The most terrible woes which came upon Israel during their career in the land of Canaan were the result of departing from the worship of the true God and bowing down to idols and false gods.

The worship of the true God has been revealed to us. He has revealed Himself in our day. Mortal men have beheld the Eternal Father and the Redeemer, Jesus. And we know that they live. We know also that our Father in heaven should be the object of our worship. He will not have any divided worship. We are commanded to worship Him, and Him only.

In the revelation of God the Eternal Father to the Prophet Joseph Smith there was no revelation of the feminine element as part of the Godhead, and no idea was conveyed that any such element "was equal in power and glory with the masculine."[12]

Therefore, we are warranted in pronouncing all tendencies

[10]Exodus 20:3.   [12]Elizabeth C. Stanton, *The Woman's Bible.*
[11]*Ibid.*, 20:5.

to glorify the feminine element and to exalt it as part of the God-head as wrong and untrue, not only because of the revelation of the Lord in our day but because it has no warrant in scripture, and any attempt to put such a construction on the word of God is false and erroneous. (May 15, 1895, *JI* 30:314-7)

CHAPTER 11

FREE AGENCY, FOREORDINATION, AND
PREDESTINATION

THE FREE AGENCY OF MAN. We must remember, to begin with, that God our Eternal Father has given unto each of us our agency. There is no human being born on the earth from whom God has withheld his or her agency. We have as much right to exercise our agency in our sphere as God the Eternal Father has to exercise His agency in His sphere, just as much. It is not sacrilege, it is not any infringement upon the power of our God to indulge in this thought or to have this belief. It does not detract in the least from His glory, from His power, nor from our dependence upon Him as an infinite and almighty Being to entertain this view of ourselves. . . .

ADAM AND EVE EXERCISED AGENCY. It was so in the beginning—in the very commencement of the work of our God upon the earth when He placed Adam in the garden and gave Eve unto him for a wife. He set before them the principle of knowledge—that is, He told them what they should do; He told them what they should refrain from doing. He told them that if they did certain things, certain penalties should follow. . . . There was no attempt on the part of our Father to interfere with the agency of Adam in this respect. He left him perfectly free, and in the exercise of that freedom Adam did partake of the tree of knowledge of good and evil. His wife, Eve, was deceived in eating of the fruit; she partook of it, being beguiled, yet in the perfect exercise of her agency, and after she had partaken of it and become subject to the penalty that God had pronounced—the penalty of death and expulsion from the garden—then she came and told Adam what she had done. (Sept. 28, 1884, JD 26:188)

FREE AGENCY A NECESSARY PART OF PLAN OF SALVATION. Men could not be perfectly happy and could not be heirs of God and joint heirs with Jesus Christ if they did not have their agency. Satan exercised his agency and became the devil. He loved evil and chose it. We have no doubt that in the beginning, before he became totally abandoned, he was

taught the right way, he was plead with, entreated and prayed
for. The revelations teach us that he was an angel of God, that
he was, in fact, a son of God. He had the same opportunity of
choosing the good that Jesus had; but he was disobedient and rebellious. He fought against the Father and became a fallen
angel, even a devil. He could do this, because he was a free
agent.

All the sons and daughters of God are also free agents. Satan,
therefore, tempts them. It is necessary they should be tempted.
Without this the plan of salvation would not be perfect. On the
one hand the Father entreats us to obey His laws, to keep His
commandments and to cherish His Holy Spirit. On the other
hand Satan tempts us to do wrong, to commit sin, to disobey
God. He spreads temptations before men to lead them astray.
We are not compelled to listen to him. He cannot force us to
do evil. If we do wrong, it is because we choose to do so, for we
are free agents.

The Lord Himself will not compel us to serve and obey Him.
It is pleasing to Him to have us do so. But, when we do so, it
is because it is our choice and in the exercise of our agency. If,
then, we should be so blessed as to hereafter reach the heaven
where God the Father dwells, it will be because we have obeyed
His laws and not because He has forced us to go there. . . .

To enjoy the sweet, mankind must know something about
the bitter. They must have the opportunity of exercising their
faculties and testing their powers. Unless they were exposed to
temptation they never could know themselves, their own powers,
their own weaknesses nor the power of God. If Satan had no
power to tempt mankind, they would be in a state where they
could neither know good nor evil; they could not know happiness
nor misery. All their powers would lie dormant, for there would
be nothing to arouse them. They would be destitute of that experience which prepares men to become like God, their Eternal
Father.

We may depend upon it, therefore, that the proper way to
take away the power from Satan is to teach mankind not to listen
to him. They are free agents. They can reject him. He has no
power to lead them astray if they will not listen to him. When
they cease to listen to him, he will be bound. The time is com-

ing when for one thousand years Satan will be bound. (Jan. 1, 1880, *JI* 15:6)

PRINCIPLE OF FREE AGENCY.   This is a fundamental principle of the Gospel of the Lord Jesus Christ, and we as His followers should clearly understand it.   If we do wrong (and we have it in our power to do wrong) we must be responsible for that.   We do it because we elect to do it and not because we are compelled by some power over which we have no control to commit this wrong.   On the other hand, if we do right, it is because we exercise our agency in that direction and not because there is a power exercised over us which compels us to do right. . . .

A GOSPEL OF PERFECT FREEDOM.   The Gospel of the Lord Jesus Christ is one of perfect freedom.   Every soul has the right to choose whom he will serve, whether God or Baal, and no individual who does that which is wrong can reproach God therefor.   Unfavorable circumstances may surround human beings at their birth which may have influence upon their subsequent careers.   But our Great Creator in judging His children will make full allowance for these.   Man, having his agency, need not, unless he so wishes, become the entire creature of these circumstances.   It becomes his duty to contend against that which is evil and, by the help of God, to overcome evil inclinations and rise above evil surroundings.

It is for this purpose that God gives His Holy Spirit unto His children, that under its influence and by its power they may be able to resist evil, to overcome the temptations that may be in their pathway and to strengthen themselves in the practice of those virtues which He has enjoined upon us as necessary to make us acceptable in His sight. (April 27, 1890, *DW* 40:833)

SALVATION DEPENDS ON EXERCISE OF AGENCY. We have the choice in the exercise of our agency.   Man can be saved if he will.   There is no power on earth or in hell that can prevent his being saved, if he exercises his agency to that end. Do you understand that? If you ever go to hell, it will be because you yourselves choose to go there and not because any power forces you to go there.   There is no power on earth or in hell that can compel a man to go to hell or to be damned if in the exercise of his agency he chooses to serve God.   Therefore, when men lift up their eyes in torment, the misery of their torment will be increased by the knowledge that they themselves through their own action and through the exercise of their own agency have brought upon them this condemnation and not because any human being forced them there, for there is no such thing possible.

There may be circumstances that are unfavorable to man.... His punishment will be according to the knowledge possessed, to the light he has, to the opportunities that God has given unto him —his punishment will be in accordance therewith. (Jan. 18, 1885, DNW 34:50)

A FREE EXERCISE OF AGENCY. If, when He sends forth his Prophets, He were to manifest His power, so that all the earth would be compelled to receive their words, there would be no room then for men to exercise their agency, for they would be compelled to adopt a certain course and to receive certain teachings and doctrines regardless of their own wishes and will. . . .

This agency God has given unto man, and hence it is that when He sends his truth and His servants to declare it unto the people, He does it in such a way that man is left to the free exercise of his agency in receiving or rejecting them; at the same time we are assured that whoever receives that truth will also receive the convincing power of the Spirit of God to bear testimony to him that it is divine. . . .

When the people demanded miraculous signs of Joseph Smith to convince them of the truth of his testimony, they would not or did not exercise their agency but wanted some overpowering evidence to convince them. The Lord does not operate in that way among the children of men. He sends forth His servants with the truth. (March 23, 1873, JD 15:369-70)

ALL MANKIND ELECTED TO BE SAVED. All mankind are elected to be saved. No man is a tare unless his conduct makes him such. He is not predestined to be a tare or to be damned, but he is predestined to receive, if he will, salvation and glory in the presence of God. . . .

We shall stand before the judgment seat of Christ, and each of us will have to answer for the deeds done in the body, whether they be good or whether they be evil; the judgment that will be pronounced upon us will be a righteous judgment. If we have done wrong, we shall have to atone for that wrong. If we have done that which is right in the sight of God, if we have walked before Him uprightly, confessing our sins and obtaining the forgiveness of them as we have gone along from day to day, then the reward that will be bestowed upon us will be because of our faithfulness in keeping the commandments of God. (Feb. 17, 1895, *DW* 50:417-8)

OBEDIENCE TO GOSPEL AN EXERCISE OF FREE AGENCY. When a man yields complete obedience to the will of the Lord in all things, some pretend to think that he must of necessity lose his free agency and at once become a puppet for others to handle. Those who hold this idea must entertain a very low estimate of human nature, for they would have us believe that to love sin and delight in its practice is the natural condition of the human family; nor do they appear to be willing to admit that a man may freely and without constraint love God and keep His commandments. But we contend that the idea that the sinner is the only free agent is entirely false and further that it is the sinner who is the slave; and he who dances on the devil's ground and keeps step to his music has to serve a hard taskmaster. . . .

On what grounds can we assume that the obedient man uses his agency any less freely than he who chooses to disobey? Because a man or a youth chooses to serve God and obey His laws, is he any less free in doing so than his unwise fellow who prefers to live without God in the world? Cannot a man as freely serve God as he can the devil and tread the path to heaven as voluntarily as he can descend the road to hell? We think so; why not?

The fact is that some who take no pleasure in doing the will of God confound ideas when they talk about entire and unreserved obedience to God destroying man's free agency. They really mean that he who keeps God's laws has no license to sin; but it is this license to sin and not the power, permission and opportunity to choose between right and wrong that is withdrawn. A man is just as much a free agent in avoiding sin as in committing it, in doing good, as in doing evil. . . .

The laws of the Lord are perfect; they are adapted to our eternal natures and worthy of our divine origin; they are to us peace and salvation, and we see nothing unworthy of our manhood in choosing to obey them. It is they who reject so great a salvation that manifest their blindness and folly and show how great is their ignorance of true and heavenly wisdom.

OBEDIENCE TO PRIESTHOOD NECESSARY. Here some one may assert that he has not one word to say against a man being obedient to God, but it is this obedience to other men to which he objects. Who is meant by this expression "other men"? We reply, the Holy Priesthood—the servants of God. Just as well might a man say he believes in obeying the king but does not believe in obeying his ambassadors or his representatives. How can a man obey God and disobey the Priesthood, who teach God's will? They are the channel of communication between heaven and earth; they are the mouth pieces of Jehovah, and when we hearken to them, we obey Him. (June 20, 1874, *JI* 9:150)

FOREKNOWLEDGE AND FOREORDINATION. People confound foreknowledge with foreordination. Because God foreknows a thing, it does not follow that He has foreordained it. He foreknew that Pharaoh would fight Israel and would reject the testimonies which Moses and Aaron bore to him. But Pharaoh had the full use of his agency. It was in his power to have accepted the message which Moses delivered; it was in his power also to reject that message. He chose to reject it, and God magnified His name in the earth by showing His wonderful works among the Egyptians. But He did not foreordain Pharaoh to be damned. His foreknowledge extends to the uttermost end of life. He knows all about us.

Jesus knew that one of His Apostles would be a devil. But it was not foreordained that Judas should be a devil. He chose that part himself, in the exercise of his agency. He betrayed the Son of God and brought upon himself the dreadful fate which befell him. So with Esau. He had equal opportunities with Jacob. Cain had equal opportunities with Abel. God told him that his offering would be accepted if he would do right. God plead with him; his father, no doubt, also plead with him to forsake sin and unrighteousness. But he took the other course.

Do not be deceived and allow any such thought to enter into your hearts that you are fated to be damned, that you are fated to commit sin, that you are fated to be surrounded by inextricable circumstances which break you down. There is no such doctrine in the Gospel of the Son of God. We have our free and unfettered agency. (April 7, 1889, *DW* 38:677)

FOREKNOWLEDGE A N D PREDESTINATION. I would like you to clearly understand that foreknowledge is one thing and predestination is another, and there is a great distinction between the two. They must not be confounded one with the other. . . . That men are foreordained there can be no doubt entertained by those who believe the Gospel but not to be damned. Every human being is ordained to be saved, if he will be. If he is damned, it is because he chooses the path that leads to condemnation. . . .

Have we not seen in our day men violate the commands of God in, what some might term, little things and go on, step by step, from one degree of sin to another, until they would betray the Lord's Anointed? And can any who were familiar with such cases and who watched the gradual descent of these men to evil, doubt for a moment that they had their agency? They chose to commit sin. They had their agency in doing so. They did not repent, and the most dreadful results followed.

God knew His Son Jesus Christ before He was born in the flesh, and He was ordained before the foundation of the earth was laid. He was the Lamb slain, we are told, before the foundation of the earth. That is, it was known that He would be slain; it was known that a generation would be found upon earth at the time the Savior came who would be so hard in their hearts that they would reject Him and crucify Him. God foreknew this. He predicted it. . . . But you must not imagine that because of this those who murdered the Savior were predestined or compelled to do what they did. On the contrary, they did it because they wished to do it. In the exercise of their agency they chose evil rather than good. They hated virtue; they hated purity. Full of the traditions of their fathers, they hated the Son of God, and they hated Him to prison and to death. . . .

ALL FOREORDAINED TO DO GOOD. We were sent here on earth foreordained to do good, to keep the commandments of God and to be saved; for God loves all His children and would save every human soul. He would not that any one should be lost; but He desires the salvation of all. All will be saved except the sons of perdition. This is the grand truth that God has revealed unto us in these last days, that every human being will be saved except a certain class who commit the unpardonable sin—they who shed innocent blood, they who are accessory thereto, or who consent to the shedding of innocent blood. For them there is no salvation, we are told. . . .

PUNISHMENT AFFIXED TO EVERY SIN. Every sin not of this unpardonable character will receive forgiveness, sooner or later. But will it not be punished? Yes. There is punishment affixed to every sin. No man can commit sin without receiving the punishment therefor. He will have to expiate that sin, either in this life or in the life to come. For there is a penalty affixed to every transgression of the laws of God, and we shall have to pay the penalty unless we repent of our sins, and by going forth into the waters of baptism, obtain a remission of them, according to the promise which God has given. In this way our sins can be remitted and be blotted out, and we be relieved from the penalty that is affixed to sin. . . .

MEANING OF ETERNAL PUNISHMENT. Because God's punishment is eternal punishment, it does not necessarily follow that the being who receives it is consigned to it eternally. For instance, a prison might stand for a hundred years. It might be a place of punishment. A person consigned to that prison might go in there and expiate his crime in the prison by suffering a certain punishment, and after the time pronounced as the punishment had expired he could emerge therefrom. Still the prison exists.

So it is with God's punishment. His punishment is eternal punishment, because He is eternal; but it does not follow, as the Lord has said with great plainness, that a person who is consigned thereto will endure it eternally. The Lord Jesus Christ has died for all men, and He will draw all men unto Him. But there are degrees of punishment affixed to sin; and in proportion to men's crimes they will be punished. But they will not be consigned to endless punishment—that is, to suffer it eternally. (April 27, 1890, *DW* 40:834-5)

PREDESTINATION A FALSE DOCTRINE. While we believe fully in foreordination, we do not think it wise to carry this idea to the extent that we are told that some . . . have carried it. That a man's time of departure is absolutely and unchangeably fixed by Providence is not warranted by the word of God.

One of the commandments which Moses was inspired to give to the Children of Israel was: "Honor thy father and thy mother: that thy days may be long upon the land which the Lord thy God giveth thee."[1] What is implied by this commandment? It is that length of days is given to the obedient child who honors his parents and that the disobedient and rebellious child should not live long upon the land.

Solomon says, "The fear of the Lord prolongeth days: but the years of the wicked shall be shortened."[2] The Bible is full of promises to the righteous and of warnings to the wicked. Length of life, the good things of the earth and a peaceful departure when this life is ended are all promised to the righteous. If the time of man's departure from this life were unchangeably fixed, of what use would it be for men to live lives of temperance with the hope that they would prolong their days thereby?

The Lord, in the Word of Wisdom, gives a promise to those who will observe that Word and who remember to keep and do His sayings. He says: "I, the Lord, give unto them a promise, that the destroying angel shall pass by them, as the children of Israel, and not slay them."[3]

It is clear from this that length of life is promised to those who keep this word of counsel. Others may fall a prey to the destroyer, but they will escape and will live on the earth to an age that is not promised to ordinary men. The teachings of the Elders constantly to the people are to live in obedience to the word of the Lord and they will have health and strength given to them; they will run and not be weary; they will walk and not faint. . . .

Our children should be taught to have faith so that like the young men of whom Helaman writes they will escape, even in deadly battle, the fate that more wicked people, or people of less faith, meet. . . . How incorrect an idea it is to suppose that each man has his hour of death fixed, from which he cannot escape. (June 15, 1889, JI 24:276-7)

---

[1] Exodus 20:12.
[2] Proverbs 10:27.
[3] D. & C. 89:21.

CHAPTER 12

FAITH AND TRUST IN GOD

FAITH IS OUR STRENGTH. The strength of the Latter-day Saints is their faith. By that they can accomplish anything they set their hearts to do if it is right. God will be with them and sustain them. He has done it all the time. We have accomplished apparent impossibilities through the power and blessing of God and the faith of the people. If we have faith, we can accomplish all things that are required at our hands. . . . We can do everything that is required of us by the principle of faith actively exhibited in works. (Oct. 6, 1898, CR 5)

It has been my experience and observation that whenever the Latter-day Saints are called upon to perform a work and they go to with their energy, their might and with the spirit of union to accomplish that work, the effects upon their character are always of a beneficial nature. It results in great good to the individual and to the people. . . .

God intends that we shall be a people of great faith—a people of such faith that we shall carry to a successful termination any labor or duty that He may require at our hands. . . .

ZION TO BE BUILT BY FAITH. It is time, with the experience we have had now as a Church, that we should be a people of unbounded faith, willing to believe that all things are possible with God and that when He commands us to do anything, we should go to with our might and with unyielding determination to accomplish that end according to the mind and will of God. This is the kind of people God expects us to be. If we are going to build up Zion in power and in great glory upon the earth, it will be by this principle of faith, by putting our trust in God, listening to His word, receiving it in the proper manner from that authority which He has placed on the earth to give His word unto His people. Zion cannot be built up in any other way. . . .

THE EARTH IS THE LORD'S. The heaven of heavens is the Lord's. The cattle on a thousand hills, the fish that swim in the sea and everything there is upon the face of the earth—all are His.   He has His agents by the thousands ready to do His bidding and to interpose in behalf of His children. They are invisible to us perhaps, though occasionally one may see them; but they are nevertheless around us, and we can feel their heavenly presence.   Now, how easy it is for them to overrule and control and shape things to suit the Lord and His purposes.

He has done this all the time in connection with this work. He has turned aside our enemies when it has seemed as though we should perish.   He has made the wrath of men to praise Him. He has defeated their machinations, and their well-laid plans He has brought to naught.   And He is able to do this always and will do it if we will only have faith in Him and believe that He can do this and put unfaltering trust in Him.

All that is necessary is to know what is the right thing to do. How shall we know it? We can know it by receiving it through the constituted authority that God has placed on the earth to represent Him.   When the word of the Lord comes through that authority and a command is given to us to do a certain thing, let me tell you, in the name of the Lord Jesus, that can be done if we will do it. . . . If we will do this, there is nothing that can prevent the accomplishment of the work that is entrusted to us. (April 17, 1898, *DW* 56:705-7)

OUR FAITH IN THE ALMIGHTY. Obedience to the Gospel brings men into very close and intimate relationship with the Lord.   It establishes a close connection between men on the earth and our Great Creator in the heavens.   It brings to the human mind a feeling of perfect confidence in the Almighty and in His willingness to listen to and answer the supplications of those who trust in Him.   In times of trial and difficulty this confidence is beyond price.   Trouble may come upon the individual or upon the people, disaster may threaten and every human hope may seem to be overthrown, yet, where men have availed themselves of the privileges which obedience to the Gospel brings, they have a sure standing place; their feet are upon a rock that cannot be moved.

This is the secret of the wonderful calmness and serenity of mind which the Latter-day Saints have shown in the midst of the persecutions through which they have passed.   They have had unshaken confidence in the ability and willingness of God to save them.

It has been a matter of surprise to many people that the Latter-day Saints should feel as they did when they were driven forth as homeless wanderers into the wilderness. . . . Trusting in the Lord and in His providence, they launched forth into the wilderness, feeling unshaken confidence in the Lord's willingness to lead them to a land where they could live in peace, undisturbed by enemies. . . .

While they did not have a clear understanding as to the exact point to which they were aiming or the character of the country which they would reach, still the testimony of the Spirit of the Lord was such that they could not hesitate about starting. They felt sure they would be led to a suitable place. They had the same confidence then which they have had in all their trials since. (Oct. 15, 1893, *JI* 28:639)

DEVELOPING FAITH LIKE THE ANCIENTS. The Lord has shown His people that He is able to take care of His own work, to carry out His own purposes, and to fulfill His promises. . . . The testimonies of the servants of God have been amply sustained wherein they have said that whatever might occur, and however fiercely the work of God might be warred against, it would stand impregnable and unshaken and would proceed in its onward march unchecked by the attacks that should be made upon it. This is and ought to be a great source of comfort to all who are connected with the Church of Jesus Christ of Latter-day Saints.

God has spoken. He has laid the foundation of His work. He has promised that it shall be built up and that no power shall prevail against it. As one of the Prophets has said, "What shall one then answer the messengers of the nation? That the Lord hath founded Zion, and the poor of His people shall trust in it."[1] This prediction is literally fulfilled in our case. We do put our trust in Zion, the Lord having founded it. (Jan. 1, 1893, *JI* 28:24)

TEACH CHILDREN TO HAVE FAITH. Let us, as a people, cling to the old faith, to the old doctrine that has come down to us through the Bible that God is, that He is to-day as

---

[1]Isaiah 14:32.

much as He ever was and put our trust in Him. Let us train up our children to the faith that He is a God who hears and answers prayer, so that they will have faith in Him, that in times of trial, in times of difficulty, when they are encircled by danger and it would seem as though there were no possible way of escape from the danger with which they are threatened, they can humble themselves and call upon God with a faith that cannot be overcome, to deliver them and to give unto them those blessings which they need. It is the greatest comfort that a human being can have to be in close communion with his Father in heaven or her Father in heaven. (June 27, 1880, JD 22:57-8)

FAITH—THE FOUNDATION. Faith lies at the foundation of our religion, and it is impossible to grow in a knowledge of the truth or to please God without it. A person who has not faith walks by sight, and he is harassed with doubts and fears. Appearances are nearly always against the work of God and the fulfillment of His purposes, for His ways are not man's ways, and His thoughts are not man's thoughts.

It is frequently the case that that which man would desire and advise is the very thing that would bring disappointment; and that which man would often imagine to be fraught with evil is controlled by our all-wise Creator for the accomplishment of His purposes in the advancement of His glory and the salvation of His people. . . . Many movements that the Church has been compelled to make through the persecutions of the wicked and which were intended by the wicked as deadly blows against the work of God have been converted into means of doing great good and enlarging the work and bringing to pass the Lord's purposes. We have been forced to do things that, if left to ourselves, we would not have done, and yet they were necessary to be done to bring to pass the fulfillment of the word of God. (Feb. 1 ,1890, JI 25:84)

GOD WILL NOT BE DICTATED TO. God by His infinite power can bring to pass marvelous changes and that, too, in a short space of time. He has His own way of doing things, and all that He asks of His people is to follow His guidance. This is His work, and He will care for it. He will not be dictated to by man as to how He shall proceed; but He will show man that having laid the foundation of this work He is able to carry it through.

Every man who has observed the progress of events must be impressed with the shallowness of human wisdom and foresight and how utterly unable man's power is to cope with the circumstances which are from time to time thrown around the Church of God. We are compelled to seek for refuge in the wisdom and power of our God; and though many things may be done that are contrary to the way we would have had events controlled, it takes but a little time to show the faithful that the way that God has wrought is infinitely superior to the way man would have done. It was true inspiration which prompted the poet to write:

> God moves in a mysterious way
> His wonders to perform. . . .

It is a blessed consolation to know that God possesses such power that He can fulfill every promise that He makes and that He not only has the power but that He is willing to hear the humblest of His children and to respect their supplications and give them the righteous desires of their hearts. (Jan. 1, 1892, *JI* 27:20)

GOD'S OWN WAY OF BUILDING UP CHURCH. God has taken His own way to build up His Church and to accomplish that which He seeks to bring to pass. . . . It is a cause of stumbling among the nations of the earth that God does not accompany the work that He has established by such signs as they think He has the power to give. They say, "If God the Eternal Father has the power that is attributed to Him and this is His work, why does He not accompany it by manifestations and signs that would carry irresistible weight and conviction to the minds of all those unto whom it is brought. It would be a very easy thing for Him," they say, "if He wished to convince the world of the truth of this being His Gospel, to give such signs and manifestations as would compel men and women to receive and to believe it to be His work."

This is man's idea about the work of God. But God, our Eternal Father, has not seen fit to take this method. He places us in circumstances where we are compelled to exercise faith, to put our trust in Him and to seek by faith for that knowledge which He is willing to bestow; and it is not His object, neither would it be consistent with His purpose to convince all men and all women concerning His work whether they would be convinced or not. (Jan. 18, 1885, *DNW* 34:50)

It is natural for human beings, when in difficulty and surrounded by unpleasant circumstances, to form an idea in their own minds as to the manner in which they would like to be extricated and to come off triumphant; and this has proved a means of disappointment to a great many members of our Church in times that are past. The Lord has not saved them in the manner that they felt was best. He has not come up to their expectations, and they have not had faith enough to trust Him to the uttermost. Now, it is in this manner that the patience and faith of the Saints are tried. It is most presumptuous for man to mark out the line of deliverance which God shall adopt. Man with his human knowledge cannot possibly comprehend all the influences that are at work or the purposes to be accomplished. (Jan. 15, 1890, *JI* 25:38)

MAKE GOD YOUR FRIEND. If men do not suit you, make God your friend. He says: "Cursed be the man that trusteth in man, and maketh flesh his arm."[2] The man that trusts in his fellow man is likely to be deceived. Men will fail, husbands will fail, wives will fail, children will fail, parents will fail, but God never fails. He never grows cold or indifferent. He is always the same unchangeable being, and His promises can be relied upon to the very uttermost. . . . We should be pure in thought, pure in the sight of the eye and the conception of the thought, pure in act and pure in word. If we live this way, God will dwell with us, and He will be our friend all the days of our lives. He will not leave us in the midst of trouble. We may go through six troubles, and He will be with us in the seventh. He will be with us in the deep water. He will be with us in the fiery furnace. He will be with us under all circumstances, if we serve Him. I bear testimony to this. (Dec. 13, 1891, *DW* 44:5)

GOD'S REQUIREMENTS FOR HIS PEOPLE. Now God requires of us, as His people, that we shall do that which He commands us to do, no matter what that may be. The Lord never had a people on the face of the earth without making require-

---

[2]Jeremiah 17:5.

ments of them. He required Noah to do a certain work; He required Abraham to do a certain work; He required certain things to Joseph, Moses and the children of Israel; and in every age when He has had a people on the earth He has required them and His servants to depart from the path trod by men generally who followed their own devices and who were guided by their own wisdom and counsel.

He has made these requirements upon all His people, not upon the Latter-day Saints alone, not for the first time upon us who live in this generation but in every age and generation when He has had upon the earth a people whom He recognized He has given them peculiar commandments and made requirements of them that called for the exercise of faith and that tested their courage and also their sincerity in the cause which He had established. The history of God's dealings with the children of men are full of incidents of this character. . . .

SHOWING FAITH BY WORKS. God requires that we who live in this generation shall show our faith by our works. It is an easy thing in one respect for people to float with the tide, to sail with the stream, to have their sails spread to catch the popular breeze and to go along with the current as it flows. This is the way the great majority of mankind has gone; it is the broad way to which Jesus referred, when He said so many walked therein; but He designated the path which led to Him as a straight and narrow path, a path upon which few entered, for it was a path upon which those who walked would be tried and tested, and their sincerity proved. And this is the path He calls upon us as a people to walk in. (Aug. 23, 1874, *DNW* 23:530)

CHAPTER 13

OBEDIENCE—HEAVEN'S FIRST LAW

OBEDIENCE IS HEAVEN'S FIRST LAW. The Lord has shown in all His dealings with the children of men that He places a high value upon obedience. We frequently hear it stated that "order is heaven's first law." This is a quotation from the English Poet, Pope; but the statement is a mistake. Obedience must precede order, and order is the result of obedience. Careful reflection leaves no doubt that obedience is heaven's first law. . . .

Obedience is a great lesson that children should learn. Every child should obey with the greatest respect the commands of his parents. A child should listen with humility to its parents' teachings and should constantly honor its parents. In like manner, as they grow to manhood and womanhood, they should listen to and honor the counsel of the Priesthood. Our Father in heaven has bestowed His Priesthood upon men, and if we would honor Him, we must honor the authority which He has bestowed, namely, the Priesthood. (April 1, 1886, *JI* 21:104)

OBEDIENCE A MOST IMPORTANT PRINCIPLE. No principle pertaining to the Gospel is of greater importance than obedience, for without obedience no blessing can come upon the people. Men may talk all their lives about their faith; but, if they do not obey, they can not obtain the promised blessings. For instance, a man may say that he believes in Jesus and that He is the Son of God; he may believe in baptism and the laying on of hands; but can he get his sins remitted or receive the Holy Ghost if he should not obey baptism or the laying on of hands? . . .

What is the nature of the obedience that children should show to their parents? Can they stop and argue with them and say, when they are told to do a certain thing: "Father, or mother, would it not be better to do this in some other way?" No well-behaved child will do this, but he will go promptly and do what is required of him. Children may not understand everything their parents ask them to do; but still this should not prevent them from obeying. Parents ask their children to do many things which they, probably, fully understand but which their children do not. A child who has good parents and has been properly trained has faith that its parents will ask it to do nothing but what is right, and the spirit of obedience is so strong within it that it goes without hesitation and obeys their commands.

It is in this manner that God should be obeyed. To begin with, we must have faith in Him. When we have a proper degree of faith, it is easy and joyful to obey every requirement of God, whether we understand it or not. God's ways cannot be fully understood by man; they are frequently beyond our comprehension; though if we try to do as He tells us, He gives us such pleasure and peace that we are convinced we are right. . . .

It is this kind of faith and obedience that is needed in these days. God has given us a Prophet to lead us. We must obey him, if we would have the blessing of God to rest upon us. Never let doubts arise in your hearts about him or his teachings and counsels; for, if Satan can persuade you to doubt, he has gained a great victory over you, and he will lead you captive as he will. (Sept. 25, 1869, JI 4:156)

ALL OF GOD'S CREATIONS OBEDIENT EXCEPT MAN. By this principle of obedience order is maintained throughout the universe amid all the creations of our God. Even the animals obey the laws of their creation, and there is no plant or creature, no element with which we are acquainted which disobeys or breaks the laws of its creation, which God has given for its government. Man alone of all the creations of our Father exhibits disobedience and fails to observe the laws which his Creator has given unto him. By obedience he can ascend from this condition of existence to dwell with his Father eternally in the heavens to become, in fact, a god; but he can by disobedience sink far below all created things. The earth is cursed because of man's disobedience. Even the animal creation suffers from it. But the day is coming when man's obedience will be the means of blessing the earth and all the animal and vegetable creations. . . .

DISOBEDIENCE TO COUNSEL DISPLEASING TO GOD. There are great promises made to those who are obedient. The Lord told the children of Israel that if they honored their fathers and mothers they should live long in the land. He has said unto us in His revelations that "the willing and obedient shall eat the good of the land of Zion in these last days."[1] The obedient are numbered among the children of Ephraim, and the Lord says that "the rebellious are not of the blood of Ephraim."[2] He further says that "they shall be plucked out."[3] They "shall be cut off out of the land of Zion, and shall be sent away, and shall not inherit the land."[4]

From the beginning of this Church until the present the men and women who have been obedient to the counsel of God's servants have always been the most favored. President Young, during the lifetime of the Prophet Joseph, was always noted for his strict obedience to the Prophet. Brother Joseph never made any requirement of him that he did not strictly comply with. The same may be said of the other faithful men who, during his lifetime, were associated with him. But the disobedient and the rebellious have been, as the Lord said they should be, cut off. Oliver Cowdery was with Joseph when John the Baptist came to them and ordained them to the Aaronic Priesthood. He was the second Apostle in the Church also and a witness of the Book of Mormon, the angel of the Lord having shown him the plates. But he was disobedient to the Prophet, and he could not stand. It might be thought that he was so near to Joseph and so favored of God that it was not necessary for him to do exactly as the Prophet told him but not so. There is an order in the Church of Christ which all must observe, and no one can be disobedient without bringing the displeasure of the Lord upon him. This is a principle which all should learn. . . .

Remember that God has chosen men to be His servants and has given them power to regulate His Church and to lead and guide His people, and He will honor them if they do right, and those who refuse to obey them He will condemn; and no man in this Church, from the beginning until the present time, ever refused to obey the counsel of God's servants without losing His Spirit, and where they have not repented with heartfelt sorrow, they have lost their standing in the Church. . . .

NOT TO BE COMMANDED IN ALL THINGS. Our Heavenly Father requires something more of us than to be merely obedient to a commandment when he gives it to us. He desires

---

[1]D. & C. 64:34.   [3]Ibid., 64:36.
[2]Ibid., 64:36.   [4]Ibid., 64:35.

us to strive to do good of ourselves without waiting to be commanded to do so. He says, "It is not meet that I should command in all things; for he that is compelled in all things, the same is a slothful and not a wise servant; wherefore he receiveth no reward."[5] He adds that "men should anxiously be engaged in a good cause, and do many things of their own free will, and bring to pass much righteousness; for the power is in them."[6] He says also: "He that doeth not anything until he is commanded, and receiveth a commandment with doubtful heart, and keepeth it with slothfulness, the same is damned."[7]   (Sept. 18, 1875, JI 10:222)

BLESSINGS THE RESULT OF OBEDIENCE TO LAW. Among the important items of instruction given by Joseph the Prophet on April 2, 1843, . . . are these words:

> There is a law, irrevocably decreed in heaven before the foundations of this world, upon which all blessings are predicated—
> And when we obtain any blessing from God, it is by obedience to that law upon which it is predicated.[8]

This statement is beautifully in harmony with the teachings of the holy scriptures, and it will serve as a most useful guide to all who are in search of the blessings which the Lord has in store for those who serve Him.

If we enjoy bodily health, we know it is through obedience to the laws of our physical nature; and no one can reasonably expect to retain health of body and mind if he neglects to conform to those laws. The same rule will apply to spiritual matters. If we have received a knowledge of the truth of the Gospel of Christ, it has been obtained through obedience to its rules, as it is only on condition of such obedience that this knowledge is promised. If we have received a forgiveness of our sins, it is by repenting of them, for we know that there is no remission of sins without repentance.

If we desire further blessings of the Lord, we should not expect to receive them only upon further compliance with His laws. Obedience to one requirement does not entitle us to all blessings; and yet we should seek to gain all the blessings promised

[5]Ibid., 58:26.   [7]Ibid., 58:29.
[6]Ibid., 58:27.   [8]Ibid., 130:20-1.

to the faithful. The gifts of our Heavenly Father ought to be highly prized by everyone, and they should be diligently sought after. Just how they are to be obtained is made plain by the Prophet in the words already quoted—"When we obtain any blessing from God, it is by obedience to that law upon which it is predicated."

In the revelations of the Lord given to the Church in our day are many commandments which the Saints are required to observe, and accompanying these commandments are most glorious promises to all who will obey; and if it requires any sacrifice on our part to observe these laws, the reward that follows is a hundred-fold recompense for such sacrifice. (Oct. 1, 1900, JI 35:655)

OBEDIENCE IN ALL THINGS. The Latter-day Saints ought to know that obedience to the first or primary principles is not all that is required of them. Every principle of our whole religion teaches us that we must progress from one degree to another, until we shall see as we are seen and know as we are known; and, in fact, until we fully comprehend all truth, and obey every ordinance necessary to fit us for a residence in the Kingdom of God. (March 22, 1856, WS 43)

DISOBEDIENCE ONLY THING TO BE FEARED. There is only one thing connected with this work—speaking for myself individually—concerning which I have any fear, and that is ourselves. I never had any feeling of fear while I was at Washington, and the clouds were dark and menacing, and our enemies were threatening and active in their preparations to assail us; I never had, I can truthfully say, any fear as to the result of their operations so long as the Saints at home were united and were seeking to keep the commandments of God. . . .

God . . . has plainly given a promise unto this people, this Church:

But verily I say unto you, that I have decreed a decree which my people shall realize, inasmuch as they hearken from this very hour unto the counsel which I, the Lord their God, shall give unto them.

Behold they shall, for I have decreed it, begin to prevail against mine enemies from this very hour.

And by hearkening to observe all the words which I, the Lord their God, shall speak unto them, they shall never cease to prevail until the

kingdoms of the world are subdued under my feet, and the earth is given
unto the Saints, to possess it forever, and ever.[9]

Now, here is a promise that the Lord has given, He says,
by a positive decree. It is a promise given with conditions, and
if the conditions should be observed, we may rest assured that
the promise in its entirety will be fulfilled. There are no res-
ervations about it, only the reservation connected with the condition upon which it is made. "They shall prevail"—that is if
they keep His commandments and if they observe the counsel
which He has given unto us. Now in the next paragraph He says:

> But inasmuch as they keep not my commandments, and hearken not
> to observe all my words, the kingdoms of the world shall prevail against
> them.

Our fate, therefore, as a people—that is, as individuals at
least—is plainly pointed out unto us in these two or three
paragraphs. . . .

SAINTS TO PREVAIL THROUGH FAITHFULNESS.
There has never been an hour since the Lord gave this work unto
the Church—not one hour—that they have not prevailed over
His enemies when they have hearkened unto His words and
kept His commandments. . . . We know by experience that when
the Latter-day Saints have been most faithful, have been most
diligent, when they have been most zealous in preaching the
Gospel, in building temples, in carrying out the word of our God
as He has given it unto us, then the anger of our enemies has been
most fierce against us. But notwithstanding the fierceness and
the heat with which it has burned, it has been powerless against
this people to injure us or to interfere in any manner with our
growth and with the accomplishment of the purposes of God
entrusted to us. (Dec. 2, 1883, JD 24:359-60)

THE OBEDIENT ARE HAPPY. My theory is that when a
man is conscious or a people are conscious that he or they are
in the path of duty, doing that which is right in the sight of
God, they should always be happy, no matter what the circumstances may be which surround them. I think that God has

9*Ibid.*, 103:5-7.

created us to be happy,[10] and my belief is that he placed happiness within the reach of all, and it is man's own fault if he is not happy and does not enjoy himself every day of his life. This is one of my reasons for liking my religion, this system called "Mormonism," because it bestows full happiness and joy upon its believers. They can be happy in the midst of the most adverse circumstances; they can rejoice when their lives are imperilled. (July 12, 1874, *JD* 17:121)

---

[10]"Happiness is the object and design of our existence; and will be the end thereof, if we pursue the path that leads to it; and this path is virtue, uprightness, faithfulness, holiness, and keeping all the commandments of God." (*Teachings of the Prophet Joseph Smith,* page 255-6)

CHAPTER 14

REPENTANCE—THE PATHWAY TO HAPPINESS

ALL MAY RECEIVE BLESSINGS OF REPENTANCE. Repentance will always bring a blessing. Faith in the Lord Jesus Christ will always bring a blessing. I do not care what nation a man may belong to nor what church he may enter, if he will only repent of his sins, it will bring a blessing to him. . . . God will accept the repentance of His children. No matter what a man's standing or what his connections may be . . . if he truly and sincerely repents of his sins, the blessing of repentance will rest down upon him. This may seem strange to you; it is nevertheless true.

Of course, if he were a Mohammedan, he would not have faith in the Lord Jesus Christ; he would not believe in the Son of God as the Redeemer of the world; but so far as repentance goes and turning away from sin with a determination to live a purer and better life, the blessing of God would rest upon that individual. If he believed in Jesus, then the blessing of that belief would rest upon him; and the man who is in that condition of faith has the advantage, so far as that goes, over the unbeliever.

But will repentance save people? Is that all that is necessary for salvation? No! That is only one of the requirements which the Lord makes of us. He requires of us that when we hear the name of Jesus and are taught the mission of Jesus we shall accept Him as our Savior, as the Son of God, as our Redeemer, and have faith in Him. Then we are required to repent of all our wrongdoing. How shall we know that which is wrong? Do we derive the knowledge of it from books alone? No! (Dec. 31, 1893, DW 48:162)

ONLY ONE PLAN OF SALVATION. I doubt not that hundreds, in various nations and generations, who have been in ignorance of the true Gospel and far removed from those who had authority to administer its ordinances, have had their sins blotted out. God has looked in mercy upon them and on account of their sincerity has witnessed unto them that He accepted the broken spirits and contrite hearts which they offered unto Him.

I cannot doubt this; but wherever the Gospel of Jesus Christ is preached in its fullness, none can obtain the remission of sins only in the way that God has pointed out, and that is by baptism by one having the authority from God to administer that ordinance. (July 14, 1872, JD 15:115)

ALL ARE SINNERS AND NEED REPENTANCE. We cannot commit sin and retain His Spirit. That is an impossibility. Apostles have tried it; others who were men of God have tried it; but they have signally failed. They could not retain the Spirit of God and at the same time commit sin. . . . No man can hope to enjoy the favor and blessing of God who commits sin and does not repent of it. And it will be so unto the end of time. There are two things that are irreconcilable—sin and the Spirit of God. The Spirit of God will not tolerate sin. Therefore, if we hope to escape darkness and apostasy, we must refrain from sin.

Of course, every human being is a sinner. No man or woman ever lived on this earth, excepting the Son of God, who was not a sinner. The Presidency of this Church, the Twelve Apostles and all the Prophets that ever lived upon this earth are and have been sinners. It is one of the consequences of the fall. We are subject to sin and temptation. But, while this is the case, it is the privilege of every human being to live so that his sins will be forgiven and not be held against him.

It should be the aim of all who desire to live in the enjoyment of the Spirit of God to try and retain that Spirit in its fulness; for when the Holy Ghost is with us, then God is with us; and when we are in the fellowship of the Holy Ghost, we are in the fellowship of the Father and the Son.

While I say we are sinners, I believe it is possible for us to live so as to have no sin held against us. We should have the spirit of repentance constantly in our hearts. Our hearts should be touched and softened by it, so that we will be mellowed under its influence and that we shall have such a horror of sin and such a desire for righteousness that when we become conscious that we have thought or said or done anything contrary to the mind and will of God, we will instantly bow down and acknowledge our sins before the Lord and repent of them with all our hearts and obtain forgiveness for them. (Nov. 2, 1895, *DW* 51:802)

GOSPEL PRINCIPLES SAME IN ALL AGES. If it was necessary in the days of Jesus and of His Apostles that men should believe in Jesus and repent of their sins, it is necessary today; and no human judgment nor human council can do away with that necessity. God is the Being to grant salvation, and He is the Being to withhold salvation, and He is the Being to pronounce the terms upon which salvation shall be obtained. Therefore, as God did make faith in Jesus a doctrine that was necessary for man's salvation, it is still necessary. Though ages may have passed, this has not changed. It cannot be changed.

It takes as much to save a man in this generation as it did eighteen hundred years ago. There may be any amount of enlightenment, of wisdom and of knowledge, but however great this may be, it does not affect in the slightest degree the principle that men must believe in Jesus as the foundation of their faith and of their salvation. They must also repent of their sins. No sophistry, no human wisdom, no human device can remove from the plan of salvation the necessity of the repentance of sin; the Gospel of Jesus Christ demands absolutely that sin must be forsaken, and in order for it to be forsaken it must be repented of.

Therefore, if men say that you can be saved without faith and without repentance, or if the whole world should say this, would it affect in the least degree the salvation of men? Would men be saved because the whole world said they could be without these vital principles? Certainly not. God, who grants salvation, and who is the Author of salvation, has placed these principles in His Gospel as essential to salvation. (Sept. 18, 1892, *DW* 45:450)

SEEDS OF WRONGDOING SOWN IN HEART. We have compared the word of God to a seed. We can also compare wrongdoing to a seed. The seeds of wrongdoing are sown in the human heart. If there is not care taken to uproot these seeds, they also will grow; and if permitted to go on unchecked, if nourished and cherished, they will increase and become strong, and they will bring forth fruit also—the fruit of evil.

How shall we prevent the growth of this evil seed? How

shall we cherish the growth of this good seed? . . . Prayer, coupled with repentance, is one of the means of doing this. God extends His arms of mercy and loving kindness to all His children and beseeches them to turn to Him and repent of their sins. Our sins may be as scarlet, but if we will repent of them, He will make them white as wool. No matter what our sins may be, save the unpardonable sin, if we will repent of them with all our hearts and confess them in humility before God and make atonement for them to the extent of our ability, He will forgive them. Be comforted, then, all ye penitent sinners! Be comforted, all ye people; for there is none of us but has committed sin. We are all offenders in the sight of God's exalted purity. (Feb. 17, 1895, *DW* 50:419)

ALL WRONGDOING MUST BE FORGIVEN. Nothing will escape the recollection of Jehovah; no act of our lives can be hidden; no word that we have ever spoken that has been harsh, cruel and wrong will ever be forgotten or blotted out, unless we have obtained forgiveness for it. . . . We will get the measure measured to us that we measure to our fellow men, just as sure as God has spoken.

If we have been merciful, kind, sympathetic, filled with charity and love, we will have these repaid to us; but if we have not exercised these heavenly qualities, we may depend upon it, unless we have repented and made atonement, they will be measured to us in the same manner that we have measured them to others. God is just, and He cannot even wink at iniquity, much less countenance it. (Jan. 14, 1894, *DW* 48:350)

REPENT DAILY AND ENJOY HAPPINESS. When we get up in the morning, let us examine ourselves to see whether the Spirit of God is with us and so at night before we commit ourselves to slumber, review the acts and words of the day and ask God to show unto us wherein we have come short that we may repent; thus, repenting every day and having the forgiveness of our sins every day, there will be no account recorded in heaven against us to be expiated after this life.

If we indulge in an improper thought, ask God to forgive us and not rest satisfied until we are forgiven. Let us live the lives of Latter-day Saints so that every one of us will exemplify in our lives the principles of the Gospel. (Feb. 16, 1896, *DW* 52:387)

Let us repent of our sins as we go along, and not let them accumulate against us. Let us be able to look our brethren and sisters in the face and feel that we have done them no wrong. If we have done wrong, confess that wrong and obtain forgiveness from our brethren and sisters; then we can go to God and ask Him to accept of us and blot out that transgression that it shall not be held against us. If we live this way, our lives will be happy, peaceful and full of joy. We will diffuse happiness and good feeling all around us. Our children will feel the influence of that spirit which we carry, and they will imitate us.

Develop a keen sense of justice and of righteousness in our children, and the son will say, "Why, my father would not do such a thing, and I will not do it;" or, "My mother would not do such a thing, and I will not do it." . . . Thus righteousness will be perpetuated in the land. (Jan. 14, 1894, *DW* 48:351)

It is not repentance at the time of baptism alone. Some people have an idea that because they have entered the waters of baptism and repented of their sins then that is an end of it. What a mistake! We need to have this spirit of repentance continually; we need to pray to God to show us our conduct every day. Every night before we retire to rest we should review the thoughts, words and acts of the day and then repent of everything we have done that is wrong or that has grieved the Holy Spirit. Live this way every day and endeavor to progress every day. We may indulge in many things that are not right, indulge in wrong thoughts, be actuated by wrong motives, may have wrong objects in view. . . .

Therefore, we need to repent every day and every hour, everyone of us. There is none of us so perfect but that we need to do it, and if we do not we will grieve the Spirit of God and check our progress. We need not hug the delusion to our bosom that because we are members of the Church and hold the Priesthood, therefore we can do things that other men cannot do and not grieve the Spirit and be condemned therefor. We cannot. I bear testimony to that. (Jan. 22, 1898, *MS* 61:117-8)

NO NEW YEAR'S RESOLUTIONS. Among Latter-day Saints there ought to be no occasion for what is called "swearing-off" or for the general making of resolutions of improvement on

New Year's day. Every day should witness with them a determination to lay aside weaknesses and take on more of the graces of godliness. Each day furnishes opportunity to look closely into one's habits, to examine and discard the worthless and cleave unto that which is elevating and holy.

The partaking of the Sacrament in the Sunday Schools and Ward meetings, when done worthily, of itself implies an earnest endeavor towards improvement. Every time a true Saint, whether old or young, kneels in prayer, he or she should consider anew the duty of leading a better life, one more in conformity with the precepts and example of our Great Master. Not alone on New Year's, therefore, but on every day, should people seek to effect an improvement in their habits of life. (Jan. 1, 1897, JI 32:23)

REFORMATION IS PROGRESSION. There exists, so long as mankind are imperfect, a continual necessity of reformation. When a Latter-day Saint ceases to perceive the necessity of reformation or doing better than he has been doing, it should be an evidence to him that he has not the light of the Spirit as he should have it and that he has ceased to progress. If he is fully possessed of the Spirit of the Lord, he will progress, and, if he progress, he will see ample cause to do better to-day than he did yesterday, this week than last week and the present year than the preceding year. His experience, if he should live his religion, will increase daily, and with the aid of that experience he will comprehend more perfectly the duties devolving upon him and will be more capable of discharging them every day that he lives than the preceding one. So, the man or the woman who is living up to the light of truth is continually reforming—progression implying reform. . . .

No man or woman who has not ceased to progress and who has no need of deep and heartfelt repentance will ever allude to any previous period of their lives as a time of superior enjoyment —so far as the Spirit and power of God are concerned—to that then experienced. For, however unfavorable the circumstances by which they may be surrounded, if they undeviatingly pursue the course which the Lord has pointed out, present light, intelligence, gifts of the Spirit and happiness will contrast very favorably with the amount of these blessings experienced by them at any previous time. If it were not so, could the people of God be said to progress, increasing in faith and preparing for the revelation of the Lord Jesus? The Saints may put it down as a truth that if they do not feel to enjoy the power of God more at the present time than they ever did in their lives before, there is something wrong, and they have need to critically examine themselves and repent with all their heart, or they will get worse and worse until they are completely destitute of the light and intelligence of the Lord. (Jan. 31, 1857, *WS* 326-7)

PENALTY FOR SIN MUST BE PAID. There is connected with every crime and every sin that man commits a penalty. This is an inexorable law, an unchangeable law, and the effect of it cannot be avoided. We must endure the penalty of our sins. . . . We have to endure the penalty of the violation of the laws of God. There is only one way in which the punishment can be avoided, and that is by obeying the law that God has given. That law is a superior law. He says:

"Believe in my Son Jesus Christ, repent of your sins, be baptized by one having authority, and you shall have the remission of your sins." This is the only way by which we can escape the penalties of violated spiritual laws.

The Lord has made this exceedingly plain in these days so that we can understand it. Those who take a wrong course must endure the consequences of their wrong. . . .

Therefore, when we commit sin, we should understand that we have to expiate that sin. We cannot transgress the laws of God with impunity; and if we commit certain sins, we are debarred from entering into the presence of God and into that glory that He has in store for His faithful children. (April 27, 1890, *DW* 40:836)

INDIVIDUAL SALVATION OUR GREATEST WORK. This work of self-improvement, under the power and influence of the Gospel of Jesus Christ, is a work given to each of us. It should be the great work of our lives; it should be the chief thought of our hearts. There is nothing greater. . . .

The greatest work we can do is to so live that we ourselves shall be saved, that our own acts shall be correct and our will and desires and passions be brought into subjection to the will of God. There is no work that I know of so great and important to me as this. . . .

This Gospel of our's is a practical Gospel. It is not like our Sunday apparel to be put on today and put off tomorrow; it ought to be carried with us in all the transactions of life, applied to everything we think, say and do and always be remembered by us. (July 27, 1879, JD 20:291)

SALVATION AN INDIVIDUAL MATTER. The great duty devolving upon you and me is to see that we are individually saved. . . . It is for each of us to look at ourselves and examine our own hearts, look at and scrutinize our own conduct, doing that which is right in the sight of God ourselves.

Are we individually complying with those requirements which Jesus gave his Apostles? If we are, it is well with us. If we are not, it matters not how many others are doing wrong; it does not help my case or excuse you in the least degree. But it is for me to do right by myself; it is for me to carry out and practice in my life the principles revealed and which I know to be true; and then whether those on the right or those on the left do wrong, it makes no difference so far as my individual salvation is concerned. . . .

THE DUTY OF SELF-EXAMINATION. It is our duty to indulge in and practice self-examination and self-condemnation if necessary. The man that looks at himself in the light of the Spirit of God and who is a humble man will not find much fault with his fellow-man; for the presence of his own faults arise before him continually when he sees another man's weaknesses, and instead of filling him with self-pride and self-justification and feeling self-righteous, it produces a feeling within him of commiseration for others, and the spirit of charity takes possession of him, and undoubtedly a prayer ascends from his heart to God in behalf of him who had given way to weakness, desiring the Lord to deliver him that he might not be left to be overcome by the adversary. (Sept. 15, 1878, JD 20:95-6)

NO GUARANTEE OF FAITHFULNESS TO THE END. If we will pray unto God continually to show unto us our weaknesses and shortcomings by the light of his Holy Spirit, we then may hope that we will be able to persevere until the end of our lives. I can say for the encouragement of all who are struggling that God is very, very merciful. He is willing to forgive all who come unto Him in humility. All who will ask Him for light, He will give light. All who ask Him for strength, He will give strength. All who ask Him for peace, He will give peace. All who ask Him for joy and happiness of soul, to them He will give these blessings. None will go away unsatisfied.

This is the way to preserve ourselves in the truth so that we can walk without deviation in the straight and narrow path that leadeth unto God. The humblest can do it. The most ignorant can do it. The child can do it. It is not for the wise alone. It is not alone for those who have experience. It is not alone for those who have talent. Every soul can do it, no matter how unlearned or how weak that soul may be. And unless we do this, there is no guarantee for any man in this Church, no matter how great his office may be, that he will be faithful to the end unless he keeps the commandments of God, so that God will be with him.

I believe, however, there are men that have obtained such faith with God that He would not allow them to go astray; He would take their lives from the earth before He would suffer it. As our beloved President has often said to us himself, the Lord would not permit him to do anything that would lead this people wrong. I believe that with all my heart. . . .

KEEPING COMMANDMENTS THE BEST COURSE. But it is far better for us to live. God does not want us to die until we have filled our missions. He does not want to take us away to prevent us from apostatizing. Better to stay here and battle with sin and show our integrity and faithfulness to the very last moment of our existence than have to be taken off to save us. Of course, this is far better than to live and deny the faith; but the best thing is to live and keep the commandments of God, enjoying the fellowship and communion of the Holy Ghost all our days. This is the better course for us to take, and by our faithfulness set an example to our children and to everybody else. (Feb. 17, 1895, DW 50:419)

ONLY SIN CAN INJURE THIS WORK. There is only one thing that can injure this work, and that is the sins of the people themselves. You can injure it—that is, you can injure yourselves in connection with it. There is no man can prevent another from receiving salvation. God has not placed it in the power of man to prevent either a man or a woman or a child from receiving salvation. He has placed that within the power of the individual himself or herself. If a man be damned, it is because he takes a course to be damned; he breaks the laws of God. . . .

CHURCH TO BE CLEANSED OF SINNERS. There are practices being indulged in among us that are sins in the sight of God, and the officers of this Church will be held accountable for them unless they take a course to eradicate them from the midst of the Saints.

There should be no man allowed to remain in this Church who is a Sabbath-breaker, and when you know that there are men and women or children who are Sabbath-breakers, you should take steps to have them warned, to have them reproved and if they will not repent to have them severed from the Church of God.

No man in this Church should be allowed to have a standing in it who is a drunkard; God does not approve of drunkenness; and if there are any drunkards remaining in the Church, hear it, O ye Bishops, and O ye officers, you will be held accountable for their sins—the condemnation will rest upon you.

The same with men who blaspheme, either young or old, who take the name of God in vain, they ought not to be permitted to remain in the Church. It is a sin in the sight of God, and He will visit a people with condemnation who permit these things to exist in their midst.

And so with fornication. No fornicator, no adulterer nor adulteress should have a place among us. They should be warned; they should be dealt with; they should be cut off from the Church. And so with every other sin. We have been too lenient, and have permitted things to exist which are wrong in the sight of God. (Dec. 7, 1884, JD 26:46-7)

CHAPTER 15

BAPTISM—A COVENANT WITH GOD

BAPTISM THE SAME IN ALL AGES. The Gospel, like its Author, is unchangeable and everlasting; it is the same in time and eternity. So, necessarily, are its laws and ordinances. The Gospel was preached to Adam, and he was baptized. The results of baptism were then, as they have ever since been and are now, admission into the Church of Christ and the remission of sins. Baptism was recognized as an ordinance in the service of the true God by the Antediluvians, the Hebrews, the Nephites and by all who worshiped Him correctly, as much so before the advent of the Savior in the flesh as in these latter days. Those who, in those earlier years, sincerely repented and were baptized by one having authority received the remission of their sins, equally with ourselves who accept that ordinance in this dispensation. (Feb. 1, 1894, *JI* 29:78)

OUR COVENANT WITH GOD. When we went forth into the waters of baptism and covenanted with our Father in heaven to serve Him and keep His commandments, He bound Himself also by covenant to us that He would never desert us, never leave us to ourselves, never forget us, that in the midst of trials and hardships, when everything was arrayed against us, He would be near unto us and would sustain us. That was His covenant, and He has amply fulfilled it up to the present time and has shown that we can tie to the promises that He has made. We have proved these things through experience. (Aug. 6, 1893, *DW* 47:346)

BEING BORN AGAIN. Who that is old enough, that can recollect his baptism or her baptism or their first association with the Church and their first enjoyment of the truth, whose hearts do not burn to-day at the recollection of the feeling they had of the sweet and heavenly influence that came to them when they first became acquainted with the everlasting Gospel as preached by the Elders. There was, as it were, a new life opened before them, even the gates of heaven seemed to be opened to them, and they saw the Kingdom of God as they never had seen it and never had understood it. Truths that they had read carelessly and indifferently, without comprehending them, came to their minds with an assurance and with a strength and force and power that they never had comprehended previously. (Aug. 23, 1884, *JD* 25:297)

ORDINANCES ARE NECESSARY. Although an individual who does not believe in obeying ordinances but who is moral and conscientious is more to be admired than the man who, though obeying ordinances, is neither moral nor conscientious, yet this does not make the ordinances nugatory. Such a man we may admire; but, though we may admire and prefer his honesty before the hypocrisy of the other, yet this does not argue that the observance of ordinances ought to be slighted or that he would not be still more admirable and preferable were he obedient thereto. Neither can mankind, if ordinances have been made obligatory, be justified for refusing to become obedient to them because there is a spirit of contention and strife indulged in by professing followers of Christ. (May 10, 1856, *WS* 101-2)

BAPTISM ONLY ONE ROUND OF GOSPEL LADDER. Baptism is . . . only one of the rounds in the Gospel ladder which reaches from the depth of the degradation into which poor humanity has fallen to the Celestial Kingdom of God. But the poor prisoner who wishes to escape from his dungeon must take step after step up the ladder until he reaches the top and can breathe once more the free air of heaven, or he will not be benefited; the ladder is his means for attaining the desired end— liberty. The Gospel is our means of gaining our important end —salvation. But we must obey every principle, or we cannot be saved; we must take every step up the ladder, or we cannot get into the Celestial Kingdom. The moment we set bounds to our faith and works, that moment our salvation ceases. . . .

No individual is justified in neglecting a present duty in order to be better able, as he thinks, to perform a future one. No man can be depended on to do his duty in another sphere or position in life if he does not do so in the one he at present occupies. We must keep our path clear as we go. Let the pages of our lives be free from blot or stain every day, or else the record of our folly and neglect of duty may stare us in the face some day when we shall bitterly regret having given way to such weaknesses. (March 28, 1863, *MS* 25:202-3)

THE AGE OF ACCOUNTABILITY. The revelations of God to the Church in relation to little children are as comforting as they are clear and definite. They are indeed rays of pure light, contrasted with the darkness of the creeds of men. . . .

The word of the Lord through the Prophet Joseph Smith dissipates all doubt and sets at rest all disputes, where it is fully understood. In a revelation given in September, 1830, the Lord said:

But, behold, I say unto you, that little children are redeemed from the foundation of the world through mine Only Begotten; wherefore, they cannot sin, for power is not given unto Satan to tempt little children, until they begin to become accountable before me.[1]

In a revelation given in April, 1830, we find this:

No one can be received into the Church of Christ unless he has arrived unto the years of accountability before God, and is capable of repentance.[2]

In another revelation given in November, 1831, the following law is declared:

And again, inasmuch as parents have children in Zion, or in any of her stakes which are organized, that teach them not to understand the doctrine of repentance, faith in Christ the Son of the Living God, and of baptism and the gift of the Holy Ghost by the laying on of the hands, when eight years old, the sin be upon the heads of the parents.

For this shall be a law unto the inhabitants of Zion, or in any of her Stakes which are organized;

And their children shall be baptized for the remission of their sins when eight years old, and receive the laying on of the hands.

And they shall also teach their children to pray and walk uprightly before the Lord.[3]

It will be seen from a careful reading of these passages that no special age is set as the time when children "begin to become accountable" before the Lord, yet—though there is as much difference in the capabilities of children to comprehend, as there is in their size and complexion—it is made clear they should be baptized at eight years of age. The Redeemer of the world was sinless, yet He was baptized to fulfill all righteousness.

---

[1]D. & C. 29:46-7.   [3]*Ibid.*, 68:25-8.
[2]*Ibid.*, 20:71.

PARENTS' RESPONSIBILITY. We think it safe to say no condemnation will attach to children for acts committed by them prior to their reaching the age of eight years. As soon as children can understand the difference between right and wrong, they can and should be taught the doctrine of repentance, also faith in Christ the Son of the living God and of baptism and the gift of the Holy Ghost. And sin will be on the heads of their parents if they do not teach their children those principles of salvation. Children who understand right from wrong and are taught the law of God in reference to faith, repentance and baptism are accountable for their own sins and also for refusal to submit to the ordinances of the Gospel.

When parents teach their children a right and set them a good example and exercise proper parental influence over them, the parents are not responsible for the sins of the children. When parents neglect these duties, the sin of that neglect will rest upon them, and they will have to answer for it.

All intelligent beings are accountable for the exercise of the agency given to them. Responsibility increases with the development of the creature, and condemnation comes in proportion to the sin, which is gauged by the understanding of wrong and the intent and purpose of the transgressor. (Aug. 1, 1896, JI 31:449-50)

PROPER WORDING OF BAPTISM ORDINANCE. The form of baptism given by the Lord for the baptism of those who are entering into the Church is found in the Book of Doctrine and Covenants. This is the form which should be followed in the baptism of all who present themselves for admission into the Church.

Under President Young's administration, when action was being taken in regard to the United Order, he taught some of the brethren to use the words "into the United Order" in the ceremony of baptism. In the same way the words "for the renewal of your covenants" were used at the time of the Reformation in 1856.

It is always safe, however, for those who officiate in baptisms to confine themselves to the written word. The Lord has given the form, and unless there is some special occasion, when

the man holding the keys suggests another form, it is unsafe and
unwarranted to depart therefrom. (April 1, 1891, *JI* 26:218)

The man holding the keys has the right to instruct the
Elders to modify or change that form, according to circumstances
which may arise from time to time in the Church; but where no
such modification is given, the safe and proper course for the
Elders and Priests in baptizing is to follow the words which the
Lord has given. (Sept. 1, 1891, *JI* 26:535)

BAPTISM FOR REMISSION OF SINS. Baptism is commanded of the Lord and is the ordinance given by Him by which
His children can enter into covenant with Him and obtain the
forgiveness of their sins. After having obeyed this ordinance and
become members of the Church, if people commit sin, they should
repent and confess their sins. If they have sinned against their
brethren or their sisters, they should confess their wrong-doing
to those whom they have wronged, and if to the Lord, they should
confess their sins to the Lord and obtain forgiveness; for the Lord
has promised to forgive all those who truly and sincerely repent
of their sins. . . .

RENEWAL OF COVENANTS BY RE-BAPTISM. There
have been times in the Church when the Prophet of the Lord has
been led to call upon the people to reform and to repent of their
sins, and the people have been aroused from their lethargy and
seen their sinfulness, and they have been permitted to renew
through baptism their covenants with the Lord. This was nota-
bly the case after the Church was led to the valley of the Great
Salt Lake. After the lengthy and trying journey across the
plains, in which the patience of the people was tried and their
faith was severely tested and improper things were done in many
instances because of peculiar circumstances in which the people
were placed, the Saints desired to renew their covenants with the
Lord. The Prophet of the Lord, himself, set the example, and
it became a custom for all who came across the plains in those
weary and trying days to renew their covenants by baptism upon
their arrival in the valley.

There were cases also of persons committing sins of such a
character that after they had confessed them their brethren and
sisters felt they could fellowship them better and more cordially

if they would renew their covenants by baptism. There were other instances where persons absented themselves from the Wards and from association with members of the Church and were gone some time, living under circumstances where they became cold and indifferent, if not sinful, and when they returned and became convinced that they had not lived as they should have and made confession of this, they desired to be re-baptized.

Other persons may have been baptized in their childhood and grown to be men and women without having seriously thought of their religion or the duties devolving upon them as members of the Church; on becoming convinced of the error of this indifference and neglect, they naturally desired to renew their covenants by baptism in order to regain the fellowship of the Saints. There would have been no impropriety in re-baptism in those or in other cases of that kind.

But it is far better for the Latter-day Saints to live day by day so as to not be under the necessity of renewing their covenants by this means. If the Church observes the sacrament properly, sins are confessed and forgiveness is obtained before partaking of the bread and the contents of the cup. (April 15, 1895, *JI* 30:242-3)

TRANSGRESSION AND REBAPTISM. It is not necessary for men and women who transgress to always be re-baptized. A transgressor should make a confession of his sins as publicly as they are known; that is, to use the language of the Lord, in the Book of Doctrine and Covenants,

If thy brother or sister offend many, he or she shall be chastened before many.
And if any one offend openly, he or she shall be rebuked openly, that he or she may be ashamed[4]. . . .

If any one entertains the idea that by baptism alone he can obtain forgiveness and be restored to the fellowship of the Holy Ghost, he is much mistaken. Repentance and the confession of sin are necessary in the case of a man who violates the law of God; and no matter how often he may be baptized without these conditions being observed, he is not promised that his sins will be forgiven. The Lord says also:

---

[4]*Ibid.,* 42:90-1.

If any shall offend in secret, he or she shall be rebuked in secret, that he or she may have opportunity to confess in secret to him or her whom he or she has offended, and to God, that the church may not speak reproachfully of him or her.[5]

Upon these points the law of the Lord is very plain. If these conditions be complied with—that is, repentance and confession of sin—the members of the Church are assured that they will be forgiven.

Whenever the ordinance of baptism is administered, it should be made plain to those who are candidates that to have it attended with the desired blessing there must be sincere and heartfelt repentance. (Jan. 1, 1892, JI 27:27-28)

REPENTANCE AND CONFESSION NECESSARY. It is repentance from sin that will save you, not re-baptism. If you have been baptized, then, if you commit sin, repent of the sin, confess it and make the confession as broad as the knowledge of the sin; confess it to your brethren and sisters, and ask their forgiveness; and do not imagine that when you commit sin you can slip into the waters of baptism and you are all right again. Do not delude yourselves. . . . Sinners, be not deceived by such a fallacy. Something more than this is necessary. We need to repent of our sins and to confess them to God. We need to come before the Lord with broken hearts and contrite spirits and before the Church with the spirit of confession. We should not be afraid to confess our sins; for there is no man among us that is not a sinner. . . .

The Lord, also, is moved with compassion; the angels are moved with mercy and sympathy; and the Lord Jesus, who stands as a mediator between our Father and ourselves, is filled with compassion for His brethren and sisters when they commit sin and repent of it. Oh! all heaven is moved by the repentance of a sinner and stirred up with a desire to help the poor creature who confesses his sins and repents truly and sincerely. (Oct. 6, 1897, CR 55)

---

[5]Ibid., 42:92.

CHAPTER SIXTEEN

THE BIRTH OF THE SPIRIT—THE SPIRIT OF GOD

ORDINANCE OF CONFIRMATION TO BE UN-CHANGED. We should seek to preserve the ordinances which God in his mercy has restored in their ancient power to the earth pure and free from any innovation and change. By so doing the blessings which are to be obtained through that medium will be bestowed, accompanied by the power in which they are desired and sought.

The greatest blessing that can be pronounced upon the heads of those who are being confirmed as members of the Church is to seal upon them in the name of Jesus and by the power of the Holy Priesthood the Spirit of the Lord. All that is said in addition to this at such times has too frequently the effect of feeding the vanity of the persons thus blessed. What necessity is there for more than this?

Can an Elder seal upon the head of any individual any blessing or gift which the Holy Spirit cannot bestow? If not, which all must admit, when the Holy Spirit is sealed upon a person's head, they have received that which comprehends within itself every other blessing which is in the power of the Priesthood at that time to bestow. (Feb. 15, 1862, MS 24:107)

WORDS USED IN CONFIRMING. The words used in the temple in confirming members in the Church are, "Receive ye the Holy Ghost," and though there may be some deviation from that by some persons, that is the phraseology used not only in the temple but by the Elders generally; for the First Presidency have so instructed. (Sept. 15, 1900, JI 35:617)

THE NEW BIRTH OF THE SPIRIT. The gift of the Holy Ghost is given to all those who obey the commandments of God. If grown persons or children of a proper age are baptized, having repented of their sins, the Lord has promised to give them the Holy Ghost. Under the influence of this Spirit they become new creatures. They are born again. Their hearts are changed. The old desires and feelings that they have had are either changed or brought into subjection to the will of God.

If this change does not take place, it is because the person who has been baptized and who has had the laying on of the hands for the gift of the Holy Ghost has not sought for these blessings with diligence. Everyone who submits to the ordinances of the Gospel with sincerity and determination to serve God will undergo this change. All such will be delivered from the bondage of sin, and the consequences of the fall will be mitigated.

It is very desirable that the Latter day Saints should understand that by obeying the Gospel it is their privilege to become new beings. They should exert themselves to obtain all the blessings and gifts which God has promised to those who take this course. He will give them power through the aid of the Holy Ghost, to overcome every evil inclination.

ANGELS OBEYED GOSPEL. We think angels are very holy beings. How did they become holy? How can they dwell in the presence of God? They have become holy through obeying that Gospel which is taught to us. Every child who obeys that Gospel can become an angel in character and disposition. There was a time when angels were mortal as we are, and they were tempted as we are. But they resisted temptation. By the aid of God's Holy Spirit they conquered their evil inclinations. They were born again and continued to resist evil until they became angels. (Dec. 15, 1900, JI 35:823)

CORNELIUS AND THE HOLY GHOST. A great many, to prove that baptism and laying on of hands are not necessary, have cited the case of Cornelius, who, though he was not baptized, received the Holy Ghost. The case of Cornelius is the only case of the kind on record, and there were strong reasons why it should be as it was with him. The Gospel and its ordinances were administered only to the Jews; Cornelius was a Gentile, and between the two races strong prejudices existed, the Jews looking upon the Gentiles as far inferior to them. Cornelius and his household were the first Gentiles to whom the Gospel was preached; they received it, and the Lord, to show to the Apostles that the Gentiles were entitled to the ordinances of salvation as well as the Jews, if they were willing to comply with the requirements of the Gospel, conferred the Holy Ghost upon Cornelius and his family. . . .

Peter took this, as the Lord intended it, as an evidence that the Gentiles as well as the House of Israel were entitled to the Gospel. And he had them baptized and without doubt laid his hands upon them to confirm upon them the gift they had received.

Had Cornelius, at that hour, stood upon his dignity and said, "There is no necessity for me to be baptized for the remission of my sins, God having given me the Holy Ghost without obeying that ordinance, and having already received the Holy Ghost, I have no need to have hands laid upon me," there is not a doubt in my mind but what that precious and inestimable gift would have been withdrawn from him, and he would not have enjoyed it after. It could only be continued to him on condition of his obeying the ordinances which God had placed in his Church and which he required all the inhabitants of the earth to submit to without hesitation; and without doubt Cornelius wisely went forward and obeyed those ordinances. (Aug. 15, 1869, JD 14:50-1)

ONENESS AN EFFECT OF HOLY GHOST. One of the peculiarities of the Holy Ghost, as we read of its effects in the scriptures, was to unite the hearts of those who received it and to make them one. . . .

All that is recorded leads us to suppose that if the Holy Ghost were to be bestowed upon an inhabitant of Europe, upon another person in Asia, another in Africa, and upon a fourth in America and again upon another on the islands of the sea, that these individuals, were they to come together and converse upon the plan of salvation, would entertain precisely similar views respecting that plan. To think otherwise would be to make God, our Heavenly Father, the author of strife and division. (Jan. 31, 1869, JD 12:363)

A SPIRIT OF HEAVENLY PEACE. What joy, peace, love and union have been bestowed upon those who have embraced the Gospel of Jesus Christ! What light has been shed upon their minds in relation to the Scriptures! No sooner have they gone forth into the waters of baptism for the remission of their sins and had hands laid upon them for the Holy Ghost than it has seemed as though a heavenly peace has taken possession of them. . . . It has been "like the dew from heaven descending." It has descended upon the people and filled them with peace and has knit their hearts together in love; and they have rejoiced in the power which God has manifested in their behalf. (Jan. 31, 1869, JD 12:370)

THE TEST OF A TRUE PROPHET. In all the churches of which we have any knowledge there has yet to be heard the promise made by one of its ministers to the humble believer who submits to its ordinances that he shall receive the Holy Ghost as they did in ancient days, with its accompanying gifts and blessings and powers. . . . Joseph Smith made this promise. The world have the opportunity of testing it. If people did not receive the Holy Ghost, then he was an imposter. If they did receive it, then his ministry was sealed by the power of God, and it was indisputable.

The best possible means was given to the human family of testing his claims and his statements. He was either an impostor, trying to deceive the people, or he was a man of God; for it cannot be supposed that heaven would lend itself to an impostor or that heaven would aid in any manner in fostering a deception. (May 27, 1883, JD 24:136)

GOSPEL TRUTH SPIRITUALLY DISCERNED. Hence, for men spiritually unenlightened to be unable to comprehend the things of God is not peculiar to the dispensation in which we live, but it has been so in every age when God made known His will to the children of men. Such individuals may come in contact with the greatest of Heaven's children and may associate with them day by day, and yet through not having that spirit they will fail to recognize their nobility of character and that they are divinely inspired. . . .

No man with his natural wisdom can comprehend the things of God; man never did do it and never can do it. Priests may study all the arts and sciences and finally graduate at a theological college; and after they have passed through it all, they have no more conception of God and the things of God than if such a Being had never existed. A man filled with the power of God might go to them, and they would not understand him; if he told them the most precious things ever uttered by mortal lips, they would not comprehend it and would be far more likely to reject him than not, because they are imbued with prejudices and preconceived ideas respecting God and His works. (March 3, 1867, JD 11:334)

SPIRIT OF GOD STRIVES WITH ALL MEN. We have the sweet influence of the Spirit of God pleading with us to do that which is right, pleading with every human being that does not drive it from him, for every human being has a portion of the Spirit of God given unto him. We sometimes call it conscience; we call it by one name, and we call it by another; but it is the Spirit of God that every man and woman possess that is born on the earth. God has given unto all His children this Spirit. Of course, it is not the gift of the Holy Ghost in its fullness, for that is only received by obedience to the commandments of God—to the Gospel of our Lord and Savior Jesus Christ. But it is a Spirit that pleads with men to do right.

The heathen have it. There is no degraded Indian in these mountains or valleys who does not have a portion of that Spirit pleading with him to do that which is right. It pleads with all the heathen, the Pagan as well as the Christian, the Methodist and Baptist as well as the Latter-day Saints. Everywhere through the earth where man dwells this Spirit rests upon him. It comes from God. It pleads with man to do right. It pleads with man to resist the blandishments of Satan. No man ever did a wrong but that Spirit warned him of it to a greater or less extent. (Sept. 28, 1884, JD 26:191)

THE VOICE OF CONSCIENCE. Some call it the light of conscience, the voice of conscience. No man ever committed a wrong that listened to that voice without being chided for it, whether he be Christian or heathen, whether he has lived according to the light of the Gospel or been in entire ignorance of it. Every man has within him a spirit which comes from our great Creator, and if we grieve it not, it leads us, guides us, though we may not know the Gospel, as has been the case with many thousands and millions of human beings. It leads all the children of men when they listen to it; it leads them in the path of peace, in the path of virtue, and in the path of happiness; but if they violate that spirit or grieve it, if they go contrary to its monitions, if they harden their hearts against and sin against it, then it departs, and another spirit takes its place, namely, the spirit of the evil one. (Nov. 9, 1884, *JD* 26:85)

A WITNESS OF TRUTH. This is not, as I say, confined to one class, nor to one nation nor to one creed; it is as extensive as the human family. Wherever the human family live, they have that spirit with them. Hence it is that when the Gospel is preached, when the Elders bear testimony to the truth of the Gospel and men and women hear it, they will be judged by that testimony; that is, that testimony will stand against them unless they listen to it and obey the Gospel.

Therefore, the servants of God in ancient days, as in our day, could go to the various nations of the earth and proclaim the truth and warn the people, and the people would be under condemnation if they did not receive the testimony of the servants of God; for the witness of the Spirit would be in their own hearts and it would testify to them.

God has not left any of us without a witness. He may withdraw it from us through our hardening our hearts and committing sin, and we may be left in the dark; but otherwise, there is in every human breast a witness of the truth. (Dec. 31, 1893, *DW* 48:162)

A STILL SMALL VOICE. It requires the utmost care upon the part of the people who have received the Spirit of the Lord by the laying on of hands to distinguish between the voice of that Spirit and the voice of their own hearts or other spirits which may take possession of them. Experience and watchfulness will enable the Saint to recognize the voice of the Holy Spirit.

It is a still, small voice in the hearts of the children of men. It is not boisterous, loud or aggressive, and if those who receive it carefully watch its suggestions, it will develop more and more within them, and it will become an unfailing source of revelation. But the necessity always remains of exercising care in distinguishing its voice from the voice of other influences in the heart. (Dec. 1, 1886, *JI* 21:364)

WALK IN THE LIGHT. We see the power of Satan, the knowledge of Satan and his cunning. He understands the avenues through which he can approach us best; he knows the weaknesses of our character, and we do not know the moment we may be seduced by him and be overcome and fall victims to him. Our only preservation is in living near to God, day by day, and serving him in faithfulness and having the light of revelation and truth in our hearts continually so that when Satan approaches we will see him and understand the snare that he has laid for us, and we will have the power to say, "Oh no, God being my helper, I will not yield to it; I will not do that which is wrong; I will not grieve the Spirit of God; I will not deviate from the path that my Father has marked out for me; but I will walk in it."

Can we do this without the light of the Spirit? No, we cannot see where the path upon which we have entered will lead to; we cannot tell what the results will be; but when the light of the Spirit of God illuminates our minds and we are enlightened by it, we plainly see the results; and if we do not see them at the time, the Lord soon reveals them to us and shows us that if we continue to take that course we will grieve his Spirit and fall victims to the adversary. (Oct. 8, 1865, *JD* 11:173-4)

SPIRIT OF GOD PRODUCES HAPPY FEELINGS. Do not allow darkness and gloom to enter into your hearts. I want to give you a rule by which you may know that the spirit which you have is the right spirit. The Spirit of God produces cheerfulness, joy, light and good feelings. Whenever you feel gloomy and despondent and are downcast, unless it be for your sins, you may know it is not the Spirit of God which you have. Fight against it and drive it out of your heart. The Spirit of God is a spirit of hope; it is not a spirit of gloom. (Jan. 14, 1894, *DW* 48:351)

There is nothing on earth, nothing that man can taste or experience that is so sweet, so happifying, so full of delight, as the presence of the Spirit of God. It fills the soul with joy that is inexpressible. (Oct. 6, 1895, *DW* 51:644)

THE RIGHT COURSE TO TAKE. And when you are disturbed in your feelings and assailed with doubt and do not feel happy, withdraw yourselves from the world, leave the cares that press you, lay them aside, withdraw to your secret chamber, and bow yourselves down before your God and entreat him, in the name of Jesus, to give you his Spirit, and do not leave your chamber until you are, as it were, baptized in the Spirit of God and full of peace and joy, all your cares and troubles dissipated and dismissed. This is the course we should take as Latter-day Saints. (July 12, 1874, *JD* 17:130)

A TEST OF THE SPIRIT. Paul advised the people to whom he wrote to try the spirits, whether they were of God or not; and one of the signs—a most important one in that day— was whether the spirit would confess that Jesus was the Christ. That was the crucial test in those days because Jesus had been born a little while before and had been crucified, and He was denounced as an impostor and a man worthy of death. Therefore, the Apostle could well say, "Every spirit that confesseth that Jesus Christ is come in the flesh is of God."[1] But that rule would not apply today with the same force that it did then because the belief in Jesus is almost universal. Times have changed. Jesus is now accepted, and there are comparatively few men who will openly avow their unbelief in Jesus. But the same reasons exist now for trying the spirits that did then to see whether they are of God or not.

I hope no one will think I am sacreligious or that I am lowering my Savior when I say that when I hear a man confess that Joseph Smith is a Prophet I think he has some of the Spirit of God within him, because it is a good deal of a test nowadays. A man who will admit that a man who lived such a life as Joseph Smith is reported to have lived and died such a death as he did is a Prophet of God satisfies me as to whether he is speaking by the Spirit of God or not.

Tests vary according to times and circumstances. That which might have been a very excellent test 1900 years ago might not be so much of a test now. Yet when a man today confesses Jesus he does speak by the Spirit of God. There is no doubt about that. That has not changed. It is the Spirit of God that prompts men to acknowledge Jesus, just as much now as it ever did. But it is not such a test now as it was in ancient days. There were very few then that dare do it; and whenever they did it, they did it, it may be said, almost with the fear of their lives before them,

---

[1] I John 4:2.

because the whole world was arrayed against the Savior and ready to pounce upon any man who acknowledged Him to be the Son of God.

ALL GOOD COMETH FROM GOD. But we can test the spirits now. Everything that is good cometh from God, I care not where it may be. Do other churches have good in them as well as the Church of Christ? Certainly. . . . There is truth throughout the earth. Men are possessed of it everywhere. Even the pagans possess it, and according to the light which they have and their lives being in accordance with that light, they are accepted of God.

Every sincere man who lives up to the light that he has is accepted of God to that extent. Before God in his infinite wisdom and mercy revealed the everlasting Gospel in this dispensation, there were great numbers of faithful men and women living on the earth, and according to the light they had, lived acceptably to God. . . .

The earth had many, many such people in it, and the various sects had these people in them. So it is today. Our Elders are commanded to go out and find these people; to find the honest, the meek, the humble and the people who want to know about God. (Sept. 18, 1892, *DW* 45:451)

GOD TO REVEAL HIMSELF. Now, listen to the voice of His Spirit. Cultivate that Spirit and seek for it by night and by day. If you will do this, I say to you that God will reveal Himself unto you as He has never done before; the visions of eternity will be open to you; angels will minister unto you, and the power of God will descend upon you, as individuals and as a people. I tell you this in the name of the Lord and as His servant. This will most assuredly be the case with this people if they will do as the Lord requires at their hands and exercise faith and put away evil from them. (April 17, 1898, *DW* 56:708)

STRAYING FROM THE TRUTH. It requires continual vigilance on the part of those the Lord has placed as authorities in His Church to prevent the growth of fashions and forms that are contrary to the spirit of the Gospel of the Lord Jesus Christ. Incidents frequently occur in the experience of the Church of Jesus Christ of Latter-day Saints which illustrate the manner in which the primitive Church, established by the Savior, fell into the grievous errors that resulted in the withdrawal of the power of God from it. It requires constant watchfulness now to prevent aberrations from the right path, even with the full organization of the Priesthood in the Church.

In the ancient Church the Head of the Church—the Savior Himself—was slain; His Apostles whom He had chosen to take charge of the ministry and to build up His Church in the earth were also slain; and every man that had that authority was taken from the people. Little by little the organization strayed from the truth and from the correct manner of administering ordinances, etc., and darkness soon prevailed.

In our own day the same results would follow if it were not for the authority of the Apostleship exercising continued watchfulness over the Church. Paul pointed out the necessity of this authority always being in the church. . . .[2]

AVOID USE OF PREPARED ORDINANCE FORMS. The Lord Himself has given us, by revelation, the manner in which we shall ask a blessing in administering the sacrament and the form of words that we shall use in baptizing. Moroni has, also, in the Book of Mormon, told us how Priests and Teachers were ordained among the Nephites. Beyond this the Lord has not gone.

The Holy Ghost has been given for the express purpose, among other things, of inspiring men to perform all the duties which belong to the Priesthood; and it is but little less than sacrilege for any man, in and of himself, to frame a form of ordination for others to adopt. Where this has been done, it has doubtless been done with the best of intentions, but, nevertheless, is it not an assumption of one of the functions which belong to one of the Godhead—the Holy Ghost? Where these forms are adopted, those who use them are in a position where, if the Holy Ghost should inspire them to say anything to a person whom they were ordaining or setting apart or blessing, they could not do so without departing from this prepared form. . . .

SPEAK BY POWER OF THE SPIRIT. Now, there can

[2]Ephesians 4:11-14

be no objection to the Elders thoroughly studying every principle which belongs to the Gospel and in mastering all the proofs within their reach that will sustain the truth of those principles. It is the duty of every man bearing the Priesthood and who ministers the word to do this and to fill his mind with all the good things he can obtain to give to the people. But it is contrary to the instructions which the Lord has given and to the practice of the servants of God to arrange beforehand what they shall say to the people while ministering the word of God unto them. It is true there may be some special occasions when it may be necessary for men to speak on certain subjects; but even when this is the case, if they do right, they will leave it to the Spirit of God to direct their minds as to the manner in which they will present the subject. Under the guidance of the Holy Ghost they may speak upon collateral subjects or even upon subjects that had not been thought about by them.

No man can be a true minister of the word of God who does not leave himself to be dictated by the Spirit of God. Whenever he attempts to arrange beforehand what he shall say to the people and the manner in which he shall treat the subject, he checks the Spirit to that extent and prevents the free flow thereof to him. The Lord does not want His servants to talk mechanically to the people but to speak to them under the influence and by the power of the Holy Ghost. It is that power and that alone that can give to the speaker the bread of life which the people stand in need of. And when the servants of God are dictated by that Spirit, the people who listen to them are edified, and convincing power attends their words, and the Elders themselves are also benefited by that which the Lord gives. (March 15, 1898, JI 33:212-4)

CHAPTER 17

MIRACLES AND SIGNS—GIFTS OF THE GOSPEL

GOD PERFORMS NO MIRACLES. God always acts in accordance with well-defined and understood laws and does not violate the laws of nature in the least in performing all his wonderful works. Because men, not comprehending how such works are performed, term them miraculous, it does not necessarily follow that there is a suspension of the laws of nature in such cases; neither does it follow, because men can partially comprehend a law according to which certain results are produced, that God has nothing to do with it. Everything that the Lord himself performs or which he commands his servants to perform is plain and simple and easily understood by Him—it is no miracle to Him, because He comprehends the law by the observance of which such things are produced.

Mankind term such works miracles and supernatural, because they have not progressed sufficiently to understand how they can be done without the suspension of the laws of nature. Did they fully understand all the laws of nature, however, they would then perceive that in the performance of these "miracles" no law of nature is in the least violated but rather that they are produced by the superior knowledge of these laws which the person has who works them or the Being who permits them to be worked. (Nov. 1, 1856, *WS* 235-6)

It was no suspension of law on the part of our Savior that caused Him to gather from the elements the bread and the fishes necessary to feed the multitude. It was no suspension of law that caused Him to open the eyes of the blind or to cause the sick to be healed. (May 4, 1884, *JD* 25:150)

CESSATION OF MIRACLES WAS GRADUAL. Speaking of the cessation of miracles in the early Christian church, Burton, in his Ecclesiastical History (Vol. II, page 233) remarks that "their actual cessation was imperceptible, and like the rays in a summer's evening, which, when the sun has set, may be seen to linger on the top of a mountain, though they have ceased to fall on the level country beneath."

There has been an impression in many minds that miracles ceased with the death of the Apostles and that they were not designed for the Church or its officers after their day. . . . But Burton, in the words we have quoted above, truly describes the manner in which these miraculous gifts and powers disappeared from among men. They were not withdrawn all at once; but they gradually faded away like the rays of the declining sun until they disappeared altogether and darkness set in.

There was a cause for this. Faith had decreased. Mankind would not have the pure word of God. They persecuted and slew the men who had the Priesthood and who received revelation from God. The result was the Church was gradually overcome, the authority which the Lord acknowledged was withdrawn and spiritual gifts departed.

SPIRITUAL GIFTS COMMON FOR TWO CENTURIES. For upwards of two centuries after the birth of the Lord Jesus these spiritual gifts were common in the Christian Church.

Justin Martyr, one of the early Christians, published a composition which is called "Dialogue with Trypho," in which he defended Christianity against the attacks of Judaism. This was not far from the year A. D. 150. In this "Dialogue" he says:

> Among us also you may see both males and females possessing gifts from the Spirit of God.

In one of his "Apologies" the same writer says:

> For many of our Christian people, exercising in the name of Jesus Christ, who was crucified under Pontius Pilate, have cured, and are even now curing, many demoniacs in your own city and in all parts of the world, though these persons could not be cured by all other exorcists, and enchanters and sorcerers. But ours have overcome and driven out the demons that possessed these men.

It seems from this testimony that in Justin Martyr's time, upwards of one hundred and fifty years after the birth of the Lord, the spiritual gifts were in the Church and also the power to cast out devils.

Quadratus, who was Bishop of Athens in the early part of the second century, is credited with the power of working miracles. One of the old writers, who had the works of Papias before him, states:

(Papias) relates that a dead man was raised in his time, and moreover that another wonderful thing occurred to Justus, who was surnamed Barsabas, namely, that he drank a deadly poison, and suffered no unpleasant effects, on account of the grace of the Lord.

The writer does not say how it was that Justus came to drink this poison; but if it is true that he did drink it, it is altogether likely he did it without knowing what it was and not to give the people a sign or to show them the power that the Lord had given to him.

Irenaeus speaks of miracles as still common in Gaul (the land now known to us as France) when he wrote, which was nearly at the close of the second century. He says:

On this account also His true disciples, receiving grace from Him, perform miracles in His name for the benefit of men, as each of them has received the gift from Him. For some truly and really expel demons; . . . and others have foreknowledge of the future, and visions, and prophetic utterances. Others heal the sick and make them well, by the imposition of their hands. And even now, as we have said, the dead have also been raised, and have remained with us many years.

He says again:

As also we have many brethren in the church having prophetic gifts, and speaking in all foreign tongues, and bringing to light the secrets of men, for a good purpose.

Tertullian and other writers of about the same period are witnesses to the continuance at their day of the power of casting out devils.

Papias, Quadratus, Justin Martyr and Irenaeus, whose names we have mentioned, were all martyred on account of their religion. Most of those in eminent positions in the Church in that day were martyred. The world hated not only the Apostles but all who held the Priesthood and destroyed them from the face of the earth.

PERSECUTION CEASED WITH LOSS OF GIFTS. The testimony of these men concerning the spiritual gifts which were in the Church is important. Is not the cause of the disappearance of these gifts plain to be seen? How could these heavenly gifts be continued in the Church when all who possessed them were hunted and slain?

Persecution of the Church ceased when there were no more victims to be offered up, when no man remained who received revelation from heaven, when the Church no longer possessed spiritual gifts. The Church and the world were then alike reduced to a dead level, true faith no longer remained and the causes of hatred with the world against the Church had all vanished.

If they vanished like the rays of the setting sun, shall they not return like the rays of the rising sun? (Dec. 15, 1888, *JI* 23:376)

SOME MIRACLES A RESULT OF FAITH. That men, unauthorized of God, will in Christ's name perform wondrous works, is evidenced from the words of the Savior. He tells us that in the great hereafter men will come to him and say, "Have we not prophesied in thy name? and in thy name have cast out devils? and in thy name done many wonderful works?" And He will say unto them, "I never knew you: depart from me, ye that work iniquity."[1] They had never received authority from Him to use His name. Nevertheless, they will state they had used it and that, too, if they can be believed, effectually in performing many wonderful works.

We hear of miracles being performed in the Roman Catholic, the Methodist and other churches. Some of these, doubtless, were works of impostures, but all were not. In many cases they were the result of true faith in the power of Jesus' name; in many instances those who received the blessings were living up to the best light they had, dim though it might be. (March 1, 1894, *JI* 29:144-5)

GOSPEL NOT DEPENDENT ON MIRACLES FOR SUPPORT. The Gospel of Jesus was not and is not dependent on miracles alone for the evidence necessary to support its truthfulness. . . . By a careful perusal of the Scriptures we find that Jesus did not work miracles to convince the people of the truth of His system, neither did His Apostles. If they had recognized this as being the correct way of converting men, they certainly would have adopted it; and no man could have been condemned for not embracing their doctrines who had not beheld a supernatural (as we have it) exhibition of power. He, however, before His ascension into heaven, in speaking to His disciples, plainly

---

[1]Matthew 7:22-3.

and pointedly said that these signs or exhibitions of power should follow them that believed—they were to be the consequences of faith and not the only foundation for faith to be based upon. . . .

Although miracles may be performed independently of a correct system, yet, we do maintain that whenever the Gospel of Jesus is preached in its purity, they must also of necessity—if there can be any reliance placed on the words of our Savior—accompany it. The principle of faith and obedience to the commandments always did and always will produce this power; and when obtained and enjoyed by these means, it will be one evidence, among a host of others, that the doctrine they have embraced is an emanation of the Deity. We can not conceive how men can prove to their own satisfaction that the Gospel of Christ as recorded in the Bible is true or that the Bible itself is what it purports to be on any other principle than this; indeed, it is the only principle upon which definite knowledge can be obtained. If the miracles recorded in the Bible were the only evidence that we had to rely upon for the truth of these things, we should consider our faith had but a poor foundation, and we certainly should be fearful of an attack upon it. (March 8, 1856, WS 20-1)

SIGNS ALONE DO NOT GIVE A TESTIMONY. The healing of the sick and the speaking in tongues are two of the gifts which the Lord has promised to those who obey His Gospel. Where these gifts exist in the Church, they are, as far as they go, evidences of the true Gospel. But while that is so, there have been cases of the sick being healed by those who were not members of the Church of Jesus Christ; and there have been cases in our own Church where persons have spoken in tongues under a wrong influence and spirit. Therefore, these signs alone do not give a testimony of the truth of the Gospel; neither are they a testimony that the person or persons who do these things are true servants of God.

The signs which Jesus said should follow the believers are a great comfort to those who possess them, and they are a cause of rejoicing to those who witness them. But experience has taught the Church that those who embrace the Gospel because they see signs, and depend upon them alone for evidence of the truth of the Gospel, do not have a good foundation for their faith, and they frequently fall away. Something more than these is needed as a foundation for faith and as a testimony of the truth of the Gospel. The reliable testimony must come from within—that is, the Saint should have the testimony of the Holy Ghost within. Outward signs and evidences go to corroborate and strengthen the inward testimony.

After this explanation we may . . . say that the seeing of the sick healed and the hearing of one speak in tongues and these alone are only a partial testimony of the truth of the Gospel. In and of themselves they are not sufficient to furnish such a testimony as Latter-day Saints ought to have. (July 15, 1898, JI 33:513)

SIGNS NOT GIVEN TO CONVERT PEOPLE. Jesus Himself gave no signs to convince unbelievers. When applied to Himself to give a sign, He said it was a wicked and an adulterous generation that sought for a sign and no sign should be given them. And on one occasion, when He visited a certain place, it is recorded of Him that He did no miracle because of the unbelief of the people. Now, it would seem that if signs had to be given to convince the people that would have been the best place Jesus could have labored, a place where unbelief was most prevalent, and where He himself was appealed to. But He refused to do so.

He did not come for the purpose of giving men signs. They were told in the Scriptures that "these signs shall follow them that believe;"[2] they should not come to convince men and to make them believe. . . .

MIRACLES WROUGHT BY FALSE PROPHETS. In fact we are told in the scriptures that the day would come when miracles should be wrought by false prophets, and men would be deceived by false evidence of this character. It is an easy thing to deceive the senses; we see it every time our theatre is occupied by a magician—we see things done that hoodwink our senses. Our eyes are deceived; our ears are deceived; all our senses are deceived by shrewd, cunning men, by men who are experts in manipulating various articles, and if they were to

---

[2]Mark 16:17.

set themselves up as the apostles of some system and declare
that these were the evidences of the divinity of that system and
we should believe this sort of evidence, we might be converted
to error.

All those who are familiar with the Bible know the experience of Moses before Pharaoh. There was scarcely a miracle
that Moses wrought that the magicians of the king did not
imitate, and every miracle that was wrought only tended to
harden the heart of the king and make him determined that
he would not let the children of Israel go; so we see that miracles
in and of themselves are no evidence of the divinity of any
system, nor of the power and the authority from God of the
men who work them. . . .

THOSE CONVERTED BY SIGNS WEAK IN FAITH.
I do not believe that men can be convinced as they should be
convinced by such manifestations. It has been a matter of remark among those who have had experience in this Church
that where men have been brought into the Church by such
manifestations, it has required a constant succession of them
to keep them in the Church; their faith has had to be constantly
strengthened by witnessing some such manifestations; but where
they have been convinced by the outpouring of the Spirit of
God, where their judgment has been convinced, where they have
examined for themselves and become satisfied by the testimony
of Jesus in answer to their prayers and to their faithful seeking
unto the Lord for knowledge—where this has been the case,
they have been more likely to stand, more likely to endure persecution and trial than those who have been convinced through
some supernatural manifestation of the character to which I
have alluded. (July 24, 1881, *JD* 22:360-2)

GIFTS GIVEN FOR PERFECTION OF SAINTS. The
Prophet Moroni explains more fully even than Paul does concerning these gifts. He said "that if the day cometh that the
power and gifts of God shall be done away among you, it shall
be because of unbelief."[3] Not because God is not willing to
bestow gifts upon His children, for as this Prophet says, "God
is not a partial God, neither a changeable Being; but he is un-

---

[3]Moroni 10:24.

changeable from all eternity to all eternity."[4] His dealings with the children of men are alike. If they come to Him with faith and obey His Gospel, He is bound by the promises that He has made to bestow upon them the same blessings and not to discriminate between His children; for if He did so, He would not be a just Being. But justice is His attribute, and He deals justly with His children. He gives unto them His gifts and blessings according to their faith. To one He gives one gift, to another He gives another gift.

These gifts are given by Him for the perfection of His people, that in this vale of tears, shut out as we are from His presence, a veil of darkness having been drawn, as it were, between us and Him, those who will exercise faith in His promises and will keep His commandments may receive the aid that is necessary to enable them to walk before Him and to enjoy His power. . . .

GIFTS DISTINGUISH SAINTS FROM THE WORLD. He can receive the evidences from the Lord, by the exercise of faith, that will convince him of the existence of his Father in heaven and also of His willingness to hear and answer the prayers and supplications which are addressed to Him in sincerity.

It is for this purpose that these gifts are bestowed, that those who do obey the commandments of God shall have privileges, blessings and powers that those who do not take this course cannot have. The bestowal of these is to create a distinction between the people of God and those who are not His people, to give them that superiority which the enjoyment of these gifts bring. . . .

OUR DUTY TO SEEK AFTER GIFTS. How many of you are seeking for these gifts that God has promised to bestow? How many of you, when you bow before your Heavenly Father in your family circle or in your secret places, contend for these gifts to be bestowed upon you? How many of you ask the Father in the name of Jesus to manifest Himself to you through these powers and these gifts? Or do you go along day by day like a door turning on its hinges, without having any feeling upon

4Ibid., 8:18.

the subject, without exercising any faith whatever, content to be baptized and be members of the Church and to rest there, thinking that your salvation is secure because you have done this?

I say to you, in the name of the Lord, as one of His servants, that you have need to repent of this. You have need to repent of your hardness of heart, of your indifference and of your carelessness. There is not that diligence, there is not that faith, there is not that seeking for the power of God that there should be among a people who have received the precious promises we have. . . .

If any of us are imperfect, it is our duty to pray for the gift that will make us perfect. Have I imperfections? I am full of them. What is my duty? To pray to God to give me the gifts that will correct these imperfections. . . . They are intended for this purpose. No man ought to say, "Oh, I cannot help this; it is my nature." He is not justified in it, for the reason that God has promised to give strength to correct these things and to give gifts that will eradicate them. . . . That is the design of God concerning His children. He wants His Saints to be perfected in the truth. (Nov. 26, 1893, *DW* 48:34-5)

The Lord has said in a revelation to the Church that the Saints should "seek ye earnestly the best gifts, always remembering for what they are given; for verily I say unto you, they are given for the benefit of those who love me and keep all my commandments."[5] How many Latter-day Saints are there who supplicate the Lord for the gifts which they need? . . .

Every defect in the human character can be corrected through the exercise of faith and pleading with the Lord for the gifts that He has said He will give unto those who believe and obey His commandments. (Oct. 1, 1896, *JI* 31:572)

WE ALL NEED GIFTS. Is there any one among us that does not need these gifts? I need prophecy. How can I magnify my office, how can I stand in my calling, how can I do my duty to the Latter-day Saints in the office to which God has called me, unless I have the gift of prophecy? That gift I should seek to have increase upon me. The gift of revelation should increase

---

[5]D. & C. 46:8-9.

within me. I should seek for the gift of wisdom, to have it increase within me, the gift of knowledge also. Should we not all do so?

You need to have patience, long-suffering, forbearance. A presiding officer in the Church needs the gift of instruction, the gift of counsel and, when needed, the gift of reproof and warning. He needs to understand the plan of salvation and what constitutes godliness; he needs to have the gift of healing and the gift of the discernment of spirits.

We all need to have the gift of a broken heart and a contrite spirit, for that is the offering that is acceptable to the Lord. When we come to Him with broken hearts and contrite spirits, He hears us, and He accepts the offering. It is the offering that He asks at our hands. . . .

GIFT OF TONGUES. If I were called on a mission to a people speaking a foreign language, I should pray constantly for the gift of tongues and for the gift of the interpretation of tongues. . . . I know that such a gift is within the reach of those who seek for it. It is not alone given to us to get up in our testimony meetings and speak in tongues and somebody interpret it. That is very comforting and a very desirable gift when it is governed properly. It appeals to many people; they think it is a wonderfully great gift. But in my experience it is a gift that is apt to lead people astray unless it is properly controlled. Under its influence people sometimes give way to a wrong spirit. . . .

This gift, as I have said, is a desirable gift; but it is especially desirable for our Elders who go to foreign lands. They should seek for it with all earnestness and faith. I testify to you that there is such a gift as the gift of interpretation of tongues.

So in relation to all these precious gifts. Why, what is our religion if we divest it of these gifts and we do not possess them? It is a powerless thing. But with the bestowal of these gifts, with the Lord giving them to us according to our needs, each one in his or her place, there is power in our religion.

GIFTS FOR MOTHERS. The sisters have as much right to these gifts as the brethren. They have the right to go unto God and ask Him in the name of Jesus to bestow upon them such gifts as they need. How good a gift it would be for a mother to have the gift of governing her children, the gift of wisdom to train them and to point out to them the path that they should pursue. The mother who seeks for these gifts and exercises them before the Lord will have great joy in her children and will get amply rewarded for all the faith that she has exercised and the prayers she has offered in their behalf. . . .

PATIENCE AND INTEGRITY. The Lord said to Joseph in the beginning, "Be patient in afflictions; for thou shalt have many."[6] So it is with all of us. We have great afflictions from time to time. It seems to be necessary that we should be tried and proved to see whether we are full of integrity or not. In this way we get to know ourselves and our own weaknesses; and the Lord knows us, and our brethren and sisters know us.

Therefore, it is a precious gift to have the gift of patience, to be good-tempered, to be cheerful, to not be depressed, to not give way to wrong feelings and become impatient and irritable. It is a blessed gift for all to possess.

The gift of integrity also is a splendid gift. Men may do many wicked things, and repent of them and the Lord will forgive them, if they have integrity. I value that gift exceedingly. . . . The gift of integrity is a good thing. It is good also to have steadfastness, valor and courage in the hour of trial and danger—in the hour when men's lives are in danger. (Feb. 12, 1899, *MS* 62:355-7)

DISCERNING OF SPIRITS. One of the gifts of the Gospel which the Lord has promised to those who enter into covenant with Him is the gift of discerning of spirits—a gift which is not much thought of by many and probably seldom prayed for; yet it is a gift that is of exceeding value and one that should be enjoyed by every Latter-day Saint. . . . No Latter-day Saint should be without this gift, because there is such a variety of spirits in the world which seek to deceive and lead astray. In a revelation to the Church upon the spirits which have gone abroad in the earth the Lord says:

Behold, verily I say unto you, that there are many spirits which are false spirits, which have gone forth in the earth, deceiving the world.[7]

[6]*Ibid.*, 24:8.   [7]*Ibid.*, 50:2.

The Lord warns the Saints and says: "Beware lest ye are deceived."[8] And that they may not be deceived, He commands them to seek earnestly the best gifts.

The Apostle John says:

Behold, believe not every spirit, but try the spirits whether they are of God: because many false prophets are gone out into the world.[9]

This counsel of the beloved Apostle applies as much to us in these latter days as it did to the Saints of his age. All manner of spirits have gone forth to deceive, to lead astray and to obtain possession of the children of men; and many people yield to them because they are invisible and cannot, perhaps, think that they can be possessed by invisible influences. Anger, backbiting, slander, falsehood and various passions are manifested by people under the influence of false and deceptive spirits. . . .

Now, the gift of discerning of spirits not only gives men and women who have it the power to discern the spirit with which others may be possessed or influenced, but it gives them the power to discern the spirit which influences themselves. They are able to detect a false spirit and also to know when the Spirit of God reigns within them. In private life this gift is of great importance to the Latter-day Saints. Possessing and exercising this gift they will not allow any evil influence to enter into their hearts or to prompt them in their thoughts, their words or their acts. They will repel it; and if perchance such a spirit should get possession of them, as soon as they witness its effects they will expel it or, in other words, refuse to be led or prompted by it.

The gift of discerning of spirits, also, is one that is of great importance to the Elders who are laboring in the ministry. We have known Elders become so filled with zeal and so desirous to do good, or what they supposed to be good, that they exposed themselves to the influence of the adversary. They would be filled with a species of what has been called "wildfire," and, carried away by zeal, they would go too far; they would say and do imprudent things and yet, being prompted by the purest and best motives, would feel entirely justified in their course. In the history of the Church there have been many illustrations of this.

---

[8]*Ibid.*, 46:8.   [9]I John 4:1.

Elders can work themselves up beyond that which is proper and wise and be led to say and do many imprudent things and overstep the line of propriety. Now, the gift of discerning of spirits is necessary to keep these kind of feelings in check.

The gift of discerning spirits is not only necessary for this purpose, but it is necessary in the branches of the Church. Newly baptized members, anxious to obtain the gifts, are liable sometimes to be taken advantage of by the adversary and to imbibe or yield to a wrong spirit. A newly organized branch of the Church, where the gifts are manifested, especially the gift of tongues, has to be watched with great care. The Elders laboring in the branch or presiding in the conference must be in a position to discern between the Spirit of the Lord and other spirits that may seek to steal in. . . .

In all the situations in life, therefore, in which Latter-day Saints can be placed there is great need for them to possess the gift of discerning of spirits. Fathers and mothers need it for their own benefit. They need it in their families, in the training of their children. All Saints need it to enable them to escape from the many evil influences that are abroad. The Elders need it for their own sakes; they need it also in the government of the branches, of the conferences, of the wards, of the stakes and, indeed, the entire Church. It is a great and blessed gift, and it should be sought for by all. (Oct. 1, 1896, *JI* 31:572-4)

GIFTS OF GOSPEL NOT CONFINED TO GENERAL AUTHORITIES. I hope the idea will never prevail among our people that God confines his gifts and graces to the First Presidency or to the Twelve Apostles or to the Seven Presidents of Seventies. I know that God is the God of this people, and every young man or middle-aged man or aged man who will seek for the power of God can obtain it, and he can declare the truth of God in the power and demonstration of the Holy Ghost, and it is just as good as if it were told by the President of the Church or by one of the Twelve Apostles. . . .

The field is white for the harvest, and laborers are wanted. It is beyond the power of the First Presidency and Twelve to do all the labor. Therefore, the Elders are called to the ministry, and they should seek for the gifts and for the power and authority of the Holy Priesthood and exercise it and not think because they are not Apostles or Presidents that therefore they have not the right to teach and to speak with authority. If you have any doubts upon this, read . . . what the Lord says upon this point.[10] (Oct. 5, 1894, *DW* 49:642)

[10]D. & C. 68:2-12.

CHAPTER 18

UNITY—A PRINCIPLE OF STRENGTH

THE PRINCIPLE OF UNION. The principle of union . . . is one of the most delightful features connected with this Church. I would not give much for a system of religion that did not make its followers one and did not unite them, because it would fail in the most essential feature. One cannot conceive of a pure religion that would lack the great qualification of making those who believed it and espoused it one in their feelings, in their faith and their actions.

All our ideas of heaven cause us to feel that dissension and division, strife and factional differences and contention concerning any important point are effectually excluded from that blest abode. We picture hell, when we picture it at all, as a place where devils contend and quarrel and fight and where union and love are entirely absent. We cannot conceive of hell being a place of love and oneness, because if love reigned it would cease to be hell. If love did not reign in heaven, nor union and peace abound there, it would not be heaven.

Therefore, inasmuch as religion is given for the purpose of preparing us to dwell eternally with God our Eternal Father, it is natural that we should expect that religion would have the effect upon mankind to give them a foretaste of that bliss and union and love and peace, the full realization of which is expected to be enjoyed in heaven. I think I am justified, therefore, in saying that if a religion does not produce union among its followers, it is unworthy of the acceptance of mankind and of very little value to any of us.

A DISTINGUISHING FEATURE. The distinguishing feature of the religion taught by Jesus was that it would make His followers one; and He gave this as one of the evidences by which the world might know it was true. His last prayer was that His disciples might be one, even as He and the Father were one, thus showing that, according to the idea of the Great Founder of our religion, it was capable of making us one, even as closely as the Father and Son are one. When we come short of this ideal perfection and union, we come short of being the people of God.

CONTENTION TO BE AVOIDED. Whenever factions exist among us, whenever disunion prevails, whenever there is opposition in views concerning points of doctrine or concerning counsel, it may be set down as indisputable that the Spirit of God is not in our midst and that there is something wrong. Whenever two men in this Church differ upon points of doctrine, they may know and others who may be acquainted with the fact may know also that there is something wrong; for the Spirit of God will not teach two men different ideas. If it teaches one man a truth, it will not teach another man something that is opposite to that truth. If it gives to the presiding officer in the Church, or to a man in authority, certain counsel to give to the people, it will not give to another man different counsel. If there should be a difference, the very fact that there is such a difference ought to convince the parties themselves that the Spirit of God does not reign in their hearts.

Is it right for Latter-day Saints to contend and to have arguments? It is not right; it is not according to the mind and will of God. Whenever two Elders contend and argue, they may know and everyone may know that the Spirit of God is not there to the extent that it should be, because where the Spirit of God reigns there is no contention, no controversy. Men may differ in their views, but after they have expressed these differences then contention should cease; in fact, it should never exist. (Aug. 3, 1890, *DW* 41:484)

SPIRIT OF ONENESS SHOULD CHARACTERIZE DISCIPLES OF JESUS. It is evident that the Savior designed that the spirit of oneness and of love and union should character- ize His disciples and those who obeyed His commandments. He says . . ., "A new commandment I give unto you, That ye love one another," and He continued, "By this shall all men know that ye are my disciples, if ye have love one to another."[1] They were to be distinguished as His disciples by their love one for another. If this characteristic should be absent, there would be nothing, according to these words, to distinguish His disciples

---

[1]John 13:34-35.

from those who were not His disciples. John has also recorded that if we love Him we will keep His commandments. As disciples of the Lord Jesus, we should show our love for Him by keeping His commandments. Those who love Him not will not keep His commandments.

These features which the Lord Jesus impressed upon His disciples are the attractive features of the Gospel which He preached; and where this love and this union, which He so beautifully describes, are absent, then there is evidence that His commandments are not being kept and that those who are in that condition are not His disciples.

In these words that I have read we have the means of testing His Gospel and of proving who are His disciples. When men say they want some evidence concerning the truth of the Gospel, they have in these characteristics the tests by which they can ascertain for themselves whether those who profess to be the disciples of the Lord are such in reality. (Nov. 14, 1897, *MS* 60:146)

THE POWER OF A UNITED PEOPLE. Now, what have we to fear? The only cause of fear in my mind is concerning ourselves—divisions, differences of views, ideas concerning the course that should be pursued that may not be in accordance with the mind and will of God. It is of the utmost importance to us as a people that we should be united. Our strength, our prosperity, our success in the past have been due to union. It is the union of the people that has been hated and that has brought upon us the persecution that we have had to contend with. That is all that gives us importance in the earth. . . .

The fact that these people are united creates a dread in the breasts of those who dislike them. It is this that has given us influence, that has given us importance, that has made us what we are, that causes us to occupy the position that we do. Take this away from us, and we are indeed . . . like salt that has lost its savor, good for nothing but to be thrown out and trampled under foot of men. Take away from us as a people the principle of union, and you take away from us the salt that makes us the savor that we are today. And it is of the utmost importance for us as a people that we should keep this constantly in view. (Dec. 2, 1883, *JD* 24:361)

THE ONENESS OF THE FATHER AND THE SON. Now, can you conceive of a oneness more close, more complete than the oneness that exists between the Father and the Son? It is impossible for the human mind to get the faintest idea of any difference of opinion or expression or action between the Father and the Son. We worship them as one God—not three Gods, not two Gods but as one God. The Father and the Son are the two personages of the Deity, with the Holy Ghost as their ministering Spirit or agent. We worship them as one. We do not separate them in our thoughts and in our feelings. . . .

While they are two Personages, they are but one—one in feeling, one in thought, one in mind, one in everything, in fact, in every direction in which their power is or can be exercised. And in all the records that have come down to us from the Son of God there is one thing that stands out clearly and prominently throughout all the teachings and acts of our Lord and Savior Jesus Christ and that is His entire devotion to the Father, His complete submission to the will of the Father and His oft-expressed desire to know and to do that will. It is wonderful the submission that the Savior manifested in His life, when we think of His great dignity and the position that He occupied. . . .

DISUNITY THE SOURCE OF OUR TROUBLES. Can any of you put your finger on any serious trouble that we have had that has not had its origin in professed Latter-day Saints dissenting from us and turning against us? I tell you . . . there is no power on earth, there is no power in the domains of the damned that can shake or disturb this people if they are only united. No matter what course we may take, so long as it is in righteousness, if we are united, we can stand against the world and all its assaults. We can stand not only against visible enemies, but we can stand against the invisible hosts of darkness which Lucifer has at his command; and we can stand unshaken and unmoved amid the tempests that may break upon us, or whatever may be the character of the assault that may be made upon us. . . .

When dissension comes in our midst, when disunion manifests itself, when you see men who call themselves Latter-day Saints yielding to the spirit of Satan and rebelling in their feelings against the Spirit of God and the work of God, then there is cause for apprehension and for us to tremble, if we ever do tremble, because that is and always has been the fruitful source of our troubles, and it always will be.

CHIEF CORNERSTONE OF CHURCH SUPERSTRUCTURE. Union, therefore, ought to be the keynote of the entire people as it is the chief cornerstone of the superstructure of the Church. It ought to be more desirable than anything else among us. How shall we obtain it? Shall we have it by each man having his own way and carrying out his own designs? Was that the way Jesus, our great Exemplar, did?

"Ah! but," I have heard it said, "that takes away man's independence." There are some people who seem to have the idea that rebellion and disobedience are evidences of independence and of manhood. Well, I am glad to know that, so far as I am concerned, I never took that view. I always felt that I was just as independent in being obedient, and I know I felt much better than I could possibly feel if I were disobedient. It is not necessary to be disobedient to show independence.

A UNITED PRESIDENCY SPEAK WILL OF LORD. There are at the head of this Church, chosen by the Lord, three men who constitute what is called the First Presidency of the Church of Jesus Christ of Latter-day Saints. One is the President. The other two are his counselors. But all three are Presidents, according to the revelations. One, however, holds the keys. President Woodruff is distinguished from every other one of us by the fact that he possesses the keys of the Kingdom on the earth. He represents the Supreme authority. His voice to us, in its place, brings to us the voice of God. Not that he is God, not that he is infallible. He is a fallible man. His counselors are fallible men. The First Presidency cannot claim, individually or collectively, infallibility. The infallibility is not given to men. They are fallible.

God is infallible. And when God speaks to the Church through him who holds the keys, it is the word of the Lord to this people. Can President Woodruff do this without his counselors? I do not know what he can do, or what he might do, but I know that he does not do it. I know that President Young did not, nor President Taylor. I know that President Joseph

Smith did not. He sought the counsel of his counselors. They acted in concert. And when the First Presidency act in concert, they are a power. . . .

Now, how is it with the First Presidency? Do we have a mind of our own? . . . It is our duty to make our thoughts known upon every subject. But we should not be hard in our hearts; we should be soft and tender so that the Spirit of God will influence us. It does not do for us to be opinionated and set in our feelings and think that our view is the correct view; but to hold our hearts open to receive the manifestations of the Spirit of God.

I suppose each one of us is fond of having his own way. I know I am. I am willing to confess that I like to have my own way. But I do not like my own way well enough to want it in opposition to my brethren's way. That is our duty as the First Presidency of the Church. It is the duty of every presidency throughout the Church.

ALL WHO PRESIDE SHOULD ACT IN UNITY. The Presidents of Stakes and their counselors, the Bishops and their counselors and all who act in presiding positions should be united. It is our duty as the First Presidency of the Church to seek for this spirit of union for which the Savior prayed and to be one, to bring our feelings in subjection, and when two agree on a thing and the third cannot see it, let him say, "I am going with you. No feeling that enters into my heart shall stand between you and me."

Suppose that one man has more wisdom than another; it is better to carry out a plan that is not so wise, if you are united on it. Speaking generally, a plan or a policy that may be inferior in some respects is more effective if men are united upon it than a better plan would be upon which they were divided.

But some may ask, where comes in the inspiration of God in such cases as this? We should understand that God uses men as instruments in carrying out His purposes. He uses them according to their capacity. He gives them opportunity to exercise their agency and to work out self-development. . . .

LORD SUSTAINS COUNSEL OF UNITED LEADERS. The First Presidency ought to have in the first place their hearts single to the glory of God, to have no personal feeling that will influence them in any policy but have their motives pure, and then when they unite on anything and give any counsel, I tell you that God will sustain that and carry it through; He will supplement it by His wisdom and power and make it effective.

The First Presidency are but mortal men. We can only see a certain distance. God sees to the utmost limit. There are no bounds to His sight. But there are bounds to ours. Does He require superhuman wisdom of us? No, only as He gives it to us. He points out the path, and if our motives are pure and we are united on any plan or policy, He will bless and sanctify that, and He will make it successful. That constitutes the strength of the First Presidency, their unity and the purity of their motives.

They may err—and who does not? As I said, we are fallible men. Whatever my views may be concerning the Church and its infallibility, I suppose there are none of the officers of the Church who claim infallibility. Certainly, I do not claim it for myself. But when we are united, our motives pure and we divest ourselves of every personal desire and bias and ask God to take away all hardness from our hearts and all blindness from our minds and then supplicate Him for His blessing, it will surely come. Then the Twelve Apostles and the other officers of the Church, when they carry that counsel out unitedly and in the same spirit, will be blessed, and the Church will be blessed, and, as I have said, God will supplement our weakness by His strength and our want of knowledge by His infinite knowledge and His great power. . . .

Occasionally men arise who tower above the multitude in the extent of their knowledge, such as the Prophet Joseph and others whose names I need not mention; for, as the Lord revealed to Abraham, there are differences in spirits. He spoke of the Kokaubeam or the stars and of the difference manifest in them, that one star was greater and brighter than another until Kolob was reached, which is near the throne of the Eternal; and He said it was so with the spirits of men. . . .

OUR DUTY TO SEEK COUNSEL. The First Presidency must be united. The Twelve must be united, not among themselves alone but with the First Presidency. They should come and ask counsel of the First Presidency. . . . When men do things in secret and are not willing to bring that which they have into the light of day, there is always cause for fear. We should have our hearts open and be willing for all our brethren to read our hearts and our thoughts. We should enter into no arrangement nor have any connection with anything that we have to conceal. It is not the Spirit of God that prompts concealment. Nor should we enter into things without being willing to ask counsel respecting them, no matter what they be.

It is our duty to ask counsel, to seek the mind and will of God; for God does speak through His servants, and He does give counsel through them unto the people. The Twelve ought to be in this condition. They ought not to shun the society and the counsel of the First Presidency. Do we want this for our self-glorification? The Lord knows we do not. But it is the order of the Church that the Twelve should seek counsel from those whom God has placed to preside. And they should be free in asking counsel and not do anything without it.

In the same manner the Presidents of Stakes and their counselors should ask counsel; the Bishops and their counselors should ask counsel; and the seven Presidents of the Seventies, in their place, should ask counsel also. They are under the direction of the Twelve Apostles, who are their file leaders, under the First Presidency of the Church. And one man should not give counsel without consulting his fellow servants. (April 7, 1895, *DW* 50:641-4)

GOSPEL DRAWS PEOPLE TOGETHER. There is no power of human origin that can bind men to men for any length of time. There are occasions, when some great exigency or peril arises, when people will cling together. When nations are attacked and when all their liberties and perhaps their lives are at stake, they will then move forward animated by one common impulse, and they will cling together with wonderful tenacity. . . . But apart from these great crises in the history of individuals and nations, there is no power among men that will unite and hold men together. They will differ in a little while; they will separate.

We see this in the religious world. As soon as men attempted to reform religion, as soon as they dissented from the mother

church and began to establish reformed religions, they began
to differ, and they went on differing and separating until now
the whole of Christendom is filled with churches, among which
there is no union, notwithstanding they call themselves the
churches of Christ. They have not the secret of union with them.

Now, the difference between this Church and other churches
is this: when men receive this Gospel, wherever they may be,
however widely separated they may be, as soon as they are confirmed members of the Church, they receive a spirit that fills
them with that union, and when they are brought together from
the ends of the earth, they feel alike and are drawn together.
True, they have their failings and their weaknesses; but they
possess a spirit of union that no human being is able to impart
unto his fellows. It comes from God. It is the power that reigns
in heaven. It is the power that makes heaven the glorious place
that it is described to be by all who have any conception of it,
in contradiction to hell, the place of misery and torment. . . .

If we were not united, we would not be the people of God.
It is the true sign by which the people of God may be found.
I do not care what we may claim or what our pretensions may
be, we are not the people of God when we are not united. Union
is one of the fruits of the Spirit. (April 17, 1897, *DW* 55:33)

SATAN HATES A UNITED PEOPLE. The devil does not
want the will of the Lord done. He does not want the people
united. He seeks for division, for contention and for strife. He
hates the Latter-day Saints because they act together. All his
followers hate them for the same reason. If we would split up
and divide, refuse to listen to the counsel of the man of God,
then the devil and his followers would rejoice. He tries to persuade the people that it is true independence to divide up and
every man go for himself and to refuse to do as the servants of
God say.

But remember, this is a step towards apostasy. Whenever
you see a man disobeying the counsel of the Lord through the
Holy Priesthood, you may know that unless he repents he will
apostatize. It is a sure sign of apostasy. A man may be an
Apostle, a Seventy, a High Priest, an Elder or a Bishop, yet if
he tries to divide the people and persuades them to disobey the
Prophet of God, he will surely fall, unless he repents with all

his heart. The Lord asks us to obey Him. He tells us how to do so. He does not ask for blind obedience, because He gives His Holy Spirit to all who ask for it to show them that it is right to obey.

UNITY IN POLITICAL MATTERS. But some men think that it may be right to be obedient and united in church matters but in politics it is not so necessary. They act as though it was all right to divide and quarrel in political matters. This, however, is a great mistake. The Lord says to us that we must be one, not in church affairs alone but in all things.

It would be a blessed thing for the Latter-day Saints if the Lord would choose their officers for them, and they would accept those whom He should choose. Does not the Lord know what is best for us politically? He certainly does. (March 1, 1878, *JI* 13:54)

SECTION 3

AUTHORITY AND COMMUNICATION FROM GOD

The Priesthood of the Son of God . . . is the power by which all things were created and are held in their place. Shall I startle you when I say that our Father Himself controls the universe and occupies His exalted station because of the Priesthood? Whether it is startling or not, it is nevertheless true. Our Eternal Father is the Creator of all things through the power of the everlasting Priesthood — that Priesthood which has been bestowed upon and exercised by the servants of God in our day.

—GEORGE Q. CANNON
Deseret Weekly 55:354
(August 22, 1897)

CHAPTER 19

PRIESTHOOD — POWER AND AUTHORITY FROM GOD

THE POWER WHICH CONTROLS UNIVERSE. What is that power? It is the Priesthood of the Son of God. It is the power by which all things were created and are held in their place. Shall I startle you when I say that our Father himself controls the universe and occupies His exalted station because of the Priesthood? Whether it is startling or not, it is nevertheless true. Our Eternal Father is the creator of all things through the power of the everlasting Priesthood—that Priesthood which has been bestowed upon and exercised by the servants of God in our day. (Aug. 22, 1897, *DW* 55:354)

NECESSITY OF PRIESTHOOD. It is a well authenticated and indisputable fact that God never had a people on the earth in any age whom He recognized as His peculiar people without having in their midst those who had the authority and the right to officiate in His name. They were the bearers of His Priesthood —the recipients of the power which He bestows to enable man to act in His stead and to transact that which was necessary to be transacted to fit and prepare His people to enter into His presence. For, as the Scriptures plainly teach, the Lord revealed unto the children of men, by His own voice and by the voice of His Spirit and His servants, ordinances which He expected them to observe before they could be permitted to partake of His glory.

And, as it was incompatible with His designs for Him, His Son or His angels to come down and administer in these things, it was necessary that His power should be bestowed upon men who were counted worthy, by Him, to receive this great and exceeding honor, that they might go forth in His name as His ambassadors or ministers among their fellow men and officiate in all these necessary ordinances and thus be the means, in His hands, of preparing their brethren and their sisters to inherit the glory and the exaltation which He wished to bestow upon them.

They attained unto this honor and power by their worth and faithfulness in doing the will of their God; and it was only by maintaining this character that they were enabled to retain this authority. Their words, while acting in this capacity, were as the words of God unto the people—salvation, honor and heaven's approving smiles being bestowed upon those who obeyed them, and destruction, dishonor and heavenly disapprobation following those who disobeyed; God continually manifesting His determination to honor Himself by honoring those to whom He had delegated a portion of His power.

GOD CONTROLS ITS BESTOWAL. Hence, we read, in the history of God's dealings with the children of men, that whenever an individual or a nation came in contact with one of God's anointed ones—the bearers of this Priesthood or authority—it was equivalent to coming in contact directly with Himself and the consequences were equally terrible. The Almighty always reserved to Himself the right to bestow this authority upon whomsoever He would and never recognized a man as His minister who did not obtain it by the legitimate and only correct means and from the proper source.

When this Priesthood was taken from the earth and was not in the possession of man, if God wished to again bestow it upon him, to fulfill His designs, it was always done by the direct manifestation of His will by His own voice and by the ministration of His angels, to the individual selected. When, on the other hand, this power was upon the earth, held by those whom the Lord recognized and approved as His servants and ambassadors, for an individual to obtain it it was always necessary for the one who held it, before he could with propriety confer it, to obtain a knowledge from the Lord that He approved of the individual as one worthy to hold this dignity—as one upon whom the power should be bestowed to go forth and act in His name and stead among the people. These were the only means through which this power and authority could be obtained, and any man who claimed this Priesthood or who professed to act by this authority, who had not obtained it through either of these processes, was condemned as an impostor, and everything that he did was unrecognized and disapprobated by the Lord. . . .

THE CORRECT MODE TO OBTAIN IT. Paul, in writing to the Hebrews upon the subject of Priesthood, alludes to the correct mode of obtaining it in these words: "No man taketh this honour (Priesthood) unto himself, but he that is called of God, as was Aaron."[1] Now, every reader of the Bible knows that Aaron was called to this honor through the revelations of God to Moses and that Paul . . . and . . . all the Apostles were called in like manner. . . . And when men were called and set apart in this manner, all their acts, while officiating in the sphere of their Priesthood, were sanctioned by the Lord—the Being in whose name they acted. When it was necessary for them to attend to any of the ordinances which the Lord had instituted for His creatures to obey, the person who submitted to it in the proper spirit obtained a knowledge from the Lord that He had approved and blessed the operation; thus, every one of His people knew that the men who were officiating in their midst as His representatives were empowered by Him so to act; therefore, there existed no doubt as to their right to dictate and control the affairs of the Kingdom of God on the earth, and all knew that implicit obedience was both expected and necessary. The people who had in their possession knowledge of this nature were easily governed and always presented the characteristics which we find attributed to the people of God, whenever He had a people on the earth. . . .

A TRUE CHURCH TO HAVE DIVINE AUTHORITY. Who is there that has been taught to believe the Bible that can reflect dispassionately and unbiased by prejudice upon these subjects and not be convinced in his own mind that if there be a Church of God upon the earth, there must be men in that Church who are endowed by Him with the authority to act in His name in all the ordinances pertaining thereto and to whom He will make known His mind and will in the government thereof? They must also be convinced that if there be such a Church in existence, its members, so long as God maintains His character for being unchangeable, must, of necessity, enjoy the gifts and blessings which the members of His Church anciently did. (Oct. 18, 1856, WS 225-30)

SUCCESSION OF PRIESTHOOD. There are many churches that consider this question of succession of authority

---

[1]Hebrews 5:4.

as unworthy of attention. . . . There are hundreds of churches which profess to be of Christ, and yet they differ very widely in their teachings and in their religious practices. They cannot, in the very nature of things, all be right; in fact, it is contrary to the whole spirit of the Savior's teachings to imagine that there can be more than one church which He would call His. It is simply ridiculous to suppose that the Savior who prayed so earnestly to His Father for union among His disciples would fail to desire and to command that His people should be one or that the Holy Ghost would rest upon thousands of people of different denominations and teach them to be divided and disunited.

Nothing more clearly sustains the position that the Latter-day Saints take and the testimony that they bear concerning the establishment of the Lord's Church in these last days than the diversity of sects and of doctrines that are taught in the so-called Christian world. What possible hope could any earnest seeker after truth receive from these different denominations when the lack of authority is so apparent? It is not to be wondered at that sincere Protestants turn their eyes toward Rome and many of them take refuge in that church because there is a consistency in the claims of the Church of Rome to Apostolic succession. But those claims are not supported by the facts of history. That church lost the authority of the Priesthood through transgression. The Priesthood was undoubtedly taken back to God. The men who bore it were slain and none were left to continue its succession.

Hence, the position that our Church occupies is the only logical position. The Prophet Joseph Smith testified that he and Oliver Cowdery were ordained by men who once held the Priesthood on the earth. John the Baptist, who held the authority to baptize and who did baptize the Son of God himself, came and laid his hands on the heads of Joseph and Oliver and restored to men on the earth the authority which he held while in the flesh. In like manner the Apostles Peter, James and John appeared unto them and ordained them to the Apostleship and Priesthood which they held. By means of these ordinations the authority was once more restored which was necessary for the organization of the Church and for the administration of the saving ordinances of the Gospel.

We are relieved, therefore, as a people, from the necessity of discussing Apostolic succession and from contentions whether it is necessary for men to be ordained by proper authority in order to become ministers of Jesus Christ. All doubt and uncertainty concerning these points were swept away by the knowledge that the Apostleship has been restored to the earth from a source which leaves its validity without question. The position of this Church on these points is impregnable.

The proofs of what the Lord has done in restoring the authority to man on the earth again are found in the fruits which have followed its restoration. All the evidences of God's favor which attended the Church in ancient days under the administration of the Apostles of the Lord Jesus are to be found in and accompanying the Church of Jesus Christ of Latter-day Saints. That Church is distinguished from all other churches on the earth in that it possesses in fullness the gifts and graces and the divine manifestations of favor which the Church of Jesus Christ of Former-day Saints possessed. (Oct. 15, 1896, JI 31:609-10)

ON THRESHOLD OF A NEW ERA. We live on the threshold of a new era; the work that God has established in our day shall never be given to another people. The Priesthood which God has restored—the authority by which men can administer in the ordinances of God—that Priesthood shall never be taken from the earth. . . .

There is no power on earth nor in hell that can destroy the Church that God has established nor obliterate the Priesthood from the earth again as it was obliterated in ancient days. It was necessary when this Church was started that angels should come to restore that which was taken away, the everlasting Priesthood, but there will be no future necessity for this. We are at the threshold of a thousand years of peace; we are engaged in laying the foundation of that work which shall stand forever, not only the thousand years but as long as time shall last and as long as the earth shall endure. This is the consolation we have that our predecessors did not have. (Aug. 3, 1879, JD 20:250-1)

PETER HELD SAME PRIESTHOOD. The Latter-day

Saints lay claim to having received the same Priesthood and
authority which was held by Peter and his brethren—they claim
nothing less than this. The power which Jesus bestowed upon
them, the Latter-day Saints assert and testify, has been again
restored to the earth and is now held by the present Apostles
of the Church of Christ. The head of the Church upon the earth
at the present time holds the same authority which was held by
Peter, the head of the Church in ancient days. He is invested
with the same power, holds the same keys, and his counsel is
equally as binding as Peter's was when he occupied the same
position. (July 10, 1857, WS 470)

ORDINATION OF JOSEPH SMITH AND OLIVER
COWDERY. There is nothing in writing or that has come to
us orally as to why Joseph Smith and Oliver Cowdery should
ordain each other to the Priesthood they received under the hands
of both John the Baptist and Peter, James and John. But the
reason which appears plain to the First Presidency, with whom
I have conversed on the subject, is that it was necessary, after
the Priesthood had been restored from heaven by the administration of holy angels, that mortal men should ordain each other
and baptize each other and lay hands upon each other for the
reception of the Holy Ghost. This appears to be a sufficient
reason for this action on the part of the Prophet Joseph and
Oliver Cowdery.

To Joseph the keys were given. He stood at the head. And
it was proper that the ordination of all who belonged to the dispensation should come through him; and it appeared to be just
as necessary that he himself should be ordained by a mortal in
order to observe the order of heaven. (Jan. 1, 1891, JI 26:13)

PRIESTHOOD AND PREEXISTENCE. We are asked if
it is true doctrine to teach that those who hold the Priesthood
now in the flesh held it in the spirit world before they came
here. . . . We know of nothing that has been revealed and written
which warrants any one in teaching as doctrine that men who
hold the Priesthood here were ordained to the Priesthood before
they came here. Such ideas should not be advanced in public or
in private. (Aug. 15, 1895, JI 30:497-8)

JOSEPH SMITH FOREORDAINED. The Prophet Joseph and many others were ordained before the foundations of the world were laid to come forth and accomplish the labor and the work that they did. There is no room for doubt in regard to the truth of this statement that is so frequently made. In the early boyhood of the Prophet Joseph he was moved upon in a mysterious manner to seek unto God. By the exercise of a faith that was uncommon . . . unknown upon the earth, he was able to receive the ministrations of God the Father and of His Son Jesus Christ, thus showing in the very beginning of his career that he was a man or a spirit that was highly favored of God—a man to whom God desired to give particular manifestations of His kindness and goodness and power, and this was followed up from that time until his death by continued manifestations of the favor and the will and the power of God unto him.

A FACT TO REMEMBER. But it is a remarkable fact, and I wish to impress it, I think it is worthy of remembrance by all of us that notwithstanding the Prophet Joseph had all these manifestations and was a Prophet and Seer and a Revelator, he never attempted—notwithstanding the ideas that were so prevalent among mankind, and especially in the region where he lived and where he received his education—to officiate in any of the ordinances of the house of God or of the Gospel of salvation until he received the everlasting Priesthood. When that was bestowed upon him, when he received the Priesthood after the order of Aaron and was ordained by the angel who alone held the keys, who was a literal descendant of Aaron and by virtue of that descent entitled to the keys of that Priesthood, having exercised the authority thereof while in the flesh, then and not till then did he administer the ordinance of baptism for the remission of sins.

Then he refrained from acting in ordinances belonging to the Melchizedek Priesthood, that higher Priesthood by the authority of which the baptism of fire and the Holy Ghost is administered unto the children of men. Having authority to baptize in water given unto him, he did not go any farther until the Lord in His kindness and mercy bestowed upon him, through the administration of the Apostles who held the keys till the death of our Savior, the authority to administer in those higher ordi-

nances and to exercise the power and authority of this higher
Priesthood.

This illustrates most perfectly how careful men ought to
be in acting in the name of God not to overstep the bounds of
the authority conferred upon them but to carefully keep within
those limits that are assigned to them in which to exercise
authority. It is a lesson unto us as a people. We should be particular ourselves and should impress every man with the great
care that he should exercise to confine his acts to the authority
which he has received from the Almighty. . . .

PRIESTHOOD WITHDRAWN FROM EARTH. We are
building temples at the present time in which we have ordinances
administered unto us for those who have died. Why is this necessary? It is because the Priesthood of the Son of God was withdrawn for a long period of time from the earth. The children of
men have been born; they have lived; they have died without
any of the ordinances being administered unto them by those
who held the Priesthood of the Son of God.

It is true that many sought after God in a certain manner
and according to the light they had, and many obtained some
degree of knowledge concerning God. Some of them had a testimony of Him through their faith and died at peace with God.
Many of our ancestors lived in this condition, and God bore
witness to them by His Holy Spirit that He was pleased with
them. But what of that? Is that all that is necessary to place
them in a saved condition? By no means. Something more than
that is necessary to obtain for them the full remission of their
sins and to place them in a condition where they can be saved
and exalted in God's presence.

REFORMERS LACKED PRIESTHOOD. Something more
was necessary for Joseph than that he was a Revelator, a Seer and
a Prophet to constitute him a servant of God empowered to administer the ordinances of life and salvation. A Wesley, a Luther,
a Calvin, a Wycliffe and a host of others who have arisen in
the world, imbued with the highest and purest motives and
the highest and most intense desires for the salvation of their
fellow men, have labored zealously to turn men to God and to

bring them to a knowledge of the Savior; but they have not had the authority of the Holy Priesthood.

They themselves could not usher people into the Church of God. They could not legitimately administer an ordinance pertaining to the salvation of the human family. Yet, God, in many instances, accepted of them where they sought unto Him according to the best light they possessed; He accepted of them and their labors, and He witnessed unto them, by the outpouring of His Spirit upon them, that He was pleased with them and He whispered peace to their souls.

MANY FAVORED PEOPLE IN ALL NATIONS. In every land, in every nation and among the people of every creed, men and women of this kind have been found, and according to their faith and diligence their works have been acceptable to our Father. Men have thought that the Christian lands and the Christian people, so called, have been the most favored of God in this respect. No doubt they have because they have had knowledge concerning the Savior that other lands and other peoples have not had; but in pagan lands, in lands where the name of Jesus has never been heard, men have sought after God and endeavored to live according to the light that He has given unto them and the Spirit that He has bestowed upon them and which He bestows upon every man and woman born into the world. He has accepted of them, and in the day of the Lord Jesus, the heathen will have part in the first resurrection.

NECESSITY FOR TEMPLES. Our ancestors have, in common with others, been destitute of the power and the authority of the Holy Priesthood. Hence, we build temples; hence, we go into these temples and attend to the ordinances of life and salvation for our kindred who have died in ignorance of this power or were in a position where they could not have it exercised in their behalf. They could not be baptized for the remission of their sins; they could not have hands laid upon them for the reception of the Holy Ghost; they could not have any other ordinance administered unto them because the authority to administer was not upon the earth, and whatever might be done in the name of God or in the name of Jesus by those who thought they had the authority or who assumed to possess it was of no avail so far as salvation was concerned; so far as acceptance by the Lord our God is concerned it was as though nothing had been done.

Hence it is that in these last days, God having in His great kindness and mercy opened the heavens once more and sent from heaven that authority which has so long been withdrawn, God having done this, we are put in the possession of the authority to administer to each other the ordinances of life and salvation and not only to administer to each other but to exercise that authority in behalf of those who have lived before us, lived in ages that are past, so that we can connect generation unto generation until we reach back to the time when our ancestors did hold the Holy Priesthood.

In this manner the work of salvation will progress until throughout the Millennium temples will be built and the servants and handmaidens of God will go into these temples and officiate until all who have been born upon the face of the earth who have not become sons of perdition will be redeemed and the entire family be re-united, Adam standing at the head. . . .

IMPORTANCE OF KNOWING LINE OF AUTHORITY. I believe the time will come when it will be necessary for every man to trace the line in which he has received the Priesthood that he exercises. It is therefore of great importance in our Church that records should be kept and that every man should know whence he derives his authority—from what source, through what channel he has received the Holy Priesthood and by what right he exercises that authority and administers the ordinances thereof. I believe this is of extreme importance and that where there are doubts as to a man's legitimately exercising that authority, that doubt should be removed.

Every man should be careful on this point to know where he gets his Priesthood, that it has come to him clean and undefiled, legitimately; and when men are cut off from that Priesthood by the voice of the Servants of God, there is an authority on the earth which God recognizes in the heavens and that man is cut off from the Priesthood. He said in ancient days in speaking to His Apostles:

"Whose soever sins ye remit, they are remitted unto them; and whose soever sins ye retain, they are retained."[2]

"Whatsoever thou shalt bind on earth shall be bound in heaven: and whatsoever thou shalt loose on earth shall be loosed in heaven."[3]

In these last days God has, in like manner, restored this same authority of the Holy Priesthood. He has restored to man the power to bind on earth and it shall be bound in heaven. . . .

PRIESTHOOD ACTS BINDING. That which is done in the name of the Holy Priesthood will stand and will be fulfilled both in the world and out of the world, both in time and in eternity. Hence it is that when an Elder goes forth in the authority of the Holy Priesthood and baptizes a candidate who has repented of his sins, God confirms that ordinance; God remits the sins of that individual; God by bestowing His Holy Spirit witnesses unto that soul that his sins or her sins are remitted.

In like manner when an Elder lays his hands upon the head of a man or a woman who has been thus baptized and says unto that individual, "receive ye the Holy Ghost," God in heaven, bound by the oath and the covenant that He has made, bound by all the conditions that pertain to the everlasting Priesthood, will cause the Holy Ghost to descend upon that soul, and he or she will be filled therewith. He receives the baptism of fire and the Holy Ghost, and it stands on the earth, and it stands in heaven recorded in favor of that soul if he continues to observe the conditions under which that baptism and confirmation are administered. There is no human power that can deprive that individual of the fruits of that blessing which has been thus sealed upon him by authority of the Holy Priesthood.

So with other ordinances. When men go forward and attend to other ordinances such as receiving their endowments, their washings, their anointings, receiving the promises connected therewith, these promises will be fulfilled to the very letter in time and in eternity—that is, if they themselves are true to the conditions upon which the blessings are promised.

And so it is when persons go to the altar and are married for time and eternity. When the man who officiates says: "I seal upon you the power to come forth in the morning of the first

---

[2]John 20:23. [3]Matthew 16:19.

resurrection, crowned with glory, immortality and eternal lives,"
just as sure as that promise is made and the persons united (to
whom the promise is made) conform with the conditions thereof,
just so sure will it be fulfilled. There is no power anywhere in
existence that can invalidate the force, the efficacy or that can
prevent the fulfillment of that promise when it is pronounced
upon a man and woman by the authority of the Holy Priesthood
—that is, there is no power but that which they themselves can
exercise. (Oct. 18, 1884, JD 26:243-9)

NECESSITY OF HONORING PRIESTHOOD. God has
shown that however weak and imperfect a man may be, if he
will seek to magnify that Priesthood, God will honor and sustain
him. This the whole history of the Church has proved, and its
truth has been illustrated by innumerable cases; while on the
other hand, innumerable instances are found in the history of
the Church where men have lost the Spirit of God and gone into
darkness through treating the Priesthood of God with contempt.

In the early days of the Church the Prophet Joseph gave
it as a certain sign that could be depended upon, that whenever
men were found finding fault with and murmuring against the
bearers of the Priesthood, especially those whom God had chosen
to lead His people, apostasy would inevitably follow if not speedily repented of. The indulgence in such a spirit is most dangerous
and has been attended up to the present time and will be attended
hereafter with fatal consequences to the faith of those who
indulge in it.

Men have said concerning servants of God: "Oh! These
men are but mortal; they are very fallible, and they are as liable
to do wrong as anybody else." This may be true. At the same
time God does not sustain those who imagine they have a right
to criticize, find fault with or in this manner condemn His servants. They are weak and fallible; but they bear the Priesthood.
The Priesthood cannot be separated from the men; and in attack-
ing the men it is evident from the results which have followed
such a course that the Lord views such attacks as being made
upon His authority. . . .

If Satan can only destroy the confidence of the Latter-day
Saints in the Priesthood which God has bestowed, his end is
accomplished, for it is against the Priesthood that he has made

unceasing warfare. Much blood has been shed under his instigation for the purpose of destroying the authority by which the Church of Christ is established and the great works of God are accomplished.

The Latter-day Saints should reflect upon this. If we believe that our Father in heaven has visited the earth to open this dispensation and has sent angelic messengers to bestow the Priesthood upon men, can we suppose that He will not see that that Priesthood is not misused and that the men who bear it do not use it for wrong purposes? To have any other idea than this is to suppose that the Lord has either gone to sleep or taken a journey or has lost His interest in the great work which He has founded.

The revelations of the Lord through the Prophet Joseph plainly intimated to him and to the Church that if he did not do right he would be removed. President Young often told the people that the Lord would not permit him to lead the people astray. Presidents Taylor and Woodruff have made the same statement. And that which is true concerning the men who hold the keys is true in relation to the other officers of the Church.

The Lord will take care of His people, and He will not suffer His work to be thwarted. When men standing in high places do wrong, He will deal with them. He will not suffer them to persist for any length of time in wrong-doing, withdrawing His Spirit and His power from them and removing them out of their places. He has done this in the past; He will continue to do it in the future, until the Lord himself shall come to preside over His people. (Feb. 15, 1896, *JI* 31:101-2)

ENDOWMENTS TOO EASILY OBTAINED. I believe that our endowments are too easily obtained. Men and women go to the temples who do not understand the value of the precious blessings that are bestowed upon them, and I have felt for years that something should be done to change this so that instead of it being necessary for a man to receive the Melchizedek Priesthood, he will first manifest his efficiency in the Aaronic Priesthood and show his capabilities and good desires before receiving the higher Priesthood. I firmly believe that this will be so some time and that men will not get the fullness of the endowment with the ease that they have done but will receive that part which belongs to the Aaronic Priesthood. These blessings become so common that many people do not value them or know how to use them.

When the Prophet Joseph first communicated that the Lord had revealed to him the keys of the endowment, I can remember the great desire there was on every hand to understand something about them. When the Prophet would speak about his desire to complete the temple in order that he might impart unto his fellow servants that which God had delivered to him, a thrill went through the congregation and a great desire for this filled their hearts. . . .

Then, when he did communicate the endowments to a few persons before the temple was completed, the whole people were moved with desire to complete the temple in order that they might receive these great blessings therein. They were valued beyond price. A man that could go in and get his endowments was looked upon as though he had received some extraordinary blessing—something akin to that which the angels received—and it was estimated and valued in that way.

How is it now? There is a complete indifference, it may be said, in relation to it. Young people go there stupid, with no particular desire only to get married, without realizing the character of the obligations that they take upon themselves or the covenants that they make and the promises involved in the taking of these covenants. The result is, hundreds among us go to the house of the Lord and receive these blessings and come away without having any particular impression made upon them.

I think that this is deplorable. When men have gifts and blessings bestowed upon them and they do not value them, they become a cause of condemnation rather than blessing. It seems to me that there should be exceeding great care taken in this respect. I would rather—though I would not like it—a son of mine be married by a Bishop than to have him go to the temple in an unfit condition and receive these blessings. It would be far better for him.

PRIESTHOOD NOT FULLY APPRECIATED. This Priesthood that the Lord has restored is a far more important thing than even the most advanced of us can appreciate at the present time. We who bear this Priesthood act in God's stead in the midst of the people; we are the representatives of God—the ambassadors, so to speak, of the Savior, who has given us this Priesthood; and the duties of this calling are most important because they affect the salvation of the children of men. (Jan. 14, 1894, *DW* 48:349-50)

I say, every man, not any one class of men but every man bearing the Priesthood of the Son of God in this Church, should feel that there is a responsibility resting upon him and that perchance if he be not careful he may wake up in eternity and find himself under serious condemnation for having neglected to do his duty to his fellowman and to magnify the holy Priesthood that God has placed upon him. (Sept. 2, 1889, *DW* 39:461)

FAILURE TO MAGNIFY PRIESTHOOD BRINGS DAMNATION. We must honor the Priesthood we hold or that Priesthood, instead of exalting us, will be the means of damning us; instead of exalting us at the right hand of God, for which it was given, it will drag us down to a depth of misery and woe such as we never would have reached if we had not received it and failed to honor it. It is a fearful thing to receive the Priesthood of God and not magnify it, and the man who receives it should not do so to gratify some feeling he may have that he would like to hold authority that would give him some dignity or place him in a position above others of his brethren and sisters but with the consciousness that if he does not bear off the responsibilities which are involved in receiving it, it will lead him down to the depths of misery and anguish. (Aug. 10, 1862, *MS* 24:548)

MORE THAN ORDINATION NECESSARY. If men or women become members of the Church and receive the Holy Ghost, their work does not end there; it has hardly begun. They have taken merely the first steps and have scarcely passed the threshold, and before them is stretched out a field of labor of unlimited extent. If men have been ordained, the mere ordination does not bestow upon them all the knowledge and power they need, only as they live for it, constantly striving to obtain it by the cultivation of that which they already have in their possession.

It is folly for any man to think that the Priesthood will be a source of advantage or honor to him or that it will increase his knowledge or his influence, if he himself does not apply himself to the labor by diligently seeking for these blessings by faith and works. So with members. If they do not cultivate the Holy Spirit, it will not increase in them; neither will the gifts and blessings of the Gospel increase within them. (Aug. 24, 1861, *MS* 23:538)

FAITHFULNESS RATHER THAN POSITION BRINGS EXALTATION. There is no Elder, Priest, Teacher or Deacon that can increase in the power of God and the faith of the Lord Jesus Christ unless he magnifies his Priesthood and honors that which God has bestowed upon him; and the Deacon who is faithful in his calling and honors his Priesthood is far more acceptable in the sight of God than the Elder, High Priest, Seventy, or even Apostle who does not magnify his Priesthood, and he will receive an exaltation which they will not receive, for they have failed to honor the covenants they have made with God. . . .

The works of an humble, faithful brother or sister are more pleasing in the sight of God than those of the smart people, who are at one time faithful and full of great zeal and in a short period become dilatory, careless and measurably forget God and His works. . . . There are Elders who are faithful men . . . and who have always done everything that was required of them, attended to every duty placed upon them, yet they have been humble and have attracted very little attention, while other men have made a great stir and have been conspicuous among the people whose course has not been so upright. Is there any doubt as to which of these two classes is the more acceptable in the sight of God?

The man or woman who has been faithful before the Lord, I care not who they may be nor what their Priesthood may be, they may have little or no Priesthood, but the prospects of that individual are brighter before the Lord than those of the person who does not live up to the light which God has communicated unto him. I would like to have this thought fasten itself deeply in the minds of the Saints that God will reward every man and woman according to their works. If they are faithful, they will be exalted, and, I care not what their position may be nor what

Priesthood they may have, if they are unfaithful, they will receive no reward. (Aug. 10, 1862, *MS* 24:547)

BE CONTENT TO SERVE ANYWHERE. If there be one duty of more imperative importance than another which the Elders of Israel should learn, it is that they should be at all times perfectly content to fill any calling and labor in any capacity that the Lord through His servants may designate. . . .

The only principle upon which position should be sought and held by the servants of God is that they might thereby be more useful—that the field of their usefulness might be enlarged. No man should seek to hold a position to gratify a vain ambition to excel. And whatever the position that may be assigned him, he should therewith be content. If an Elder's happiness be affected by the prominence or obscurity of his station, it is an evidence that he is dependent upon something beside the Spirit of God for happiness; if he be appointed to labor in a humble position by those who have the authority and he strives to fill that appointment honorably, he will be happy—his happiness will be perfect; his joy will be full; should his station be ever so exalted, he could be no more than this. . . .

It is not in occupying this or the other honorable and prominent station that the Elders should find gratification alone (though, of course, it is gratifying to them to know that they have the confidence of the Lord and their brethren); it is in knowing, whatever their station or calling may be, that they are in the position which the Lord, through His servants, wishes them to occupy and that they have His approval and His sweet and precious Spirit imparting unto them happiness and peace.

An Apostle, however eminently gifted, can act without the least loss of dignity or without derogating in the least from his high office in any position or calling connected with the salvation of the children of men or the building up of God's Kingdom upon the earth. And though others of more limited experience and holding only a portion of the Priesthood held by him may, while he is thus acting, be acting in more prominent positions, yet it does not in reality detract an iota from his dignity, his usefulness or the reward which, if faithful, is promised to him. If this is true respecting an Apostle, it is true respecting a High Priest, a member of the Seventies, an Elder or any of the bearers of the Priesthood. (Aug. 23, 1862, MS 24:536-8)

CHURCH LEADERS NEED BUSINESS QUALIFICA-
TIONS. Now, it is doubtless a fact that in selecting men to hold ecclesiastical positions some attention is paid to their energy and business qualifications. The Latter-day Saints need men who are capable of managing affairs and sustaining themselves credit-ably to be their guides and to take the lead in temporal things, as many Bishops have to do. It would not be wise to disregard business qualifications, when coupled with other characteristics that are suitable, in choosing a man to hold as important an office as that of a Bishop or President of Stake. But it certainly would not be proper to select men for their business qualifications or their money-making faculty alone. Such men would prove failures as leaders of the people in the things of God. And the history of our people proves that men have not been selected for position because of these qualities alone. . . .

Business capacity, talent for management and skill in the accumulation of property are gifts not to be despised; and when a public man possesses them and has, in addition, a love for the truth and a determination to serve God and keep His command-ments and deal justly with his neighbor, they certainly are no disadvantage whether possessed by an Apostle, a President of Stake, a Bishop or any other officer in the Church but are de-cidedly an advantage to him and to the community over which he is called to preside. (March 15, 1887, JI 22:50-1)

PROMISES TO THOSE WHO MAGNIFY PRIESTHOOD.
To the Latter-day Saints this Gospel and this Priesthood come on the one hand accompanied by great blessings and promises and great power and exaltation, and on the other hand they come accompanied by dreadful penalties, by degradation and con-demnation greater than it would be possible for any being to reach unless he had had the opportunities which the Gospel and the Priesthood bring and afford. . . .

We are promised in the plainest of all language that those who receive this Priesthood receive the Lord. . . . They are to receive the Father's Kingdom, and if they receive the Father's

Kingdom, they are to receive all that the Father hath for all that he hath will be given unto them.

Can you conceive of this? Can any human being conceive of the immeasurable extent of the glory here promised—the immeasurable extent of exaltation here offered unto all those who receive the Priesthood of the Son of God and who magnify it? It is impossible for mortal man to have the least conception even when his mind is enlightened by the Spirit of God—that is, the least conception compared with the immeasurable extent of the glory that is here promised. We can have some conception of it; we can have some foretaste of it when we receive the Spirit of God, when it rests down upon us in power; but to conceive of the fullness of this glory is impossible for any being in this mortal condition of existence. . . .

HIGHER PRIESTHOOD NECESSARY FOR EXALTATION. Now, this Priesthood which God has restored in these last days through Peter, James and John is the Priesthood that continueth in the Church of God in all generations. The Church of God cannot be without it; for without it the power of Godliness is not made manifest to man in the flesh. A people can progress to a certain extent with the Aaronic Priesthood, but there is a limit to their progress. There are bounds beyond which they cannot pass. They cannot attain to the fullness of the glory of God the Eternal Father without the presence of the Melchizedek Priesthood. . . .

Without this Priesthood, without its ordinances, without its powers, without its gifts, "no man can see the face of God, even the Father, and live."[4] Therefore, it is essential that if a people should be exalted unto the presence of God, they should have this Melchizedek or greater Priesthood and the ordinances thereof, by the means of which they are to be prepared or they shall be prepared to enter into the presence of God the Father and endure His presence. . . .

PRIESTHOOD MUST BE OBEYED FOR FULLNESS OF GLORY. God designs to have us led in that path which will bring us into His presence. He designs that this whole people called Latter-day Saints shall have the laws of His Celestial King-

---

[4]D. & C. 84:22.

dom revealed unto them line upon line, precept upon precept, here a little and there a little, until they are brought into His presence, until every man and woman and child who belongs to this Church shall be able to endure the presence of God and live, until by means of this Priesthood, this higher Priesthood, every man will be prepared to receive the fullness of the celestial glory and this by obedience to law, not by hardness of heart, not by rebellion, not by rejecting the counsel of God through His servants, not by taking our own way. . . .

These Latter-day Saints must obey the Priesthood of the Son of God and be led by it in all things, or they never will enter into the presence of God our Eternal Father, never, worlds without end. God has placed this Priesthood in the Church for the express purpose of leading His people forward, just as Moses endeavored to lead the children of Israel forward by giving unto them His law, by revealing unto them His will, by instructing them in the things of righteousness and leading them forward until they should attain unto the fullness of His glory. (Aug. 31, 1884, JD 25:290-4)

NECESSITY OF FAITH IN AUTHORITIES. A faithful Latter-day Saint may not be able to understand all the movements of the Church nor all the motives of the authorities of the Church in giving counsel or in taking action upon different questions; but will a man of this character censure them, assail them or condemn them? Certainly not. He will be likely to say: "I do not understand the reasons for this action; I do not see clearly what the presiding authorities have in view in doing this; but I will wait and learn more. This I do know, that this is the work of God and that these men are His servants and that they will not be permitted by Him to lead the Church astray or to commit any wrong of so serious a character as to endanger its progress or perpetuity." This would undoubtedly be the feeling of a man living close to the Lord, because the testimony of God's Spirit would bring this to His mind and make him feel sure that God had not forgotten nor forsaken His Church. (Oct. 15, 1896, JI 31:618)

GOD BLESSES THOSE WHO MAGNIFY CALLING. He is ready to bless every man in His Church who will magnify

His office and calling. He is ready to bestow the gifts and qualifications of that office upon every man according to his diligence
and faithfulness before Him. But the idle man, the slothful man,
the man that shirks his responsibility, the man that avoids duty
. . . every man that does this God will take from him His gifts
and His blessings; He will withdraw them and give them to the
faithful one. He will clothe His faithful servants with the power
that belongs to the Priesthood in proportion to the diligence and
faithfulness in seeking to magnify their calling and to live near
unto their God. Mark this and let it bear with weight upon your
mind for I tell you it is so.

You may ordain a man to be an Apostle, but if he does not
seek to magnify that office and Priesthood, the gifts of it will not
be with him as they would be with a man who does seek to
magnify his calling; no matter how great his ability, the power
of God will not accompany him unless he seeks for it for God
will be sought after, and God will be plead with for His gifts
and graces and for revelation and knowledge; He will be sought
after by His children, and then when He is sought after, He will
bestow. (Dec. 14, 1884, *JD* 26:62)

THE PRIESTHOOD WILL NEVER MISLEAD PEOPLE.
Why we had better distrust the solid earth itself on which
we stand and think it trembling and unreliable than to think
that the Priesthood cannot be relied upon—that Priesthood which
God Himself, accompanied by His Son Jesus, came to earth to
prepare the way for its restoration. I would just as soon think
of the starry heavens falling into chaos; I would just as soon think
that the throne of our Father in heaven was in danger of being
shaken to its foundations as I would think that the Priesthood
of God . . . would be permitted by the Lord to mislead this people.
Never! Never!

The Father did not come down from heaven Himself, accompanied by His Son Jesus, for any such purpose as this. The Lord
did not pour out His Spirit as He has done upon the honest in
heart wherever the Elders have gone to leave this work alone,
to be mismanaged and the people to be led astray. The Lord has
not led us to these mountains and blessed us as He has done for
this purpose. No, no!

Though impenetrable darkness should surround us, we

ought, as a people and as individuals, to cling to that truth which the Lord has revealed concerning this work; cling to the Priesthood; cling to the "rod of iron," which is the word of God, and the word of God comes through the Priesthood. Let each one say, "I will serve God no matter what happens; I will cling to His Priesthood, which God has put in His Church to govern it, no matter what the consequences may be." That is the integrity we should cherish and which we should teach to our children. Unless we do, we will never accomplish that which God designs for us. . . .

THOSE WHO OPPOSE PRIESTHOOD TO BE CURSED. It is a serious thing to fight against the Priesthood of the Son of God, no matter who holds it. The men who do bear it are fallible men and when they bear it properly, are conscious of their own weaknesses and infirmities. They feel not only as if they were utterly unworthy of the authority the Lord has placed upon them but incapable of exercising it. But they have been chosen by the Lord, and He will sustain them and bear them off triumphant always, as He has done thus far. And no man can lift his heel against the Priesthood of the Son of God without the curse of Almighty God coming upon him, unless he repents. . . .

It is a dreadful sin to fight against or in any manner oppose the Priesthood of the Son of God, and everyone of us should repent of such opposition with all our hearts. . . . When men have attempted to exercise the authority of the Priesthood in an improper manner, the Lord has withdrawn His Spirit from them. . . . He will have a pure people, who will be led by His servants. When a man ceases to be a true servant of the Lord, the Lord withdraws His Spirit from him, and leaves him to himself. Happy would that man be if he should die before he did this. (April 5, 1897, *DW* 54:674)

PROPER METHOD FOR ORDAINING. We have been asked by several different persons whether, in ordaining a brother, it is right to confer the Priesthood first and then ordain him to the particular office to which he is called or to directly ordain him to that office in the Priesthood. That is, in ordaining a man an Elder, should the one officiating say: "I confer upon you the Melchizedek Priesthood and ordain you an Elder, or, I ordain you an Elder in the Melchizedek Priesthood, or whatever the office conferred may be?"

So far as we know, the Lord has revealed no particular form or words to be used in the ceremony of ordination to the Priesthood as He has done in the rite of baptism, neither has He given any direct instructions on the point presented by the enquirers. Certain it is that both forms have been and are being used by those officiating, and it is equally certain that the Lord recognizes and honors those ordained in either way. Consequently, we are of the opinion that both are acceptable to Him and will be until it pleases Him to give the Church further light on the subject, either by direct revelation or by inspiring His servants of the First Presidency of the Church to direct exactly what shall be said.[5] (Feb. 15, 1894, *JI* 29:114)

A STREAM CANNOT RISE HIGHER THAN ITS FOUNTAIN. The question is asked if there are any cases on record in the Church where men holding a lesser degree or office in the Priesthood are authorized under any circumstances to ordain to the greater offices in the Priesthood and it be lawful and right.

There is no record or book or history which authorizes or justifies such action. A stream cannot rise higher than its fountain. In the affairs of the Kingdom of God a man cannot bestow that which he has not received. This is illustrated in the history of all religious movements since the days when the true Priesthood was taken from the earth. Men have endeavored to ordain their fellow-men to an authority which they themselves did not hold. The result has been failure. God does not acknowledge the bestowal of any authority which He does not authorize; and before a man can legally in the sight of heaven ordain his fellow-man to an office, he must have the authority himself from God. In other words, he himself must have been ordained to that office

---

[5]"To prevent disputes over this subject that may arise . . . we draw attention to the fact that until recently, from the days of the Prophet Joseph Smith, ordinations to the Priesthood were directly to the office therein for which the recipient was chosen and appointed. . . . In reference to the form of procedure . . . our beloved and departed President, Joseph F. Smith, when questioned concerning them, decided, as of record, 'It is a distinction without a difference,' and 'either will do.' Persons, therefore, who have been ordained in either way hold the right to officiate in all the duties of their respective offices in the Priesthood." (So stated the First Presidency of Heber J. Grant, Anthon H. Lund and Charles W. Penrose, *Gospel Doctrine*, Second Edition, Page 686).

of the Priesthood which he attempts to bestow. (Jan. 1, 1891, JI 26:13)

THE POWER IN ORDINATION. Some brethren are appointed to preside over missions, and very likely they feel entirely inadequate to the labor; the duties seem far beyond their ability to perform; but they are set apart for that calling by the servants of God, and they go forth trusting in the Lord. Does any one know of an instance where a faithful man thus appointed ever found himself lacking in the performance of his duties? No; I am sure the universal testimony would be that every man thus appointed and set apart has been made capable of filling his office and calling to the acceptance of the Lord, to the satisfaction of his brethren and to his own happiness. . . .

We see the same effect at home. Let a man be ordained to the office of a Bishop or a Bishop's counselor or a High Councilor and in every instance, if he be a faithful man, the spirit, power and gifts of his office will rest upon him. He will be filled with the same spirit which inspires the Prophet of God and those associated with him.

So with an Apostle. Let the Lord select a man out of the body of the people and make him an Apostle and what a change takes place. The spirit of the Apostleship rests upon him; the gifts of that Priesthood and calling descend upon him, and he becomes a changed man in consequence of the bestowal of those powers upon him. He receives authority; he enjoys the spirit of revelation; he is upheld by the people as a Prophet, Seer and Revelator. If he be a faithful man, he receives the gift and power of a Prophet and a Revelator and perhaps of a Seer. These are his rights because he has been ordained to that office; and God has promised that if men will serve and obey Him in all things, He will give them the necessary power and gifts. (DEN, July 14, 1900)

POWER ATTENDS ACTIONS OF CONFERENCES. It is always an impressive sight to me to see a congregation numbering so many people as this does raise their hands before the Lord to sustain the names of men who are presented to them as holding office in the Church; and though we do this semiannually, in our general conferences for the General Authorities and quarterly, that is, four times a year for the local authorities, it should not be in our feelings nor in our practice the performance of an empty form but should be done in a spirit that will be acceptable unto our Father and in consonance with the responsibility that devolves upon the men whom we sustain. For when we thus sustain these men, it means more than the mere lifting of our hands or at least should do so.

It means the sustaining of these men by our faith and by our prayers and so far as works are required, by our works; and when we thus vote and thus act, there is a power and an influence accompanying such action . . . that are felt by those in whose favor we vote; they feel strengthened, and God our Eternal Father seals His blessing or causes it to descend upon those who are voted for, and there is a spirit that rests down upon them from that time forward, so long as they are faithful and are thus sustained, that manifests itself unto all with whom they are brought in contact. . . .

GOD CONFIRMS AUTHORITY OF THOSE SUSTAINED. Men may sneer at the Latter-day Saints and say this is but an empty form and that it is all pre-arranged. Men may say what they please about this. It is pre-arranged according to the Spirit and mind of God, so far as that can be ascertained. When men are chosen for office, the Spirit of God is sought for by those who have the right to select, and if there be doubt upon certain points, men are not chosen; but when they are chosen and the mind of the Lord is sought for to know whether it will be agreeable to Him that they receive this office or that they should act in those positions, and when they are thus selected and thus submitted . . . to the Conference, then if they themselves live so as to have the Spirit of God with them, they will be clothed with it, and when they seek to magnify their office, God will magnify them before the people and will show them and the people that they are indeed His chosen servants and that their ministrations are acceptable unto Him, that He confirms them by the outpouring of His Spirit and the bestowal of His gifts. . . .

The Spirit and power of God will rest upon a man if he listens to it. It will impel him to action. If he cherishes it, it will be his constant companion. It will be with him in times

when he will need it, and when he does need it, if he magnifies
his calling, the Spirit and power of the Almighty—that spirit
and power and those gifts which belong to his particular office—
will rest upon him, and he will be made equal to every emergency, to every trial and will come off victorious. (Dec. 14, 1884,
JD 26:55-9)

DOES THE CORRUPTION OF A CHURCH OFFICER
INVALIDATE HIS ACTS? A man holding the Priesthood and
in good standing in the Church may nevertheless be a sinner and
a violator of the laws of God. There have been such cases in the
Church; yet, while they held the Priesthood and performed acts
such as the ordination of men under proper circumstances, those
ordinations have not been void. A man properly ordained by
another who is in this condition would receive the Priesthood
conferred upon him, although it might be subsequently discovered that he who did the ordaining was in transgression at the
time. That would not invalidate that ordination, neither would
it be necessary for the person thus ordained to be ordained a
second time.

To deprive a man legally of his Priesthood, there must be
action on the part of proper authority. There have been
Apostles who have fallen into sin, but they held their Apostleship
until they were legally deprived of it by action of their own
council or the action of the Church. When they were excommunicated by the Council, they lost all the authority which had
been conferred upon them; and so also, when excommunicated
by the Church, they lost the fellowship of the Saints and all
the promises which had been made unto them as members of
the Church. (Dec. 15, 1891, JI 26:768-9)

EXCOMMUNICATION TAKES AWAY PRIESTHOOD.
When a person has been legally cut-off from the Church of
Christ, all the rights and privileges and authority which that
person may have enjoyed as a Saint or servant of God are forfeited, and he or she becomes, to all intents and purposes, an
alien to the covenant. On this point there can be no doubt.

There may be extenuating circumstances in some cases
which, in the sight of the Lord, may have a tendency to lighten
the condemnation which follows such action, for where persons

know but little and their ignorance is not their own fault, the Lord may view them with pity and mercy, as He has said that "unto whomsoever much is given, of him shall be much required;"[6] "but he that knew not, and did commit things worthy of stripes, shall be beaten with few stripes;"[7] yet, when proper action has been taken with a member of the Church and he is excommunicated, whether he knows much or little matters not; he is deprived of every claim to blessings which, by virtue of his being a recognized member of God's Church, he may have enjoyed.

If he should afterwards repent and come forward confessing his sins and desiring to be baptized, the ordinance of baptism, when administered properly, will be administered to him as though he were being baptized for the first time and so also with the ordinance of laying-on-of-hands; the Elder will not say "I re-baptize thee," or "I re-confirm thee;" but, "I baptize thee," etc., or "I confirm thee," etc.

If a person were renewing his covenant, as the Church was required to do at the time of the reformation in the years 1856-7, then re-baptism and re-confirmation would be proper, and all the blessings and promises and authority which such a person held at the time of his re-baptism would with propriety be sealed upon him again. Not so, however, with a man who has held the Priesthood and been cut-off from the Church; he cannot claim the Priesthood by right of having once held it; he is as a new member and should receive authority of Priesthood as he received it the first time—if he received it properly then—that is, through the spirit of revelation in the man or men who have the authority to call him to bear the Priesthood and to bestow it upon him. . . .

SUSPENSION OF PRIESTHOOD AUTHORITY. While upon this subject we will allude to another misconception which is entertained by some who hold the Priesthood. It is that when a man has had the Priesthood bestowed upon him he cannot be suspended therefrom while he remains in the Church. The view of such persons seems to be that the presiding Priesthood can ordain and bestow authority but cannot recall or suspend that

---

[6]Luke 12:48.   [7]Ibid.

authority without excommunicating the man who holds it. . . .
The power which bestows authority can, if authority be misused
or not properly magnified, withdraw or suspend it; and it does
not necessarily follow that because a man is suspended from
acting in some office in the Priesthood, he is therefore cut-off from
the Church or deprived of any of the privileges of membership.
(Nov. 7, 1863, *MS* 25:713-4)

YOUTH IN THE DEACON'S OFFICE. "Why do we
ordain boys twelve or fourteen years old to the office of Deacon,
when Paul says . . . 'Let the Deacons be the husbands of one
wife'?"[8]

Paul in referring to the branches of the Church as then
organized had in mind adults who had been ordained. Probably,
in those branches the most of the members, if not all, were newly
converted; none had been born in the Church who were at that
time old enough to hold the Priesthood. With our Elders even
in these days it is a very uncommon thing to ordain, while out
in the world, very young men to any office. Mature men are
frequently ordained as Deacons and act as such.

The circumstances which surround us here in Zion are entirely different from those which surrounded the Saints in the
days of Paul and of which he wrote. There is no impropriety
whatever in young men, even as early as at the age of twelve
or fourteen years, acting as Deacons. They receive a training
that is very valuable to them, and we know of many who have
been and are greatly benefited by acting in this position, meeting
with the Deacons' quorum and receiving such instructions as are
proper to be imparted to them in this capacity. The cases to
which Paul refers, therefore, and those that exist in Zion are
not at all parallel.

All who have had experience among the young Deacons
of the Church are doubtless convinced of the propriety of ordaining our boys early, if worthy, that they may become thoroughly
familiar one by one with the duties of the various offices and
grades of the Priesthood. (Jan. 15, 1899, *JI* 34:48-9)

HIGH PRIESTS MUST BE ORDAINED. It is true that
"the office of an Elder comes under the Priesthood of Melchiz-

---

[8]I Timothy 3:12.

edek,"[9] and "an Elder has a right to officiate in his (High Priest's) stead, when the High Priest is not present."[10] But "the offices of Elder and Bishop are necessary appendages belonging unto the High Priesthood,"[11] just as "the offices of Teacher and Deacons are necessary appendages belonging to the Lesser Priesthood."[12] "Wherefore from Deacon to Teacher, and from Teacher to Priest, and from Priest to Elder, severally as they are appointed, according to the covenants and commandments of the Church. Then comes the High Priesthood, which is the greatest of all."...[13]

An Elder is not a High Priest until he is ordained to the High Priesthood. He cannot legally act in that office by being merely set apart; he must be ordained, and the High Priesthood must be bestowed upon him. (Oct. 15, 1891, JI 26:622)

PRIESTHOOD IS PARAMOUNT. I cannot too strongly impress upon you the propriety of acting in harmony with those in authority in the Priesthood. Do not imagine that prominence in [any] organization gives you rights over the Priesthood. It does not. . . . The Priesthood is paramount always, under all circumstances; and we must honor it if we wish to be honored ourselves. (Nov. 13, 1900, JI 36:267)

WARD TEACHING AN IMPORTANT CALLING. It is a very important calling and one that the Lord will hold those responsible for who receive it. . . . Now it is just as honorable in the sight of God and is as productive of reward to act as a teacher in a Ward as it is to go abroad and preach the Gospel. Your name may not be published in the papers; nevertheless, the Lord, who is the Rewarder of the children of men, will reward you if you labor wherever you are appointed, and do so faithfully.

You should not allow your manual labor to prevent you from doing your duty as teachers. . . . And let me say to the sisters, when the teachers come to your houses, gather your families together. If you know beforehand that they are coming, take pains to keep the children at home. Show the teachers proper respect when they come to visit you. The man of the house

[9]D. & C. 107:7.
[10]Ibid., 107:11.
[11]Ibid., 84:29.
[12]Ibid., 84:30.
[13]Ibid., 107:63-4.

really surrenders, for the time being, his family into the hands of the teachers; and if the teachers are wise men, they leave the household in a far better condition than they found it because they will say words of encouragement and will teach the children; and the words of the teachers when added to the words of the parents will have great influence with the children.

Therefore, to have well governed households you must have teachers. And teachers should go filled with the Spirit of God. They may be able by the influence of that Spirit to say something that will arrest some young person in his career that is likely to lead to evil. Boys and girls may be out late; they may not regard the entreaties and counsels of their parents. Teachers could help create an influence with these children that would be of great assistance to the parents.

It is proper that parents should gather their families together when the teachers come. I make it a rule, as soon as I know the teachers are at my place and I am there, to gather all my family together, and I sit with them; and if the teachers do not ask questions that are searching enough to bring out what I want, I suggest to them certain lines of inquiry; for I want my children to be benefited by the visit of the teachers. I know it is of great good, and I am pleased always when they come to my house. I try and give them all the honor I can, and I thank them with a grateful heart for their visit because I know that they come at inconvenience to themselves very frequently.

I do not care how searching they are in their inquiries. Of course, I would not want them to ask impertinent or indelicate questions. No wise man will do that. But those questions that are necessary to find out my true condition I want them to ask; and I want them to ask each member of my family and search them and find out their true feelings. Teachers do come to my house and ask me as freely as they would a member of the Church that held no office. They ask me concerning my faith, whether I sustain the authorities of the Church, whether I believe President Woodruff is the man to lead the Church, what my feelings are concerning the principles of the Gospel, whether I attend to my family and secret prayers, whether I help the poor and pay my tithing and whether I attend meetings regularly. My teachers are encouraged by me to ask these questions of me and my family to find out our true condition; and if they see anything in us that is not right, they may check it and tell us.

This is the way teachers should do. If men will follow this up, they will get a spirit, a power, a light and a testimony from God that will be of immense advantage to them. I would like to see the teachers in all the stakes zealous. Wherever the teachers are active there is a good condition. In this way the teachers maintain the morale of the Ward; that is, they teach a standard of purity that everyone with right feeling will strive to attain to. (June 20, 1892, *DW* 45:259)

WARD TEACHERS MUST LIVE GOSPEL. Experience has proved that no one can teach a principle with any success who does not practice it. . . . We hear of teachers in Wards who are called upon to visit the Saints who do not themselves perform the duties that as teachers they are required to enforce upon the attention of the families whom they visit.

It is said that there are brethren who act as ward teachers who do not pay their tithing. How any man in this condition can act conscientiously and sincerely as a teacher it is difficult to understand. One of the chief duties which devolves upon a teacher, in visiting the families of the Saints, is to inquire concerning the payment of tithing, fast offerings, etc. Now, how can any man discharge this duty in a proper manner who himself neglects these requirements?

Can a man who is guilty of neglecting his prayers enforce upon families whom he may visit the importance of prayer and the benefits which flow from prayer? Can a man who is dishonest teach honesty? Can a man whose own life is that of a sinner teach others to be saints?

Everyone can answer these questions for himself. It is when men feel the importance of duties so strongly that they never fail to perform them that they are capable of teaching others their importance and of showing them the benefits which flow to those who observe them. (Feb. 1, 1898, *JI* 33:124-5)

TEACHERS TO SEEK FOR SPIRIT OF REVELATION. Teachers, do you inquire where these girls and boys are at night? Do you inquire of the parents if the children keep good hours?

Do you inquire if they are at parties at improper hours and with improper companions and improper surroundings? You should do this. It is well enough to inquire how they feel toward the Presidency of the Church or to the Twelve or to the Presidency of the Stake or to their brethren and sisters. But there are other questions which may be asked, and which are equally as important as these. And if you live as you should do, the Spirit of the Lord will suggest these to you when you enter into the house.

You can very properly inquire concerning the habits of the young people, and perhaps by doing so you may stop some soul from committing some more deadly sin and be the means of rescuing some young person, either girl or boy, from pursuing the downward path that leads to destruction. Teachers, therefore, should be exceedingly careful, when they enter the houses of the Saints, to endeavor to obtain the spirit of revelation that the Lord will suggest to them the very things to ask and to say. (May 19, 1889, *DW* 18:18-9)

POWER OF PRIESTHOOD IN RIGHT HAND. When one hand only is used, it should be the right, for in the right hand is the power of the Priesthood. You who have received your endowments will, doubtless, know this. Therefore, when you lay your hands upon the head of an individual—whether it is to heal the sick, to ordain to the Priesthood or to confirm upon him the Holy Ghost—let your right hand always be used; and when you administer with one hand alone, let it be with your right.

Again, when you lay your hands upon the heads of persons, for any purpose which I have mentioned, do so in the name of Jesus Christ and by the authority of the Priesthood which you have received. Do not be content with expressing your intention "to confirm" the individual or "rebuke disease" or "to ordain" to such and such office in the Priesthood; but say that you do confirm the individual a member in the Church of Jesus Christ of Latter-day Saints, etc., and so, also, in regard to other ministrations. (Jan. 5, 1864, *MS* 26:210-1)

WORDS USED IN ORDINANCES. Where the Lord has condescended to reveal the exact words to be used in the performance of any ordinance of the Church, these words should be used without change or deviation, but where the Lord has not done so, it is improper, not to say impious, for men to trench upon the authority of the Holy Ghost and undertake to write or dictate forms when the Lord Himself has not thought it well so to do. It is the privilege of every man who is called to officiate in the ordinances of the Church to enjoy a portion of the Spirit of the Lord. On that Spirit he should rely when called upon to administer as a servant of the Lord, and we look with great disfavor on the tendency shown by some to have set forms prepared and used whenever there is an ordinance to be performed. We regard it as a dangerous departure from the Lord's way, one that is likely to result in grievous errors.

If a man holding the holy Priesthood is called upon to officiate in any of the duties of his calling, he should be sure that he does that which he intends, and if the Lord has given no exact formula, let him trust to the Spirit of the Lord to fill his heart and inspire his tongue, and if he is doing his duty, he will not go far wrong. Our Heavenly Father will not hold him a transgressor for a slip of the tongue or a verbal inaccuracy caused by nervousness or misapprehension; on the other hand, every officer should do his very best when ministering in the things of God; carelessness or slovenliness in the handling of holy things or the performance of sacred rites is very displeasing to Him in whose name we are officiating. (Nov. 15, 1898, *JI* 33:764)

HOW TO BLESS CHILDREN. Of course, where children are of a sufficient age to sit up alone, it is proper for the Elders to lay their hands upon them. But it has been a practice where infants are blessed for the Elders to take them up in their arms and bless them without laying their hands upon their heads. There is a power and efficacy in the laying on of hands, and where it is convenient, it is well for the Elders, if there are more than one, to lay their hands lightly upon the infant's head. Where there is only one, it is not a difficult thing for a man to hold the child so that its head will rest in his hands. There has been no fixed rule upon this point, so far as we know; but it has been the practice among the Elders, where they could lay their hands upon the heads of the children in blessing them, to do so.

When children were brought unto the Lord Jesus, "he took

them up in his arms, put his hands upon them, and blessed them."[14] It seems from this reading that He not only took them up in His arms, but He put His hands upon them. (May 1, 1891, JI 26:276)

SOME ADVICE REGARDING BLESSINGS. Every Elder who lays his hands upon a child to bless it should be careful that he is not led by fancy or by a desire to say some wonderful things instead of being prompted by the Spirit of the Lord. For when the Spirit of the Lord does not dictate, however many blessings an Elder may promise and fine things he may say, disappointment is sure to follow. The parents of the child have their expectations raised only to be dashed again to the earth. It is too often the case that in blessing children the Elders entertain the idea that they ought to pronounce upon its head every good thing they can think of. . . .

We would not have the Elders check the spirit of prophecy; but we would wish them to know that they have it and that whatever promises they may make are uttered by its promptings. A child may be blessed, and the power of God may be invoked in its behalf in a prayer offered up in the name of Jesus and in the spirit of faith, which shall be recorded on high, and yet heaven and earth not be ransacked for blessings to be pronounced upon its head.

Be the blessings ever so great and important that are placed upon the heads of children, it should ever be remembered that they are all conditional. Their fulfilment depends to a very great extent upon those who have the children in charge. If they train them up in the fear of the Lord, there is a far greater likelihood of their receiving and enjoying such blessings than if they had trained them up in a total disregard of His commandments and the truth. (Feb. 15, 1862, MS 24:106-7)

[14]Mark 10:16.

CHAPTER 20

THE APOSTLESHIP—PROPHETS, SEERS, AND ·REVELATORS

LIVING PROPHETS REJECTED BY WORLD. The world entertain certain ideas concerning truth; they entertain certain ideas concerning God and concerning His servants, and when men come to them with something that conflicts with these ideas, they are led to reject them, and it is not until a man has died, not until in many instances his blood has been shed that he is recognized as a Prophet of God. . . . It takes time to bring men to esteem Prophets. It has taken centuries to sanctify the memory of the Son of God; centuries have rolled on before He was recognized by the world as the being whom his disciples testified He was. . . .

In the same way it will take time to make the merits of the predictions of Joseph Smith recognized. Will they be recognized? Yes. (June 12, 1881, *JD* 22:177-8)

THE SIN OF THIS GENERATION. This is the condemnation of our present generation. A great Prophet has arisen in their midst. They do not believe it. They do not believe that Joseph Smith was a prophet of God. They basely and cowardly slew him. Yet, he was a Prophet of God, just as much as Elijah or as Isaiah or as any of the ancient Prophets. . . .

This is the sin of this generation. This man came in their midst bringing to them gifts from God, bringing to them a message of love and salvation, and they cruelly and basely slew him in the most abominable manner. But like all the Prophets, his blood has not been avenged. . . . God will hold this generation to a strict accountability for these acts, just as sure as He did the generation who slew the Apostles and those who lived contemporaneous with the Apostles. (May 27, 1883, *JD* 24:139-40)

Never at any previous time in the world's history has a Prophet come forth having stronger evidence to support him in claiming to be a servant of God in possession of the Spirit of the

Lord than has this Prophet (Joseph Smith). It was necessary that it should be so that this generation might be left without excuse. The work was to be a great and mighty one; and though in the commencement the means seemed inadequate to produce it, yet, like the tree grown from the mustard seed of which Jesus spoke, it is destined eventually to overshadow the earth and afford shelter to all who are willing to accept it. (*Liahona* 30:543)

APOSTOLIC SUCCESSION. The Scriptures plainly teach that the Apostleship was an office of the Priesthood as necessary to be filled as that of the Evangelist, Pastor or Teacher. . . . Paul, himself an Apostle, though not one of the Twelve, says, in his Epistle to the Ephesians, that these officers—Apostles, Prophets, Pastors and Teachers—were to be placed in the Church "for the perfecting of the saints, for the work of the ministry, for the edifying of the body of Christ: till we all come in the unity of the faith, and of the knowledge of the Son of God, unto a perfect man, unto the measure of the stature of the fulness of Christ. . . ."[1] The Pastors and Teachers were not the only officers necessary in the Church to accomplish these desirable results—the Apostles and Prophets were also needed.

Paul, in another epistle, when writing to the Corinthians about the organization of the Church, says that God had set in the Church, "first apostles, secondarily prophets,"[2] etc. These were the principal officers in the Church, the foundation, with Jesus Christ as the chief cornerstone, and the Church of Christ could not exist without them. If Paul, then, can be relied upon as a competent judge of the nature of the office of an Apostle, we may be assured that it is the nature of their office to have successors and that, inasmuch as mankind are not in the situation which they are to be brought into by the aid of Apostles, Prophets, Pastors and Teachers, they ought to be in the Church at the present and will have to be continued in the Church, or this happy state of things will never be brought about. . . .

QUORUM TO BE PERPETUATED. We find that in ancient days when a vacancy occurred in the quorum of the Twelve Apostles selected by Jesus, the remainder of the Apostles

---

[1]Ephesians 4:12-13.   [2]I Corinthians 12:28.

chose one to fill his place as a witness of Jesus, and he was numbered with them. If it was not the nature of the office to have succession, why was Matthias chosen to fill the place of an apostate? Why did not the eleven act without attempting to fill the place of him who had forfeited his office?

If it were necessary that the eleven should ordain one, to make the number complete of those whom the Lord had chosen as His special witnesses, and they had the power to do so, if there had been eleven vacancies instead of one and but one man holding the Apostleship left, he also would have had the right, by parity of reasoning, to have ordained the eleven. The fact that one was ordained, however, is in itself a sufficient evidence that the nature of the office demanded succession and that so long as Christ's Church remained upon the earth, while there was a soul to be saved, a heathen to be converted, or a testimony to be borne to the world that Christ was the Son of the Eternal Father and had indeed risen and they were His witnesses, so long the Apostleship would be necessary. . . .

It is His will that Apostles should be in His Church whenever it is organized upon the earth; and it is through the want of them and their teachings that we now witness the disunion and strife so prevalent around us and, most of all, among the sects who profess to be His. It is for want of these officers that the inhabitants of the earth have not arrived at the unity of the faith, have not attained unto the knowledge of the Son of God and are tossed to and fro and carried about by every wind of doctrine, as they have been and are at the present time. (July 12, 1856, *WS* 160-2)

PROPHETS AND APOSTLES NECESSARY. If the Scriptures the Jews had and the Scriptures we at present have are examined, it will be found that there is a greater amount of evidence in our possession in favor of the idea of living oracles or Prophets and Apostles being raised up and inspired in these days than there was among the Jews in the days of the Apostles to support them in believing that they would make their appearance at that time. In fact the Scriptures cannot be fulfilled until these things take place. . . .

Since the creation of man and the first revelation of God's will unto him, we have no account of the Lord ever having a people upon the earth or a system which He recognized as being His without also having men of this description—men with whom He could communicate and through whom His mind and will could be made known to the people. They were the living oracles possessing living Priesthood through which they could obtain light and intelligence from the Almighty to expound with authority to the children of men; and their words, whether delivered orally or written, were equally binding upon the people with the words of any preceding servant of God. That this was the case all sacred history bears abundant evidence.

The necessity of inspired men, in order that the prophecies may be fulfilled, must be apparent. Man has always been the instrument which the Lord has used to accomplish His purposes. But apart from the prophecies which set forth in unmistakable language that the days of revelation and intercourse between the Deity and man will again be restored, there is an abundance of evidence to prove that there cannot be a Church of Christ on the earth without having Prophets and Apostles as its officers. . . .

MEANING OF SCRIPTURES DISTORTED. Men instead of making their belief conform to the Bible have endeavored to distort it and make it correspond with their ideas and systems; when the plainly written word would not admit of that, they have endeavored to hide their errors and the incorrectness of their position by stating that the Scriptures have a spiritual meaning, and they do not literally mean what their language denotes, but they require to be spiritualized to be understood.

Miserable subterfuge! What a cunning device of the adversary of souls and his agents to entrap and deceive mankind! Impress upon the people that these are no longer necessary, and they will cease to look for them; persuade them to believe that the word of God has a different meaning from the one apparent on its face, and they will see nothing condemnatory of sin and the commission of gross wrong; Satan's victory and triumph will then be easy. . . .

If men believe the Bible, they must believe as Latter-day Saints, and if there is a Church of Christ upon the earth there must of necessity be Prophets and Apostles, and if there are Prophets and Apostles, they have the right to teach and instruct mankind in the principles of the Lord's Kingdom, and their teachings and counsels are entitled to consideration and obedience. (April 26, 1856, WS 82-5)

JOSEPH SMITH A PROPHET BEFORE ORDINATION. It is a remarkable fact that Joseph Smith had gifts before he was ordained. He was a Seer, for he translated before he was ordained; he was a Prophet, for he predicted a great many things before he was ordained and before the Church was organized; he was a Revelator, for God gave unto him revelations before the Church was organized. He, therefore, was a Prophet, Seer and Revelator before he was ordained in the flesh.[3] Did you ever think of it? Brother Joseph Smith was a Prophet, Seer and Revelator before he ever received any Priesthood in the flesh. . . .

He was ordained a Prophet, doubtless, before he came here; but that ordination did not give him the right to immerse men and women in the waters of baptism, neither did it give him the power to lay on hands for the gift of the Holy Ghost. He had to await the authority from on high. (May 8, 1881, JD 22:267)

LIMITS OF AUTHORITY NOT OVERSTEPPED. That authority was not conferred upon him when he first saw angels and had some of the gifts of which I have spoken. It required the laying on of the hands of some personage or personages who had the authority of the Holy Priesthood.

No, Joseph never ran until he was sent. He exhibited in this the qualities of the man that he was; there are few men, as we well know, who, if they had obtained the gifts that he possessed, would not have overstepped the limit of their calling and authority and done something beyond their province. But Joseph did not err in this way; he had been too well taught of the Lord, and therefore he waited. . . .

KEYS AND APOSTLESHIP RESTORED. He . . . received the authority of the Melchizedek Priesthood under the hands of those who last held the keys of that Priesthood upon the earth. When Jesus, you will remember, took His three disciples into the mount, He was transfigured before them, and Moses and Elias administered unto them, and at that time Peter was or-

---

[3] "Every man who has a calling to minister to the inhabitants of the world was ordained to that very purpose in the Grand Council of heaven before this world was. I suppose that I was ordained to this very office in that Grand Council." (*Teachings of the Prophet Joseph Smith,* Page 365).

dained to hold the keys of that dispensation. He held the keys in conjunction with his brethren, James and John.

They came and unitedly laid their hands upon the heads of Joseph and Oliver and ordained them to the authority that they themselves held, namely, that of the Apostleship. In this way they received the authority of the Melchizedek Priesthood and could administer in the ordinances that belong to that Priesthood, one of which is the laying on of hands for the gift of the Holy Ghost. Until that time they had not received that ordinance. . . .

There is no doubt in my mind that Joseph Smith was called just as the Son of God, our Lord and Redeemer, was called before the foundation of the earth, as Jeremiah in his record says he was, and was ordained to be a Prophet, Seer and Revelator and to stand at the head of this last dispensation. Although this was the case, it was still necessary that he should be baptized and have hands laid upon him for the reception of the Holy Ghost and also be ordained to the Priesthood of Aaron and Melchizedek. . . .

KEYS OF OTHER DISPENSATIONS BESTOWED. In addition to this the Prophet Joseph informs us in his letter addressed to the Saints when he fled away from Nauvoo to escape the hands of his enemies that "It is necessary in the ushering in of the dispensation of the fullness of times, which dispensation is now beginning to usher in, that a whole and complete and perfect union, and welding together of dispensations, and keys, and powers, and glories should take place, and be revealed from the days of Adam even to the present time." He, therefore, received the ministration of divers angels—heads of dispensations —from Michael or Adam down to the present time, every man in his time and season coming to him, and all declaring their dispensation, their rights, their keys, their honors, their majesty and glory, and the power of their Priesthood.

PROPHET JOSEPH PRESIDES OVER DISPENSATION. Joseph, the head of this dispensation, Prophet, Seer and Revelator, whom God raised up, received from all these different sources, according to the mind and will of God and according to the design of God concerning him; he received from all these different sources all the power and all the authority and all keys that were necessary for the building up of the work of God in the last days and for the accomplishment of His purposes connected with this dispensation. He stands at the head. He is a unique character, differing from every other man in this respect and excelling every other man.

Because he was the head, God chose him, and while he was faithful, no man could take his place and position. He was faithful and died faithful. He stands, therefore, at the head of this dispensation and will throughout all eternity, and no man can take that power away from him. If any man holds these keys, he holds them subordinate to Joseph Smith.

OTHER PROPHETS SUBORDINATE TO PROPHET JOSEPH. You never heard President Young teach any other doctrine; he always said that Joseph stood at the head of this dispensation, that Joseph holds the keys, that although Joseph had gone behind the veil, he stood at the head of this dispensation and that he himself held the keys subordinate to him. President Taylor teaches the same doctrine, and you will never hear any other doctrine from any of the faithful Apostles or servants of God, who understand the order of the Holy Priesthood.

SALVATION WITH HIS PERMISSION. If we get our salvation, we shall have to pass by him; if we enter into our glory, it will be through the authority that he has received. We cannot get around him; we cannot get around President Young; we cannot get around President Taylor; we cannot get around the Twelve Apostles. If we ever attain to that eternal glory that God has promised to the faithful, we shall have to pass by them. If we enter into our exaltation, it will be because they, as the servants of God, permit us to pass by, just as the revelation says, "pass by the angels, and the Gods, which are set there,"[4] to our exaltation.

You know that Jesus said to His Apostles in ancient days that they should "sit upon twelve thrones judging the twelve tribes of Israel."[5] And Paul says, "The saints shall judge the world."[6] This is true. Joseph, then, stands at the head and then every man in his place after him until you come down to the

---

[4]D. & C. 132:19. [6]I Corinthians 6:2.
[5]Matthew 19:28.

Elder, the most humble Elder of the Church who has proclaimed the Gospel of the Son of God to the inhabitants of the earth. He will sit as a judge to judge those who have received or those who have rejected his testimony. He will stand as a swift witness before the judgment seat of God against this generation.

He will lift up his voice testifying as to that which he has done, and men will be condemned, and men will be justified and women will be justified according to the testimony of the faithful servants of God, each one in his place and station, but Joseph holding the keys and presiding over all, subordinate, however, to him from whom he received the keys, as he (Peter) will be subordinate to the Son of God who placed them upon him, each one in his dispensation, each one in his place, each exercising the authority of his Priesthood, each man honoring God according to his faithfulness and diligence in magnifying that Priesthood and calling that God has placed upon him, and each woman in her place receiving her share of glory and honor according to her faithfulness in keeping the commandments of God and honoring the Priesthood. . . .

JOSEPH POSSESSED ALL KEYS AT DEATH. When Joseph died, he had embodied in him all the keys and all the authority, all the powers and all the qualifications necessary for the head of a dispensation to stand at the head of this great last dispensation. They had been bestowed upon him through the providences of God and through the command of God to his faithful servants who lived in ancient days. There was no end scarcely, in many respects, to the knowledge that he received. . . . In this respect he stands unique. There is no man in this dispensation can occupy the station that he, Joseph, did, God having reserved him and ordained him for that position and bestowed upon him the necessary power. . . .

ALL KEYS BESTOWED ON TWELVE. While he was in possession of all his faculties and likely to live for many years to lead the Church—in fact the people believed that he would live to redeem Zion—when he was thus situated, impressed by the Spirit and power of God, he called together our leading men, and he bestowed upon the Twelve Apostles all the keys and authority and power that he himself possessed and that he had received from the Lord. He gave unto them every endowment, every washing, every anointing and administered unto them the sealing ordinances and taught them the character of those ordinances. . . .

And filled with the power of God, he blessed them and placed those keys and this authority upon them and told them that he had thus ordained them to bear off the Kingdom. There was no key that he held, there was no authority that he exercised that he did not bestow upon the Twelve Apostles at that time. Of course, in doing this he did not divest himself of the keys; but he bestowed upon them these keys and this authority and power so that they held them in their fullness as he did, differing only in this respect that they exercised them subordinate to him as the head of the dispensation. He ordained them to all this authority without withholding a single power or key or ordinance that he himself had received.

Thus, you see, these men whom God chose to hold the Apostleship received all this authority from Him. Hence, he told the people before he was taken, "I roll this kingdom off on to the shoulders of the Twelve. . . ."

DESIRED HYRUM TO SUCCEED TO PRESIDENCY. I was but a boy at the time, but I remember it very distinctly. He evidently wanted his brother Hyrum also to be preserved, and for some time before his martyrdom talked about him as the Prophet. But Hyrum, as you know, was not desirous to live away from Joseph; if he was to be exposed to death, he was resolved to be with him. (Oct. 29, 1882, JD 23:359-63)

LIFE PRESERVED UNTIL WORK COMPLETED. God preserved his life until every key, every authority, every power and every gift that he had received from the eternal worlds, through the ministration of angels, from the days of Adam down to the days of Moroni, was again restored to the earth and sealed upon the heads of men, and then it proved more difficult for Satan to accomplish his purpose. He slew Joseph; but it was too late to prevent him communicating that authority which he had received; and the Church organization was preserved on the earth.

Joseph lived long enough, as did our Elder Brother Jesus, to accomplish the work God sent him to do. He laid the foundation of the Church. He laid it so deep that it will never be overthrown. He bestowed upon man the everlasting Priesthood, with all its authority, from the Apostleship down to the authority of a Deacon, with every key, every endowment and every ordinance necessary to accomplish the work of God upon the earth. (Sept. 2, 1883, JD 24:375)

RELATION OF NEPHITE TWELVE TO TWELVE AT JERUSALEM. You remember reading in the Book of Mormon that the Twelve on this continent, whom the Savior chose after His resurrection, are to be judged by the Twelve Apostles that were at Jerusalem. It was with Peter, who was the senior Apostle there, that the keys rested. He was at the head of that dispensation; therefore, those that received the Apostleship on this land were to be judged by the Twelve at Jerusalem. There the keys were; and it was right and proper that Peter, with James and John, should come and bestow them upon him who was to be the head of this dispensation, namely, Joseph Smith. (Oct. 29, 1882, JD 23:360)

JOSEPH SMITH HELD APOSTLESHIP. My views are that the Lord chose in the first place an Apostle, Joseph Smith, to commence the building up of the Kingdom of God; and he did not organize the Church till he received the Apostleship. And as the work progressed he chose High Priests and other Apostles and Seventies to go forth to the nations and act for him as he could not leave Zion himself. But he needed aid in building up the Kingdom—helps in the work of the ministry—and he called these men and bestowed upon them a portion of the Priesthood he himself held, to go forth and act for him. He could not divide himself up and have a part go here and another part go there; therefore, he sent them with authority to act in his stead and he acted in the place of Jesus. The authority, then, originated in the Apostleship; and as he was the first Apostle, by virtue of that authority he presided in every place where there were Saints. (Jan. 3, 1862, MS 24:113-4)

PROPHETS, SEERS AND REVELATORS. The question has been asked as to why the Twelve Apostles are sustained as Prophets, Seers, and Revelators.

In Section 21 of the Book of Doctrine and Covenants, the Lord says that a record shall be kept, and in it Joseph shall be called a Seer, a Translator, a Prophet, an Apostle of Jesus Christ and an Elder of the church.

In the 4th, 5th and 8th paragraphs the Lord says:

Wherefore, meaning the church, thou shalt give heed unto all his words and commandments which he shall give unto you as he receiveth them, walking in all holiness before me;

For his word ye shall receive, as if from mine own mouth, in all patience and faith.

For by doing these things the gates of hell shall not prevail against you; yea, and the Lord God will disperse the powers of darkness from before you, and cause the heavens to shake for your good, and His name's glory.

In Section 28, paragraphs 2, 3 and 7, the Lord says:

But, behold, verily, verily, I say unto thee, no one shall be appointed to receive commandments and revelations in this church excepting my servant Joseph Smith, Jun., for he receiveth them even as Moses;

And thou shall be obedient unto the things which I shall give unto him, even as Aaron, to declare faithfully the commandments and the revelations, with power and authority unto the church. . . .

For I have given him the keys of the mysteries and the revelations which are sealed, until I shall appoint unto them another in his stead.

In the 43rd Section, paragraphs 2-7, the Lord says:

For behold, verily, verily, I say unto you, that ye have received a commandment for a law unto my church, through him whom I have appointed unto you to receive commandments and revelations from my hand.

And this ye shall know assuredly—that there is none other appointed unto you to receive commandments and revelations until he be taken, if he abide in me.

But verily, verily, I say unto you, that none else shall be appointed unto this gift except it be through him, for if it be taken from him, he shall not have power except to appoint another in his stead.

And this shall be a law unto you, that ye receive not the teachings of any that shall come before you as revelations or commandments;

And this I give unto you that you may not be deceived; that you may know they are not of me.

For verily I say unto you, that he that is ordained of me shall come in at the gate and be ordained as I have told you before, to teach those revelations which you have received and shall receive through him whom I have appointed.

The same principle is set forth quite fully in paragraph 7, of Section 132, in which the Lord says:

And I have appointed unto my servant Joseph to hold this power in the last days, and there is never but one on the earth at a time on whom this power and the keys of this priesthood are conferred.

These quotations from the revelations clearly show that while the Prophet Joseph lived he alone had the authority to give written commandments and revelations to the Church. Oliver Cowdery was ordained, as Joseph was, to the Apostleship, and was the second Elder in the Church; yet the Lord clearly defined how far he could go in the exercise of the authority that he had received. In paragraphs 4, 5 and 6, Section 28, speaking to Oliver, the Lord says:

And if thou art led at any time by the Comforter to speak or teach, or at all times by the way of commandment unto the church, thou mayest do it.

But thou shalt not write by way of commandment, but by wisdom;

And thou shalt not command him who is at thy head, and at the head of the church.

Oliver Cowdery could speak or teach by way of commandment to the church, but he was not authorized to write commandments.

In Section 68, paragraphs 4 and 5, speaking to some of the Elders, the Lord says:

And whatsoever they shall speak when moved upon by the Holy Ghost shall be scripture, shall be the will of the Lord, shall be the mind of the Lord, shall be the word of the Lord, shall be the voice of the Lord, and the power of God unto salvation:

So, not only had Oliver Cowdery the right to speak and teach by way of commandment to the church, but all the Elders who spoke by the Holy Ghost had the same right; yet they did not have the authority to write commandments or to give laws for the government of the church.

In the 42nd Section, paragraphs 12-17, the Elders, Priests and Teachers of this Church were informed by the Lord the manner in which they should teach, and He authorized them to lift up their voices by the Comforter, and they were to speak and prophesy as seemed good unto the Lord. There was no limit placed upon them in speaking and prophesying, so long as they did so under the influence of the Spirit of God. But they were expressly commanded that they were not to teach if they did not receive the Spirit.

These revelations show very clearly the distinction which exists between the head of the Church and the other officers of the Church. The latter might prophesy and teach and instruct and even write by way of wisdom to the Church; but it is the privilege of the head alone to give written revelations and commandments to the Church, for the guidance and government of the Church. This distinction should always be kept in mind so that it may be understood that though men may hold the same authority, as in the case of the Apostles, yet there is only one who has the right and privilege to hold the keys and to exercise the authority belonging thereto.

Now, to turn to the question: "Can a number of men be Prophets, Seers and Revelators and yet not interfere with the rights of him who stands at the head?"

There is no reason why this should not be the case. By reference to Section 124, paragraphs 91-95, it will be seen that the Lord, by His own voice, appointed Hyrum Smith to be "a prophet, seer and a revelator unto my church, as well as my servant Joseph." . . .

Hyrum was to have the same blessing and glory and honor and Priesthood and gifts of the Priesthood that were once put upon Oliver Cowdery. Oliver Cowdery had received these gifts and powers from the Lord; but he fell away, and the Lord by this revelation selected Hyrum Smith to receive all that Oliver Cowdery had lost, so he was, to all intents and purposes, a Prophet, Seer and Revelator the same as the Prophet Joseph. But, as in the case of Oliver Cowdery, he had to look to Joseph as his head and did not have the authority to write commandments to the Church; for this belonged only to the President of the Church.

There are many now living who can doubtless recall how frequently the Prophet Joseph mentioned in public that Hyrum was a Prophet. He led the Saints to understand by his remarks that Hyrum had received this power and authority. Here, then, were two Prophets, Seers and Revelators, both appointed by direct revelation from the Lord, and these revelations are written.

But, in addition to these, on March 27, 1836, the Prophet Joseph Smith called upon the "quorums and congregation of

Saints to acknowledge the Twelve Apostles who were present as Prophets, Seers and Revelators,"[7] and they were thus sustained. Their being ordained to this authority and sustained as such does not lead to confusion nor to the least conflict of authority, any more than the reception of the gift of prophecy by the Elders leads to any conflict between them and the President of the Church. The remark of the Prophet Moses upon this point is so applicable and so beautifully expresses the correct idea that we insert it. Two young men had been prophesying in the camp of Israel, and Joshua asked Moses to forbid them. Moses replied: "Enviest thou for my sake? would God that all the Lord's people were prophets, and that the Lord would put his spirit upon them!"[8] (Jan. 1, 1891, JI 26:26-28)

APOSTLESHIP EMBODIES ALL AUTHORITY. President Brigham Young, during his lifetime, set forth with great plainness the authority of the Apostleship. We do not quote his exact language; but he said that when a man was ordained an Apostle he received all the authority of the Priesthood that a man could hold on the earth in the flesh. It comprehended all the offices of the Priesthood. . . .

The Prophet Joseph Smith and Oliver Cowdery were ordained Apostles before the organization of the Church. By virtue of that authority Joseph acted. (July 1, 1890, JI 25:404-5)

The Apostleship, now held in this Church, embodies all the authority bestowed by the Lord upon man in the flesh. . . . The Lord has given unto His people and to His Church every gift and every qualification and every key which is necessary to lead this people into the Celestial Kingdom of our Father and our God. There is nothing wanting.

When the Lord restored the Apostleship to the earth, he restored all the power that was possible for a human being to hold in the flesh. . . .

AUTHORITY THAT SAVES. The same spirit of revelation that Moses had, concerning which God speaks through the Prophet Joseph Smith, has rested upon men that have held the keys of this Kingdom, whether it was during President Young's

---

[7]History of the Church 2:417.   [8]Numbers 11:29.

life or at the present time—that same spirit of revelation rests upon him who holds the Presidency as senior Apostle in the midst of the people of God. The Apostles of this Church have all the authority; they have all the keys, and it is within the purview of their office and calling to have all the spirit of revelation necessary to lead this people into the presence of the Lamb in the Celestial Kingdom of our God. (Nov. 2, 1879, JD 21:269-70)

AMBASSADORS FOR CHRIST. The Prophet Brigham . . . acts in his present position by virtue of his authority as an Apostle of the Lord Jesus Christ. That Apostleship makes a man an ambassador in Christ's stead unto the people. He has power to bind on the earth, and the Lord, whose ambassador he is, will ratify it in the heavens; he has power to loose on the earth, and it will be loosed in heaven. Every act necessary to be performed for the salvation of man he has the right to attend to, and it will be equally as legal and binding as though the Lord Jesus himself had done it, because he is His legally authorized and empowered ambassador. This is the power of the Apostleship as plainly set forth in the Scriptures, and anything less than this is not. (April 24, 1857, WS 392)

ONLY ONE CHANNEL FOR RECEIVING PRIESTHOOD. The Priesthood which the Lord bestowed upon His Prophet Joseph is the only Priesthood that any man can receive. What I mean by that is that it must come to us in that direct channel, and it cannot be received through any other channel. There have been men who have professed to have had the ministration of angels and to have received revelations and to have authority to lead the Church and to give revelations to the Church, having been called to do this as they have claimed outside of the Priesthood given to the Prophet Joseph Smith. I wish to impress upon the minds of my brethren that all such pretensions, you may know for yourselves, are false. No man can, no man ever will, receive this Priesthood of which we are the bearers unless he receives it through the channels which God has appointed. . . .

Suppose any number of men should pretend that they had been visited by holy messengers and had received manifestations from God, can you for a moment imagine that God would give any authority, except it were given in the line or channel which He has prepared and through which the Priesthood has already come? Can anyone think that the Lord would send His holy angels from heaven to lay hands upon Joseph and Oliver—chosen vessels for this purpose—and restore the everlasting Priesthood, as He did, and then allow some side person to receive it in some surreptitious and illegal manner? . . .

NO POWER LACKING. Some have got the idea that there is something lacking, some absence of power which some great Prophet, a Prophet greater than anybody we have ever had, will have to restore. Such ideas unsettle people in their minds and faith and produce dissatisfaction and discontent. I am looking for great manifestations of the power of God; but I am not looking—I never have been—for any great and wonderful thing of this kind to occur. Prophets will undoubtedly continue to arise. We shall have men with various gifts. The Prophet Joseph was succeeded by the Prophet Brigham, who . . . was one of the mightiest Prophets that ever lived.

FEW EVER GIFTED LIKE PROPHET JOSEPH. Of course, there is a difference in men's gifts. Very few men have ever lived on the earth who have been gifted like the Prophet Joseph. We would not make any comparison between any Apostle and the Savior, and it is scarcely right to make a comparison between any Prophet and the Prophet Joseph. He was chosen expressly to lay the foundation of this great work, and the Lord gave him wonderful power and wonderful revelations. He received a continued stream of revelation from the time that the Father and the Son visited him until the time of his death. He was a great and mighty spirit. I always try to avoid making comparisons between servants of God; but I doubt whether there ever was a Prophet who received so much light in the same length of time, for he died in comparative youth, being only thirty-eight years of age. (March 3, 1889, *DW* 38:386-7)

NO PRIESTHOOD AUTHORITY OUTSIDE CHURCH. At the death of the Prophet Joseph Smith, and probably for many years subsequent to his death, some people seemed to have the feeling that when he died there died with him some power and some authority and some knowledge that could not be regained very readily and was out of the possession of those who presided over the Church.

This feeling may prevail to some extent at the present time —the feeling that some great one has to arise in our midst in order to revive the old power and restore it to the Church and to perform the mighty works that God has promised shall be performed in connection with His Zion of the last days. I do not believe that all the Latter-day Saints understand as they should —I speak now in general terms—the authority, the gifts and qualifications which God bestowed upon His servant Brigham; and there were many who, after the Prophet's death, were not disposed to accord to President Young the same rights, the same authority, the same gifts that they were willing to accord to the Prophet Joseph. . . .

Those who look for some increased manifestation of power to come in some form outside of that which we recognize as the governing authority of the Church are in danger of being deluded and being led astray. Such persons . . . are in just the condition that the adversary would like people to be in that he may have influence with them. . . .

Where there is a feeling to look for some authority outside of our present organization of the Holy Priesthood, you can readily see how the adversary could take advantage of it and puff vain, weak men up with the idea that they are to be some great ones. No greater mistake can be indulged in than for any person to suppose that there is not that authority in the Church at the present time that is necessary for the establishment, for the government and guidance and for the building up and complete control of the Church and Kingdom of our God upon the earth according to the pattern which He has given. (Oct. 29, 1882, JD 23:357-9)

THE KEYS OF THE APOSTLESHIP. Every man who is ordained to the fullness of Apostleship has the power and the authority to lead and guide the people of God whenever he is called upon to do it and the responsibility rests upon him. . . . And while it is the right of all the Twelve Apostles to receive revelation and for each one to be a Prophet, to be a Seer, to be a Revelator and to hold the keys in the fullness, it is only the right of one man at a time to exercise that power in relation to the whole people and to give revelation and counsel and direct the affairs of the Church—of course, always acting in conjunction with his fellow-servants.

And while we say that the Twelve Apostles have the right to govern, that the Twelve have the authority, that the Twelve Apostles are the men who preside, we do not mean that every one of the Twelve is going to give revelation to this great people, that every one of the Twelve has the right to counsel and dictate and regulate the affairs of the Church as emergencies may arise, independent of the rest. The Church is not governed like Zion's Co-operative Institution, by a Board of Directors; this is not God's design. It is governed by men who hold the keys of the Apostleship, who have the right and authority.

Any one of them, should an emergency arise, can act as President of the Church, with all the powers, with all the authority, with all the keys and with every endowment necessary to obtain revelation from God and to lead and guide this people in the path that leads to the celestial glory; but there is only one man at a time who can hold the keys, who can dictate, who can guide, who can give revelation to the Church. The rest must acquiesce in his action; the rest must be governed by his counsels; the rest must receive his doctrines. . . .

When revelation comes to this people, it is he who has the right to give it. When counsel comes to this people, as a people, it is he who has the right to impart it; and while the Twelve are associated with him, one in power, one in authority, they must respect him as their President, they must look to him as the man through whom the voice of God will come to them and to this entire people. . . .

NO ORDINATION REQUIRED TO PRESIDE. In relation to ordination a great many people have imagined that it was necessary to ordain a man to succeed another, that it would impart a particular efficacy or endow him with some additional power. Ordination is always good and acceptable; blessings and setting apart are always desirable to those who have to go forth to prepare them for God's service; but it is not necessary that an Apostle should be ordained to stand at the head of the people.

When the exigency arises, he has already got the fulness of authority and the power of it. . . .

If every man of the Twelve but one were slain, the remaining one would have the right to organize a First Presidency of the Church, to choose Twelve Apostles and to organize the Church in its fulness and power and to preside over it. And his acts would be accepted of the Lord and binding upon the people. This is the authority of the Apostleship. If every Apostle anciently had been slain but John the Revelator, as they all were, and there had been faith and men enough left, he would have had the right to ordain other Apostles and set in order the entire Church and carry forward the work as the Lord should dictate it. So in our day. As I have stated, it is not necessary for a man who has received this power and these keys to be ordained and set apart to act; he can act in any position.

COUNSELORS NOT SET APART. President Young, when he chose Brother George A. Smith to be his First Counselor in the place of Heber C. Kimball, did not lay his hands upon his head to confer upon him any additional power or authority for the position because Brother George A. held the Apostleship in its fulness, and by virtue of that Priesthood he could act in that or in any other position in the Church. He chose other Assistant Counselors; he did not set them apart; there was no necessity for it as they already held the Apostleship. And if he had, he could only have blessed them; he could not bestow upon them any more than they already had because they had all that he himself had, that is when he chose them from the same Quorum. He did choose several of his Assistant Counselors from the Quorum of the Twelve; he did not put his hands upon them to set them apart nor to give them the authority and power to act as his Counselors; they already held it.

It is well for the Latter-day Saints to understand the principles of the Holy Priesthood and the power thereof that it may be known by you where the authority rests, who has the right to teach and guide and counsel in the affairs of the Kingdom of God. The Lord has revealed it in plainness so that a wayfaring man, though a fool, need not err therein.

Was it necessary that Elder Taylor should be set apart to preside over this people? Was it necessary that the Twelve

Apostles should be set apart to preside over this people? No, it was not for they already possessed the power, authority and ordination. Was it necessary for the Prophet Joseph Smith to set apart Brigham or Heber or Willard or any of the rest of the Twelve Apostles? No, for the same reason; they had received the fulness of the Holy Priesthood, the full endowment and the keys and the authority and the fulness of the Apostleship; therefore, it was not necessary.

NO IMPROPRIETY IN A BLESSING. It might have been done; there would have been no wrong in doing it; there would be no impropriety in blessing a man; there would be no impropriety in a man like Joseph or Brigham, favored of God with the power to move the heavens to bring down blessings upon the children of men, I say, there would be no impropriety in such men laying their hands upon any man and blessing him; the Lord would bless him, if he were thus blessed. But I am now speaking of the authority and power of the Holy Priesthood. The blessing of such men or by such men would not bestow upon him any additional authority or any more keys, presuming that he already had received the fulness of the Apostleship. (Oct. 8, 1877, JD 19:233-6)

GREAT RESPONSIBILITY RESTS ON GENERAL AUTHORITIES. Our history, as a Church, has been like a drama. No scenes acted upon the theatrical stage ever possessed more engrossing interest than have the scenes of our lives as Latter-day Saints. And there is a constant change of circumstances. We are invironed by new difficulties, and it requires constant watchfulness on our part to avoid taking a wrong step or committing ourselves in some direction that might be injurious to us.

Therefore, God has ordained that there shall be Prophets and Apostles, whose duty it is to guide and counsel, to instruct, to reprove when necessary, to warn; and great responsibility rests upon them in connection with these duties. I tremble at the very thought of it. I am filled with feelings that cause me to shrink when I think about the great responsibility that God has placed upon the leading Elders of this Church.

The welfare, the future happiness and the prosperity of the

people are to a great extent entrusted to those men who are called to be the shepherds of the flock of Christ. I often ask myself, how can I appear before the Lord Jesus, my Master, if He should call me to account for the charge that He has placed upon me; can I stand up and say I have not obstructed the work with which I am connected; I have not obscured the light of heaven; I have not acted in any way to divert the rays of truth from shining in the midst of the children of men—I ask myself, can I stand in this position and look upon the face of God without feeling condemned and that my garments are unstained with the blood of this generation, that I have been a faithful minister of the Lord, a faithful shepherd of the flock of Christ, a watchman who has never slept at his post, who has never failed to utter the cry of warning when danger has menaced the Zion of God? This is a feeling it seems to me every man who bears the holy Priesthood ought to have. (Sept. 2, 1889, DW 39:461)

SHEPHERDS AND WATCHMEN. Great responsibilities rest upon the officers of the Church of Jesus Christ of Latter-day Saints. The souls of the children of men are entrusted to their care. They are called shepherds of the flock of Christ, and if the sheep of the flock are injured or destroyed, the blame rests upon the shepherds. They are also called watchmen. They must stand and give warning of the approach of danger. They tell the people to prepare to escape threatened evil. If they are not watchful and vigilant, trouble may fall upon those whom they are appointed to guard and care for. (July 1, 1886, JI 21:200)

SHEPHERDS OVER THE FLOCK. I cannot lift my hand against this people and be prospered in it, nor can any other man. No man can join with the enemies of this people and hope to succeed; for God will desert him no matter how high his standing may be, and all who follow in his footsteps will find themselves dreadfully deceived.

We may as well warn you of this and tell you the truth, whatever may be said about it. We do not want any of your blood clinging to our garments. We do not want to stand in the positions we do and hold our peace and see the people misled and going astray. God has placed us as shepherds over His flock, and if we do not look out for the flock, He will smite us and remove us. We are placed as watchmen upon the walls of Zion, and if we do not give warning when we see danger, then we are culpable and will be condemned of God.

Now, if you want to know why we talk this way, understand that this is the reason: We are responsible to the Lord for you, and we cannot shirk that responsibility. Our opponents may be offended at these remarks and misquote them; but that does not make a particle of difference. Must we stand and let the people go astray and not lift up our voices in warning? Why, we might as well die today and be done with it and let somebody else come and take our places and do the work. What is the use of our being in this position unless we are men and have the willingness to declare the whole counsel of God as it comes to us? (April 5, 1897, *DW* 54:675)

ONLY ONE TO GUIDE SHIP OF ZION. It is my privilege as an Apostle of the Lord Jesus Christ to have the revelations of Jesus. It is my privilege to live so as to have the gift of prophecy and to have wisdom and knowledge from God. It is my privilege to have all these gifts and blessings resting down upon me by virtue of my calling. If I am faithful thereto, they will rest upon me. But it is not my privilege to guide this ship. It is not my privilege to write revelations or commandments to this Church. Much as I may rejoice in the knowledge of God, much as I may be possessed of the revelations of Jesus, that is not a privilege which has been accorded unto me, nor has it been accorded unto any other Apostle or officer or member of this Church but one, and that is the man whom God has chosen to hold the keys.

WATCH THE CAPTAIN. Therefore, in times of danger, whatever my own feelings may be—and as those who are acquainted with me know, I have pronounced opinions generally upon every subject that is brought up—notwithstanding this characteristic, I look always, and always have looked, to the man whom God has placed to preside over His people. I watch his demeanor. I know that it is for him to give the signal. It is for him to direct the movement of the crew of the Ship Zion. It is for him to direct how she shall be steered, so far as human power is necessary for this purpose; and when there are no indications of fear on his part, when he feels serene and confident, I know that I can do so with the utmost safety and that this entire people can trust in that God who has placed a Prophet, a Seer, and a Revelator to preside over His people upon the earth. (Dec. 2, 1883, JD 24:366-7)

I look at our President—I always did watch the captain of the ship with peculiar interest, when on the ocean surrounded by icebergs or when in the midst of great storms, as I have been a few times. I watched his eye and his demeanor, and I fancied, and I think very correctly, that I could form a good idea of our peril by watching him. I have been in storms when everybody on board excepting the Elders expected to go down.

I did the same thing when a boy, watching the Prophet Joseph, the few opportunities that I had of doing so. I did the same with President Young when he lived. In times of threatening danger and of anxiety I noticed the spirit that moved upon him as well as its operations upon myself. I do the same to-day with President Taylor; I have watched his bearing and have listened to his words; and I have taken notice of his spirit, as I have also of the brethren associated with him.

I have witnessed but one spirit and felt but one feeling and have had but one thought impressed upon me by their demeanor; and this spirit and the impression it makes corresponds exactly with my own. I feel that I am in accord with him and with them, and while this is the case, I feel that there is no real danger for Zion. (Oct. 8, 1882, JD 23:276)

UPHOLD THE LIVING PROPHET. The trouble is, the Prophets of God walk around among you, and you see them all the time. "Why I saw Lorenzo Snow today, and he is just like any other man. I saw Joseph F. Smith, and if I had not known, I might have taken him for anyone else. I saw some of the Apostles, and they are like other men." And because they are like other men, therefore, they must be rejected. It is not supposed that they have more power than others. That is a mistake that the world has always made.

There was Moses, one of the mightiest Prophets that ever lived. Did the children of Israel see anything particularly mighty in Moses? No; he was one of them, and they saw nothing exceptional about him. Then there was Nephi, another mighty

Prophet. Did Nephi's brethren see anything mighty in him? Why, no; there was nothing to distinguish him particularly; and yet he was a mighty Prophet whom God had raised up. So it was with the Son of God himself, the mightiest being that ever trod the earth. He descended from the throne of His Father and came to earth; but men saw nothing in Him different to other men, and they crucified Him. Thus it has been in every age. There have only been a few who have ever discovered the power of God as manifested through His servants.

It is so today. Who recognized Joseph Smith as one of the mightiest Prophets that ever lived? Why, the Saints themselves received with reluctance the truths he taught; and men slew him and may possibly have thought they were doing God's service in doing so. So it has been with those who have followed him and have held the keys of authority. They have passed among their fellow men and received but little recognition. Men could see all their faults and failings and could talk about them one to another; but they could not see the divinity in them. It is the same with the servants of God in our midst today. They are but mortal men, and we see their weaknesses and their defects of character. These become magnified in our eyes, and we talk freely about them. The result is, we receive their words with reluctance; we question the word of God that comes through them and wonder if it is not alloyed with something of their own.

What we all need is faith—faith in God, faith to believe that which He tells us. (Oct. 8, 1899, *CR* 50-1)

PURPOSE OF APOSTLES. The Apostle Paul says that the Apostles were placed in the Church expressly to keep the Saints from being carried away by every wind of doctrine and by the cunning craftiness of men. You watch the men that listen to the Apostles, to the authority that God has placed in His Church, and you will find that they are not carried about by cunning craftiness of men nor by every wind of doctrine. But the people that neglect and deride that authority, they are carried about in that manner.

Men may say it is wrong to obey the Priesthood. I tell you the world will not be saved unless it is through the exercise of the authority of the Priesthood of the Son of God under His own direction. We may as well look that squarely in the face as not. (Nov. 22, 1896, *MS* 59:66)

NECESSITY OF VISITS BY AUTHORITIES. There is a constant necessity for the visits of those whom God has called to preside over the affairs of His Church and to hold the Apostleship of the Church in the midst of the various Stakes of Zion. . . . The Lord has not left His people without proper care, and He has not left His servants destitute of his word and of a knowledge of His will but has given these to them at the very time when they have been needed. No evil or difficulty has ever occurred in the Church or outside of the Church affecting us that we have not been warned of by the servants of God and prepared for by their teachings, their counsels and their warnings. (Sept. 2, 1883, *JD* 24:368-9)

FUTURE APOSTLESHIP REVEALED. It is a very responsible station for a man to stand as an Apostle of the Lord Jesus Christ, to stand as one upon whom the responsibility rests of counseling the people, of directing them and of imparting to them such instructions as are needed by them, and I naturally shrink from this responsibility. I never did desire prominence among men. The Lord revealed to me when I was quite young that I at some time would be an Apostle. I never told it to any human being; but on more than one occasion I have gone out and besought the Lord to choose some one else and to relieve me of that responsibility. I have besought Him earnestly, time and again, that if I could only get my salvation and exaltation without being called to that high and holy responsibility, I would much rather He would choose some other person.

These have always been my feelings concerning responsibility in this Church; yet I have endeavored to the best of my ability when responsibility has been placed upon me to bear it off with the help of God the best I could. . . . I feel that it is one of the greatest blessings a human being can have bestowed upon him to be chosen a servant of Jesus Christ and to enjoy the power and the gifts and the blessings that ought to rest upon those who are thus chosen.

LORD SUSTAINS THOSE CALLED. There is this to comfort all those upon whom this authority is bestowed—the

Lord is always able and always willing to sustain His servants in the performance of all the labors and duties which He assigns unto them. He does not leave men to themselves when He calls them to office; but He gives them gifts and graces and qualifications and the Spirit suited to the duties devolving upon them and the labors which they may have to perform.

Notwithstanding my own weakness and the realization of my own incapability, I can testify to you this day that the Lord has always, through my life and my varied labors, blessed me beyond what I, in many respects, could have expected. And I have seen that this has been the case with my fellow servants; He has been exceedingly kind to them. He has bestowed His Spirit upon them, and He has given unto them knowledge and wisdom, revelation and counsel to impart unto the people and to guide them in the performance of the various labors that have devolved upon them. So it has been with this entire people. (Feb. 23, 1890, *DW* 40:377)

LEADERS DON'T ASPIRE TO OFFICES. Honor the Priesthood of the Son of God. Let no word be spoken in your streets or in your dwellings or in your associations derogatory to the work and the servants of God or that would in any manner grieve the Spirit of God.

It is true, His servants are fallible men. No one knows their fallibility better than they do themselves, speaking generally. They know how much they shrunk from bearing the responsibility which God has placed upon them. Joseph F. Smith and George Q. Cannon, who are here today, never wanted the office that they hold. We both would have avoided it if we could. We did not seek for power but have endeavored to protest against receiving it. Nothing but the command of God would have induced us to have taken it. But God did command; He did make this requirement of us, and we are here today, standing in the position we do, unsought for by us.

So it is with all of us. All you who know Wilford Woodruff know that that man never had any aspiration to preside over this Church. He presides today because God required it at His hands. Therefore, should you not uphold these men? Should you not pray for them? Should you be envious of them? Should you speak evil of them and be jealous of them? I say, No; for if you do, God will be angry with you.

I have spoken about the First Presidency of the Church; but I need not confine these remarks to them; they apply with equal force to the Twelve Apostles, and to the Presidents of Stakes. . . . The same thing applies, no doubt, to the High Council and to the Bishops and to all the servants of God. Men do not obtain place in this Church because they seek for it. If it were known that a man was ambitious to hold a certain office in the Church, that fact itself would lead to his defeat because his desire would not be granted unto him. This is the case with the officers of this Church. . . . We are responsible to God. God chose us and nominated us, and it is for Him to straighten us out when we do wrong. (April 17, 1898, *DW* 56:707-8)

FIRST PRESIDENCY CHOSEN BY GOD. When I was first called to be a counselor to President Taylor, I besought him and the Council with all the energy of my soul not to call me to act in that position but to call some one else; I felt that everyone of the Council was more fitted for that position than I. And when President Woodruff called President Joseph F. Smith to be his counselor, he expressed himself in the same manner and besought President Woodruff not to choose him, or at least to select someone else in preference to himself. In this spirit we have accepted the duties of our positions—not for personal gratification, not to give us prominence but to do that which we have felt to be the will of God. And I do know that God chose Wilford Woodruff, that God chose Joseph F. Smith and that God chose George Q. Cannon to be the First Presidency of this Church. I can bear testimony to that with all my heart. . . .

OPPOSING AUTHORITY A DEADLY SIN. Whoever arrays himself in any manner against the authority which God has placed in His Church for its government, no matter who it is —one of the Twelve Apostles even or any number of them— unless he repents, God will withdraw His Spirit and power from him; and He will show the world; He will show the Church; He will show the officers of the Church that that which He has spoken in the past concerning the authority of the Holy Priesthood and the respect and honor which He requires His servants and people to show to it is true and must be carried out, or He will withdraw His Spirit and power from those who take a different course. If any of you have indulged in the spirit of murmuring and fault-finding and have allowed your tongues to give utterance to thoughts and words that were wrong and not in accordance with the spirit of the Gospel, let me say to you here today that you ought to repent of it with all your hearts and get down into the depths of humility and implore Him for the forgiveness of that sin—for it is a most deadly sin.

The men who hold the Priesthood are but mortal men; they are fallible men; they are sinners. No human being that ever trod this earth was free from sin, excepting the Son of God, from the beginning throughout all the ranks of the Priesthood in every generation. Every human being has been a sinner and has been forced to confess before the Lord that he was a sinner. None is exempt in this respect; there is no exception, aside from the Lord Jesus Himself. This is true concerning the Presidency of the Church; it is true in relation to the Apostles.

Nevertheless, God has chosen these men. He has singled them out. They have not done it themselves; but He has selected them, and He has placed upon them the authority of the Holy Priesthood, and they have become His representatives in the earth. He places them as shepherds over the flock of Christ, and as watchmen upon the walls of Zion. And He holds them to a strict accountability for the responsibility and for the authority which He has given to them, and in the day of the Lord Jesus they will have to stand and be judged for that which they have done and the manner in which they have exercised this authority. If they have exercised it wrongfully and against the interests of His work and the salvation of His people, woe unto them in the day of the Lord Jesus! He will judge them, and, if worthy of condemnation, He will condemn them.

But He does not give the authority to judge and condemn to man, only in the regularly constituted councils of His Church; and those who lift their voices and their heels against the authority of the Holy Priesthood, I tell you today, as a servant of God— and I wish these young men and young women to hear my testimony this day and to remember it as long as they live— they will go down to hell, unless they repent.

EXAMPLES OF OPPOSING PROPHET. There are many examples in this Church of a character to prove what I here state. Oliver Cowdery, who received the same blessings and the same ordinations as the Prophet Joseph, ordained to the Lesser Priesthood at the same time as Joseph, ordained to the Melchizedek Priesthood by the same angels who visited Joseph, afterwards in the Kirtland Temple beheld the Son of God Himself and received the keys of the gathering from Moses and the gospel of Abraham and the promises that were made to Abraham from Elias and afterwards the keys for the turning of the hearts of the fathers to the children and the children to the fathers from Elijah—this man, so favored of God, after all this, lost the Spirit of God through opposing the Prophet Joseph!

He might in one sense, and doubtless did in his feelings, rank himself as the peer of the Prophet; but God had given to Joseph the keys of the Priesthood and the authority to preside, and because Oliver Cowdery did not honor that Priesthood and that authority, God withdrew His Holy Spirit from him, and he lost his standing in the Church, and his Priesthood was taken from him and given to another, as you will find by reading the revelations. God gave the same authority that Oliver Cowdery held to Hyrum Smith, the brother of the Prophet Joseph and the father of Brother Joseph F. Smith here. Before his death Oliver Cowdery came back, humbly penitent, and was baptized into the Church again.

Not only this man but no less than six of the Twelve Apostles lifted their heels against the Prophet of God; they murmured at him, questioned his authority, told lies about him or believed lies about him, and as a result they lost their standing, and others were chosen to take their places.

Sidney Rigdon, whom God designated as a spokesman for the Prophet Joseph, a man of great eloquence and of many gifts, a man who was favored of the Lord with that wonderful vision which is recorded in the 76th Section of the Book of Doctrine and Covenants, who with Joseph beheld the glories of the Celestial, the Terrestrial and Telestial Kingdoms, . . . this man fell. Why did he fall? Because he not only murmured against the Prophet of God, but he even murmured against God because of the afflictions the Lord permitted to come upon him in Missouri.

Willam Law, who was a counselor of the Prophet Joseph, took the same course, and he lost his Priesthood and became one of the bitterest enemies of the Church of God. There is scarcely any room to doubt but what he was guilty of contributing to the shedding of the innocent blood of the Prophet and the Patriarch of the Church. (Feb. 16, 1896, *DW* 52:385-6)

DON'T SPEAK EVIL OF LORD'S ANOINTED. There is one thing that the Lord has warned us about from the beginning and that is not to speak evil of the Lord's anointed. He has told us that any member of the Church who indulged in this is liable to lose the Spirit of God and go into darkness. The Prophet Joseph said time and again that it was one of the first and strongest symptoms of apostasy.[9] Have we not proved this? Have not his words upon this subject been fulfilled to the very letter? No man can do this without incurring the displeasure of the Lord. It may seem strange, in this age of irreverence of iconoclasm, to talk in this way. Nevertheless, this is the truth.

God has chosen His servants. He claims it as His prerogative to condemn them, if they need condemnation. He has not given it to us individually to censure and condemn them. No man, however strong he may be in the faith, however high in the Priesthood, can speak evil of the Lord's anointed and find fault with God's authority on the earth without incurring His displeasure. The Holy Spirit will withdraw itself from such a man, and he will go into darkness. This being the case, do you not see how important it is that we should be careful? However difficult it may be for us to understand the reason for any action of the authorities of the Church, we should not too hastily call their acts in question and pronounce them wrong. (Oct. 6, 1896, *DW* 53:609)

CONSENTING TO DEATH OF GOD'S ANOINTED UNFORGIVEABLE. It is a terrible thing for a man to consent to the death of God's anointed—to shed innocent blood or to be accessory thereto. It were better for such a man never to have

---

[9]"I will give you one of the Keys of the mysteries of the Kingdom. It is an eternal principle, that has existed with God from all eternity: That man who rises up to condemn others, finding fault with the Church, saying that they are out of the way, while he himself is righteous, then know assuredly, that that man is in the high road to apostasy; and if he does not repent, will apostatize, as God lives." (*Teachings of the Prophet Joseph Smith*, Page 156-7).

been born or if a millstone had been tied around his neck and he had been cast into the depths of the sea, for such a sin can never be forgiven in this world nor in the world to come; and the heaviest of woes are pronounced upon those who commit such crimes. The men who were guilty of this crime towards him placed it out of Joseph's power to render them the aid which they will yet require. (Jan. 1, 1880, *JI* 15:11)

LEADERS NOT DEPENDENT ON PEOPLE FOR SUPPORT. There is one thing about the leading men of this Church, they do not depend upon the people for their support. It is not necessary for them to tickle their ears by fine speeches and pleasant things. They can say rough things, unpleasant truths because they are independent; they can live without the aid of the people by the industry of their own hands, and they are not afraid of some of their Deacons or some of the congregation taking exceptions to their manner of speech and cutting off their salary.

Why, if such unpleasant truths were told as have been told to the Latter-day Saints by ministers of different denominations, who do you think would give them a call? Would they receive a call to some other place and be paid a higher salary? No, their style would be too unpleasant to be popular. Well, I have hope for this people while this is the case, and I pray that we shall always have men here who are not afraid to tell you and me our faults and warn us of them and reprove us, for "better the reproof of a friend than the kiss of an enemy." (Oct. 6, 1879, *JD* 20:338-9)

BRIGHAM YOUNG'S POLICY. It is true that God has designed that the tithings shall be used, among other things, for the support of the Priesthood. But I should deplore the day when the Priesthood of the Son of God would depend upon the tithings of this people for their support. It would be something that I should dread. I always admired the policy of President Young in this respect. During his lifetime he never would allow any man to draw a fixed amount from the tithing for his support; but he allowed the tithing to be administered, under the direction of himself and counselors, to the brethren as they might need so that no thought should enter into the minds of a certain class that because they held official position in the Church they would therefore have a right to live upon the tithings of the Church.

It is incumbent upon all who hold the Priesthood or any portion of it to labor freely in the offices to which they are ordained. . . .

NOT A SALARIED PRIESTHOOD. The Lord is determined to have a Priesthood that will not be a salaried Priesthood. Because a man gets an office in the Church—for instance, one of the Seven Presidents of Seventies or an Apostle—he should not imagine that immediately he is ordained to that office he will have a fixed salary or that he can depend upon the tithing for his support or, because he is a Bishop, that he will think, "Well, this office of Bishop has a fixed salary, and I will depend upon that to sustain me." This would reduce the Priesthood to the level of political office.

It is not the design of God that such a condition should exist in His Church. When men are ordained to office in the Priesthood, they should seek to honor the office regardless of pay. If the idea of the emoluments which might be attached to an office were in their minds, they would show themselves unworthy of the office. But, when men are devoted to the work of the ministry and their whole time is occupied and they are likely to need assistance, shall they not be helped? Certainly; for the Lord has given authority for the tithing to be used in such cases— to that extent and no more, not for a fixed amount to be attached to an office but for help to be rendered according to the needs of the individual. Thus, if Elders are in want, help them; but if they can sustain themselves, let them do it by their own labor and then pay their tithing just as other folks do. That is the true law of the Lord in regard to this people. (Nov. 12, 1893, MS 56:34, 36)

Our theory is that a man who can not sustain himself and also teach others how to sustain themselves is unfit for a leading position, and he becomes a drone in the great hive. On that account we compel or require every minister in this Church to sustain himself. Jesus said that he who is greatest among you let him be the servant of all, and we have carried this into effect —the servant of the whole people is the President of the Church. (Sept. 8, 1872, JD 15:152)

CHAPTER 21

SUCCESSION IN THE PRESIDENCY

SAINTS DIDN'T UNDERSTAND COMING MARTYR-
DOM. Though he [Joseph Smith] had spoken for some time past
in a manner to convey the idea that he was not to remain long
in their midst and had often remarked in public and in private
that the authority and the burden and responsibility which
rested upon him he had transferred to the Twelve Apostles, yet
none seemed to realize that the time for his departure from this
life was drawing near. For some reason it seemed as though the
minds of the people were incapable of comprehending such an
event.

Joseph and the work of God which he had established appeared so inseparably connected in their minds that they had
not conceived it possible for that work to progress without him.
Hence, his words, in reference to his leaving them, were not
understood and were almost passed unheeded; and another consequence was, he was not watched over with that vigilance and
shielded with that care that he should have been. His friends
did not perceive this then, but afterwards they did and sorrowed
over it. (Jan. 8, 1870, *JI* 5:6)

JOSEPH DESIRED HYRUM TO BE HIS SUCCESSOR.
Joseph wrote to those of the Twelve Apostles who were absent
on missions to come home immediately, as he was anxious to
have them with him; he felt that trouble was thickening around
him; and no doubt he desired to have his friends—the men he
could rely upon—near to him in the hour of difficulty. He was
anxious to get Hyrum, his brother, out of the way. He advised
him to take his family on the next steamboat to Cincinnati. If
anything happened to himself, he was anxious that Hyrum
should live. Said he: "I wish I could get Hyrum out of the way,
so that he may live to avenge my blood; and I will stay with
you and see it out." But Hyrum could not be moved. If Joseph
suffered and died, he was determined to suffer and die with him.
Said he to the Prophet: "Joseph, I cannot leave you."

Joseph saw from a letter of the Governor's and by the spirit that was manifested that there was no feeling of mercy towards the Saints or disposition to treat them with any degree of fairness. He was well convinced that if he and his brother Hyrum could get out of the way and the Saints would be still and go quietly about their business, trouble would be avoided. In speaking upon this point he said: "There is no doubt they will come here and search for us. Let them search; they will not harm you in person or property, not even a hair of your heads." He remarked to Brother Stephen Markham that if he and Hyrum were ever taken again, they would be massacred, or he was not a Prophet of God. He added: "I want Hyrum to live to avenge my blood, but he is determined not to leave me."[1] (Jan. 22, 1870, JI 5:14)

TWELVE ARE ENDOWED WITH KEYS. By virtue of the ordination he received, Joseph had the right and the authority to confer this Priesthood upon others. He called Twelve Apostles, and they were ordained under his authority by the direction of the Lord, and those Twelve were endowed with the keys. Previous to his death the Prophet Joseph manifested great anxiety to see the temple completed, as most of you who were with the Church during his day well know. "Hurry up the work, brethren," he used to say, "let us finish the temple; the Lord has a great endowment in store for you, and I am anxious that the brethren should have their endowments and receive the fullness of the Priesthood." He urged the Saints forward continually, preaching unto them the importance of completing that building, so that therein the ordinances of life and salvation might be administered to the whole people but especially to the quorums of the Holy Priesthood; "then," said he, "the Kingdom will be established, and I do not care what shall become of me."

These were his expressions oft repeated in the congregations of the Saints, telling the brethren and sisters of the Church and the world that he rolled the Kingdom on to the Twelve, and they would have to round up their shoulders and bear it off, as he was going to rest for awhile and many other expressions of a like nature, the full meaning of which the Saints did not realize at the time.

---

[1]History of the Church 6:546.

Prior to the completion of the temple, he took the Twelve and certain other men, who were chosen, and bestowed upon them a holy anointing similar to that which was received on the day of Pentecost by the Twelve, who had been told to tarry at Jerusalem. This endowment was bestowed upon the chosen few whom Joseph anointed and ordained, giving unto them the keys of the Holy Priesthood, the power and authority which he himself held, to build up the Kingdom of God in all the earth and accomplish the great purposes of our Heavenly Father; and it was by virtue of this authority on the death of Joseph that President Young, as President of the Quorum of the Twelve, presided over the Church. (Dec. 5, 1869, *JD* 13:49)

APOSTLES HAD WARNINGS OF DREADFUL HAPPENINGS. On the day of the murder of the Prophet and Patriarch those of the Twelve Apostles who were on missions, as well as other Elders, had warnings that something dreadful had happened. They felt cast down, and a spell of horror seemed to rest upon them. Some wept without knowing why they should do so except that they were filled with unaccountable sadness and gloom. The succeeding night was a miserable one to them. When they received the news of the death of Joseph and Hyrum, the cause of these feelings was explained, though it was difficult then for several of them to believe that they were dead. (Aug. 6, 1870, *JI* 5:127)

MARTYRDOM OF PROPHET JOSEPH CHURCH'S DARKEST HOUR. Even when Joseph was slain—probably as dark an hour as the Church ever saw—and when men cast about not knowing where to look and whom to follow, there was in the hearts of the people of God an unshaken faith that the Lord would not leave His people and suffer the work that He had established to be overthrown.

Up to the time of the Prophet's martyrdom the anticipation of the Latter-day Saints was that he would live to lead the people of God until Jesus should come. I suppose that there was not a feeling in the Church, not a thought among the faithful Saints that the Prophet would not live, not only to be the means in the hands of God of laying the foundation of the work but, if I may so speak, of laying its capstone and completing the work and witnessing the redemption of Zion as the leader, the Revelator and the Prophet of God.

Those of you, therefore, who are not familiar with those times can well imagine what a shock it was to the people to find that the enemy had obtained power to take his life and how it naturally tried their faith and would have caused them to have despaired had it not been for this promise . . . which was given to the Prophet in the beginning, namely, that the work that he was the instrument in the hands of God of founding should never be overthrown. And from that day to this, through all the vicissitudes and changes which have occurred, that promise has shone out brightly and filled the hearts of the Saints with hope, and they have never yielded to despair. (Dec. 23, 1894, *DW* 50:321)

PEOPLE NOT LEFT WITHOUT A SHEPHERD. When Joseph was taken, how was it then? Were the people left without some man or men to stand up in their midst to declare to them the counsel of their Almighty Father? No! The Lord did not leave His people without a shepherd. He had anticipated the dreadful tragedy which would rob us of His anointed one, rob us, the Church of Christ, of our Prophet and Patriarch. He had anticipated this, and previous to this horrid tragedy He inspired His servant Joseph to call other men, upon whom He bestowed all the keys, all the authority, all the blessings, all the knowledge so far as endowments were concerned, so far as the power to go unto God and ask Him in the name of Jesus and obtain His mind and will was concerned. . . .

A body of men were endowed with this power when Joseph was taken, and the earth was not robbed of that Priesthood which God had sent His angels from heaven to restore once more to the children of men and to act on the earth in the plenitude of its power. There was no more need, therefore, for angelic visitation to restore it. It was not taken back to God by the slaying of the Prophet and Patriarch but remained with mortal men here on the earth. (Dec. 14, 1884, *JD* 26:60)

INCIDENTS FOLLOWING THE MARTYRDOM. After the martyrdom of the Prophet Joseph Smith several persons arose claiming to be the successor to the Prophet. Prominent among these was Sidney Rigdon, who had been with the Prophet Joseph as his counselor and spokesman. He claimed that the Church was then fourteen years of age and should have a guardian and plainly stated that he was the man who should be that guardian.

All the Twelve Apostles were absent on a mission to the Eastern States excepting Elders John Taylor and Willard Richards, who were with the Prophet and Patriarch in the jail at the time of their death. Brother John Taylor was shot in a number of places and for weeks his life trembled in the balance. Rigdon was also absent from Nauvoo when the Prophet was killed; but, as he was nearer to Nauvoo than the Twelve were, he reached there first and held several meetings before the Twelve arrived.

It was at this time that he appointed a day for the Church to meet and choose a guardian. The people felt like a flock without a shepherd. The general feeling had been that the Prophet Joseph would live to preside over the Church, at least till old age, and some thought that he would live till the Savior would come. No one looked for his death. It was, therefore, a most unexpected blow, and as no one had thought of such a thing, the bulk of the people were at a loss to know who should take the presidency of the Church. (Oct. 1, 1877, JI 12:222)

BRIGHAM YOUNG ASSUMES MANTLE OF JOSEPH. President Brigham Young was in the stand and arose and addressed the people. . . . It was the first sound of his voice which the people had heard since he had gone east on his mission, and the effect upon them was most wonderful. Who that was present on that occasion can ever forget the impression it made upon them!

If Joseph had risen from the dead and again spoken in their hearing, the effect could not have been more startling than it was to many present at that meeting. It was the voice of Joseph himself; and not only was it the voice of Joseph which was heard, but it seemed in the eyes of the people as though it was the very person of Joseph which stood before them.

A more wonderful and miraculous event than was wrought that day in the presence of that congregation we never heard of. The Lord gave His people a testimony that left no room for doubt as to who was the man He had chosen to lead them. They both saw and heard with their natural eyes and ears, and then the words which were uttered came accompanied by the convincing power of God to their hearts, and they were filled with the Spirit and with great joy. There had been gloom and in some hearts, probably, doubt and uncertainty; but now it was plain to all that here was the man upon whom the Lord had bestowed the necessary authority to act in their midst in Joseph's stead. . . .

On that occasion President Brigham Young seemed to be transformed, and a change such as that we read of in the Scriptures as happening to the Prophet Elisha, when Elijah was translated in his presence, seemed to have taken place with him. The mantle of the Prophet Joseph had been left for him. . . . The people said one to another, "the spirit of Joseph rests upon Brigham;" they knew that he was the man chosen to lead them, and they honored him accordingly.

In his remarks to the congregation he alluded to the fact that instead of himself and brethren finding them mourning the death of their great leader, as Israel did the departure of Moses, they found them holding meetings to choose his successor. But if they wished to obtain the mind and will of the Lord concerning this subject, why did they not meet according to the order and have a General Assembly of the several quorums, which constitute the spiritual authorities of the Church, a tribunal from whose decisions there was no appeal. In a moment the few words he spoke upon this subject threw a flood of light upon it. The Elders remembered then the proper order. He desired to see an Assembly of the quorums at two o'clock that afternoon, every quorum in its place and order, and a general meeting also of the members.

The tones of his voice, his appearance, everything he said and the spirit which accompanied his words, convinced the people that the leader whom God had selected to guide them stood before them. He was the master spirit on the occasion. . . . Probably no few words that were ever uttered by a servant of God gave greater relief and satisfaction than those spoken that morning by President Young; for at no other period in the history of the Church had the people beheld such a crisis. (Oct. 29, 1870, JI 5:174-5, 182)

BRIGHAM YOUNG FOREORDAINED TO PRESIDE. Look at the singular combination of circumstances which caused Brigham Young to be President of the Twelve. Reflect on the remarkable combination of events which made him the leader of Israel, showing plainly, in my mind, that long before he was born, yes, probably before the earth was organized, Joseph Smith and Brigham Young were chosen, the same as Jeremiah was. (Dec. 5, 1869, *JD* 13:52)

BRIGHAM YOUNG LED CHURCH BY REVELATION. God has borne testimony to the acts and teachings of His servant Brigham and those of his servants, the Apostles, who received the keys in connection with him. God sustained him and upheld him, and He blessed all those that listened to his counsel. No man that ever obeyed all his counsel and teachings was ever cursed but was always blessed of God, while those who disobeyed his counsel did not prosper. We have all seen this.

He led the people by the power of God into this wilderness, taking upon himself such responsibility as no other man dare take, which, of course, he was inspired of God to do. In various ways God sustained him to the time of his death. All the authority, all the power, all the keys and all the blessings that were necessary for the guidance of this people he held. He held them as his fellow-servants, the Apostles, held them; only he, being the senior, had the right to preside and did preside, God sustaining him in so doing.

NO MANIFESTATION REQUIRED AT HIS DEATH. Then, when he died, there was no need for any peculiar or overpowering manifestation such as was witnessed when the Prophet Joseph died because the authority of the Priesthood was recognized, and among the Twelve there was no dissent. We all knew the man whose right it was to preside, there being no doubt upon this matter. We knew he had the authority. We knew that there was only one man at a time upon the earth that could hold the keys of the Kingdom of God, and that man was the presiding Apostle.

Other names had at one time preceded President John Taylor in the order of the Twelve. There were various reasons for this. Two of the Apostles had lost their standing and upon deep and heartfelt repentance had been again ordained to the Apostleship. In both instances this had occurred after the ordination of President Taylor to that calling. Still, for many years their names were allowed to stand in their old places and preceded his in the published list of the Twelve. . . . For some years attention was not called to the proper arrangement of the names of the Twelve; but some time before President Young's death they were arranged by him in their proper order. Not long before his death a number of the Twelve and leading Elders were in Sanpete when, in the presence of the congregation in the meeting-house, he turned to President Taylor and said, "Here is the man whose right it is to preside over the Council in my absence, he being the senior Apostle."

Therefore, as I have said, when President Young died there was no doubt in the minds of those who understood principle as to who was the man—it was the then senior Apostle. He was the man who had the right to preside, he holding the keys by virtue of his seniority, by virtue of his position in the Quorum, and he became the President of the Twelve Apostles and became President of the Church.

PRIESTHOOD RIGHTFUL AUTHORITY TO LEAD CHURCH. Now, let me ask you, is it necessary that somebody should rise up outside of this Priesthood to be a Prophet, Seer and Revelator to the Church? Is it not consistent with the wisdom and government of God to acknowledge His servants who have been faithful all their lives, who have proved their integrity before Him, who have never swerved to the right or the left and whose knees have never trembled and whose hands have never shaken —is it not within His power and His wisdom to endow them with all the gifts and qualifications necessary for the guidance of His Church? Certainly it is.

There has never been a moment since this Church was organized, since the 6th day of April, 1830, when God has been without ministering servants through whom He has revealed His mind and will to the people. President Young might have received and given revelations to the people in the same manner as the Prophet Joseph did. He had the authority, and he did give his revelations to the people; he gave his counsel. President Taylor has done the same. The Twelve in their labors have done the same. They have taught the people the word of God. The Twelve have the right, every Apostle has the right, to teach the people by the spirit of revelation, by the spirit of prophecy and the power of God.

This people have been led by that power and spirit; and it was in this way that ancient Israel was led when Moses stood at their head. He had the authority; he held the keys, and he received revelation from God concerning all the people. It has been so in our day. We have had revelations; and we have revelations still. (Oct. 29, 1882, JD 23:364-6)

ONLY ONE HAS KEYS TO PRESIDE. I rejoice that God still continues to manifest His power through His anointed one and through the channel of the Holy Priesthood, having but one man at a time on the earth unto whom He gives the keys to preside over the Church and give revelations to the entire Church, as a Church and as a people. He has chosen him from among the Prophets, Apostles, Seers and Revelators to bear the keys of the everlasting Priesthood upon the earth in the flesh, he having the power and authority to act for the entire people and to receive the mind and will of God for the entire people. (Dec. 14, 1884, JD 26:61)

SUCCESSION IN PRESIDENCY. We should all be grateful for the mercy which God has shown to us in raising up such men as He has called to preside over us and over His Church, men in whose mouths has been found no guile, who have pursued the path of duty without turning to the right hand or to the left, who have been true and faithful to every trust reposed in them and who have never flinched in the hour of trial. . . .

When the Prophet Joseph Smith died, the Council of the Apostles with President Brigham Young at their head led the Church for some years before the First Presidency was again organized. There was a reason for this. After the martyrdom of the Prophet Joseph there was intense feeling against the Church. The spirit of persecution raged. There being no First Presidency, hatred was not concentrated against any one man as it would have been, doubtless, had the First Presidency been organized. The Twelve, therefore, presided over the Church until we had left Illinois and come west.

After the death of President Brigham Young, again some time elapsed before the First Presidency was organized. At the death of President John Taylor the Twelve again acted as the presiding council until the First Presidency was organized with President Wilford Woodruff at the head. And thus, it might be said, a precedent had been established, and the general feeling was that no immediate action would be taken in organizing the First Presidency.

But on September 13th [1898] at a meeting of the Apostles, while discussing the necessity for the appointment of a trustee-in-trust for the Church, the necessity also of organizing the First Presidency appeared clear to the brethren, and one after another of the Twelve spoke in favor of such action being taken at that time. After hearing their views, President Snow then arose and stated to the brethren that he had, since the death of President Woodruff, felt led to present himself before the Lord, clothed in his priestly robes, in the Temple, and the Lord had revealed to him that the First Presidency should be organized and also revealed to him who his counselors should be. He did not give any expression to this, however, until after the Apostles had spoken on the subject.

This statement of President Snow was evidence to them that the Spirit of God had inspired the remarks which they had made and approved of the work which they had proposed to do, and it caused them to rejoice greatly. For myself it was very unexpected to me for action to be taken at that time, though I was heartily in favor of it and have always felt that the First Presidency should be organized as quickly as possible or as soon as the Lord would inspire such action.

President Lorenzo Snow was called of God to occupy the position in which he stands today, and he will be sustained by the Lord as His mouthpiece to the Church and also by his counselors and the Apostles, and the whole Church will approve of the action taken and sustain it fully. . . . I can say that President Wilford Woodruff, shortly before his decease, expressed his desire that there should be no delay after his death in perfecting the organization of the Presiding Quorum. The action taken was inspired of the Lord, and it is a matter of gratification and rejoicing that this has been so soon accomplished.

KEYS CONTINUE WITH CHURCH. It is wonderful how the Church moves forward without a jar or a break in its course, notwithstanding the departure of its leading spirits. The authority of the Holy Priesthood remains; the keys continue with the Church; the order of the Priesthood is maintained, and the revelations of God are given through the designated authority for the guidance of His people. Nothing that occurs will interfere with its progress or with the consummation of the purposes for which the Lord designed it. This authority and the keys will remain with the Church, no matter what may happen or who may be taken from us, for this is the work of the Lord, and it will not be hindered by any power beneath the heavens. What an impressive lesson it must be to the world to see the Church moving thus steadily forward. (Sept. 18, 1898, *DW* 57:514)

MORE THOUGHTS ON SUCCESSION. Men vary in their organizations. Joseph possessed gifts that no man in this age possessed. Brigham Young, having a different organization, had gifts which the Prophet Joseph did not have, and he arose in the power of his Priesthood and calling, with the authority to stand as the senior Apostle at the head of the Church and to declare the word of God to the people. . . .

The revelation says that the Twelve are "equal in authority and power to the three presidents,"[2] and the Seventy "form a quorum equal in authority to that of the Twelve."[3] But the Twelve are equal to the First Presidency only when the First Presidency are absent; and if the First Presidency and Twelve were absent, the Seventy would be equal. At the time I am speaking of the First Presidency were absent. Joseph had been slain; one of his counselors had apostatized, and the other was not as he should be. Therefore, there was no First Presidency. It fell then to the Quorum of the Twelve to preside; for they held the authority equal to the First Presidency, and the First Presidency were absent. The Quorum of the Twelve has no right to preside when the First Presidency is there.

Brigham Young stepped forward with the Twelve and took the Presidency of the Church. And through his unwillingness to push himself forward, the Twelve governed the Church for three years. But the Church is not perfectly organized unless there is a First Presidency and a Twelve and a Seventy. Now,

[2]D. & C. 107:24.   [3]*Ibid.,* 107:26.

every one of the Twelve held the same powers as the Prophet Joseph, but they had no right to exercise them only in their own place and station. No one of them could rise up and exercise the authority of leading the Church.

As the Lord has plainly revealed, there is only one man on earth at a time who has the right to hold the keys and to preside, though others may have equal power, authority and ordination and be equal in every other respect. Only one man is called to lead. There were twelve men with Brigham, but Brigham held the keys. He was the senior Apostle and had the right to exercise that authority. When the First Presidency was organized, he still, with his counselors, had the right to preside over the Church. (*DEN*, July 14, 1900)

THE MAN FOR THE HOUR. There has been a peculiar providence in the selection by the Lord of the men who have been called to occupy the leading places in this great work. We look at Joseph; he filled a sphere that was exceptional among the sons of men. He was perfectly adapted for the work he was called to do. Probably few Prophets ever were so endowed with gifts and graces as was he. Everything connected with his history gives evidence of the fact that he was inspired far beyond many of the Prophets of whom we have read and that he was especially fitted for the performance of his great mission.

The Lord permitted his enemies to take his life. He fell a martyr; and, at the time it seemed that no one could be found to fill his place. But the Lord raised up another—Brigham Young. He had his peculiar gifts and endowments, and he filled his sphere and accomplished a mighty work. He was a man remarkable for his talents, and the Lord sustained him. He passed away, and then President Taylor succeeded to the Presidency. A man who had been a martyr, it may be said, for he bore to his grave wounds received when the Prophet Joseph was killed; but he was spared to become a champion of liberty. A man who was always full of integrity and zeal and who carried on the work, while he lived, in such a manner as to show the people that the Lord had made no mistake in his selection.

Next came Wilford Woodruff. We all know how well he filled the place. A more childlike man, I do not believe, ever lived. Free from show, free from ostentation, free from the defects which beset many men. I never knew a man so childlike, unassuming and free from jealousy and vanity. He was the embodiment of childlike simplicity of faith and, at the same time, a man of undaunted courage. It required a man of such peculiar gifts to do what he did. As natural men, neither Brigham Young nor John Taylor could have issued the Manifesto. They would have required to have been changed by the influence of the Spirit of God. Wilford Woodruff, because of his peculiar organization, could do it and did it. I think it one of the bravest acts a man could perform. I cannot believe that Brigham Young or John Taylor could have done it as he did, and it has always seemed to me that the Lord chose him specially to do this work, and he did it in a manner to please God and the people.

Now I look at Lorenzo Snow. His life has been prolonged, and the Lord has raised him up to fill his sphere under the peculiar circumstances in which the Church is situated; and there can be no doubt that he will perform the work in a manner to please the Lord, he having those peculiar gifts and graces which will enable him to glorify God. (Nov. 10, 1900, *Era* 4:143-4)

LACK OF REVERENCE FOR PRIESTHOOD. My mind of late has dwelt considerably upon the want of reverence there is among us for the Priesthood of the Son of God. Now, I may say some things in this connection that may not be suitable in the opinion of some; but I have strong feelings on this subject. I have felt that too much reverence can not be shown to the Priesthood of the Son of God. I think it has been a characteristic of my life to entertain extreme reverence for the men who bear the Priesthood.

THE PROPHETS WERE PERFECT MEN. I had this feeling when a boy in the days of Joseph. To me Joseph was perfect. I could not see, and I did not hear anything that ever made any impression upon me to the contrary. It was so with my feeling for President Young. I was intimately associated with him the last twelve years of his life. I saw him in private and in public. I saw him when he laid aside, it might be said, his reserve and would unbend and talk with familiarity. There was one feature in his character that won my admiration, and I have not lost it to this day—I never heard President Young utter an expression that would weaken anybody's respect for the Prophet Joseph. He admired him; he looked upon him as the Prophet of God, as he was. I do not think that anyone else ever heard an expression from him that would tend in any manner to weaken respect or reverence or love for the Prophet Joseph Smith. I admired that in his character. And though I was closely associated with him, I never saw a fault in Brigham Young. I expect many would think this very foolish in me and that I must have been very blind. Perhaps I was; at any rate, I wanted to be. I never wanted to see his faults. I think it was Pope who said:

> Be to her faults a little blind,
> And to her virtues over kind.

That was the feeling I had concerning President Young. I wanted to be blind to the faults of the man of God. I knew he was a fallible man, a human being; but I did not want to sit in judgment upon him nor to criticize his words and acts. To me he was God's servant. God had chosen him out of all the men on earth to hold the keys—that power, awful in some respects, which God commits to one man on earth at a time. He had chosen him, and who was I that I should sit in judgment upon him and criticize him? I never felt as though I dared do it. I never had the disposition to do it.

The Lord took him, and He gave us another man to hold the same authority, to occupy the same position, to exercise the same powers; and I felt towards him as I did towards Brother Brigham. I knew him intimately also, had known him, I may say, all my life; but during his Presidency over the Church we were thrown very closely together because we both had to go into exile. I might repeat the same in regard to Wilford Woodruff, who succeeded President Taylor. I knew these men as intimately as one man could know another, and I can only say this: more angelic characters, men of sweeter dispositions I do not believe ever lived. They were men who were as perfect as human beings could be. They loved God supremely. They loved their Priesthood and the cause of God with all their hearts. They would have been willing, if necessary, to have laid down their lives at any time for the truth. . . .

This is my testimony this day in the presence of these assembled thousands, that a more perfect man than President Young I never knew. So I may say of his two successors.

Now we have a man who has taken the same place by selection and appointment of the Almighty—President Lorenzo Snow. He is a man who has proved himself through long years of fidelity to the work of God. He stands here in our midst as the Prophet of God, the man holding the keys, the man who can bind on earth and it will be bound in heaven, the man who can loose on earth and it will be loosed in heaven, the man who has the power (which, however, he exercises very rarely, if at all) to forgive sins, to curse and they shall be cursed, to bless and they shall be blessed.

I have said it is an awful power. It is; and it ought to be and is exercised with the greatest care and discrimination. God has chosen this man; He has delivered him from perils and from death and has brought him at his present age to be the President of His Church. Had He a purpose in this? Undoubtedly He had. God foreknew who should hold the keys after Wilford Woodruff passed away, and he selected this man—a perfect man, as far as we know, as far as fidelity to the truth and willingness to submit to anything, even to death if necessary for the truth— to hold the same position and to exercise the same authority. . . .

REVERE AND SUSTAIN THE PROPHET. I tell you that there never was in this Church within my recollection such an absence of respect and reverence for the authority of God as there is now among this people. . . . Why is it? Many men seem to think that their way is better than any one's else; and though we believe and testify that God has a Prophet in our midst through whom we can get the word of the Lord, we despise that word, so much so at least that we will not ask for it for fear we should be told something that does not agree with our feelings and with that which we desire to accomplish. I tell you, as sure as God lives there will have to be a change in this respect or some men will go to hell. God will not put up with it.

We have come here today to hear the word of God, and I am going to tell you what I think, if I do offend you. As a servant of God, I want to warn you of the danger you are in and of the consequences of the spirit that is being yielded to. I would no more dare to do anything of an important character without consulting the man of God than I would think of putting my hand in the fire, especially to do something that I knew he felt differently about what I did.

As I have said, God has chosen him to stand where he does —not you or me; and He knows every secret thought of men's hearts. His all-piercing eye has penetrated the innermost recesses of his heart, and He has seen all there is about him, inside and out. He knows him thoroughly, because He created him. He knew his past history; He knows his present history. And knowing this He has chosen him. What can we do better than to show respect to our God by listening to His servant, by treating him with reverence, asking his counsel and seeking for his guidance? I know we pray to God for him that he may be inspired from on high. Do you believe your prayers? Do you believe that God will and does inspire him? I hope you do; and I hope that having this feeling, you will be prompted to different action.

WE ARE DEPENDENT FOR GUIDANCE. Men may talk as they please about one man power, and they may fight us and seek to destroy us because we listen to the man of God, but the fact still remains that this whole people are dependent for guidance, when they are guided aright, upon the man who holds the keys. Our settlement in these valleys was due to the recognition of that authority; the building of these settlements throughout these valleys is due to that. And, shall we say that in some things we are willing to be guided; we think it right to be guided in matters of doctrine, etc.; but in other matters, just as important and necessary for the salvation and preservation of this people, we are not willing?

Latter-day Saints, you cannot do it. You cannot get away from this authority and remain Latter-day Saints for you sever yourselves from the Church of God, because everything you have is based on the recognition of this authority. . . .

EXERCISE OUR FREE AGENCY. We have a right to exercise our free agency in doing right, in being obedient, in listening to counsel and in doing that which God wants. I think that I am as much of a free agent when I obey God as I would be in rebelling against Him and obeying Satan. . . .

You cannot show reverence to the Priesthood without showing it to the men who bear it. . . . You who have been in sacred places know one thing, that you cannot speak evil of the Lord's anointed and be justified, and if you break your covenants in that respect, you are of course incurring severe condemnation. (April, 1900, *CR* 11-14)

JOSEPH SMITH MOST REMARKABLE MAN OF HIS AGE. Joseph Smith, the Prophet of the nineteenth century, was the most remarkable man of his age. He was only thirty-eight years old when he was martyred. Yet, inspired of God, he had revealed a sublime system of theology and had given to the world the most magnificent organization that had been witnessed since the days of the Redeemer. Truths which had been hidden by false traditions and men-like theories of salvation were brought to light by him with astonishing plainness and simplicity. Men wondered, in hearing them, how they could have been misunderstood—they seemed so simple, in such perfect agreement with Scripture and appealing so strongly and convincingly to the human mind. He was the incarnation of great qualities. A more self-sacrificing man, with the exception of the Lord Jesus, never lived.

Among the earliest communications which he received from the Lord was one which foreshadowed his probable martyrdom. But with unflinching courage he pursued the path which God had marked out. He was undaunted in the deadliest peril and in face of the most formidable opposition. He had entire confidence in the success and future triumph of the system which he was the instrument in the hands of God of founding.

He has been credited with having given to the world a new religion. In one sense, this is true. It was a new religion to our age. But it was the old religion restored in primitive purity and power—the old religion which has been taught by the Son of God Himself. A more fitting instrument to accomplish this wonderful work cannot be imagined. The youthful Prophet possessed every quality necessary for the accomplishment of the labor assigned him. His character stands out in bold relief as a beautiful example of all that is great and heroic in man for Latter-day Saints to admire and imitate. (Jan. 27, 1890, *MS* 52:52)

A MARVELOUS WORK PERFORMED. When we recollect that Joseph was only thirty-eight years of age at the time he was killed, the work which he was the instrument in the hands of God in accomplishing seems truly wonderful. Alone, with no one to help him but the Lord, he had started out with the determination to obey the commands which he received from heaven. He had not learning; he had not wealth; powerful friends he had none; but he had what were of greater value to him than all these—he had the truth and the authority from God to proclaim it. And the Lord whom he served made him mighty in word and in deed. He performed a marvellous work, and in the face of obstacles, too, that would have frightened the most of men and which he himself could never have overcome had the Lord not given him help. (Aug. 20, 1870, *JI* 5:131)

JOSEPH SMITH PROVED A PROPHET BY WORLD. The Prophet Joseph Smith's name has been known for good and evil among all the inhabitants of the earth, being regarded by some as a man divinely inspired, a Prophet of the living God, his words treasured up as the words of a Prophet should be; and by others he is looked upon as an imposter, an ignoramus, a man in fact too bad to live. This Joseph Smith, who is thus known and has this repute among various people, is gradually being lifted up and made prominent. . . .

Joseph Smith is being proved to be a Prophet, not by the Latter-day Saints alone, for we are doing comparatively little towards the vindication of his prophetic views, of this divine calling. . . . The inhabitants of the earth, numerous as they are, by their words and acts are establishing the divinity of his mission and proving that he is the man that we have testified he was from the beginning. (April 3, 1881, *JD* 23:115-6)

NO MAN EVER CHOSEN TO DO A GREATER WORK. When we reflect upon the work which has been accomplished through the instrumentality of the Prophet Joseph Smith, our hearts are filled with thanksgiving and praise to God that we have been permitted to live in the earth at a time when we can enjoy the fruits of the labors that he performed. It has been said that probably no man, excepting the Son of God himself, ever accomplished so great a work in so short a time.

Of course, a complete history is not before us of all that men of God have done in various dispensations. We know but little concerning Enoch or Noah; and especially is our knowledge very limited concerning those who lived upon this continent. After the death of our Savior and His visit to the people of this land a reign of righteousness was ushered in, and no doubt very many mighty men lived during that period. But, we think it is not too much to say that no man, always excepting our Redeemer, was ever chosen to lay the foundation of a greater work than that which has been accomplished in our time. . . .

That which has been wrought out by the Lord through this man of God is exceedingly difficult to comprehend. The work that he accomplished is so magnificent, so far-reaching, so grand in every respect that it is not easy for the human mind in a brief space of time to grasp the great results that have been achieved. (Dec. 23, 1894, *DW* 50:321)

A REMARKABLE MAN OF GOD. Probably no man that ever lived left his impress more deeply upon his people, for the length of time he resided among them, than our departed President [Brigham Young]. He was a man of extraordinary will and great firmness of purpose. He was prudent in counsel and wise in action. No hesitation, no vascillation of purpose but great tenacity and firmness in carrying out his views of right marked his course. His courage was wonderful; he never knew what it was to have moral fear. The only question in his mind was, is it right? When this was decided, he pressed forward to its accomplishment, and no obstacle could deter him.

He was the man for the times. A man more yielding and pliant could not have filled the situation he occupied as he did. The Lord raised him up and inspired him and gave him the necessary qualifications for the discharge of his high calling. He never took the glory to himself for what he did but always gave the Lord the glory and acknowledged his weakness, inability and entire dependence upon Him.

With all his strength of character, firmness of purpose and driving power, he was a modest man and a man of tender feelings. His heart was easily touched. No one ever went to him and related real causes of sorrow without exciting his sympathy. But he was one who frequently concealed his own feelings in order that he might nerve up others and make them view their difficulties as being light. (Sept. 15, 1877, *JI* 12:210)

THE GREATNESS OF BRIGHAM YOUNG. Brigham Young has been credited with having contributed greatly to the strength and success of what is called Mormonism. It is true that he was adapted to take up the work where Joseph, through martyrdom, laid it down. He possessed wonderful powers of organization and government and executive ability of a superior character—a statesman in the highest sense of the word. But he always asserted that it was Mormonism that made him. Whatever greatness he possessed was due to the principles which Joseph Smith was the means in the hands of God of revealing. It was the fruit and product of the Gospel of Jesus Christ. He embodied in his life and character those principles, and he is but a type—a superior type, it is true, in many respects—of all the people who have embraced and carried out practically in their lives the principles which are taught by the Latter-day Saints.

Possessing unbounded influence, he used his power most temperately, and his whole aim was to promote the welfare of the people. The evidences of his superior wisdom and genius are seen in every settlement that has been made throughout these mountains. Salt Lake City, through his prescience, was laid out as a metropolis. He never had any doubts as to its future or the commanding position of the territory which had been settled, and he made preparations in consonance with his expectations.

Some of his contemporaries viewed him as, in many respects, the greatest living American. Only those who are ignorant of his true character will deny to him the possession of the highest powers of statesmanship, government and philosophic wisdom. History is dealing more justly with him since he died than during his lifetime. The time is not far distant when Joseph Smith and Brigham Young will be considered the most remarkable men of their age. (Feb. 3, 1890, *MS* 52:66)

GREATNESS OF BRIGHAM YOUNG RECOGNIZED. It is said, and with more or less truth, that the generation in which a great man lives is rarely able to fully appreciate him. Of course, his immediate circle of associates, those who know his plans and motives, are competent to judge his abilities with some accuracy. But, the great majority of his fellow men, not alone those who enjoy a casual acquaintance with him but also those who know him only by hearsay, are in the very nature of things deprived of the insight into his character and achievements that would enable them to correctly estimate his influence upon the times in which he lives. When his plans see fruition, when the foundation he laid is found to possess the strength and solidity necessary to bear any superstructure that may be erected upon it, then mankind come without much hesitation to the agreement that he was a master spirit, possessed of the wisdom, foresight, energy and integrity that constitute true greatness.

Brigham Young was a man who during his lifetime received but small honor, save from his own people, for the splendid abilities with which he was endowed. By the world the very attributes which made him the conspicuous figure he was were quoted as proving that he was a man of dangerous ambition. His influence in the community was deemed conclusive evidence that he lacked but opportunity to become a despot. His clearness of judgment, quickness of decision and courageous adherence to what he believed to be the right were considered to be traits of character which, however admirable in themselves, were exceedingly menacingly in him. In short, the world which could not understand his impulses and which always misconstrued his motives would yield but a meager tribute to the qualities that in another man they would have been happy to acknowledge with the most generous applause.

As Utah has become better known, and as his life-work has been exhibited before a generation that is more willing to forget prejudice in judging a dead man, Brigham Young is coming to be regarded at something near his true stature. Men see in the greatness and stability of the Territory a testimony to the care and thoroughness with which he as its chief founder built. The consummate foresight that prompted him to select these valleys as a resting place for his people, to the rejection of more inviting regions on either side, can be admired today by thousands who come from curiosity or speculation to visit the mighty community he established. Every year adds luster to the record he made; every day brings fresh assurances that his services to his people and to the country are at last receiving their just recognition from a reluctant world. (Mar. 15, 1892, *JI* 27:179-80)

BRIGHAM YOUNG RECOGNIZED AS GREAT STATESMAN. The labors of President Brigham Young and the leading men of the Church in founding the commonwealth of Utah are gradually being recognized and looked at in their true light. . . .

There has been gradually dawning upon the minds of observing people, and especially on publicists, the fact that President Young was a statesman of a high order and that in all his labors among the people he laid the foundation for their future happiness and prosperity. Among unprejudiced people, who look dispassionately at that which he accomplished, it is now conceded that he possessed qualities of the highest order and that he was a statesman in the truest and highest sense of the word.

Men can now perceive and freely admit that his counsel to the people to cultivate the earth and to make sure their living, instead of running around the mountains hunting for silver and gold, displayed the highest wisdom because it is now acknowledged that had the people deserted their farms, neglected the production of food and devoted their time and energy to mining, the settlements of Utah, if not a failure, at least would not have been a success. After the lapse of years this is readily seen and is frequently admitted because experience has proved the correctness of his policy. Had his strong and powerful influence not been used in this direction and had the people been permitted to go hither and thither, prospecting through the mountains, instead of the happy homes and the strong and healthy settlements with which Utah is now filled there would be starving villages and poor mining camps scattered throughout the state.

The Latter-day Saints in Utah have great reason to be thankful to the kind Providence which gave them such a leader as Brigham Young, and inspired him to give the wise counsels that he constantly imparted unto them.

His expressed views as to the proper methods of managing municipal and county affairs, as well as the affairs of the Territory, had much weight with public men. He used his great influence while he was Governor of the Territory to keep down expenses, and to check all tendency towards extravagance or the contracting of public debts. (Feb. 1, 1898, *JI* 33:128-9)

Chapter 22

Revelation—The Rock Foundation of the Church

A GOD OF REVELATION. We are a people who seek to live by every word that proceedeth out of the mouth of God. I am frequently asked, "What is the great difference between your belief and the belief of other denominations in Christendom?" The great radical difference is this, that though we believe in God and Jesus Christ as they profess to believe in them, we believe in a God who can and does now give revelation, impart wisdom and bestow blessings as at any previous time when His servants were upon the earth. This is the point of divergence, and from it we continue to differ on many points. (Aug. 10, 1862, MS 24:562)

BLIND LEADERS OF THE BLIND. Puny man, especially if exalted by a little learning, is prone to reject that which is beyond his ability to grasp. Instead of the true spirit which alone leadeth to a knowledge of the things of God, your leader of modern theological thought aims to get more and more of the spirit of man. That which is the completest key to knowledge the sectarian world refuses to accept. Instead of revelation, by which alone they may know the Lord and His truth, they cling to tradition and become confused in the discrepancies and differences that they find. They are blind leaders of the blind; and it is no wonder that they move about in a maze of doubt and are all the time striving to harmonize the Word with their limited reason, tearing it away piece by piece until the children of men reach a state of utter skepticism and unbelief.

In contrast with this, how firm and clear and comforting is the faith which enables the Saints to say: "We believe all that God has revealed, all that He does now reveal, and we believe that He will yet reveal many great and important things pertaining to the Kingdom of God!"[1] Is there anything in all the world to compare in value with this belief, coupled with the absolute

---

[1] Articles of Faith No. 9.

knowledge that the Lord lives and that His own plan for the salvation of His children has been restored to man? (April 1,.1899, JI 34:218)

SPIRIT OF REVELATION NOT MYSTERIOUS. Men's ideas differ very much in relation to what a Prophet is or should be; they have certain ideas and opinion as to how he should receive the gift of prophecy and revelations, and if a man professing to be a Prophet or servant of God does not conform to those ideas, he is, of course, set down as an imposter.

The spirit of revelation is not so mysterious and incomprehensible as many imagine it to be. Men have imagined that it is something they cannot understand and that men in possession of it must differ very remarkably from those who are destitute of it. But the Lord in His dealings with the children of men never did produce these monstrosities.

His servants were not so remarkable in appearance as to strike everybody who saw them with surprise, but on the contrary they were natural men, similar in form, feature and apparel and speaking the same language as others, and because of this men could not entertain the idea that they were the servants of God or were intimate with His purposes or that they could possess more wisdom than man obtains by the exercise of his natural mind. (April 21, 1867, JD 12:41-2)

REVELATION TO ALL PEOPLE. God in ancient days was a God of revelation, and He communicates His mind and His will unto those who seek after it; not to the President of the Church alone, not to the High Priests or Seventies or any of the officers or all of them alone, but He communicates His mind and His will to all who seek after Him in humility and meekness and lowliness of heart, obeying His commandments.

To the Latter-day Saints alone? No, not even to them alone for there is no human being that is born of woman, there is no son or daughter of Adam that has ever lived upon the face of the earth who has not the right and who has not obtained at some time or other in his or her life revelations from God, but who may not have understood what those revelations were. The Latter-day Saints are not so cramped in their feelings as to imagine that they are the only and peculiar people above all others who have, in this sense, received revelation. . . .

ALL TRUTH COMES FROM GOD. God has revealed Himself at various times and in various ways to many people. The heathen have had communication from Him. All the light that exists, all the truths that are taught and all the correct principles and knowledge that have been communicated and existed among the children of men have come from God; He is the author of all. Socrates, Plato, Confucius, the heathen philosophers who knew nothing about Jesus Christ and the plan of salvation received important truths from Him, and so did many other people to a greater or less extent, according to their abilities in improving upon the knowledge communicated to them. . . .

SCIENTIFIC DISCOVERIES GOD INSPIRED. The remarkable discoveries that are being made in the world of science, in fact, all the remarkable discoveries that have been made from time to time are produced by the operations of an unseen influence upon the mind of the children of men. . . . The truth is that God is the Author; it is God that moved upon the minds of those individuals. It was God that inspired them to do as they did; it was He who led on from step to step until they achieved the results which have made them famous, and sometimes quite unexpectedly to themselves.

What is this which has led these famous men in the path of discovery? The Latter-day Saints call it the spirit of revelation, the spirit of revelation resting down upon the children of men. Some men possess it to a greater extent than others. Some have the gift in one direction, and they are capable of receiving communication from God in a direction that others are not; their minds are better prepared to receive revelation upon a given subject than are the minds of others. Some will receive great moral truths, and these men differ in their organisms; but the light they receive all comes from our Heavenly Father; it is He who gives the inspiration. And so man has progressed from one degree of knowledge to another. . . .

THE FOUNTAIN OF ALL KNOWLEDGE. We acknowledge God as supreme, the fountain of all knowledge, the fountain of all power, the fountain of all intelligence, the fountain of everything that is good. Who are men? The creatures of His workmanship, if you please, His descendants, His own children begotten by Him, descended by lineal descent from the God we worship. The same being whom we worship is our God, is our Creator, is our Father. When I worship Him, I worship Him as my Father.

That which I possess, if there be anything godlike in it, I attribute to Him as having come from Him by lineal descent. Every aspiration, every noble thought, every pure desire, everything that is good and holy and pure, elevating, ennobling and godlike comes from our Father, the God of the universe, the Father of all the children of men. In Him we move; in Him we have our being. He can extinguish life; He can create life; He can perpetuate life. There is no power that human beings can conceive of which He does not possess. The light that now shines comes from Him.

The revelation we may get, imperfect at times because of our fallen condition and because of our failure to comprehend the nature of it, comes from God. The Latter-day Saints glorify Him for it. If there is anything good or great or noble, if there is anything to be admired, it comes from God, not man. Man is but the medium, but the instrument, but the conduit through which it flows. God is to be worshipped; God is to be adored; God is to be glorified and He will be. . . .

A DUTY TO RECEIVE REVELATION. We believe in revelation. It may come dim; it may come indistinct; it may come sometimes with a degree of vagueness which we do not like. Why? Because of our imperfection; because we are not prepared to receive it as it comes in its purity, in its fullness from God. He is not to blame for this. It is our duty though to contend for more faith, for greater power, for clearer revelations, for better understanding concerning His great truths as He communicates them to us. That is our duty; that is the object of our lives as Latter-day Saints—to live so near unto Him that nothing can happen to us but that we will be prepared for it beforehand. . . .

We have got to seek after God with an earnestness, a fervor and devotion that we at the present time cannot comprehend. It is our duty as Latter-day Saints to seek for knowledge. Will

God bestow it upon us if we do not seek for it? (Oct. 5, 1879, JD 21:74-7)

REFORMERS INSPIRED OF GOD. Yes, millions of people have received the Holy Spirit to a certain extent, although not in its fulness. Luther had it when he was inspired to war against the iniquities that existed in the Romish Church. He was raised up especially to prepare the way for the manifestation of the work of God in the last days. Calvin and Melancthon had a portion of the Holy Spirit, and so had all the Reformers who followed them; and though they had not the authority to build up the Church of God in its ancient purity, they still had a work to do, and they have come in their days and generations and have labored zealously, indefatigably and fearlessly, regardless of death, inspired of God to do the work which they performed in the various lands in which they labored—Germany, France, England, Scotland and various parts of Europe and also in our land—America. John Wesley, also, was raised up and inspired of God to do a work, and he did it.

FOUNDING FATHERS ALSO INSPIRED. Not only have these religious reformers been inspired to do a work in preparing for the advent of the Kingdom of God upon the earth; but others have been raised up for the same purpose. Columbus was inspired to penetrate the ocean and discover this Western continent for the set time for its discovery had come; and the consequences which God desired to follow its discovery have taken place—a free government has been established on it. The men who established that government were inspired of God; George Washington, Thomas Jefferson, John Adams, Benjamin Franklin and all the fathers of the Republic were inspired to do the work which they did. We believe it was a preparatory work for the establishment of the Kingdom of God.

This Church and Kingdom could not have been established on the earth if their work had not been performed or a work of a similar character. The Kingdom of God could not have been established in Asia amid the despotisms there, nor in Africa amid the darkness there; it could not have been built up in Europe amid the monarchies which crowd every inch of its surface. It had to be built up on this land; hence, this land had to be dis-

covered. It was not discovered too soon; if it had been, it would
have been overrun by the nations of the earth, and no place would
have been found even here for the Kingdom of God. It was discovered at the right time and by the right man, inspired of God
not to waver or shrink; but, undaunted by the difficulty with
which he was surrounded and contending with a mutinous crew,
he persevered and continued his journey westward until he discovered this land, the existence of which God had inspired him
to demonstrate.

It was necessary that George Washington should be raised
up, that the battles of the Republic should be fought, that the
Colonies should be emancipated from the fetters of the mother
country and declared free and independent States. Why? Because God had in view the restoration of the everlasting Gospel
to the earth again, and in addition to this the set time had come
for Him to build up His Kingdom and to accomplish the
fulfilment of His long deferred purposes. . . .

Yes, glory and honor and blessings and immortality will
rest upon men who have been instruments in the hands of God
in bringing to pass his great and marvellous purposes. We have
the greatest charity for them; we know that God will save and
bless them. We know, further, that their sins were sins of
ignorance. Where there is no law, it is said, there is no
transgression. (Aug. 15, 1869, JD 14:55-6)

INSPIRED MEN IN ALL NATIONS. There have been
many faithful men in all nations and among all people unto
whom God has given great light and knowledge. He gave light
and knowledge to Luther and Calvin and Melancthon and Cranmer and George Whitefield and John Wesley and Edward Irving
and Alexander Campbell and to Confucius, Socrates and Plato
and many other philosophers and teachers. He did not confine
His knowledge to one nation or to one people or to one sect but
has given faithful men considerable knowledge among all nations.
There have been men among the Catholics who have had knowledge concerning the things of God, and also among the
Protestants and among the Mahometans and among the fire-
worshipers and idolaters who lived up to the best knowledge they
had.

Confucius and other Chinese philosophers who knew little

about the worship of the true God possessed a knowledge of many important principles. Great moral truths were communicated unto them and they taught them. They were just as true, many of them, as if they had been taught by an inspired Prophet of God. So with Mahomet, he taught many grand truths. So with Socrates, he possessed principles of truth which were divine in their origin. And there is no sect or party upon the face of the earth that we have ever read or heard about that does not possess some principles of truth.

What, then, is the difference between these men and their teachings and the teachings of the Apostles and Prophets? Did the latter comprehend all the truth and no one else comprehend any? No, certainly not. God has been merciful to all His children and has rewarded all men according to their diligence and faithfulness before Him. But this is the superiority that the Gospel of the Lord Jesus possesses. Its great Teacher is the Redeemer of the world. He came with power and authority from the Father to teach the truth in its fullness, in its perfection, unmixed with error. There was no falsehood in His teachings or doctrines and so also with His Apostles and inspired servants.

INSPIRED MEN LACKED PRIESTHOOD. God has placed in His Church the Holy Priesthood and given unto man the keys thereof. It is true that some of His servants who bear the Priesthood may go astray and teach incorrect doctrines, but the authority and power are bestowed by which error can be discarded and truth established and taught in all its plainness and purity. Thus, there being at the head of the Church a man who bears the Holy Priesthood and who holds the keys thereof and others associated with him who bear the Apostleship, they know the truth in its purity and can discern false teachings and expose the false doctrines which they propagate. This is the superiority of the Church of Jesus Christ over all other churches now upon the face of the earth. This is the advantage that the Prophet Joseph and the Prophet Brigham have over wise men of antiquity, the philosophers and teachers and leading men who did not possess the keys of the Holy Priesthood.

Confucius, Socrates, Mahomet, Plato and the noted men of antiquity, as well as those who had live in modern days, who taught truth, had not the keys of the Holy Priesthood nor the power and authority thereof to guide them in their teachings; hence, they ran into errors, and this gave rise to a great variety of views and doctrines and to schools of divinity that have existed and that still exist among the children of men. The truth which they had was not unmixed with error, and many times the error was in larger proportion than the truth. This of course made everything uncertain, and the great cause of thankfulness which we as a people now have is the removal of this uncertainty and the bestowal of reliable knowledge, pure unadulterated truth. (Feb. 1, 1877, *JI* 12:30)

MAHOMET LED BY SPIRIT OF GOD. I believe myself that Mahomet, whom the Christians deride and call a false prophet and stigmatize with a great many epithets, was a man raised up by the Almighty and inspired to a certain extent by Him to effect the reforms which he did in his land and in the nations surrounding. He attacked idolatry and restored the great and crowning idea that there is but one God. He taught that idea to his people and reclaimed them from polytheism and from the heathenish practices into which they had fallen. . . . But while this was the case it was the Spirit of God that did it. (Sept. 2, 1883, *JD* 24:371)

MANY WISE MEN IN ALL NATIONS. Many wise men were raised up, and though they did not have the Priesthood, the Lord gave them clear views of truth.

Zoroaster, if all accounts be true of him, was a great reformer, if he was not a Prophet. Much pure truth was given to him, but his followers have departed from his teachings. So with the followers of the religious teachings of Chinese sages including Confucius.

There can be no doubt that Mahomet had much truth revealed to him, and he was raised up to do a great work; but his followers have departed in many directions from his teachings.

Buddha, also, was no doubt inspired of the Lord to teach many important principles, and his doctrines have had vast influence; but his followers, like the followers of other great reformers, have departed from the original truths which he taught.

In every nation men have been raised up and been called

of the Lord to effect reforms among their fellow-men and to teach important truths. Many of the so-called Christians arrogantly believe that they have been favored above all the rest of the world. In some respects they have been; for they believe in Jesus as the Son of God, and they have His teachings in considerable purity. But other nations and races have not been forgotten by the Lord. They have had great truths taught to them; and in many instances they have profited by them. There have been millions of people, probably, whom the Christians call pagans, whose lives have been as acceptable to the true God as the lives of the same number of so-called Christians. The reason of this is plain; they lived up to the light which God had given them, and this is all that He could require of them. (Aug. 15, 1886, JI 21:248)

GOD RESPONSIBLE FOR SCIENTIFIC DISCOVERIES. This is termed a scientific age, an age of discovery and improvement, and it is without question rightly named; but to whom shall the credit of these discoveries and wonders be attributed? It is fashionable, we know, in the world at the present time to attribute them to the genius of man and to view them as the fruits of his intellectual progress. It needs but a little reflection, however, to convince us that man is but the unwitting agent of a higher and, to some extent, unseen power who operates through him for the accomplishment of His purposes.

Man is, as yet, but at the threshold of the chambers which contain inexhaustible stores of knowledge of every kind; he is but just commencing to learn his A-B-C's in the great science of life. As he progresses, his comprehension expands, his faith increases, and he is prepared to make more rapid advancement in the boundless field of knowledge that is spread out before him. This advancement will not, however, be confined to the knowledge necessary for man's temporal progress but will also include everything that pertains to his spiritual improvement.

There has not only been an extraordinary revelation of scientific truths during the last twenty-five or thirty years, but there has also been a wonderful outpouring of religious truths. The last dispensation, of which Prophets have written and poets sung when God would again make bare His arm in the deliverance of His people, has been ushered in. To thoroughly disseminate this knowledge, scientific truths were revealed, and science assumed her proper position as handmaid to religion. It was necessary that this should be the case that the accomplishment of the designs of the Almighty might be brought about with the requisite speed.

In making and perfecting their discoveries, therefore, the scientific men of the age are but instruments in the hands of a superior power that is operating with them for the accomplishment of His plans. Viewed in this light, the sudden and wonderful stride that has been made in discoveries and improvements is easily accounted for; but how few there are who will thus view it!

MORMONISM AIDED BY SCIENCE. It would be very difficult to persuade men that they are really building up and forwarding the interests of the Kingdom of God, or what they term "Mormonism," (indirectly, it is true, but still forwarding it) by their labors in the cause of science. . . . Yet, it is the truth. That under rated and despised system called "Mormonism" has to spread, conquer and triumph and gather together from all nations those who are willing to serve God and keep His commandments. For it to do this speedily the aid of science and the resources of wealth are required. Through the triumphs of science those bearing the Priesthood of the Almighty and going forth in obedience to His commands prove indeed "swift messengers"[2] and are enabled to traverse sea and land with an ease and celerity unknown to previous generations. . . .

The Lord is rapidly bringing His designs to pass; and though the world may not feel to acknowledge His hand in all these things that are transpiring in their midst, yet it is His hand nevertheless, and they will hereafter know that in revealing this flood of light, by which men are enabled to make such progress in scientific truth, He had in view the rolling forth and establishment of His great Work. (Jan. 10, 1857, WS 300-1)

DEAD PROPHETS HONORED. Magnificent structures are reared to the memory of the men who once talked with God. There is not a city in Christendom where there are no temples reared bearing the names of the men who suffered martyrdom

---
[2]Isaiah 18:2.

because they were the servants of God—St. Peter, St. Paul, St. Mark, St. Andrew; and all these sainted personages were once despised, derided, persecuted, cast out and finally killed.

What was their crime? They professed to have received revelation from God, to be His servants and to have received authority to act in His name; and because they did this, men sought to kill them. Not many generations had passed away, however, when they became the honored among men. They were extolled and held up as examples. Sanctity was attributed them. Miraculous power was attributed to anything that had been in their possession. The places of their martyrdom were considered sacred. And anything that could be done has been done by different generations to show that if they had lived contemporary with them they would not have persecuted them or slain them. (Dec. 13, 1891, *MS* 54:51-2)

THE ROCK FOUNDATION. The rock upon which this Church is built and the foundation stone thereof is new revelation from God to men, and that revelation being of divine origin it must of necessity agree with the revelations which have already been given; hence, the doctrines taught by the Prophet Joseph Smith and the organization of the Church as he was directed to accomplish it was all in perfect harmony with the truths contained in this book (the Bible). It can not be otherwise and be what it professes to be.

It made no difference to Joseph Smith whether he read and was familiar with every doctrine taught by the Apostles; he was under no necessity of framing his teachings therewith that there should be no difference between that which he taught and that which had been taught, because the same spirit that revealed to the ancient Apostles and Prophets and inspired them to teach the people and leave on record their predictions and doctrines taught him also and enabled him to teach exactly the same truths.

JOSEPH SMITH SURPRISED AT BIBLE EVIDENCES. I remember hearing related Brother Parley P. Pratt's first interview with the Saints at Fayette, Seneca County, where the Church was organized. Those of you who remember Brother Parley know his familiarity with the Scriptures, especially with the prophecies. On that occasion he was called upon to speak; the Prophet Joseph was not present at the time. He brought forth from the prophecies of Isaiah, Jeremiah, Ezekiel and other Prophets abundant proofs concerning the work which the Lord had established through His servant Joseph; a great many of the Latter-day Saints were surprised that there were so many evidences existing in the Bible concerning this work. The Church had been organized some five months, but the members had never heard from any of the Elders these proofs and evidences which existed in the Bible. And, if I remember correctly, he told me that Oliver Cowdery and the Prophet Joseph himself were surprised at the great amount of evidence there was in the Bible concerning these things.

LEADERS TAUGHT REVEALED DOCTRINE. The Prophet Joseph was inspired of God to teach the doctrines of life and salvation, and he did so without reference to what the ancient Prophets had said. I have heard President Young make the same remarks. He said that he never consulted the Book of Covenants; he never consulted the Bible or Book of Mormon to see whether the doctrines and counsels which he was inspired to give corresponded with these books or not. It was a matter that gave him no particular concern from the fact that he endeavored always to be led by the Spirit of the Lord, to speak in accordance therewith; hence, these men have had very little care resting upon their minds as to whether their doctrines and counsels were in harmony with the doctrines and counsels of those who preceded them.

It was for them to seek to know the mind and will of the Lord and comprehend His Spirit as it rested upon them, to speak in accordance therewith; and the doctrine that has been taught under the inspiration of that Spirit will be found to be in perfect harmony with the doctrines which have been taught by men inspired of God in ancient days. (Sept. 16, 1877, *JD* 19:104-5)

THE NATURE OF REVELATION. There is a passage in one of the revelations which the Lord gave to the Prophet Joseph Smith before this Church was organized that explains to some extent the nature of the Spirit by which this people have been and are led. It is in a revelation given through the Prophet to

Oliver Cowdery in relation to the translation of old records. The Lord said:

> Yea, behold, I will tell you in your mind and in your heart, by the Holy Ghost, which shall come upon you and which shall dwell in your heart. Now, behold, this is the spirit of revelation; behold, this is the spirit by which Moses brought the children of Israel through the Red Sea on dry ground[3]. . . .

In this manner the Church has been built up from the beginning. . . . But a great many people have imagined that when the Holy Ghost descended upon men or women they were completely transformed and that it was a supernatural influence which could be witnessed and felt by those surrounding the person receiving it. On this account many misapprehensions have arisen in regard to the way this Church has been governed. Some members of the Church have imagined that it has been necessary for angels to come and point out to the leaders of the people every step they should take or that some other supernatural power had to be exhibited to enable the servants of God to do as they have done in leading the people.

THE GIFT OF THE HOLY GHOST. There is a higher gift than the gift of the ministering of angels, and that is the gift of the Holy Ghost. This is the Spirit described in this revelation which I have quoted to you. It is with the Prophet and becomes, so to speak, a part of him. God dwells with His servants through the Holy Spirit, which manifests unto them the very things they should do. As this revelation says:

> This is the Spirit by which Moses brought the children of Israel through the Red Sea on dry ground.

This people have been led to these valleys by the same Spirit. Every step that has been taken in building up the Church has been under the influence of that Spirit. It is that that has constituted the strength of the people of God, because when the servant of God gave forth the mind and will of God as revealed to him through the Holy Spirit, those who were with him, being possessed of the same Spirit, were led to understand that that was the very thing that should be done. . . .

BRIGHAM YOUNG LED BY HOLY GHOST. When the

---

[3]D. & C. 8:2-3.

people of God first came to this land, as soon as the Prophet Brigham gazed upon this valley, he said this was the place. How did he know that? By the influence of the Spirit of God, which rested down upon him. Under that influence he was able to say to his companions with entire certainty and confidence that they should make this their stopping place, that this was the place designated by the Lord where His people should build a city.

Did an angel manifest that to him? I will not say that an angel did not come to him, but I will say that it was the inspiration of the Holy Ghost that rested upon him. His mind was light and clear, and he could see plainly that this was the right spot; whereas, if this had not been the place designated by the Lord, his mind would have been dark, and he would have had no assurance that this was the place designed of the Lord as the place of settlement.

This is not the experience of the leading men of the Church alone; it is the experience of all the Elders. . . . In a thousand ways, the Spirit of God manifests unto the servants of the Lord the course that they should take. This is a very remarkable fact with the history of this people. . . .

REVELATION TO LEAD THE CHURCH. President Young passed away. President Taylor then, being the senior Apostle, took the lead, and the spirit of revelation and of leadership rested upon him. He received revelations (some of which he wrote) for the Church. Previous to the death of President Young he had no right to receive revelation for the Church, but after President Young had passed away he did have that right, because he was the senior Apostle and held the keys of presidency. When he passed away, then the power and the gifts rested upon President Wilford Woodruff, and he was filled with the spirit to lead the people—the same spirit by which Moses led the children of Israel through the Red Sea on dry ground. He could tell the people what to do and how to do it, because God was with him and gave him the necessary light for that purpose.

Now, the same authority, gifts and powers rest upon President Lorenzo Snow and he has the right to stand as the mouthpiece of the Lord to the Church to tell the people what to do and how to do it; in other words, to give them the mind and will of the Lord as they may need it. He has the spirit today, just as

Brother Brigham had the spirit when he said to this whole people, "Let us move South." By the Spirit of God he saw that that was the right move to take, and he foresaw what the results would be, if not entirely, at least in part. Under the influence of the same spirit the whole people responded to the call.

· So it has been in all the great movements that have been made in the history of this Church. . . . The spirit . . . rests upon the man who presides, and he has the right to say what course shall be taken. If a move is made, he has the right to say whether it is right or wrong. If it is right, the Spirit of God makes it plain to him, and he sees it just as clearly as I see this path in the center of this building. If it is wrong, everything is dark, obstacles appear in the way, and he is made to know that it is not the right move to take.

A UNITED ACTION REQUIRED. As I have said, there is but one man who has this right. If it were otherwise, confusion would ensue. . . . At the same time, when the Presidency and the Twelve meet together, they have a perfect right to express their views freely, as they may be led; but because they express their views and perhaps are positive in their expression, it does not follow that their views should of right be adopted. No, it is the right of the man who presides, after hearing all that may be said, to say what the mind and will of the Lord is; and though his decision may be contrary to all the views expressed, it is nevertheless his right to say what is the thing to do. No limit is placed upon the expression of views concerning all questions affecting the policy of the Church, but there must be union of action and concentration of faith and obedience to the law which God has revealed. . . .

THE ASSURANCE OF REVELATION. How the possession of this gift relieves the man of God. What an appalling responsibility it would have been for President Young to have led the Latter-day Saints into the wilderness if he had not had this spirit of revelation with him. Think of thousands of people following him, taking his advice and counsel, and he uncertain as to what to do. No, Brigham was never uncertain. A faithful Prophet of God is never uncertain. He is not assailed by doubts. Everything he does is decisive because he knows what he is doing is right. The sense of responsibility is taken from him to that extent.

So it has been in every move that has been made. As a people we have done most daring things—things which have startled the world. Why? Because the man at the head has known the mind of the Lord. He has known the voice of the Spirit of God and has given heed to its monitions. In doing so he has felt perfectly safe in whatever action he has been led to take, knowing that the Lord would control it for good. (*DEN*, July 14, 1900)

THE RIGHT TO INDIVIDUAL REVELATION. Every individual has a right to a personal knowledge of the truth and of the mind and will of God concerning his own personal affairs. Our Father does not ask you to walk in darkness nor by another's light, but it is His good pleasure to give each one of you the light of His Holy Spirit in your own souls. By this light you have a right to examine all things that you may hold fast to that which is good. It is your privilege to know for yourselves, not only if Joseph Smith was a true Prophet but whether Wilford Woodruff is God's own choice of a leader in His Church, if the Twelve Apostles are approved of Him and all things whatsoever which concern you to know.

I would not give much for a Latter-day Saint who does not know these things because the want of this knowledge proves that individual slothful and lax; they who have it are awake and active, ready at all times to put a shoulder to the wheel and aid in rolling forth the great work of the last dispensation; herein lies the strength of the latter-day work. . . .

GOD RAISES UP AND INSPIRES SUITABLE LEADERS. In the days of Joseph Smith many of the Saints were so firmly persuaded that none but the Prophet could lead the Church of God that when he had laid down his life for his testimony, they actually looked for him to be resurrected at once and sent back to his earthly duties; but we may all rest assured that the Lord always knows where to lay His hand on the tool which this work requires. He has given the keys and powers of His Holy Priesthood to His servants on the earth and has promised that they shall never be taken away from now until the Savior shall come. . . . Thus God will continue to raise up and inspire suitable men, so that we shall never be without an efficient leader. . . .

SEEK TO RECEIVE THE HOLY SPIRIT. It is indeed our right and privilege to have the companionship of the Holy Spirit of the Lord, and we need it. Even children may have it if they will and need not be left to walk alone on earth. Every woman should win and keep it for herself and never try to walk by another's light. If she puts her whole trust in another, even if he be her husband and a good man, he will surely some time fail her. Let her learn to stand alone so far as human aid is concerned, depending only on God and the Holy Ghost.

PUT TRUST IN NO MAN. Do not, brethren, put your trust in man though he be a Bishop, an Apostle or a President; if you do, they will fail you at some time or place; they will do wrong or seem to, and your support be gone; but if we lean on God, He never will fail us. When men and women depend on God alone and trust in Him alone, their faith will not be shaken if the highest in the Church should step aside. They could still see that He is just and true, that truth is lovely in His sight and the pure in heart are dear to Him.

Perhaps it is His own design that faults and weaknesses should appear in high places in order that His Saints may learn to trust in Him and not in any man or men. Therefore, seek after the Holy Spirit and the unfailing testimony of God and His work upon the earth. Rest not until you know for yourselves that God has set His hand to redeem Israel and prepare a people for His coming. . . .

A RULE TO JUDGE REVELATION. I will give you a rule by which to judge if you have received the Holy Ghost. It gives strength; it gives hope; it gives wisdom; it gives joy; it gives love of God and man; and if you follow its guidance, it will lead you into the presence of God because it is the Spirit of God and the power of God. All that His servants know of His will comes to them by that Spirit because it is the spirit of revelation and the only source whence such knowledge can come. It dwells in the hearts of men and does not mask a man outwardly nor change his appearance so that he may be known in that way to possess it, and this we may know from the fact that even the Savior was with difficulty recognized as the Son of God, even by His own disciples. (Feb. 15, 1891, *MS* 53:658-9, 673-5)

REVELATION A RIGHT AND A DUTY. It is my duty, as a servant of God, to qualify myself by faith for the office that God has given to me. It is the duty of the First Presidency to do this that we shall not be stagnant and that the Church will not stand still but that we shall be alive and filled with the spirit, power and gifts of our office and calling that the revelations of Jesus will be given to us and the Twelve Apostles, also, until angels will minister to us, the heavens be opened to us, the revelations of God be multiplied upon us, until everything necessary for the guidance of this people to redemption will be revealed to us. This is our duty.

It is also the duty of every officer in the Church in his place and station . . . to live in such a way that there will be constant communication between the heavens and each soul. In this respect this Church is different from all others. Every member of this Church in his place has as much right as the President of the Church to have knowledge from God. . . . Every member is stirred up and exhorted to seek for knowledge for himself and herself. If all would do this, then the Church would be easily guided because the people would know for themselves and would be of one heart and mind and understand alike. And that will be the case sooner or later. But the thing that prevents it now is the commission of sin. People will commit sin and darken their minds and thus weaken their faith and their hold upon the truth, and they fall away. (Dec. 12, 1897, *DW* 56:67)

THE FAITHFUL TO BE TAUGHT BY THE LORD. As a people we do not live up to our privileges. We do not have the knowledge of the things of God that we should have. There is not that amount of revelation enjoyed by us which there should be. . . . Now, if we live as we should, there is no event of any importance that could occur but we would have some intimation respecting it; we would be prepared for it. We would be prepared for every public event that affected us; every private event, everything of this character that could occur to us that would affect us in the least degree would be known by us at the very time. . . . All who belong to this Church and have taken the course which

God has pointed out and have humbled themselves in obedience to the commandments of God and endeavored to carry out these commandments have this promise made unto them that they will be taught of the Lord. . . .

THE STILL SMALL VOICE. This is a gift of itself, to be able to distinguish that which suggests itself to our own hearts and that which comes from God. And we are misled sometimes by our own feeling because of our inability to distinguish between the voice of the Spirit of God and the suggestions of our own spirit. There is a still, small voice in the heart of every human being. There is an influence comes with every son and daughter of Adam that is born into the world. What! Outside of the Latter-day Saints? Certainly, we are all the children of God. There is an influence born with every person that to a certain extent is a spirit of revelation. . . .

WALKING IN THE LIGHT. I proclaim it as a truth that when a man or a woman enters into this Church and is baptized, repents of his or her sins, humbles himself and herself in the depth of humility before the Lord determined with His help to forsake their sins, to put them away from them, I say, when a man or a woman comes to the Lord in the spirit and lives so that the Holy Ghost will rest upon them, there will be no event of any importance from that time forward but what they will have some intimation respecting it, some premonition, and they will walk in the light, some to a greater extent than others, because some are more gifted than others; some live in such a manner as to have this developed within them to a greater extent. But if they continue to cultivate this spirit, to live in the light of it, it will become a principle of unfailing revelation to them. . . .

It is the design of God that it should be so. But it is dim within us because of the generations of unbelief and wickedness of heart which have existed. We have inherited a great amount of unbelief from our fathers; it has come down to us. (July 25, 1880, JD 22:103-5)

ALL MAY RECEIVE PERSONAL REVELATION. It is the privilege of every one to receive revelation. It is the privilege of every mother to receive revelation from God for guidance in the training of her children, to be in communication with the

Father through the Holy Spirit. It is the privilege of children to
have the same Spirit and to have knowledge from God through
that Spirit. What for? To teach the parents? No! If their parents are in the path of duty, it is not so, but it is, as I have said,
the privilege of every man, woman and child in the Church to
have revelation, to have knowledge, to be instructed of the Lord.
(Dec. 14, 1884, *JD* 26:63)

ONLY ONE CHANNEL OF REVELATION. Now, there
is only one way in which the commandments of God can be
revealed unto us. God has not left this in doubt. He has not left
us to grope in the dark respecting His methods of revealing His
mind and will unto His children. In the very beginning of the
work of God in these last days, to remove all doubt upon this
subject, God gave revelations unto this Church in exceeding great
plainness, and there was one principle that was emphatically
dwelt upon and enforced, namely, that there was but one channel, one channel alone, through which the word of God should
come to this people.

The word of God was not to come from the people up. It
was not vox populi, vox dei, but it was to be vox dei, vox populi—
that is, the voice of God and then the voice of the people—from
God downward through the channel that He should appoint, by
the means that He should institute, that word should come to
the people, and when obeyed by the people would bring the union
and the love and the strength consequent upon union and
love. . . .

A PROMISE OF FAITHFULNESS. It is through this source
that commandments must come to the people of God. It is
through this source that the word of God has come to this people
during the years that have now elapsed. The prosperity of this
people, their success, and the triumphs that have attended this
work are due to this, that God has chosen one man and through
him has given His word unto His people. . . . I am willing to stake
my reputation—I never claim to be much of a Prophet, I do not
talk much about prophecy—but as a servant of God I am willing
to stake my reputation in making this statement, that if you will
listen to the voice of God as manifested through His servant who
stands at our head, you never will, from this time forward until

eternity dawns upon you, you never will be overcome by your enemies or by the enemies of God's Kingdom. (Dec. 2, 1883, JD 24:362-5)

ONLY ONE SOURCE OF AUTHORITY. He that cometh in by any other way than by the door, you know what is said of him; he that climbeth over the wall, he that receiveth authority from some source outside of that which God recognizes, we as a people are not bound to receive anything that may be communicated to him. Out of that which is communicated in that way, there may be nineteen truths out of twenty statements; but there will be error, there will be falsehood, there will be something that will mislead, because there is not the authority from God to lead and to act. (Dec. 14, 1884, JD 26:64)

SCRIPTURES AN INSUFFICIENT GUIDE. As Latter-day Saints, we need constantly the guidance of Jehovah. We have the Bible, the Book of Mormon and the Book of Doctrine and Covenants; but all these books, without the living oracles and a constant stream of revelation from the Lord, would not lead any people into the Celestial Kingdom of God. This may seem a strange declaration to make, but strange as it may sound, it is nevertheless true.

Of course, these records are all of infinite value. They cannot be too highly prized, nor can they be too closely studied. But in and of themselves, with all the light that they give, they are insufficient to guide the children of men and to lead them into the presence of God. To be thus led requires a living Priesthood and constant revelation from God to the people according to the circumstances in which they may be placed.

MANY REVELATIONS NOT SUITED TO PRESENT CONDITIONS. A great many people fall into error very frequently by quoting and seeking to apply to present conditions revelations which were given to the Church in early days and which were especially adapted to the circumstances then existing. Of course, it is appropriate to quote from the revelations concerning principle; but in many instances the revelations that are contained in the Book of Doctrine and Covenants are not, I may say—and I say it with some degree of care—suited to the circumstances and conditions in which we are placed. They were given to the Church at a time when just such revelations were required. Nor must we fall into the idea that the world has adopted, that the Bible is all that is necessary for man's salvation.

The Bible is of exceeding great value to us. The Book of Mormon is likewise of inestimable value. The Book of Doctrine and Covenants is also beyond price. And these records are of great advantage to the people. . . .

WE NEED THE LIVING WORD. It is of infinite importance that we should value and preserve these records because in them is contained the revelations of God to His children in former times. But with all these there is still something more needed for our salvation, and that is the living word of God. We need the revelations of Jesus adapted to our condition and circumstances day by day and for the guidance and control of the Church of Christ in the various circumstances in which it is from time to time placed.

ONLY APPLICABLE REVELATIONS ARE BINDING. When men get into the dark, through committing adultery or some other sin that grieves the Spirit of God and causes it to be withdrawn from them, you will frequently find them falling back upon the Book of Mormon and the Book of Doctrine and Covenants and quoting therefrom to show how the authorities of the Church are departing from the word of God as revealed in these books. I have often noticed it, and no doubt you all have. They appear to be oblivious to the fact that the Lord gives revelations suited to the circumstances and conditions of the people.

There are revelations in that book concerning counsel and the management of affairs that are not binding upon us only so far as they are applicable to us. When, however, it comes to the revelations concerning principle, then those revelations are unalterable and they will stand as long as heaven and earth will endure, because they are true.

I wish you would see this distinction and in reading the book have it in your minds. Seek to become familiar with the conditions of the people at the time and with the circumstances in which they were placed, and then you will see that many things that are said there were necessary in those days but are not intended for us at the present time.

COUNSEL OF LEADERS IS REVELATION. As I say, we need continued revelation. It is needed today and will be until we are led back into the presence of the Lord Jesus. Now, Elders come and ask for counsel. That counsel, when given under the inspiration of the Lord, is revelation just as much as if it were written.

There are some people that attach a great deal of importance to something that is written. We have heard it stated by men who are in the dark that the leaders of the Church do not have the same revelation now as in the days of the Prophet Joseph. I have not heard it about President Woodruff, but I have about other leaders. Now, this is a great mistake. We err when we indulge in any such idea as this. I want to say to you that this Church would stand still; it would not progress; we would lose the power of God if the spirit of prophecy and revelation were not with us now.

NOT ALL REVELATION WRITTEN. Brother Brigham Young used to say—and I always have appreciated his remark—that he did not want to write revelations because the people would be held to a stricter accountability than they were. The Prophet Joseph wrote enough for the guidance of the Church in many directions. At the same time the spirit of revelation is wanted constantly in addition to these written revelations.

What written revelation is there concerning the organization of these Stakes as we see them? Here is this Davis Stake with a Presidency and High Council; what is there written in the Book of Doctrine and Covenants to sustain this? In the 102 Section we find a plan given for the organization of the High Council and over that High Council the Presidency of the Church presided. But as we are now organized there is nothing specially written concerning it. How then have these Stakes been organized? Did President Young organize them out of his own mind, or did he organize these Stakes according to the revelation of God? He organized them by revelation just as much so as if he had written the revelation. God did not require him to write it, and yet the Stakes are organized. And Zion is now as perfectly organized as circumstances will admit.

We have our Ward organizations and our Stake organizations, and they extend throughout the length and breadth of

Zion, and everybody is brought within their compass. These Ward organizations have become quite perfect. How has this been done? Has it been done by written revelation to the Church? Has it been done by anything that is recorded in the Book of Doctrine and Covenants? No; there is scarcely anything in that book that gives any clear idea of the Ward organizations that at present exist. How have they been organized? By the spirit of revelation in and through the man whom God chose to hold the keys.

CHURCH KEPT PERFECT BY REVELATION. And so there are constantly arising reasons why there should be revelation from God. Does it come? Certainly it comes and at the time it is needed. In this way the organization of the Church is kept perfect; and it will continue to be so until Christ comes. The books would not do it; the knowledge in the books would not do it. It is not designed that they should. Changes are necessary from time to time, and it requires supreme and divine wisdom to make these changes in accordance with the plans of Jehovah. Therefore, there is in the Church this spirit and gift of revelation.

God gives to every man according to his office and calling. It is not given to one man alone, (only so far as the guidance and control of the Church is concerned); but every man that has the Priesthood, from the President of the Church down to the Deacon in his office and calling, has the right to revelation and also has the spirit of revelation if he is living as he should do. . . .

COUNSELS OF PRIESTHOOD LEADERS ARE BINDING. God has placed this Priesthood in His Church for the express purpose of teaching the Church, and the Church should listen to the teachings of the servants of God. They should give heed to those teachings strictly, and if they do not, they incur a grave responsibility. The counsels of the servants of God may not be written; nevertheless, they are binding; and there will be a day come, a solemn day for all mankind and one which we ought to think about occasionally, when everyone will have to answer for the deeds done in the body.

We will have to stand at the bar of the Great Judge to be judged. All the writings of the men of God testify to this fact.

And if we have disobeyed the Lord, and if we have not listened to His counsels, those who gave those counsels will stand as swift witnesses against this generation. . . .

THIS GENERATION BLESSED WITH MUCH TEACHING. I have questioned very much whether there ever was a generation that lived upon the earth that had the amount of teaching and persuasion and every kind of inducement held out to them to serve God and to be true and faithful to their covenants as have these Latter-day Saints. It has been, so to speak, a constant stream flowing from God through His servants, who have risen early and labored late and have worn themselves out in teaching the people, telling them the counsels of God and giving unto them the word of God in the greatest simplicity and plainness. . . .

What will be the effect if these counsels that have been given in such profusion are rejected? The consequences will be most serious to those who reject them. Already we see the operation of the judgments of God in this respect. Many men whom I knew in boyhood in the Church have gone into oblivion. Whole families have disappeared, and their names are no longer numbered among the Saints of God. Instead of having a posterity that shall be numbered with the righteous, their children are unknown among us. What a dreadful fate! Why is this? The cause is easily ascertained. It is because they have not listened to the counsels which God has given; they have rejected His word; they have departed from the path of righteousness; they no longer are numbered with the Saints of God, and they and their children will perish.

And it will be so with us if we do not keep the commandments of God, for God has prophesied through His servants that there shall be great calamities and great destruction among the children of men. I say, we already see the operation of those things among ourselves and the dreadful results of disobedience. And so it will be from this time onward.

The Lord has said that His Spirit will not dwell in unholy tabernacles. We may be baptized; we may be ordained; we may have our endowments; we may have the sealing ordinances; we may have all the blessings that pertain to the Gospel and to the Priesthood, but if we do not live so as to enjoy these and to re-

ceive the fulfillment of the promises, they will only prove a condemnation to us, and they will prove our eternal damnation;
the Lord has not spoken in vain concerning these things. Therefore, we should give heed to the words of light and salvation
which God reveals to us through His servants from time to time,
and we should teach our children to do the same. (*DEN*, Sept.
21, 1895)

WRITTEN REVELATIONS NOT NECESSARY. Is it
always necessary to write revelation? Sometimes it is necessary;
sometimes it is not necessary, just as God willeth. When the word
of God is given through His servants, as, for instance, this morning through President Taylor making a certain promise, that
promise is just as binding as if written. If we live for it, it will
be fulfilled just as much as if it were written. God has bestowed
the spirit of revelation upon His servants. (Oct. 29, 1882, *JD*
23:366)

BRIGHAM YOUNG SPOKE BY REVELATION. Talk
about revelation! You go and read the sermons of President
Young, and if you do not believe now that he was a Prophet, I
think after you have read them you will be sure he was, because
he talked as a Prophet to this people concerning their future, and
his words were full of godlike wisdom, and he poured them out
in a constant stream during his lifetime. (April 6, 1891, *MS*
53:450)

UNWRITTEN REVELATION BINDING. Though we do
not receive written revelations (the men who have held the keys
have not always felt led to write revelations as the Prophet Joseph
did), the servants of the Lord do receive revelations, and they are
as binding upon the people as though they were printed and
published throughout all the Stakes of Zion. The oracles of God
are here, and He speaks through His servant whom He has chosen to hold the keys. . . . We have been blessed as a people with
an abundance of revelation. Some have deceived themselves with
the idea that because revelations have not been written and
published, therefore there has been a lessening of power in the
Church of Christ. This is a very great mistake, as we will find
out sooner or later.

CONFERENCE ADDRESSES ARE WORD OF LORD. This Church has been continually led by the spirit of revelation. The spirit of revelation has been here in our conference. The addresses that have been delivered have been made under the inspiration of the Holy Ghost, and they are the word of God unto this people, binding upon them, and they will be judged by these words that we have heard. If we do not listen to these instructions and counsels and abide by the word of God as it is given to us from time to time, we shall be held to a strict accountability. (Oct. 7, 1900, *MS* 63:18)

MANY UNPREPARED TO RECEIVE HIGHER TRUTHS. I recollect upon one occasion previous to the death of the Prophet Joseph hearing him make a remark from the stand which made a deep impression upon my mind at the time. He said that if he were to reveal unto the people the principles and the doctrines which God had revealed unto him, there were men upon the stand that would go around the streets of the city seeking to shed his blood. I do not give his exact words but the idea. I was young at the time, and I immediately began investigating my own feelings to know what doctrines brother Joseph could possibly teach that would have that effect upon my mind. Although I did not fully comprehend his remark, I believed it, for I believed every thing he said. Yet, not many months elapsed before I comprehended his words; for, soon afterwards one of the men who sat on the stand and heard that declaration and whose name he mentioned went about the city plotting to shed his blood. (Oct. 23, 1864, *JD* 10:343)

THE LORD COMMANDS AND THEN REVOKES. There is a certain class of individuals who think, because it is said that the Lord is the same "yesterday, to-day and forever,"[4] His course of action towards the human family never changes and that He never gives a revelation to His servants or a command to His people which He revokes afterwards. It is certainly true that the Lord is unchangeable in His justice and mercy; but He may deem it wisdom and more compatible with His designs and purposes to reverse to-morrow that counsel which He may give

[4]D. & C. 20:12.

to His people to-day. To think that the Almighty acts otherwise is but a narrow comprehension of His power and greatness.

The Lord controls the affairs of the earth according to the varied and changing circumstances of the inhabitants; and what may be necessary—whether in the character of His revealed will or the judgments He may see fit to send upon the earth—in one generation or dispensation may be necessary to change in another generation or dispensation that His purposes may be effected to His honor and glory. It is a lesson we have had from the Prophet Joseph. He has told us that we should not set our stakes. (Jan. 2, 1864, MS 26:182)

REVELATION ACCORDING TO CAPACITY TO RECEIVE. There are differences in spirits. There are different grades of intelligence among the spirits of men. We are not all on a dead level. God sends forth occasionally a man that towers like a giant in the midst of his fellow men. The Prophet Joseph was of that kind. There have been innumerable examples of men not of our Church of that kind, whose knowledge, foresight and intelligence were so far ahead of their compeers and those who lived contemporaneously with them that they could not come up to them. This Church could not come up to Joseph. He towered above us. He would have revealed things to us, if we had been prepared, that would have been far greater than those that we have received.

But the Lord deals with His children mercifully. He gives them intelligence according to their capacity to receive it. Therefore, wise men such as Joseph and others give the counsel that is adapted to the conditions and circumstances of the people though they may see that it is not exactly what ought to be. Better to give the people something they will obey, if it is not the fullness of the law of God; better to lead them on until their capacity is enlarged and they are prepared to receive higher principles and truths. That is the way God has done with His people.

LINE UPON LINE REVEALED. There are many things that the leading men of this Church can see and understand that they cannot impart to the people nor ask the people to do. Why? Because they know that the people would not come up to the requirement and that therefore they would be disobedient. Better to give them line upon line, precept upon precept, here a little and there a little than to give them something that they could not receive and that they would rebel against. That is the manner in which the Lord deals with His children, and it is the manner in which wise men inspired of the Lord deal with their fellow men.

Speaking as a First Presidency, if we could have our way, there are many changes that we would make; but you know how difficult it is to have people see alike upon many points. (April 7, 1895, *DW* 50:643)

MANY TRUTHS WAITING TO BE REVEALED. The heavens are full of truth and of everything that is good and noble, and many things are revealed to the servants of God which they are commanded not to reveal to the people. Why? Because it would try their faith. Joseph had things revealed to him that he did not make known. . . . There are things which God reveals pertaining to the celestial glory and the higher worlds that the people are not yet prepared to receive. We will all have to grow in faith before these things can be made known. . . . The heavens are full of knowledge. (April, 1900, *CR* 57)

MANY TRUTHS YET TO BE REVEALED. The Lord has not yet revealed to us all that is to be revealed. There are many great and glorious principles and truths pertaining to exaltation in the Celestial Kingdom of God which we are not yet prepared to receive. . . . From the day that God established this Church to the present the stream of revelation has continued to flow uninterruptedly. It flows pure for us to drink at until we are filled to repletion; and if we do not drink, it is our own fault. The servants of God are not to blame for they have been laboring by day and by night from the beginning with us, as a people, to prepare us for the great things that are at our very doors and that God intends to perform in this generation. . . .

DISCOURSES FILLED WITH REVELATION. Men talk about revelation—I said a few moments ago that men compared the present day with the past and compare it unfavorably. When I look at what God has done for us up to the present, instead of there being room for unfavorable comparisons between the past and the present, I am pleasingly astonished at what has been and is being done. It has been one constant stream of revelation from that day to this.

Read the discourses of the First Presidency and the Twelve, and you will see that they are filled with revelation, with light, with knowledge, with wisdom and with good counsel unto this people. Have this people ever seen the day when the counsel of God's servants has not been sufficient to guide them in the midst of difficulties? No; we never have. There has not been a single minute that this people has been left without the voice of God; there has not been a single minute since this Church was founded to this time that the power of God has not been plainly manifested in our midst. . . .

REVELATIONS TO BRIGHAM YOUNG. When I contemplate how we have been led, how the revelations of God have rested upon His servant Brigham, and how he has been enabled to guide this people safely through the difficulties which laid in their path up to this time, I am filled with gratitude to God our Father for raising up Prophets in this our day. Posterity will look with wonder upon the Work which has been acomplished in this day. (Oct. 23, 1864, JD 10:344-5)

ACCEPTANCE OF REVELATIONS. It seems nonsensical that the Prophet of God could not deem the revelations he received authentic until they had the approval of the different quorums of the Church. They were authentic and divinely inspired whether any man or body of men received them or not. Their reception or non-reception of them would not affect in the least their divine authenticity. But it would be for the people to accept them after God had revealed them. In this way they have been submitted to the Church to see whether the members would accept them as binding upon them or not. Joseph himself had too high a sense of his prophetic office and the authority he had received from the Lord to ever submit the revelations which he received to any individual or to any body, however numerous, to have them pronounce upon their validity. (Jan. 1, 1891, JI 26:14)

PROPER COURSE TO TAKE IN PRIESTHOOD MEETINGS. What is the proper course for officers and Elders in this

Church? Why, if I were going to a Priesthood meeting where there were important matters to attend to, it is my duty, as a servant of God, to go to that meeting with my mind entirely free from all bias. I have my views; but I should not be set in my views; I should not be wedded to them. I should enter that assembly with my mind entirely free from all influence that would prevent the operation of the Spirit of God upon me. I should go in a prayerful spirit, asking God to write upon my heart His will, not with my own will already prepared and determined to carry out my will regardless of everyone else's views. If I were to go and all the rest were to go with this spirit, then the Spirit of God would be felt in our midst, and that which we would decide upon would be the mind and will of God because God would reveal it to us. We would see light in the direction where we should go, and we would behold darkness in the direction we should not go. . . .

APPLIES TO FAMILIES. Now in the family this same thing applies. There are many things arise in families. The father and the mother get together. They want to come to some conclusion respecting some enterprise, perhaps; it may be respecting a son or a daughter—the course to take in relation to that son, the best advice to give to that daughter. How should they come together? Should it be with their minds fixed, the mother determined that she is going to have her way, the father determined that he is going to have his way, he being the head? No; the father and the mother should come together, and every member of the household, with a spirit to wait upon the Lord, to wait for the manifestation of His mind and will, not with any preconceived ideas and a predetermined plan; when that is the case, then the manifestation of the mind of the Lord is withheld so that we cannot, under such circumstances, receive the light of the Spirit.

HOW TO RECEIVE REVELATION. It is the privilege of the Latter-day Saints to have revelation; it is the privilege of fathers, of mothers, of children, of every member of this Church, young or old, to receive revelation, under proper circumstances and when needed. And this is the way to receive it. This is the way that the Church of Christ is guided. Many suppose that the

Lord, when He wants a thing done, sends His angels to tell us what to do. He may do so under certain circumstances. But the guide that God has given unto the Presidency of this Church and unto the Apostles and unto all who stand in responsible stations is the Spirit of God, the Holy Ghost. It is by its guidance and by the light which it gives that this Church is led. And it is obtained by waiting patiently for the Lord to make known His will and preparing ourselves for it, asking Him to give it. It comes then in power. It comes with the clearness of the light of the sun. It comes overpoweringly so that there can be no doubt left in the mind as to the correctness of the course.

In this way this Church has been led from the beginning. It is being led in that manner now, and it will be led in that manner until Jesus himself shall come. If the Church is led in this manner, then, of course, you can see that every department of the Church ought to be led in like manner and by the same influence. When the Holy Ghost is with you, then God is with you, and the power of God is with you for the Holy Ghost is one of the Godhead. This is the precious privilege that God has given unto those who have entered into covenant with Him. It may not come with any outward demonstration.

A STILL SMALL VOICE. You remember about the Prophet Elijah. He stood upon the mount before the Lord. "And, behold, the Lord passed by, and a great and strong wind rent the mountains, and brake in pieces the rocks before the Lord; but the Lord was not in the wind; and after the wind an earthquake; but the Lord was not in the earthquake; and after the earthquake fire; but the Lord was not in the fire; and after the fire a still small voice." It was in the "still small voice" that God manifested himself.

So it is with us. When that still small voice is heard in our hearts and we listen to it, it will guide us in the way of truth and reveal unto us everything necessary for our salvation and exaltation. If we follow it carefully, we will walk in the path that will lead us to the presence of God. Then, when we dwell in His presence, we shall see as we are seen and know as we are known. But now we have to walk by faith and not by sight, and

[5]I Kings 19:11-12.

the Holy Ghost is given to guide us in the path that God has marked out. (Aug. 3, 1890, *DW* 41:484-5)

NO GUARANTEE OF FAITHFULNESS. It would appear, looking at matters naturally, that if men and women had tested the word of God, had received revelation from God, had knowledge poured into their souls concerning this being the work of God, they would always be faithful to the truth; but it is not so, and this is evidence of the great power which the adversary exercises over the hearts of the children of men. Men may behold the heavens opened and see Jesus, they may see visions and have revelations given to them, and yet if they do not live as they should do and cherish the Spirit of God in their hearts, all this knowledge and these revelations and wonderful manifestations fail to keep them in the Church, to preserve them from the power of the adversary and to deliver them from the snares that he spreads for the feet of all the children of God. (Oct. 6, 1875, *JD* 18:83-4)

THE URIM AND THUMMIM. There is no record of a transmission of the Urim and Thummim from one continent to another. It is in the highest degree improbable that the Urim and Thummim that the Jaredites had was the same that was had among the children of Israel. It seems entirely clear that the Jaredites, and after them the Nephites, had the Urim and Thummim that the brother of Jared used and that the Urim and Thummim used among the children of Israel was one that had been prepared for use among them.

The continent of America, as we now call it, was as though it were a distinct world, so far as the other hemisphere was concerned. Its existence was unknown. There was no connection between the people that dwelt on this land and the people that dwelt on the other continents. While, therefore, it is but reasonable to assume that the Lord permits the use of but one Urim and Thummim at a time on the earth, in the case of the Jaredites and the Nephites such a rule might not apply because, as we have said, they were as widely separated from the rest of the world and as unknown to those who lived on the eastern hemisphere as if they dwelt on a different planet. (Jan. 15, 1897, *JI* 32:52)

CHAPTER 23

TESTIMONIES—THE STRENGTH OF THE CHURCH

THIS GENERATION HELD ACCOUNTABLE. Jesus said when he was upon the earth: "And this is the condemnation, that light is come into the world, and men loved darkness rather than light.[1] They were held to a strict accountability after light was revealed. . . . When God communicates His mind and will unto His children by the medium of angels, by the medium of Prophets, by the medium of holy men whom He has raised up, those who hear that testimony, those unto whom that message is communicated are held to a strict accountability to obey the same or be held in great condemnation for their rejection of it.

If you will read the history of God's ways of dealing with the children of men throughout all ages, you will find that it is invariably the case that judgments and calamities, the fiery indignation of the Almighty always follow the rejection of His truth when that truth is proclaimed by his authorized servants, such as are Apostles and Prophets. . . .

JOSEPH SMITH'S TESTIMONY BINDING. It is a remarkable fact abundantly sustained in the history of God's dealings with the children of men that He does not hold mankind guiltless because there are only a few who are the oracles of truth in their midst and who have the authority to proclaim that truth. If there was but one Prophet on the face of the earth and he had no followers but stood alone in the midst of the nations of the earth, his warnings would be followed by terrible results if they were disregarded by those who heard them. The Lord does not look upon men according to their numbers; the importance of His work and His dealings with the children of men is not to be measured by the number of those who adhere to the principles that He proclaims.

When Joseph Smith stood alone, when he had only two or three followers and he declared unto those by whom he was surrounded that God had spoken to him from the heavens, that God had revealed the everlasting Gospel in its ancient purity

----
[1] John 3:19.

and power, that God has sent His holy angels to him and that those angels had laid their hands upon his head and upon the head of Oliver Cowdery and ordained them to the everlasting Priesthood, his testimony was as binding upon those who heard it as if millions of men had testified to the same truths. His testimony was binding from the moment that he commenced to bear it to those by whom he was surrounded, and the accountability of the people who listened to him and heard his voice and heard his testimony began from the moment that he opened his mouth and bore testimony of these things. . . .

THE TESTIMONY OF THE HOLY GHOST. God has not left the inhabitants of the earth without a witness; God has not left them without some testimony which they can obtain to assure them that the words of God's servants—that is the true servants of God— which they hear are from Him. When He called Joseph Smith and Oliver Cowdery and when He sent his angels to lay their hands upon their heads to ordain them to that Priesthood which had been withdrawn from the earth, He also sent His Holy Spirit to accompany their words and to seal the testimony with power upon the hearts of all that were honest and who prayerfully sought for a knowledge from God concerning the truth of their words.

When Joseph Smith and Oliver Cowdery laid their hands upon other men's heads and ordained them to the same Priesthood which they had received from heaven, God confirmed the ordination by bestowing the Holy Ghost upon them, and when they went forth and proclaimed the truth, the Holy Ghost accompanied their words; those who were desirous of knowing from God respecting the truth of their testimony had the opportunity of receiving a knowledge direct from heaven that it was of God, and on this very account condemnation commences because light hath come into the world, and when men reject it, they reject it because they love darkness rather than light. . . .

THE DUTY OF MANKIND. What is the duty of the inhabitants of the earth when a man comes as Joseph Smith did and as the Elders of this Church are doing proclaiming the truths which I have alluded to? Why, they being in ignorance of God, they having no revelation from God, they not having heard the voice of angels, they being split up into parties and sects and divided and quarrelling respecting the points of doctrine which Christ revealed, they being in this position should humble themselves and ask God in the name of Jesus and in mighty prayer to reveal unto them whether the testimony of the these men who come with this new revelation be true or false.

That is the duty of every living soul upon the face of the earth who hears the testimony of God's servants concerning this truth, and there never has been, from the time that Joseph Smith made his first proclamation until this day, a time when a man who took this course did not receive a witness from on high, the testimony of Jesus Christ, that these truths proclaimed by the servants of God are divine and from heaven. . . .

CONDEMNATION ON THOSE WHO REJECT GOSPEL. Who have rejected this Gospel? The indifferent, those who would not take the trouble to investigate it, those who would not take the trouble to bow in submission before the Lord and ask His testimony concerning it, those who thought it beneath them, those who have been too proud or too rich or too well situated or who, for some other reason, have failed to take any interest in this work; these are they who are not members of this Church and who have failed to obey this Gospel when they heard it preached in its simplicity and its purity amongst the nations of the earth.

Well, now, will this generation escape condemnation? I say unto you, nay. There will be a heavy condemnation fall upon this generation because of their inattention to these things. Judgments and calamities will be visited upon the inhabitants of the earth in consequences of neglecting the word of God written in the Scriptures and also the word of God to His servants in these days. (Aug. 3, 1879, JD 20:245-8)

TESTIMONY ACCOMPANIES WORDS OF TRUTH. There is a testimony accompanying the words of truth spoken in soberness that carries conviction to the heart of every honest person who hears it, and there is no man or woman to whom it is declared but what has a secret conviction that there is something more in it than they are willing to allow. (April 21, 1867, JD 12:40)

PEOPLE CONDEMNED BY TESTIMONIES. The testimonies of the servants of God . . . ought to make an impression upon the minds of those who hear them—they ought to have weight for the reason that those who bear them declare in solemnity in the presence of God that they know that which they testify is true; and when a man or any number of men arise in the presence of their fellow men and declare in words of truth and soberness that certain things are true, that they know them to be true, that they are willing to bear testimony of them before God and the people and to suffer all things for their truth, even to death itself, it should make an impression upon the human mind and inspire those who hear these testimonies with a disposition to at least investigate and withhold their condemnation. Because, unless a man knows something to the contrary, unless he has had a testimony that these things are false, he is not justified in condemning them.

There is only one way in which they can be fairly condemned and that is by proving their falsity, by obtaining knowledge that is directly in contradiction to that which is borne testimony to. In this consists the condemnation of the inhabitants of the earth at the present time as it has consisted in every age when God has had a work to do upon the earth. (Jan. 6, 1884, JD 25:22-3)

INDIVIDUAL   TESTIMONIES — STRENGTH   OF CHURCH. In the Church of Christ there is a fountain opened, so to speak, at which not only the head of the Church may drink but every individual member also in the Church; and while the head of the Church holds the keys by which revelation is obtained for the Church as a whole, still every member has the privilege of receiving revelation also for himself and through such means knowing that that which the head of the Church teaches or is empowered to reveal does indeed come from the Almighty. It is this that makes every faithful member of the Church a witness of the truth, and it imparts a strength and unity which cannot be obtained in any other way. . . .

In the Church of Jesus Christ of Latter-day Saints the members not only have this in their favor, but in addition they themselves have a testimony, through the Spirit, concerning that which is taught. This brings every individual member in close relationship, through the Holy Ghost, with the Father and the Son. There is no man to stand between his fellow-man and the Creator; but each has access to Him through the same gift or power that every other has. In this way and by this means man is uplifted, and all can stand upon the same plane as the children of a common Parent and all have direct communication with Him. (Jan. 1, 1893, *JI* 28:18)

Therein lies the strength of this Church. One man alone does not govern and control. He gives the word of the Lord, and in every heart the Spirit of the Lord bears testimony that that is the word of the Lord. (Feb. 18, 1900, *MS* 62:245)

In this way the Prophets Joseph and Brigham led the Church. The Lord told them His will, they told it to the people, and if the people had the Spirit of the Lord, they knew it was true. (March 1, 1878, *JI* 13:54)

GOD'S SPIRIT ACCESSIBLE TO ALL. The Gospel of Jesus Christ or "Mormonism," as it is termed, teaches men that the Lord is accessible to all who humbly seek Him in the appointed way. The head of the Church is not the only privileged person, though he stands as Prophet, Seer, and Revelator to the people. No man that is faithful to his God and his religion, whether he be in Utah or called by duty to minister in foreign lands, will be unprepared for the reception of principles which are being revealed to the head of the Church. He possesses that Spirit which Jesus said should lead men into all truth. That Spirit, if sought after and cherished, reveals these principles to him, and he thereby becomes a living witness of their truth. This is what constitutes the potency of "Mormonism," or, more properly, the Gospel, and is the means by which its believers are bound and cemented together from the head downward. Elders faithful in their callings, then, are not kept in ignorance by the head of the Church not letting them know too much. (July 3, 1857, *WS* 465)

A DUTY TO WALK IN THE LIGHT. It is every person's duty in this Church, and it is the constant exhortation of the leaders of the people to seek for and enjoy the presence of the Spirit of God so that none will be wholly dependent upon another human being for enjoyment and happiness and for a knowledge of the truth but that each may receive a testimony that this is the Church of God, that the Priesthood has really come from Him and that the men who exercise this Priesthood are not pretenders but are indeed that which they profess to be. This is the bounden duty of all the members of this Church so that they may not be assailed by doubts but that they will walk in the light. In this way a great people can be built up, for these are the elements of greatness.

It seems to be one of the faults of human beings, however, to lean upon others and to do that which others do regardless of their own convictions instead of developing their own qualities that God has endowed them with. How often you see men and women justify themselves for doing things because somebody else does them. (Oct. 14, 1894, *MS* 56:754)

TESTIMONY OF HOLY GHOST MOST CONVINCING. Some people think, "If I had only the ministration of an angel, it would satisfy me." Do you know that when you receive the Holy Ghost you receive something that is greater than an angel? The Holy Ghost is one of the Godhead. When we are baptized, we are baptized in the name of the Father and the Son and the Holy Ghost. Jesus, therefore, instead of visiting the Gentiles Himself, sent the Holy Ghost to them, His companion, so to speak, in the Godhead, the ministering Spirit of the Father and the Son; and when He gives it unto you, you receive God; and it is a much more powerful testimony and ought to be a more convincing one than the ministering of an angel. The ministering of an angel appeals to our outer senses. We see with our eyes. But we may be deceived, for Satan, it is said, is able to transform himself almost like an angel of light. But not so with the Holy Ghost. When that descends upon a man, he knows it, and the testimony which it gives cannot be taken away. . . . When the Holy Ghost descends upon a man, God is with him as long as he retains that Spirit, and it is a Spirit that will always bear testimony to him. (Sept. 4, 1892, *DW* 45:388)

A TESTIMONY A PRECIOUS GIFT. If you know of any young persons who think they have no testimony, just say to them that if the Lord were to withdraw His Spirit from them they would be apt to find the awful condition they would be in.

I heard of one man who thought he did not have any testimony of the authenticity or divinity of the Book of Mormon, and he asked the Lord, if the Book was true, to withdraw from him His Spirit for a space of time as a testimony to him that he might know by that evidence that it was divine. The Lord answered his request. The effect was of the most startling kind. His experience was of such a terrible nature that he prostrated himself in supplication before the Lord for a speedy return of the precious gift he had voluntarily cast from him. After suffering past description the Spirit returned; he knew for himself then that the Book of Mormon was true and that this Gospel was the plan of life and salvation. Such an experience was awful, and it ought to be a lesson to every member of the Church.

Many undervalue, if they do not despise, the precious gift which God has given them. Instead of cherishing and cultivating it, they think it of no worth. Of course, where this is the case, the gift does not grow. Faith does not increase, neither does it blossom into knowledge, and gradually the Spirit of the Lord is withdrawn. (*Young Woman's Journal* 4:124-5)

A TESTIMONY THAT GROWS. The presence of the Holy Ghost will give every man and woman who possesses it a testimony concerning the truth of the Gospel. Full knowledge may not dawn upon the mind at once, but it will grow and increase until the person will have perfectly satisfactory evidence that this is the work of God. Some people, however, are not satisfied with this. They want something of a more marvelous character. And because they do not receive or witness it, they become a prey to doubt. This should not be. Whenever it is the case, there is something wrong in the individual. Either he has not obeyed the ordinances in the right spirit, or he has not understood the nature of the blessing God has given him. (Sept. 15, 1892, *JI* 27:562)

WHY TESTIMONIES ARE LOST. I have heard some people express wonder why individuals deny the truth who have once borne testimony to it; but, if we understand truly the spirit of the Gospel, we will know that while under the influence of the Spirit of God we can bear testimony to the truth, but when that Spirit takes its departure from us, we are left to ourselves, and we do not really see it as we once did for the darkness in our minds makes it impossible to do so.

I have known those whose faith did not grow beyond a certain point. Up to that point they could say Joseph Smith was a Prophet of God and that everything was right, but beyond that they would deny him and the doctrines he taught because they had lost the Spirit of God.

We would, perhaps, think that if we ever had the Spirit of God sufficiently to see the truth that we would ever afterwards know it was of heaven; but it is only by retaining the Spirit of God, by cultivating it and by keeping it bright in our bosoms that we or they can remain true. Those who have seen holy angels have afterwards denied the truth, though they would not deny that which they had seen and known while they had the Spirit. There are no circumstances in life in which we can be placed where we will not require the Spirit of God to guide us safely through them—there is no point of our lives, present or to come, that we do not want the light of that Spirit. (July 17, 1863, MS 26:501)

A KEY TO RETAIN A TESTIMONY. The only way to maintain our position in the Kingdom of God is to so conduct ourselves that we may have a living testimony of the truth continually dwelling in our bosoms, to live so that the Spirit of the Lord may be a constant and abiding guest with us, whether in the privacy of our chamber, in the domestic circle or in the midst of the crowded thoroughfares, the busy scenes and anxious cares of life. He who will pursue this course will never lack for knowledge; he will never be in doubt or in darkness, nor will his mind ever be clouded by the gloomy pall of unbelief; on the contrary his hopes will be bright; his faith will be strong; his joy will be full; he will be able each succeeding day to comprehend the unfolding purposes of Jehovah and to rejoice in the glorious liberty and happiness which all the faithful children of God enjoy.

It is not enough that we knew the truth of this work yesterday or the day before or a week or a month or a year ago; we ought to and must, in order to be happy, know it to be true to-day. . . . We can only retain the testimony of the truth in our heart by living near unto God. If we call upon Him in faith to bless us and seek to enjoy the companionship of the Holy

Spirit, so ordering our lives that God can, consistently, bless us and the Spirit of the Lord can abide with us, we receive strength to overcome every evil and our minds instinctively recoil from the commission of any act which might grieve that Spirit or bring a stain upon our own character or upon the divine cause in which we are engaged. (April 5, 1863, MS 25:275-6)

GOSPEL COMPARED TO A SEED. The best evidence that men can get, so far as I know, concerning the divinity of the work of God is to take the course recommended by the servant of God. . . . He compared the word of God to a seed.[2] If it were received in the heart and it began to swell and to sprout and to grow, those who received it might know that it was a good seed.

This is the effect that the preaching of the Gospel has had upon the honest in heart in every land where the Elders of this Church have gone. The word of God has been like seed. It has fallen in many instances in good ground, and where it has thus fallen, it has sprouted and grown and brought forth fruit which, as the Prophet said, is sweeter than all sweetness, whiter than all whiteness and purer than all purity.

I am sure the Latter-day Saints will see the appropriateness of the figure used by the Prophet in their own case. When they heard the Gospel, they knew but little about the power of God; but they received it in their hearts; they cherished it; they nursed it; it began to swell and to sprout and to grow; it has filled them with light, with joy and with peace, and they know beyond all question that the seed which they have received in their hearts is a good seed and that the fruit it has borne has been good fruit. It has satisfied the longing of their souls, and they testify before God and angels that it is the truth that they have received.

They may never have seen an angel; they may never have seen the dead raised to life; they may never have seen the blind made to see or the deaf made to hear; they may not have even seen the sick healed by the laying on of hands; but because they have not seen these mighty works, it has not deprived them of a knowledge concerning that which they have received. That has rested upon them in power, and they know for themselves it is of God. They have cherished the seed; they have dug about it and nourished it, and it has grown in their hearts until it has pro-

---

[2]Alma 32:28.

duced most precious fruit, filling their souls with joy, with peace
and with a heavenly feeling. And this is a greater testimony than
visions or dreams or angelic manifestations or the power of God
manifested through the healing of the sick because it is a living
testimony in the soul of man.

SEED GROWS UNDER INFLUENCE OF PRAYER.
There are instances, however, such as this Prophet alludes to,
where men do not cultivate the seed and do not watch over it;
they do not, in other words, pray. Prayer is to the soul like the
irrigating stream to our dry and parched fields and orchards.
Prayer nourishes, strengthens and imparts vitality to the seed.
The seed grows under the influence of prayer. But where prayer
is neglected, the results are just as we see them when we neglect
to irrigate our fields and orchards. That which is planted there
begins to wither and dry up.

So it is with the word of God in the human soul; it must
be watered by the Spirit of God. Prayer must be exercised in
order to invoke the power and blessing of God to rest upon it.
Then the seed grows; the tree grows and flourishes; its branches
spread abroad and fill the whole man, and he knows that it is
the word of God that he has received. He has a living and abiding
testimony in his heart concerning it, and doubt has no room
within him. But let him neglect his prayers, let him neglect to
cultivate the seed and to watch over it, then it begins to wither,
and he begins to doubt and to ask himself whether this is indeed
the work of God. This is not because the seed was not good; it
is because of the neglect of the individual. (Feb. 17, 1895, *DW*
50:418)

THE STRENGTH OF THE CHURCH. There is no coun-
sel given by the Presidency of the Church, no step taken nor no
policy pursued that they have to depend upon their personal
influence to have the people believe because the people can go
to God themselves, if they have doubts upon any point, and call
upon Him, in the name of Jesus, to reveal to them whether that
which is done or taught is from Him or not. They need not be
in doubt. They need not run around asking questions about
matters which may appear mysterious to them; they can go to
the Lord in their secret places, and He will remove their doubts

and answer their questions; He will throw light upon their minds respecting the matters about which they may be disturbed. . . .

THE WAY THE CHURCH IS LED. So it will be to the end. The Presidency of the Church have to walk just as you walk. They have to take steps just as you take steps. They have to depend upon the revelations of God as they come to them. They cannot see the end from the beginning as the Lord does. They have their faith tested as you have your faith tested.

So with the Twelve Apostles. All that we can do is to seek the mind and will of God; when that comes to us, though it may come in contact with every feeling that we have previously entertained, we have no option but to take the step that God points out and to trust to Him, as we were often told by President Young, for the results. That is the way this Church is led. There is no being, save the Lord himself, who knows the end from the beginning. Who of us would be tested if we were in that condition?

It is just as necessary that the Presidency and the Apostles should be tried as it is that you should be tried. It is as necessary that our faith should be called into exercise as that your faith should be called into exercise. We can see a certain distance in the light of the Spirit of God as it reveals to us His mind and His will, and we can take these steps with perfect security, knowing that they are the right steps to be taken. But as to what the result will be, that is for the God of Israel to control. That is the way in which the Church of God has always been led, and it will always be led in that way until He comes who is our King, our Lawgiver and our President, even Jesus Christ. (Oct. 5, 1890, *DW* 41:649-50)

EVERY MAN A PROPHET. The genius of the Kingdom with which we are associated is to disseminate knowledge through all the ranks of the people and to make every man a Prophet and every woman a Prophetess that they may understand the plans and purposes of God. For this purpose the Gospel has been sent to us, and the humblest may obtain its spirit and testimony, and the weakest of the weak may obtain a knowledge respecting the purposes of God. . . .

If we do anything, let us do it understandingly. If we hear

any principle taught from the stand that we do not understand, let us seek to comprehend it by the Spirit of God. If it be not of God, we have the privilege of knowing it. We are not required to receive for doctrine everything that we hear. We may say, "I do not know whether this is true or not; I will not fight it, neither will I endorse it, but I will seek knowledge from God, for that is my privilege, and I will never rest satisfied until I have obtained the light I require."

If you hear a doctrine that does not agree with your feelings or that you do not believe, take this course; do not reject nor endorse hastily without knowing or understanding. By taking this course you will develop the principle that God designs we should possess, and we will thus become a wise and understanding people, for we will be based on the rock of revelation. (April 21, 1867, *JD* 12:46)

WE ARE INDEPENDENT WITNESSES. Every man and woman who has joined this Church ought to be and is in the most of instances standing as an independent witness of the truth of that which God has done. You divide this entire congregation into units and let each one stand alone, surrounded by those not of their faith, and he or she is, though solitary, still a witness independent of all others of the truth. Then you bring these individuals together, each one understanding the Gospel and having received a testimony of its divinity, and they constitute a body which, in some respects, is entirely incomparable. (Nov. 22, 1896, *MS* 59:65)

SPIRITUAL TRUTHS NOT DISCERNED BY OUTER SENSES. We are asked whether it is possible for a man, by means of his five senses alone independent of the Holy Ghost, to know that Joseph Smith is a Prophet of the living God. . . .

To begin with the perfect use of our senses is only given to us by the aid of the Spirit of God and the light that cometh from Him; and while it is possible for men to reason upon various subjects and satisfy their minds concerning truth, still the highest testimony that a human being can have respecting Joseph being a Prophet or of our Lord Jesus being the Savior is the testimony of the Holy Ghost. The Lord has given light and intelligence to His children by means of which they are able to arrive at a knowledge concerning many things. This is done through the instrumentality of the Spirit of God. Men can satisfy themselves that Jesus is the Savior of the world by reasoning upon it and adducing evidences that are open to the outer senses, and yet they cannot reach such a conclusion without the aid of the Spirit of God. Paul says: "No man can say that Jesus is the Lord, but by the Holy Ghost."[3] The same may be said in relation to the knowledge of Joseph Smith being a Prophet of God.

For a man to say he knows a spiritual truth by the aid of his outer senses, is a rash and ill-considered expression, and it should not give rise to discussion. (Oct. 15, 1890, *JI* 25:627)

THE VALUE OF THE TESTIMONY MEETINGS. These Fast-day meetings which are being held on Sunday give every member of the Ward who feels desirous to bear testimony the opportunity of doing so, and it will lead to the people becoming better acquainted with each other and being greatly strengthened in their faith and encouraged by the testimonies of their brethren and sisters which they listen to. These can be made the most interesting meetings in the Church. They always have been noted as being exceedingly beneficial to the people. Men and women are led, in listening to the testimonies of their brethren and sisters, to examine the grounds they have for their own faith in the Gospel. It gives an opportunity also when there is anything improper advanced for the presiding officer to correct it, thus removing wrong impressions and belief in unsound doctrines from the minds of the people. . . .

Testimony meetings differ from the other public meetings in that they give the members of the Church an opportunity of expressing themselves concerning their religion and making their religion much more practical—at least, to them—than it would be if they were merely hearers of the word. Those who attend these meetings become interested in them. They are not mere listeners, but they have the opportunity of expressing their own feelings and views, and by this they feel themselves more identified with the work of God than they otherwise would. . . .

When a man or a woman stands up to bear testimony concerning the work of the Lord and set forth the evidences furnished of its divinity, it causes the other members who are present to

---

[3] I Corinthians 12:3.

think and search themselves for the proofs they possess of this being the Church of Jesus Christ. They are thus led to bear their testimony, too, in the hearing of others; or, if they have not the evidence they think sufficient to enable them to bear this testimony, they may be prompted to seek for it. This of itself has an excellent effect. They become witnesses; and having borne testimony to the work, it strengthens their faith and attaches them more closely to the principles of the Gospel. . . . When children hear testimonies of this kind from their seniors, they remember them, and they tend to strengthen their faith and to give them experience in the things of God. The gifts of the Spirit will be manifested in these meetings, and children in witnessing these and partaking of the spirit of the meetings will be greatly strengthened in their desire to do right and to keep the commandments of God. (Feb. 1, 1897, JI 32:78-9)

TESTIMONY BEARING BY CHILDREN. I hear of little children bearing testimony in the Sunday Schools and doing so by the Spirit of God, and by that they are made to feel their individual responsibility before the Lord. In my opinion this is a good thing. I believe our future will be greatly enhanced by this kind of training, and we shall have a class of people grow up among us different from all others. It may be gradual—so gradual that we will scarcely notice its growth—but the growth will take place. (April 9, 1899, CR 64)

CHAPTER 24

OBEDIENCE TO COUNSEL—THE PATH OF SAFETY

THE PATH OF SAFETY. We have to learn, if we have not already learned it, that obedience to counsel is the policy for us to pursue and that when we indulge in thoughts of an opposite character, we suffer ourselves to be led astray by the power of the adversary. Hence, it has become almost proverbial among the Saints that the path of counsel is the path of safety. Those who have had years of experience in the Church have arrived at the conclusion that the path marked out for us to walk in by those who have authority to counsel and dictate is invariably the path of safety to those who adopt it. But our traditions interfere with this. . . .

OUR RELIGION COMPREHENDS SPIRITUAL AND TEMPORAL. There is that terrible tradition, that has such strong hold of all our minds, that the Priesthood of God and the religion of Jesus Christ have nothing to do particularly with temporal matters. It is a tradition almost as old as Christianity. It has come down to us for generations and centuries and is fully interwoven in the hearts, minds and feelings of the children of men, and it is an exceedingly difficult thing to get them to comprehend that temporal things and spiritual things are alike in the sight of God, that there is no line of demarcation between the two, that the religion of Jesus Christ applies to one as much as another and comprehends within its scope temporal equally with spiritual matters. (Nov. 13, 1879, JD 13:370-2)

BLESSINGS RESULT FROM OBEDIENCE TO COUNSEL. Now, the day has come when we, as a people, will have to listen to the voice of the servants of God, to the instructions of the Almighty through his servants and obey them as implicitly as though God was in our midst. . . .

When the counsel of God comes through his servants to us, we should bow to that no matter how much it may come in contact with our pre-conceived ideas; submit to it as though God spoke it, and feel such a reverence towards it as though we believed that the servant of God had the inspiration of the Almighty resting upon him. . . .

I know that if we follow implictly the counsel of God's servants when they are inspired to give counsel, even if they may not know everything about the matter, we will be blessed if we bow to it; God will overrule everything for good, and it will result as God wishes it.

It is a great thing for us to have the counsel and instruction of the Almighty in our midst. The servants of God are inspired by the power of the Holy Ghost, and the revelations of Jesus are within them; and if we follow their counsels strictly, we shall be led into the presence of God, and I know that they are the only men on the earth who have this power, authority and knowledge. If we take a course of this kind, you can readily perceive how harmoniously everything connected with the work of God will roll forth; beauty and order will be witnessed in all the ramifications of the Kingdom of God at home and abroad, and salvation will be extended unto us. (Jan. 1, 1865, *JD* 11:71-2)

FOLLOW COUNSEL OF PRESIDENCY. When I respect and honor Wilford Woodruff, I bow to God who has chosen him. My neck does not nor never did bow to man. Those who know me know that I am unbending in that respect. I may get along quietly; I do not like to quarrel; but I never yet bowed to man. I only bow to proper authority. If I listen to Wilford Woodruff, if I look to him to see how the Spirit of God moves upon him, if I ask his counsel and take it, it is because God has commanded me. God has given him the keys of authority. Let anybody else try it and see what effect their action would have.

When Joseph F. Smith obeys Wilford Woodruff, he does it upon the same principle. We reverence him as the Prophet of God and as our leader. We listen to him and are guided by his slightest wish. It is because we know that he is the servant of God, chosen by the Almighty to fill that place, and that he holds the keys of the Priesthood to this generation on the earth at the present time. I can say truthfully that we strive to consult his slightest wish and honor him in this position, because we know that God has chosen him.

Who are we that we should withstand God? Who are we that we should withstand that which God reveals? Does this sacrifice our independence? Not in the least. And these Twelve Apostles are in precisely the same position. When they accept the counsel of the First Presidency, they do it because they believe the First Presidency to be chosen of God. They may have different views on many things, but when the First Presidency gives counsel, every man that has the Spirit of God accepts that counsel. This does not prevent him from entertaining his views and expressing them, and it does not detract from his influence. (Oct. 4, 1896, *DW* 53:738)

OBEDIENCE IN TEMPORAL MATTERS. We have to progress till we reach that state when all our labors will be under the dictation, guidance and direction of those whom God has appointed to preside over us. . . . That obedience which characterizes us in spiritual things will have to be manifested in temporal things.

Many of the people think, "I know more about this matter than my Bishop does," when some temporal matter is agitated. That feeling is running through the minds of numbers of the people; and while this is the case, your Bishops will probably not be as wise as they might be; they have not your faith to sustain them. But when the time comes that you have implicit faith and confidence in God and in those whom He appoints to preside over you, in things temporal as well as spiritual, your Bishops will have all the wisdom needed to give you the counsel you require.

This time must come; and not only must it be the case with the brethren, but it must be so with their families also for family government is the foundation of all government. Show me a community where children are brought up in holiness and purity and trained in the fear and knowledge of God, and I can prophecy future greatness and prosperity for that people. If I see a family where the children are obedient to their parents and listen to their voices as to the voice of an angel and where wives are obedient to their husbands, meeting their wishes and seeking to gratify them in everything in the Lord, I know there is greatness before that family. So with this entire people. (March 3, 1867, *JD* 11:338)

POWER AND WISDOM IN TEMPORAL AFFAIRS. Let

men reflect a moment on the position assumed by the Latter-day Saints. They profess to be sent of God and endowed with the same Priesthood and power as the ancient Prophets. Could they hold or exercise this and not have authority to meddle with municipal and civil as much as doctrinal points? Is there less wisdom, less farsightedness or penetration needed to give instruction on spiritual than on temporal subjects? To make this admission would be to give a superior importance to affairs of the body over those of the spirit.

We do not now remember an instance of a man holding the power and authority claimed by the Latter-day Saints who failed to exercise it on every occasion when necessity demanded in municipal and civil affairs as much as on doctrinal points or affairs pertaining to the spiritual improvement and salvation of mankind. . . .

There certainly would be great cause to apprehend danger from a fusion of spiritual and temporal arrangements by an illegitimate priesthood, a priesthood unauthorized by God. . . . When men are selected by the Almighty and made the recipients of His Priesthood, enlightened and taught by His Spirit, they have power and wisdom to act in spiritual affairs; and as temporal affairs require no greater amount of intelligence and authority, they can, of course, with all propriety, act in them also whenever necessity may demand. (Jan. 3, 1857, *WS* 293-4)

WE ARE STEWARDS. God our Eternal Father has placed all these possessions and blessings—that is, the possessions of the earth and the blessings connected with the earth—He has placed them in our hands merely as stewards, and we hold them subject to Him—in other words, in trust for Him—and if He calls upon us to use them in any given direction He may indicate, it is our duty as His children, occupying the relationship that we do to Him and with the hopes in our breasts that we have, to hold them entirely subject to Him. . . .

If we are expecting to reach a glory and an exaltation such as we think about and talk about and pray for, it seems to me that there should be something to be done on our part commensurate with the expectations and hopes and desires that we entertain, and I do not know myself any better test that can be brought to bear upon human beings than this test . . . of holding ourselves—that is our individual persons, with our time and the ability that God has given unto us, our wives, our children and the possessions that God has placed in our hands to control—to hold all these subject to His dictation and to His approval. . . .

AUTHORITY IN TEMPORAL MATTERS. There is an authority in the Church to whom God has given the right to counsel in the affairs of the children of men in regard to temporal affairs. When Joseph Smith lived upon the earth, it was his prerogative to do that. He stood as God's ambassador, not clothed with the attributes of God, for he was a mortal man; but he stood as the representative of God upon the earth, holding the keys of the Kingdom of God upon the earth, with the power to bind on earth and it should be bound in heaven. He occupied that position when he lived, and on his departure another took his place upon the earth and stood in precisely the same capacity to us as a people that Joseph Smith did.

That was Brigham Young. When he passed away, another stepped forward and took the same position and holds the same keys and exercises the same authority and stands precisely in the same position to us that the Prophet Joseph did or that the Prophet Brigham did when he lived upon the earth. . . .

GOD CHOOSES THE MAN FOR THE HOUR. When he spoke by the power of God, it was the word of God to this people. When he sealed a man up to eternal life, he bestowed upon him the blessings pertaining to eternity. . . . When he delegated others to do it in his stead, God in the eternal world recorded the act. . . . There is but one man at a time on the earth who holds this authority. . . .

God places him there. It is not man's act. It is God's providence. God knows the hearts of the children of men. By His overruling Providence He brings this man to the front, or He keeps him in the rear, just as it pleases Him. I believe that His providence is over all of us, and He can kill or remove as He pleases, or He can preserve in life as seemeth good to Him. And He has done so. . . .

It is His privilege to choose whom He pleases. The man whom He wants preserved is preserved. . . . I believe God manages all the affairs of this Church. I know if I do my duty He will save me, He will exalt me, and I know if you will do your duty, He will do the same for you. And if men whom He chooses are fallible, that is His business. He requires on our part obedience to His will as it is made manifest through the man whom He has chosen.

OBEDIENCE TO PRIESTHOOD A VITAL TEST. Now, this is a great point. I look upon it as one of the most vital points connected with our existence in these mountains. I look upon it as a test. It may be said that it will test the Latter-day Saints as they never have been tested—this vital doctrine of obedience to the Priesthood of the Son of God. . . .

With my feelings to-day I never can consent for any man to go in and receive a fullness of the blessings of the everlasting Gospel in . . . those buildings[1] unless I know him to be a man who is willing to yield implicit obedience to the Priesthood of the Son of God. And further, I am not willing, with my present feelings—I do not pretend to dictate in this matter; I am merely stating my own personal feelings—for any man to go into these buildings who is not willing to hold all he has got subject to the Priesthood of the Son of God and be willing to do with it as that Priesthood shall dictate. (Aug. 12, 1883, JD 24:272-7)

FOLLOWING COUNSEL OF PRESIDENCY ASSURES CELESTIAL GLORY. God has chosen us to be your shepherds, and if we do not do our duty, we shall be held responsible in the day of the Lord Jesus. But with the help of God we have been and are still striving to lead the people and teach them aright, and if you will listen to our counsels, God will save you. I know that. It may not be thought proper for me to say that, occupying the position I do, but it is the truth. If you will listen to the counsel of the First Presidency of this Church, you will be led into the Celestial Kingdom of our God. I bear this testimony to you this afternoon. (Aug. 26, 1894, DW 49:451)

DISOBEDIENCE TO COUNSEL INCURS FEARFUL RESPONSIBILITY. When men whom God has chosen to act in authority are led to give certain counsel or to take a certain course, the person who seeks to change that counsel or to divert them from that course incurs a fearful responsibility. Yet, it is

---

[1]The Temples.

frequently done. There are many people who are not willing to have the man who has the authority dictate what shall be done; they can not trust him; they have some better plan to suggest. In this way counsel is darkened; the Spirit of God is grieved, and trouble follows.

We have noticed. . . that whenever men were reluctant to adopt the plans and counsel of those in authority and urged their own in the stead that God's blessing did not rest upon them. When a man has the right to counsel and to decide what shall be done and his mind is clear on the point, there should be no division on the subject, and men who do not have the authority should never presume to suggest other plans as superior to that of the man who presides. (Feb. 5, 1870, JI 5:21)

We do not now remember an instance of trouble or difficulty experienced by any of the Saints that has come within the range of our observation but what originated either in their total disregard of plain, pointed counsel or in their hasty, unadvised action without first seeking to obtain counsel from those who had the spirit and the authority to impart it. And in every instance of this kind, if the feeling actuating them at the time had been traced to its source, it would have been found that it sprang from distrust in the integrity or ability of those placed to counsel them. . . .

The Lord requires His Saints to be obedient to his Priesthood. If any who bear it do wrong, He attends to them. We never saw an instance of an Elder acting dishonestly or taking a wrong course of any kind that did not himself suffer to a far greater extent than the obedient Saints connected with him or under his care. He injures himself far more than he can possibly injure them. When the Saints are obedient to the requirements of the Lord on this point, He overrules everything for their good so that in the end they are not the losers. (Feb. 2, 1861, MS 23:72-3)

SEEK COUNSEL FROM LEADERS. There was a time in our history when it was the prevalent fashion for the Latter-day Saints to undertake no important enterprise without first asking counsel upon the subject. . . . Experience proves that no one ever received injury through asking counsel of those who hold the Priesthood. In business affairs it can be no harm to consult friends who have experience, and if those friends are servants of God, why should not their advice be sought? The Lord having chosen them and given them the spirit of counsel and instruction and made them leaders among His people qualifies them in a high degree for this important service.

When a man has sought and obtained counsel of the Lord through His servants, he has strength and confidence that he would not have otherwise. His reflections are pleasant for he has a consciousness that he has done his duty. If embarrassment should follow, he can go to the Lord and ask for His blessing with a faith that he could not possibly exercise if he had undertaken his enterprise in utter disregard of or indifference to counsel.

It does not necessarily follow, because men seek counsel from their Bishops or their Presidents or from the Apostles or the First Presidency, that they sink their individuality or in any manner impair their own agency. I am as free a man when I ask counsel of those whom I know to be servants of God as I would be if I were to talk of my affairs to a man who is not a member of the Church. If I present to my brother or brethren my circumstances and changes which I contemplate making or enterprises which I think of undertaking, it does not follow that I have no choice of action. I am as free a man after receiving their counsel as I was before asking it, and I do not lose my individuality or merge it in the person of anyone else. (Dec. 1, 1893, *JI* 28:733)

THE BLESSING OF SEEKING COUNSEL. If I knew a man who has the counsel of God and I wished to obtain counsel, I feel as though it would be the greatest blessing I could have given unto me, under the circumstances, to be able to go to him to ask counsel concerning the course I should take. This has been my course throughout life, and I know it has been attended with blessing. . . .

Shall we, let me ask, feel ashamed of asking counsel? If a Teacher came to my house and I were in doubt concerning any matter that I wished to have counsel upon, I would gladly ask that Teacher what his views were and in this way, if possible, obtain his counsel, looking upon the Teacher as a man of God.

If an Elder were to come to my house or a Bishop or a High Priest or a Seventy or an Apostle and I were in doubt concerning something I contemplated and I wished to obtain more light upon it, I would gladly submit my case to him and ask his counsel. And if he did not come to my house and I could have access to him, I would not engage in any important enterprise without taking such a course.

In the primitive days of the Church this was universally the case. We sought counsel at the hands of the servants of God just as they did in ancient times. Kings did not go to war without seeking counsel. . . .

AN ENLIGHTENED PRIESTHOOD. One is not a sequence of the other. Every man has the right to seek unto God in the appointed way, to seek unto Him in prayer, and besides calling upon Him in prayer, to obtain His word through His appointed servants. Members of Wards should teach their children to ask counsel concerning all matters they wish to undertake, all enterprises upon which they desire to enter.

When a Bishop is living up to his duty, he has the word of the Lord for his people, and he cannot give correct counsel to his people if he is not living as he should live. The same with regard to the President of a Stake. And when the High Council come together with the President of the Stake, it is their privilege to know for themselves concerning matters and to give counsel pertaining thereunto. So it is with every council in this Church.

The light of heaven that comes from God to enlighten the minds of the children of men is not confined to one individual, to one class or to one council or quorum; on the contrary that light is diffused through the whole body of the Priesthood and the whole body of the Church according to the faithfulness of the members. We should understand this. The light of heaven— that is, the light that enlightens our minds—is as free as the light of the sun, as free as the atmosphere we breathe.

We should seek for and enjoy these privileges. I would like to see the Latter-day Saints so impressed with its importance that whenever we take a serious or grave step, we would seek the counsel of God. We should do this on our knees in our chambers, alone; and it is our privilege to seek for and obtain it elsewhere so we may walk aright before God and acceptably before Him. In this way the Kingdom of God will be built up. (Oct. 6, 1889, *DW* 39:592-3)

A HIGHER DUTY TO FOLLOW COUNSEL. Another point connected with our religion which is trying to some people is their fondness of carrying out their own will in relation to temporal affairs. . . . If I have property, it is my duty to take care of it; if I have means, it is my duty to husband it and carefully use it in a way that shall be beneficial to others as well as myself. But there is still a higher duty devolving upon me and upon every member in this Church and that is to do as we are told by the servants of God. . . .

It is necessary for our salvation and exaltation that the men who hold the Apostleship should administer unto us the ordinances in order that we may derive the full benefits which flow from them. . . . Shall we say that this same authority shall not dictate us in regard to these perishable things by which we are surrounded? . . . We must hold ourselves entirely subject to that authority which God has placed in this Church to lead and guide us. (Oct. 31, 1880, JD 22:127)

INDEX

A

Aaron, was called of God, 217.

Abominations, to be kept secret, 61.

Abraham, why tested, 113-114.

Accountability, age of, 172-173; Saints held to stricter, 93.

Adam, a perfect immortal man, 9; created in image of God, 10; fall of, 24; Gospel preached to, 170; spirit of Lucifer manifested to, 5; the first man, 68; very intelligent, 10; walked and talked with God, 10.

Adam and Eve, banished from presence of God, 8; free agency of, 137; knowledge of good and evil obtained by, 16.

Adams, John, was inspired, 307.

Adulterers, not to remain in Church, 169.

Afflictions, why given, 198.

Agencies, of God at work, 83-84.

Agency, 137-145; a fundamental principle of Gospel, 137-139; avoidance of sin an exercise of, 141; every human being given, 137; exercised by Adam and Eve, 137; exercised by Cain, 142; exercised by Judas, 142; exercised by Pharaoh, 142; exercised in rejecting Prophets, 140; exercised by Satan, 137-138; exercised by those who crucified Savior, 143; men and angels have, 14; mortality an exercise of, 16; obedience to Gospel an exercise of, 141; our right to exercise, 296; salvation depends on exercise of, 98, 139-140; Satan to be bound by man's, 86-88; seeking counsel not a loss of, 357.

Agents, God has many, 147.

Age of Disasters, the present is, 47.

Alma, compares Gospel to a seed, 344; visited by an angel, 79.

Alma (quoted concerning), secret combinations, 61; spirit world, 72.

America, discovered at right time, 307-308; Garden of Eden in, 42; has been warned, 65-66; land of Joseph, 42; prominent position of predicted, 54; Zion is, 40.

Angels, 68-85; belonging to this earth, 68; definition of, 68-69; described by Joseph Smith, 70; devil's, 20; given charge over us, 2; glorified men, 126; Holy Ghost more convincing than, 341; many under God's direction, 83; ministration of not expected, 71; ministration of to Joseph Smith, 126; not feathered beings, 69, 126; obeyed Gospel, 178; were once mortal beings, 178; who visit us, 68-69.

Anger, a spirit of evil, 19, 199.

Animals, are obedient to laws of creation, 154; created for man, 30; lives of are sacred, 30; not to be killed for sport, 30.

Anointing, received by Twelve, 283.

Antagonism, Satan's, 17.

Aphrodite, worshiped by Israelites, 135.

Apostasy, by those converted by signs, 192-193; cessation of miracles an evidence of 188-191; comes to all unrepentant sinners, 161; disunity a step towards, 210-211; examples of, 277; fault-finding against Priesthood results in, 226, 278; followed withdrawal of Priesthood, 189; key to given by Joseph Smith, 278; opposing authority results in, 236, 275-276; spiritual destruction, 51; straying from truth, 185.

Apostates, despised and distrusted, 35; don't enjoy life, 35; fall back on scriptures, 324.

Apostles: Also see Prophets.

Apostles, absent on mission at martyrdom, 285; all keys bestowed on, 257-258, 282, 284; ambassadors for Christ, 263; Brigham Young was President of, 283; Church led by, 289-290; counsels of binding, 326-327; discern false teachings, 309; don't aspire to offices, 274-275; equal with First Presidency, 291; great responsibility rests on, 268-269; had warnings of martyrdom, 283; hold fullness of authority to preside, 266-267; necessary in Church, 250-252; necessity of visits by, 273; not dependent on people for support, 279; not a salaried Priesthood, 280; opposing of a deadly sin, 275-276; order of seniority changed by Brigham Young, 287-288; Paul not one of Twelve, 250; purpose of, 272-273; Quorum was to be perpetuated, 250-251; relation of Nephite Twelve to Jewish Twelve, 258; should seek counsel from First Presidency, 208-209; shepherds and watchmen, 269-270; speak by revelation, 332; were foreordained, 11; why sustained as Prophets, Seers and Revelators, 258-262.

Apostleship, 249-280. Authority that saves, 262-3; embodies all authority, 262; future position revealed to George Q. Cannon, 273; received by Joseph Smith, 218, 254, 258; keys of, 265-266; power of ordination, 238; succession in, 250-251.

Appetites, must be controlled, 15, 104-105.

Asia, to be penetrated by Gospel, 66.

Astray, God will not permit faithful to go, 168; God would not permit Church to be led, 168.

Atonement, 24-27; of all sins, 141; should be understood, 26.

Attributes, of God and man, 1.

organized without First Presidency, 291; not to be led astray, 227; order of to be followed, 155; Priesthood rightful authority to lead, 288; principle of union a feature of, 202; Prophets and Apostles necessary in, 252; revelation the foundation stone of, 313; superiority of, 309; sustained by Bible prophecies, 313; testimonies the strength of, 336-349; to be cleansed of sinners, 169; to eventually occupy whole of Zion, 40; union is chief cornerstone of, 206.

Churches, blind leaders of blind, 303.

Civil War, a judgment on nation, 51.

Circumstances, must learn to control, 101; not to be creatures of, 139.

Class-war, foreseen, 53.

Cleansing, Church to undergo, 169; of Church going on, 62; of earth by destructions, 88-89.

Clio, the goddess of History, 135.

Commandments, complete obedience to required, 151-152; enemies to be prevailed over by keeping, 158; given only by Joseph Smith, 260; keeping of an evidence of love for Jesus, 203-204; keeping of gives protection, 50; keeping of the best course, 168; not to be given in all things, 155-156; power to keep, 147; revealed through one channel, 322; way to fulfill always given, 101-102.

Commotion, all things to be in, 46.

Collisions, of trains a sign of times, 47.

Colonies, necessity for being freed, 308.

Columbus, was inspired, 307.

Condemnation, by testimonies, 339; those who reject Gospel under, 338.

Conferences, power attends actions of, 238.

Confession, necessary for forgiveness, 176; of sins daily, 79.

Confirmation: Also see Holy Ghost.

Confirmation, birth of the Spirit, 177-187; blessings of bestowed by Holy Ghost, 177; only the beginning of the work, 229; ordinance of to be unchanged, 177; words used in, 177.

Confucius, didn't hold Priesthood, 309; great moral truths revealed to, 308; received revelation, 305.

Conscience, Spirit of God is our, 181; voice of, 181-182.

Consecration, of all to God, 112-113.

Constitution, principles of maintained by Saints, 58.

Contention, has no place in Gospel, 202; to be avoided, 203.

Conversions, not to be made by signs, 194.

Cornelius, received Holy Ghost, 178.

Corner-stone, true knowledge of God is the, 126-127.

Counsel, 350-359; a higher duty to follow, 359; apostasy follows disobedience to, 210-211; in temporal matters, 354; Bish-

ops to give, 352; blessing of seeking, 357-358; blessings of obedience to, 155, 350; Brigham Young's was revelation, 288; disobedience to displeasing to God, 154-155; disobedience to incurs fearful responsibility, 355-356; fate of those disobedient to, 327; follow that of Presidency, 351; following of leads to Celestial Kingdom, 355; gift of, 197; obedience to a vital test, 355; of Church leaders to be sought, 58, 356-357; of counselors sought by Presidents, 206; of leaders is revelation, 325; of Prophets to be sought, 296; of leaders binding, 326; of united leaders sustained by Lord, 207-208; our duty to seek, 208; Saints to prevail over enemies by following, 157-158; Spirit of God gives united, 203.

Counselors, in First Presidency not set apart, 267.

Covenants, renewal of by re-baptism, 174-175, 241; baptisms are, 170.

Cowdery, Oliver, a witness of Book of Mormon, 155; disobedient to Joseph Smith, 155; not authorized to write commandments, 260; opposed Prophet, 277; ordained to Apostleship, 260, 155.

Cranmer, was inspired, 308.

Creation, by power of Priesthood, 215.

Creations, all obedient except man, 154.

Creators, exalted beings to become, 117-118.

Cursed, earth was because of man's disobedience, 154.

Cyclones, a sign of times, 47; a judgment of God, 51.

D

Damnation, by our own acts, 98; for failure to honor Priesthood, 229; no one fated to receive, 142.

Dangers, delivered from by faith, 149; disobedience only thing to be feared, 157-158.

Daniel, visited by Gabriel, 70; saw image crumble, 55.

Darkness, an absence of Spirit of God, 20; spirit of transforms people, 85; wicked to be consigned to outer, 78.

David, quoted, 74.

Deacons, in Paul's day were adults, 242; why boys ordained, 242.

Dead, raised in early Church, 190.

Death, a consequence of fall, 25; bitter to wicked, 35; has lost its sting, 109; holds no terror for righteous, 35, 77; in world for a purpose, 12; none before fall of Adam, 68; penalty of Adam's sin, 26; should be faced calmly, 36; stimulates interest in spirit world, 75.

Decree of God, has gone forth, 56.

Deity: Also see Godhead.

Deity, 125-136; personages of, 205; worship of female gods, 135-136.

Deserts, began after fall, 26.

Desires, must conquer earthly, 15.

Desolation, to cover land, 52.

Destroying Angel, to pass by faithful, 50.

Destruction, by brightness of Christ's coming, 49; of Jaredites and Nephites, 6; of unrighteous Mormons, 60; only way to cleanse earth, 60, 88-89; spiritual, 51; to be universal, 61; to come as a whirlwind, 48; to end Satan's power, 87.

Devil, who can become, 120.

Diana, the goddess of the Chase, 135.

Disasters, age of, 47; frequency of, 46; result of shedding innocent blood, 51.

Discernment, a greatly desired gift, 198.

Discourses, filled with revelation, 331.

Disobedience, incurs fearful responsibility, 355; not an evidence of independence, 206; only thing to be feared, 157; to counsel displeasing to God, 154.

Disobedient, not to inherit Zion, 155.

Dispensation, earth to be filled by this, 21; keys of held by Joseph Smith, 254.

Dispensations, keys of bestowed, 254.

Doctrine, contention concerning, 203; not to be hastily rejected, 354; revealed to leaders, 314.

Doubt, a tool of Satan, 154; not to have concerning teachings of our Prophet, 154.

Drunkards, shouldn't be permitted in Church, 169.

Duty, following counsel a higher, 359; individual salvation our greatest, 167; mankind's, 337; none to be neglected, 171, 17; seeking after gifts our, 195-196; teaching world a true knowledge of God our, 125; to build up Zion our, 44; to live by revelation, 305, 320; to practice self-examination, 167; to seek counsel, 208; to walk in the light, 340.

E

Earth, belongs to Lord, 146-147; cleansed by destructions, 88-89; cleansed by flood, 48; created for a purpose, 12; cursed because of man's disobedience, 154; cursed by fall, 26; God once dwelt on an, 128; important period in history of, 40; redeemed from Satan's power, 88; to be cleansed, 60; to be moved in testimony, 48; to be visited by fire, 60-61; to pass away, 90-91; to receive paradisiacal glory, 90-91; to reel to and fro, 63.

Earthquakes, a sign of the times, 47; began after the fall, 26; predicted by Jesus, 47; testimony of, 46, 48.

Election, all mankind elected to be saved, 140-1.

Elias, was John the Baptist, 38; at Jesus' transfiguration, 38.

Elijah, translated, 36-37.

Embryo, men are gods in, 1.

Emigration, from spirit world, 21.

Endowment, holy anointing an, 283; Joseph Smith desired Saints to have, 282; necessary for celestial glory, 119-120; too easily obtained, 227-228.

Endure, unto the end, 103.

England, future trouble predicted for, 54-56.

Enoch, acquired great scientific learning, 10.

Ephraim, obedient numbered among children of, 155.

Erato, the goddess of Lovers, 135.

Escape, of righteous from judgments, 49-50.

Estate, this a proving ground, 6.

Eternal Increase: Also see Procreation.

Eternal Increase, glory of, 116; to be endless, 103-104; to be innumerable, 115-116; unnumbered millions to be fathered, 131.

Eternal Punishment, meaning of, 144.

Europe, prediction concerning, 57.

Eve, a lovely partner, 9; was deceived, 24, 137.

Evil, eternal nature of, 15; everyone has power to resist, 19; influences around us, 84-85; knowledge of, 16; loved by Satan, 137-138; power of to be experienced, 15; resisted by influence of Holy Spirit, 139.

Evil Influences, effect of, 19.

Evils, appeared after fall, 26.

Evolution, man not a result of, 1; true, 9, 131.

Exaltation, an equal interest in power and authority of God, 112; attained by obedience to all laws, 102, 154; by following Savior's example, 94-95; celestial marriage necessary for, 104; faithful to receive, 34; faithfulness rather than position brings, 230; higher Priesthood necessary for, 233; how God attained, 107; mortality necessary for, 13; must be willing to sacrifice all, 113; results from honoring Priesthood, 232-233; to become gods, 107, 111.

Example, set by Jesus, 27.

Excommunication, takes away Priesthood, 240-241.

F

Faith: See Trust.

Faith, 146-152; a perfect confidence in Almighty, 147-148; a tangible, 35; ancients had great, 148; circumstances require, 150-151; foundation of Gospel, 149; God will not be dictated to, 149-150; lack of tries Saints, 151; miracles performed by, 192; necessary for salvation, 162; necessary to live by, 13, 27; obedience made easy by, 154; our strength,

Subjection, complete to will of God, 104-105.

Succession, in the Presidency, 281-302; an account of, 289-290; Apostolic, 250-251; Brigham Young assumes mantle of Joseph Smith, 285-286; incidents following martyrdom, 284-285; Joseph Smith desired Hyrum to succeed, 257, 281; more thoughts on, 291; no manifestation required at death of Brigham Young, 287-288; Priesthood, 218-219.

Suicide, a dreadful sin, 29; a desertion from life's mission, 29; funerals of, 30; is murder, 30.

Suicides, a sign of the times, 47.

Sun, to be darkened, 63.

Sustain, God confirms authority of those we, 239.

Sustaining, of immortal bodies, 120.

T

Taylor, John, became President, 289; life trembled in balance, 285; no faults in seen, 294; the man for the hour, 292; was senior Apostle, 287-288.

Telegraph, spreads news of judgments, 46.

Temple, body is a, 31.

Temples, necessity for, 223-234; to be built during Millennium, 90, 224; to be entered only by those obedient to counsel, 355.

Temporal Affairs, comprehended by Gospel, 350; obedience to counsel concerning, 352; power and wisdom in, 352-353; Priesthood to counsel in, 354.

Temptation, a necessary part of Gospel, 138; Jesus was subject to, 27; why permitted, 13; resisted by influence of Holy Spirit, 139.

Tempests, a testimony of, 46, 48.

Terror, death holds no for righteous, 35.

Tertullian, witnessed miracles, 190.

Test, this life a higher, 7.

Tested, to the utmost, 6, 103-104.

Testimonies, 336-349; a key to retain, 343; accompany words of truth, 338; compared to a seed, 344; condemnation on those who reject, 338; every man a Prophet, 346; Holy Ghost gives, 337; Holy Ghost gives most convincing, 341; the strength of the Church, 339; Joseph Smith's binding, 336; not a result of signs, 192-193; people condemned by, 339; people to be judged by Elders', 182; precious gifts, 341-342; spiritual truths not discerned by outer senses, 347-348; that grow, 342; the duty of mankind in relation to, 337; the strength of the Church, 345; value of children's, 349; why lost, 342; President Cannon saw Savior, 134.

Testimony Meetings, value of, 348.

Thoughts, God comprehends all our, 127.

Thousands, to flee to Zion, 58.

Three Nephites, were translated, 36-37.

Three Tabernacles, erected by Peter, James and John, 38.

Thunderings, testimony of, 46, 48.

Tithing, used for support of Authorities, 279-280.

Torment, damned to suffer, 79; duty unperformed will cause, 17; increased by knowledge of agency exercised, 140.

Torments, of wicked, 77.

Tongues, gift of and how used, 197.

Transfiguration, doctrine of, 37-39; is not resurrection, 39.

Translation, doctrine of, 36-37; of Elijah and Three Nephites, 36-37.

Tree of Knowledge, of good and evil, 16.

Tree of Life, guarded by Cherubim, 68.

Trials, a part of God's plan, 25; all must be tried to utmost, 103-104; for our benefit, 113-114; necessity of, 13.

Trump, angel to sound, 63.

Trust, all may fail except God, 151; faith and trust in God, 146-152; necessary to cope with circumstances, 150; put in no man, 319.

Truth, all comes from God, 305; devil never tells complete, 16; knowledge of not obtained without faith, 149; much yet to be revealed, 331; of Gospel spiritually discerned, 180-181; rejection of followed by judgments, 336, 338; revealed to men of all nations, 308-309; spirit of from God, 111; straying from, 185; testimony accompanies words of, 338.

U

Union: Also see Unity, Oneness.

Union, caused persecution, 204; chief cornerstone of Church, 206; none in religious world, 209-210; principle of, 202; strength of Church, 204.

United Order, not carried out, 41; wording of baptism ordinance changed during living of, 173.

Unity: Also see Union, Oneness.

Unity, a distinguishing feature of Gospel, 202-203; a principle of strength, 202-211; all who preside should act in, 207; First Presidency act in, 206-207; hated by Satan, 210; in political matters, 211; lack of the source of our troubles, 205-206; Lord sustains counsel of leaders who act in, 207-208; the power of people who act in, 204; required among leader, 317; the strength of, 205-206; true sign of God's people, 210.

Universal, resurrection to be, 32.

Universe, controlled by Priesthood, 215.

Unpardonable Sin, committed by sons of perdition, 34; shedding of innocent blood is, 144.